IMS for the
COBOL programmer

Part 2: Data communications and Message Format Service

IMS for the COBOL programmer

Part 2: Data communications and Message Format Service

Steve Eckols

Development Team

Technical editor:	Doug Lowe
Production editor:	Judy Taylor
Designer and production director:	Steve Ehlers
Artist:	Carl Kisling

Related products

IMS for the COBOL Programmer, Part 1: Data Base Processing with IMS/VS or DL/I DOS/VS by Steve Eckols

Structured ANS COBOL, Part 1: A Course for Novices Using 1974 or 1985 ANS COBOL by Mike Murach and Paul Noll

Structured ANS COBOL, Part 2: An Advanced Course Using 1974 or 1985 ANS COBOL by Mike Murach and Paul Noll

MVS TSO by Doug Lowe

MVS JCL by Doug Lowe

OS Utilities by Doug Lowe

20 19 18 17 16 15 14 13 12 11 10 9 8 7 6 5 4 3 2 1

Library of Congress Catalog Card Number: 85-51811

ISBN: 0-911625-30-5

Contents

Preface

This book will teach you how to develop interactive application programs for IBM mainframe systems that use IMS/VS (Information Management System/Virtual Storage). IMS, which is supplied by IBM and runs on mainframe computers that are controlled by the MVS operating system, has two main functions: data base (DB) processing and data communications (DC) processing. The first book in this series, *IMS for the COBOL Programmer, Part 1*, focused on IMS's DB features and on the IMS DB subset available for VSE systems, called DL/I DOS/VS. This book, *Part 2*, covers IMS's DC features, which are available only under MVS. You use IMS's DC features to implement interactive applications which let terminal users access and update IMS data bases.

In this book, then, you'll learn how IMS DC allows for interactive applications and what the basic COBOL considerations are. You'll learn how to use Message Format Service (MFS), a facility that lets you set up screens that are easy for operators to use—whether they're entering data or retrieving information. You'll find that using MFS also lets you write programs that run more efficiently because MFS takes over some of the tasks that would otherwise have to be handled in the program. In addition, you'll learn about advanced IMS DC functions, such as how to route output to various terminals and how to write a batch program that can update IMS data bases while the same data bases are being used

1

by interactive programs. Finally, you'll learn how to use Batch Terminal Simulator, a facility for testing IMS applications.

Who this book is for

If you're a professional programmer/analyst, you owe it to yourself to learn about both the data base and data communications facilities of IMS. Obviously, that's a must if your job is developing IMS applications. But even if you're not currently responsible for designing and implementing IMS programs, you should still understand IMS either to make yourself more flexible on your current job or more marketable for another job.

If you've tried to learn IMS DC from any other sources, the experience probably frustrated you. That's because IMS DC is just plain complicated and difficult. On first thought, IBM's IMS manuals might seem like the best resources for learning IMS DC. However, because they're designed for reference, they don't help you focus on what's really important and practical. And other effective training materials haven't been available. However, this book changes that. It teaches you the essential and useful points, and does it from your perspective: application programming.

Required background

Although you'll gain a thorough understanding of IMS DC by reading this book, you need some additional background to be able to apply what you'll learn in a production environment. That's because IMS DC isn't an isolated feature, but works in combination with other software components. Specifically, to develop IMS DC application programs, you need background in three areas: (1) COBOL, (2) MVS, and (3) IMS DB.

First, you need to know how to design and code batch COBOL application programs. If you've had a basic COBOL programming course, you probably have the background you need in this area. And if you work as a COBOL programmer, particularly on an IBM mainframe, you certainly meet this prerequisite. However, if COBOL is new to you, you can pick up the information you need from Mike Murach and Paul Noll's *Structured ANS COBOL, Part 1* and *Part 2*.

(These two books, along with others I'm going to mention in a moment, are available from Mike Murach & Associates, Inc. You can use the postage-paid order form at the end of this book to order the titles I mention here, plus a variety of other data processing books that may interest you.)

The second prerequisite for learning and using IMS DC is a basic understanding of IBM's MVS operating system. Specifically, you should know enough about MVS job control language (JCL) to code job streams to perform typical program development tasks. In addition, you should be familiar with TSO, the MVS facility through which you'll enter program and MFS format set statements and request MVS services. You can learn what you need to know from Doug Lowe's books, *MVS JCL* and *MVS TSO*.

The third requirement is that you understand IMS data base processing. There are two reasons for that. First, IMS DC programs almost always access IMS data bases. And second, the techniques you use to invoke IMS DC functions are much like those you use to request DB functions. *Part 1* of this series provides you with the data base information that's necessary.

How to use this book

To be a proficient IMS DC application programmer, you need to be familiar with all of the information in this book. As a result, I encourage you to read it from beginning to end. However, you do have some options as to how you approach the content. For example, if you have experience developing applications for interactive systems, you may be able to skip chapters 1 and 2. (In fact, if you have experience as a CICS programmer, you can almost certainly skip these chapters.)

Regardless of your background, you should read section 2 (chapters 3, 4, and 5). These chapters present the IMS, COBOL, and MFS background you need to learn the more advanced material in the chapters that follow. After you've finished this section, you'll be able to develop basic IMS DC applications, either with or without MFS format sets.

The chapters in section 3 (chapters 6, 7, 8, and 9) cover Message Format Service facilities. If you're an application programmer who will not be developing your own MFS format sets, you may be able to skip this section altogether. However, some COBOL programming considerations that are closely related to MFS are presented in this section, so I encourage you to read it even if you're not responsible for developing your own format sets; if you're going to develop programs that use specialized MFS facilities, you must read at least some of the chapters in this section.

Section 4 (chapters 10, 11, 12, and 13) presents advanced IMS DC facilities. You can select which of the four chapters in this section you want to read. However, there are some relationships among these chapters that make it desirable for you to read them in sequence.

Section 5 (chapters 14, 15, and 16) shows you how to use Batch Terminal Simulator to test IMS applications separate from the production system. As you'll see, BTS lets you do thorough testing and provides you with valuable debugging information. You can read this section anytime after you've finished the material in section 2, but it will make more sense after you've learned the MFS and IMS DC features sections 3 and 4 present.

Related resource materials

To work productively as an IMS DC application programmer, you need access to several reference sources. First and foremost, you need to be able to use the set of IMS reference manuals IBM supplies. The IMS library includes a variety of manuals for different readers: application programmers, systems programmers, data base and network administrators, and system operators. Unfortunately, information that you may need can be in any of them. As a result, you should try to find out if you have access to the IMS reference library and, if so, familiarize yourself with it. The two manuals you'll find most useful are *IMS/VS Version 1 Application Programming* (SH20-9026) and *IMS/VS Version 1 Message Format Service User's Guide* (SH20-9053).

The IBM manuals provide information that applies to all IMS installations. In addition, your shop certainly has its own particular standards for program design and coding, screen layout, naming conventions, and so on, which should be documented in a standards manual. Get a copy and read it.

Also, you'll need to find out what your installation's development procedures are. For example, you'll need to know how to go about translating an MFS format set, where the output should be stored, and how to access it for testing. Because these considerations can vary from shop to shop, you'll find as you read this book that I'll often tell you to check with a co-worker or your supervisor to get particular information.

A note on the sample format sets and listings

This book contains six complete MFS format sets and eight complete
IMS DC COBOL programs. They have two purposes. First, they
illustrate the points the text makes. But second, and just as important,
they're models you can follow as you develop your own IMS DC
applications. All were developed on an IBM 3083 system using IMS/VS
Version 1 Release 3 running under MVS 3.8. Testing was done with
Batch Terminal Simulator 2.0.

Conclusion

I'm sure that there's no better way to start your IMS DC training than
to read this book. And after you have some IMS DC experience, you'll
continue to use it for reference. Of course, I'm interested in your
impressions. So please feel free to use the postage-paid comment form
at the end of this book to let me know what you like and don't like
about the book and how you've been able to use it.

Steve Eckols
Fresno, California
May, 1987

Section 1

Required background

This section presents the background information that's prerequisite to the IMS DC and MFS subject matter presented in sections 2 through 5. (Of course, you should also be familiar with the material on data base processing in *IMS for the COBOL Programmer, Part 1*.) Before you can learn how to design and develop IMS DC/MFS applications, you need to know what sorts of applications are typical on interactive systems; that's what you'll learn in chapter 1. Then, in chapter 2, you'll learn about the hardware and systems software that support interactive applications.

If you have experience developing interactive applications for IBM mainframe computer systems (such as under CICS), you can almost certainly skip both chapters 1 and 2. If you have experience developing interactive applications for other kinds of computer systems, you may be able to skip chapter 1 and the first part of chapter 2; however, the second part of chapter 2, which covers the IBM 3270 Information Display System, presents vital information you're probably not familiar with. In any event, if you think you already have a solid grounding in interactive applications and data communications systems, review the terminology lists and objectives at the ends of chapters 1 and 2. If you're comfortable with them, you can move ahead to chapter 3.

Chapter 1

An introduction to
interactive programs

For years, batch processing was the rule in the data processing industry. However, with the development of data communications facilities and display stations, interactive processing has become more and more common. In fact, most applications that are developed today are interactive.

In an *interactive* (or *on-line*) *system*, a user working at a display station interacts with the computer. On a transaction-by-transaction basis, the user enters data and receives output back from the system. There's no longer a need to batch transactions, then process them all at once. This chapter describes four types of interactive programs you're likely to encounter, as well as four considerations common to all types of interactive systems, IMS or otherwise.

Types of interactive programs

The kinds of programs you can find on interactive systems fall into four main categories: (1) inquiry programs, (2) data entry programs, (3) maintenance programs, and (4) menu programs. Although some interactive programs may combine functions and, as a result, fall into two or more of these groups, these are the basic categories.

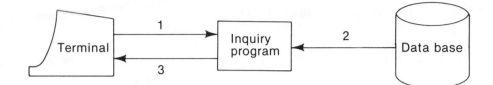

Explanation

1. The operator requests the data to be displayed.

2. The program retrieves the appropriate data from the data base.

3. The program displays the data at the terminal.

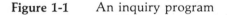

Figure 1-1   An inquiry program

Inquiry programs   An *inquiry program* is designed to respond to a user's question. Almost always, that means an inquiry program has to retrieve data stored on the computer system. Figure 1-1 illustrates a typical inquiry program. As you can see, the inquiry program here requires three steps: (1) the operator enters some value to identify the data to be retrieved, such as a segment key; (2) the program retrieves the appropriate segments from a data base; and (3) the program displays the data at the terminal.

Figure 1-2 shows three screens from a typical inquiry program. This program displays information for a selected invoice from a customer data base. In the first screen (part 1), the terminal is waiting for the operator to enter an invoice number. The second screen (part 2) shows the invoice number the operator entered. When the operator presses the enter key, the program retrieves and displays the data for the specified invoice (part 3).

The inquiry program figure 1-2 presents is simple; it accesses just one data base and, for each transaction, just one data base segment. However, it's possible to develop complex inquiry programs that provide a variety of display options and that combine data extracted from several DL/I data bases. Even so, figures 1-1 and 1-2 represent the basic operation of an inquiry program.

Data entry programs   Although inquiry programs are widely used, they don't let users key in data that's added to a system's data bases. For

The invoice inquiry program awaits operator input

```
DISPLAY INVOICE SUMMARY                              DATE:  01/23/87

INVOICE:  _        DATE:            SUBTOTAL:
                                    DISCOUNT:
                                    SALES TAX:
                                    FREIGHT:
                                              ---------

                                    BILLING:
                                    PMTS/ADJS:
                                              ---------

                                    DUE:
```

Figure 1-2   Operation of an inquiry program (part 1 of 3)

The operator enters an invoice number

```
DISPLAY INVOICE SUMMARY                              DATE:  01/23/87

INVOICE:  010000   DATE:            SUBTOTAL:
                                    DISCOUNT:
                                    SALES TAX:
                                    FREIGHT:
                                              ---------

                                    BILLING:
                                    PMTS/ADJS:
                                              ---------

                                    DUE:
```

Figure 1-2   Operation of an inquiry program (part 2 of 3)

The program retrieves the specified invoice segment and displays data from it

```
DISPLAY INVOICE SUMMARY                                       DATE:   01/23/87

INVOICE:   010000    DATE:   07/15/86    SUBTOTAL:        200.00
                                         DISCOUNT:          0.00
                                         SALES TAX:         0.00
                                         FREIGHT:          13.00
                                                       ----------
                                         BILLING:         213.00
                                         PMTS/ADJS:         0.00
                                                       ----------
                                         DUE:             213.00
```

Figure 1-2   Operation of an inquiry program (part 3 of 3)

that, *data entry programs* are used. Figure 1-3 illustrates a simple data entry program that requires only two steps. First, the operator enters data for one transaction at the terminal, and then the program updates any related data bases.

Frankly, this is as simple as a data entry program can be. More sophisticated programs involve interaction with the operator, requiring him to verify the data he entered by comparing it with information the program extracted from data bases. Still other data entry programs integrate inquiry and data entry functions.

Maintenance programs   A *maintenance program* can update a data base by adding, replacing, or deleting segments. Figure 1-4 shows a typical maintenance program. In this case, the program allows only changes to existing segment occurrences. In step 1, the operator enters a key value to identify the data to be changed. Then, the program extracts the necessary information from the data base (step 2), and displays it for the operator to review (step 3). The operator enters the changes that need to be made to the data (step 4), and the program issues the necessary calls to record the changes in the data base (step 5).

Explanation

1. The operator enters the data for one transaction at the terminal.

2. The program updates any related data bases.

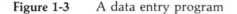

Figure 1-3   A data entry program

Explanation

1. The operator requests the data to be updated.

2. The program retrieves the appropriate data from the data base.

3. The program displays the data at the terminal.

4. The operator enters the required changes to the data.

5. The program rewrites the changes to the data base.

Figure 1-4   A maintenance program

You can think of a maintenance program as a combination of an inquiry program and a data entry program. Like an inquiry program, a maintenance program accepts a key value and retrieves data for display. And like a data entry program, a maintenance program accepts data the operator keys in and uses it to update the appropriate data bases.

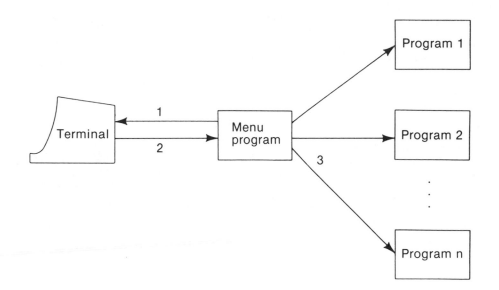

Explanation

1. The menu program sends a list of selections to the terminal.

2. The operator chooses one of the selections.

3. Control is transferred to the appropriate program.

Figure 1-5 A menu program

Menu programs A *menu program* lets an operator select the functions he wants to perform. Figure 1-5 shows a typical menu program. Three steps are required: (1) the program sends a list of processing selections to the terminal; (2) the operator chooses one of the selections; and (3) the menu program passes control to the program the operator selected. An application that's built around a set of menu programs is called a *menu-driven system*.

Figure 1-6 shows a typical menu screen. In many interactive systems, several layers of menus are required. For example, if the operator selects number 1 in figure 1-6, another menu showing selections related to order entry might be displayed.

Some interactive systems don't use menus. Instead, the operator invokes programs using explicit commands. For example, the operator might enter

        DISPINV

14   Chapter 1

```
            MASTER MENU

            1. ORDER ENTRY

            2. CUSTOMER MAINTENANCE

            3. CUSTOMER INQUIRY

            4. INVOICING


            YOUR SELECTION: _




PRESS CLEAR TO END SESSION
```

Figure 1-6   A typical menu program screen

to begin an invoice inquiry program like the one illustrated in figure 1-2. In some cases, the command can include data the program will use as it executes. For example,

```
DISPINV 010000
```

could invoke the invoice inquiry program and supply the key of the invoice segment the program should retrieve. Systems that use programs that are invoked like this are called *command-driven systems*.

Interactive system considerations

Now that you're familiar with the kinds of programs that can make up an interactive system, you need to be aware of some of the special problems interactive applications must be able to handle. In this section, I'll cover four basic problems common to all interactive systems: shared data, response time, security, and recovery.

Shared data   A batch program has exclusive control over the data bases it processes, so there's no chance that another program can interfere with its processing. In an interactive system, however, many terminal operators use the system at the same time, and they all must have access to the data bases they need. As a result, an interactive system must provide for *shared data* by coordinating updates so two programs don't update the same data at the same time.

Response time   *Response time* is another special consideration for interactive systems that isn't a concern with batch systems. Quite simply, response time is how long an operator has to wait for a transaction to be processed. A response time of several seconds is probably good, while several minutes probably isn't.

Many factors affect response time: the number of users on the system, the storage available, the speed of the disk units in use, how system parameters are set, how fast telecommunications lines are, and how application programs are written. As in the batch environment, keeping your DL/I calls few and simple will improve your programs' response times.

Security   In a batch system, *security* is easy to maintain because there's only one access to the computer system: the computer room. However, in an interactive system, terminals are located in many places, and security is a problem. Both IMS and other MVS systems software components provide security with basic logon controls that keep unauthorized users off the system and with access control features that restrict users to just the data and programs they need.

Recovery   *Recovery* from system and program failures is complex enough in the batch environment, but the additional requirements of interactive processing make it even more complicated. IMS includes sophisticated recovery features that make recovery as fast and efficient as possible. For the most part, recovery is transparent to the application programmer, so I mention it here just for perspective.

Discussion

Fortunately, many of the details of shared data, response time, security, and recovery are managed for you by IMS. As a result, the IMS application programs you develop are largely insulated from the complexities these considerations impose on the system. Nevertheless, you still need to be aware of them. When I introduce IMS functions in chapter 3, you'll see how IMS provides these services.

Terminology

interactive system
on-line system
inquiry program
data entry program
maintenance program
menu program
menu-driven system
command-driven system
shared data
response time
security
recovery

Objectives

1.   Describe the four basic types of interactive programs.

2.   Describe the four considerations that take on special importance in interactive systems.

Chapter 2

An introduction to
data communications systems

This chapter describes *data communications networks* (often called *telecommunications networks*), which let users at *local terminals* (terminals that are located at a central computer site) or *remote terminals* (terminals that aren't located at the computer site) access *host computers* (or *host systems*). Then, it describes the details of the 3270 Information Display System, the family of terminal devices that's most widely used in IBM mainframe interactive systems.

ELEMENTS OF A DATA COMMUNICATIONS NETWORK

Figure 2-1 represents a typical telecommunications network. Basically, five elements make up a network: (1) a host system, (2) a communication controller, (3) modems, (4) telecommunication lines, and (5) terminal systems. A single *terminal system* can be one or more CRT display stations, connected to the network through a terminal controller; printers can also be included in terminal systems.

Communication lines

One of the major components of a communication network is a phone connection, often called a *communication line* (or *telecommunication*

17

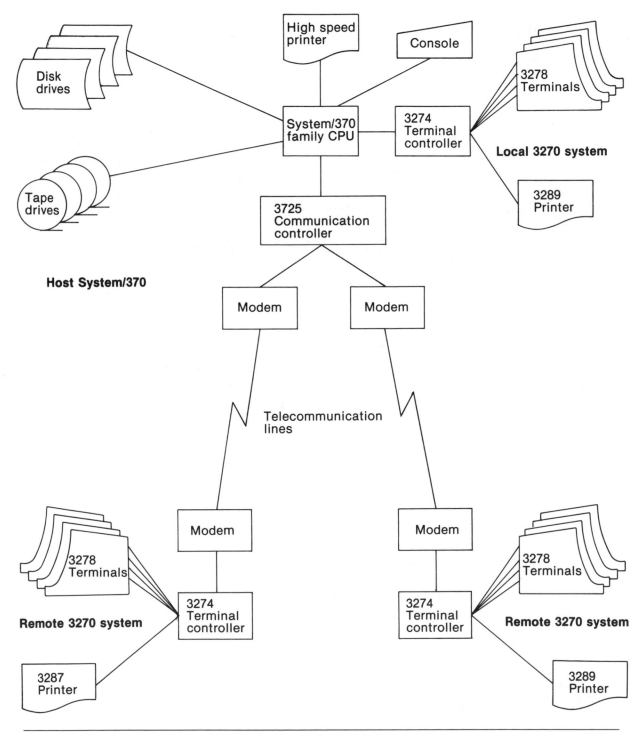

Figure 2-1   A typical System/370 and 3270 configuration

line, or just *TC line*). The TC line connects the host system with a remote terminal system. It can be set up through the public telephone system or may be privately owned.

The most common type of TC line is called a *switched* or *dial-up line*. Dialing establishes the connection in a switched line. In general, a switched line is the least expensive type of line, unless a high volume of long-distance work is done.

In contrast, a *non-switched line* (or *dedicated line*) does not require dialing; the connection is always established. If a non-switched line is set up through the public telephone system, it's called a *leased line*. If it's privately owned, it's called a *private line*. Leased or private lines are commonly used when a high volume of data is transmitted over long distances.

Non-switched lines have less interference than switched lines and, as a result, can transmit data accurately at higher speeds. Transmission speed is measured in bits-per-second, or *baud*. Typical transmission speeds for switched lines are 1200 or 2400 baud. For leased or private lines, 9600 baud is a common transmission speed.

In addition, non-switched lines permit *full-duplex* (or just *duplex*) transmission. When full-duplex transmission is used, data is transmitted in both directions at the same time. In contrast, only *half-duplex* is available for switched lines. When half-duplex transmission is used, data is transmitted only one direction at a time.

Modems

The second critical component in a data communication network is a pair of *modems*. As you can see in figure 2-1, a modem is required at each end of a TC line. A modem's function is to translate digital signals from the computer equipment at the sending end (either the host or remote system) into audio signals that are transmitted over the telecommunication line. At the receiving end of the line, another modem converts those audio signals back into digital signals.

Communication controllers

The third critical component of a data communications network is a *communication controller*. The communication controller performs the functions necessary to manage the transmission of data over the communication line.

One of the main functions of a communication controller is *data conversion*—that is, converting data into a form that a modem can process. This process is sometimes called *serialization* because it involves converting eight-bit bytes into a continuous stream of bits the modem processes one at a time. Figure 2-2 illustrates serialization. Here, two characters, A and 0, are converted from their eight-bit byte patterns into a stream of serial bits. Then, the terminal controller at the other end of the line converts that stream back to the eight-bit byte patterns for A and 0. This opposite process is called *deserialization*.

Another main function of the communication controller is *data-link control*. Data-link control insures the successful transmission of data over the communication line. Some of the functions required for data-link control are synchronizing the host with the terminal, identifying the source and destination of a transmission, and detecting and correcting transmission errors.

In addition, data-link control must convert data so it conforms to a standard *line discipline* (sometimes called a *protocol*). A line discipline is a set of rules that governs the transmission. The two most common line disciplines in an IBM communication network are *BSC* (*Binary Synchronous Control*) and *SDLC* (*Synchronous Data Link Control*).

Host system

At the center of the network in figure 2-1 is the host system. For IMS, the host system is a System/370-family processor, such as a 3080 or 3090 model. A *telecommunications monitor* (IMS data communications, CICS, or, on some systems, both) runs in the host system processor to control interactive application programs and to manage data base and file processing.

To control physical communication functions, the host system uses a *telecommunications* (or *TC*) *access method*. The TC access method serves as an interface between programs and the physical operation of the terminal network, much as the other access methods are interfaces between programs and I/O units like DASDs. The most important TC access method is *VTAM* (*Virtual Telecommunications Access Method*).

Terminal systems

A variety of terminal types can be part of an IMS DC (data communications) system. By far the most common is the 3270 Information Display

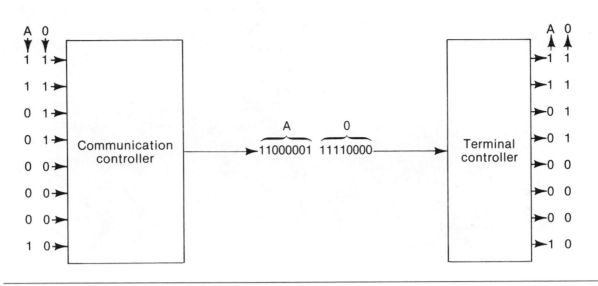

Figure 2-2 Serialization and deserialization of data

System, which I'll describe in detail in a moment. Other terminals supported by IMS include 3600s, 3790s, and System/3s.

Figure 2-1 shows two remote terminal systems attached to the host through a 3725 communication controller. The 3725 is at the host site and is connected to the two remote sites by telecommunication lines that have modems on each end.

The third terminal system in figure 2-1 is configured as a local system. Because it's at the host site, a communication controller and modems aren't necessary for it.

All three terminal systems in figure 2-1 are 3270-type systems. The 3270 Information Display System is the most common type of terminal system used with IMS DC. As a result, you need to have a basic understanding of it.

THE 3270 INFORMATION DISPLAY SYSTEM

The *3270 Information Display System* isn't a single terminal, but a subsystem of CRT terminals and printers connected to a *terminal controller* that communicates with the host. Figure 2-3 illustrates the components of a typical 3270 system. The controller, the box in the left of the photograph, is usually attached to the host through a modem and a telecommunication line, but it can be equipped for direct attachment to one of the host system's channels. The devices in this photograph are

Figure 2-3   Components of a 3270 Information Display System

older models; newer models are smaller and, as you'd expect, have a more modern style.

3270 terminal types

3270 terminals are available in a variety of configurations that display anywhere from 12 lines of 40 characters each to 43 lines of 80 characters, with one model that displays 27 lines of 132 characters. One advanced 3270-type device, the 3290, can serve as four separate display stations at the same time. However, the most common 3270-type terminals (like the 3278 Model 2 and the 3178) have screens with 24 usable display lines, each with 80 characters, for a total screen size of 1920 characters. These are commonly referred to simply as *3270 model 2* terminals; less common are 12-line *3270 model 1* terminals.

3270 display stations can be configured with several options, including alternate keyboard configurations for special applications or foreign languages. Less common features are a selector light pen that lets the operator communicate with the host system without using the keyboard, a magnetic card reader used for operator identification, color display, extended highlighting capabilities (including underscore, blink, and reverse video), and graphics.

In addition to display stations, printers can be attached to a 3270 terminal system. Many 3270 systems have a local-print feature that allows the data on the screen of a 3270 display station to be transferred to the terminal controller, then printed by one of the 3270 printers. Since this print option doesn't involve transmission of data between the 3270 system and the host, it's an efficient mode of printing.

You should realize that the word "terminal" applies to both display stations and printers in the 3270 system. When output is directed to a terminal, it's displayed at the screen if the terminal is a display station; if the terminal is a printer, the output is printed. The major difference, of course, is that printers cannot accept input data, while display stations can.

Characteristics of the 3270 display screen

The 3270 screen is a *field-oriented display*. In other words, the screen consists of a number of user-defined *fields*. As in a record or segment description, a field on a screen is a specified area that contains a particular category of information. Some screen fields let the operator key data into them, while others are protected from data entry.

A special character called an *attribute byte* (or *attribute character*) marks the beginning of a field. The attribute byte takes up one position on the screen (the position immediately to the left of the field it defines), but it's displayed on the screen as a space. The end of one field is indicated by the attribute byte that defines the beginning of the next field. So the length of a screen field depends on the position of the attribute byte that follows it. If there is no subsequent attribute byte, the field continues to the end of the screen.

Figure 2-4 shows the placement of attribute bytes in a sample 3270 display. Here, the small shaded boxes represent attribute bytes. These small boxes don't actually appear on the screen. Instead, spaces appear in the attribute byte positions.

As its name implies, the attribute byte does more than just mark the beginning of a field. It also determines a field's characteristics, called its *attributes*. The three basic attributes you'll use when you develop

```
■DISPLAY INVOICE SUMMARY■                                    ■DATE:■■01/23/87■

■INVOICE:■■0100000■ ■DATE:■■07/15/86■  ■SUBTOTAL:■   ■   200.00 ■
                                       ■DISCOUNT:■    ■     0.00 ■
                                       ■SALES TAX:■   ■     0.00 ■
                                       ■FREIGHT:■     ■    13.00 ■
                                                      ■---------■
                                       ■BILLING:■     ■   213.00 ■
                                       ■PMTS/ADJS:■   ■     0.00 ■
                                                      ■---------■
                                       ■DUE:■         ■   213.00 ■
```

Figure 2-4   Attribute bytes in a 3270 display

IMS DC applications are: (1) protection, (2) intensity, and (3) shift. Figure 2-5 shows the selections you can make for these attributes.

The protection attribute   The *protection attribute* indicates whether or not the operator can key data into a field. If a field is protected, the operator can't key data into it. On the other hand, if a field is unprotected, the operator is free to key data into it. As a result, data entry fields are often called *unprotected fields* and display-only fields are often called *protected fields*.

A third option for the protection attribute is *auto-skip*. It defines a special kind of protected field called a *skip field*. As with a protected field, an operator cannot enter data into a skip field. The difference between a protected field and a skip field is that when the *cursor* (a marker that indicates where the next character the operator enters will appear on the screen) is moved to a skip field, it automatically advances to the first position of the next unprotected field on the screen. In contrast, when the cursor moves to a basic protected field, the cursor stops, but the operator cannot enter data there. (Because of this characteristic, protected fields are sometimes called *stop fields*.)

Protection	Intensity	Shift
Protected Unprotected Auto-skip	Normal Bright No-display	Alphanumeric Numeric

Figure 2-5   Field attributes

Typically, skip fields follow data entry fields. That way, when the operator enters enough characters to fill the unprotected field, the cursor automatically moves on to the next data entry field, and the operator can continue to enter data. If a stop field follows an unprotected field, the operator has to press the tab key to advance to the next data entry field.

The intensity attribute   The *intensity attribute* indicates how the data in a field is displayed. Normal intensity implies just what it says: the data is displayed with normal intensity. If you specify bright, the data is displayed with brighter than normal intensity. And if you specify *no-display*, the field isn't displayed at all. If no-display is specified for an unprotected field, spaces are displayed no matter what characters the operator keys into the field. The no-display attribute is often assigned to unprotected fields for security reasons. For example, fields into which operators key sensitive password data are typically given the no-display attribute.

The shift attribute   The *shift attribute* indicates whether the keyboard is in *alphanumeric shift* or *numeric shift*. On older 3270 models, the numerals are located on the same keys as some of the letters, so the operator has to shift the keyboard to enter numeric data. However, if a field's attribute byte indicates numeric shift, the keyboard is automatically put into numeric shift so the operator doesn't have to press the shift key.

Newer 3270 display stations have a *numeric lock* feature that allows the operator to enter only numeric data (numerals, signs, and decimal points) into a field. On these newer terminals, the numeric shift attribute in the attribute byte activates the numeric lock feature. As a result, you'll usually specify the numeric shift attribute for numeric data entry fields. Bear in mind, however, that even when the numeric shift attribute is on, the operator can still enter invalid numeric data. For example, the operator can enter data with two decimal points or two minus signs.

Extended attributes   In addition to the characteristics defined by the basic attribute byte, fields on appropriately configured 3270 terminals can have *extended attributes*. Extended attributes provide control over special display characteristics of certain 3270 models, such as reverse-video, underlining, blinking, and color. You probably won't have to use the special characteristics the extended attributes can control.

Characteristics of the 3270 keyboard

The 3270 display station's keyboard is similar to a typewriter keyboard, with the addition of a few special keys. Although 3270 keyboards are available in a variety of layouts, the configuration in figure 2-6 is typical. The keyboard contains five types of keys: (1) data entry keys, (2) cursor control keys, (3) editing keys, (4) attention keys, and (5) miscellaneous keys. In each of the keyboard layouts in figure 2-6, one of these different groups of keys is shaded.

Data entry keys, shaded in the first keyboard layout in figure 2-6, are the letters of the alphabet, numerals, and special characters (like @, % and *). These are the keys that you'd expect to find on a standard typewriter keyboard.

Cursor control keys, shaded in the second keyboard layout in figure 2-6, let the operator move the cursor around on the screen. The simplest of these keys are the four arrow keys (up, down, right, and left). When the operator presses one of these keys, the cursor moves in the indicated direction. The other cursor control keys let the operator move the cursor in a field-oriented way. For example, the tab key (the key just to the left of the letter Q) causes the cursor to move ahead to the beginning of the next unprotected field.

The editing keys, shaded in the third of the keyboard layouts in figure 2-6, let the operator manipulate data already on the screen in unprotected fields. For example, the insert key (â) opens a space between characters to let the operator key in additional ones, and the delete key (â) lets the operator delete one character at a time. The ErInp key deletes data in all unprotected fields on the screen; the Erase EOF key erases only the data in the field in which the cursor is positioned, and then only from the current cursor position to the end of the field.

The attention keys, shaded in the fourth of the keyboard layouts in figure 2-6, let a terminal user communicate with the system. The *program function keys* (or just *PF keys*) can be used by the operator to signal a program to perform specific functions. IMS DC provides a

Data entry keys

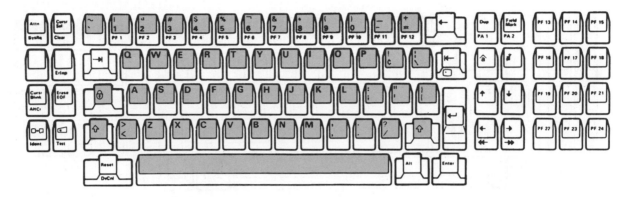

Cursor control keys

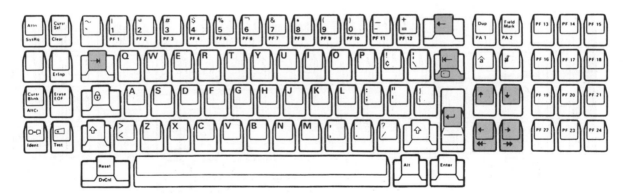

Editing keys

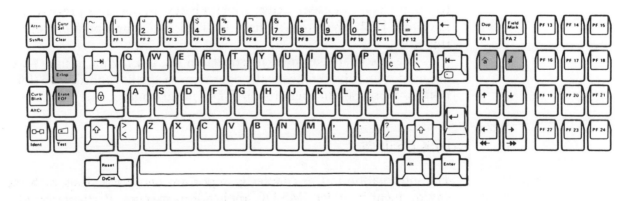

Figure 2-6   A typical 3270 keyboard arrangement (part 1 of 2)

Attention keys

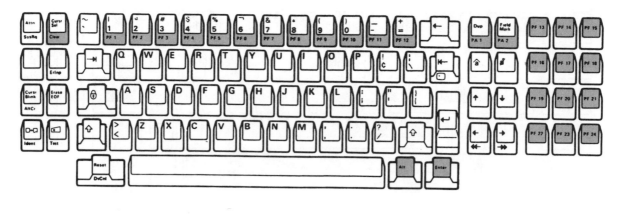

Miscellaneous keys

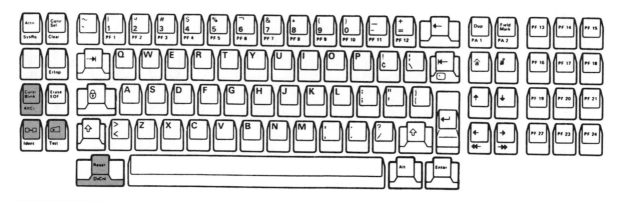

Figure 2-6   A typical 3270 keyboard arrangement (part 2 of 2)

technique you can use to detect which PF key an operator pressed. The PA1 and PA2 keys are also used by IMS for some operator control functions.

The miscellaneous keys, illustrated in the last layout in figure 2-6, are used primarily to manage the operation of the keyboard. You don't need to worry about them for IMS DC programming.

DISCUSSION

The information in this chapter is important because it deals with the environment in which IMS DC applications execute. Particularly, you need to understand the 3270 Information Display System because many of the details you'll have to contend with as you develop IMS DC applications have to do with terminal control. By using the screen and keyboard facilities of the 3270 appropriately, you can make your applications easier for operators to use and more efficient for the system to handle.

Terminology

data communications network
telecommunications network
local terminal
host computer
host system
terminal system
communication line
telecommunication line
TC line
switched line
dial-up line
non-switched line
dedicated line
leased line
private line
baud
full-duplex
duplex
half-duplex
modem
communication controller
data conversion
serialization
deserialization
data-link control
line discipline
protocol
BSC
Binary Synchronous Control
SDLC
Synchronous Data Link Control
telecommunications monitor

telecommunications access
   method
TC access method
VTAM
Virtual Telecommunications
   Access Method
3270 Information Display
   System
terminal controller
3270 model 2
3270 model 1
field-oriented display
field
attribute byte
attribute character
attribute
protection attribute
unprotected field
protected field
auto-skip
skip field
cursor
stop field
intensity attribute
no-display
shift attribute
alphanumeric shift
numeric shift
numeric lock
extended attribute
program function key
PF key

Objectives

1.   Describe the main components of a data communications network.

2.   Describe the characteristics of a 3270 display station's screen.

3.   List and describe the options of the three basic 3270 field attributes.

4.   Describe the functions of the major groups of keys on a 3270 display station's keyboard.

Section 2

Basic IMS DC and MFS facilities

This section's three chapters present the material you must understand to design and develop COBOL application programs that will run in the IMS data communications (DC) environment. First, chapter 3 describes the elements of the IMS DC environment you need to know about as an application programmer. Then, chapter 4 presents the COBOL elements you'll use as you code basic application programs for IMS DC. Finally, chapter 5 introduces a central IMS DC component, Message Format Service (MFS), that lets you develop applications that do formatted display station operations.

You need to know all of the material in this section to work effectively as an IMS DC application programmer. As a result, I encourage you to read all three chapters in sequence. If you've already read chapter 12 in *IMS for the COBOL Programmer, Part 1*, think of it as an introduction to the material in this section. What you'll learn here is in greater depth and more detail than what *Part 1* presented.

After you've finished this section, you'll be able to develop a variety of basic IMS DC applications. Although the COBOL and MFS examples in chapters 4 and 5 are simple, they nevertheless are good models that you can copy and adapt to your particular requirements.

Chapter 3

An introduction to
IMS data communications

This chapter presents the concepts and terms you need to know about
the IMS DC environment to be able to design and code applications
that will run in it. To help you understand the important concepts that
will be the foundation of your IMS DC knowledge, it presents material
from three perspectives.

First, this chapter compares programs that you may have
developed (both batch and interactive) and programs that run under
IMS DC. Second, it focuses on how IMS fits into the MVS system
environment. And third, it shows you in detail how IMS is the "control
center" for a DB/DC (data base/data communications) system by
describing the steps IMS goes through as it processes a transaction.

HOW IMS DC PROGRAMS COMPARE TO
OTHER KINDS OF APPLICATION PROGRAMS

This section compares IMS DC COBOL application programs with
other programs you may have written. First, I'll describe how IMS DC
programs are similar to batch application programs, the sort you
should already be familiar with either from job experience or from your
introductory COBOL training. This prepares you to learn the material
in the next chapter, which teaches you to design and code basic IMS DC

programs. Then, after you've seen that there's nothing mysterious about designing and coding IMS DC programs, I'll point out how they differ from other interactive programs you might have developed. When you've completed this section, you'll be less likely to make some assumptions about IMS that can cause trouble for you later.

How IMS DC programs and batch programs compare

Application programs that run under IMS DC have more in common with batch programs than you might think. If you recognize their similarities, it will be easy for you to transfer your knowledge of batch COBOL to IMS DC programming.

For a typical batch program, illustrated in the top section of figure 3-1, input is a transaction from a file containing a collection of transaction records. For each input record, a batch program does predictable processing against its data bases and writes one or more lines on a report, its typical output. Although batch programs vary in complexity and function, in general, they all loop repeatedly through a processing cycle. And usually, that processing cycle is based on processing a single input transaction record. Finally, when there are no more input transaction records, the program ends.

The bottom section of figure 3-1 shows the corresponding elements for a typical DC program. Input is an *input message*, entered by a terminal user. Input messages drive a DC program just like input transaction records drive a batch program. For each input message, the DC program does predictable processing against its data bases and sends an *output message* that's displayed at the terminal of the user who originated the input message. The program loops through this cycle once for each input message. Finally, when there are no more input messages, the program ends.

In IMS terms, a *message* is a unit of data that's transmitted between a program and a terminal; the primary inputs to and outputs from DC programs are messages. In fact, an input message like I just described is called a *transaction*. (Later in this chapter, I'll describe IMS DC transactions in more detail, and I'll present two other kinds of input messages.) As you can see, an IMS DC transaction from a terminal user corresponds to a single transaction record from a batch program's input file.

Logically, the IMS term for a program like the one in the bottom section of figure 3-1 is a *message processing program*, or *MPP*. The primary purpose of this book is to teach you how to design and code

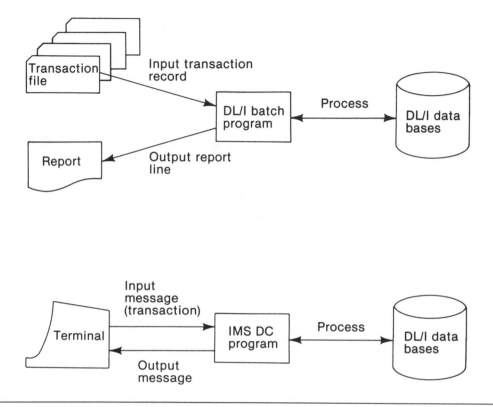

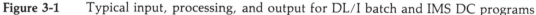

Figure 3-1   Typical input, processing, and output for DL/I batch and IMS DC programs

MPPs and how to format the screens for their input and output messages.

I want to stress that although the IMS DC program's input and output messages replace the batch program's transaction record input and report line output, the structures of the two kinds of programs are basically the same. Both kinds of programs are driven by the presence of input (either an input message or a transaction record). For each input item, the programs do predictable processing. In response to each input item, the programs produce appropriate output (a print report line or an output message passed back to the originating terminal). And when no more input is present, the programs end. If you remember these parallels, you shouldn't have any problem when it's time for you to design and code your first DC program.

However, you should keep the comparison of a DC program and a batch program in perspective. A batch program is run infrequently, typically according to a fixed schedule. That makes sense, because it takes some time for transactions to be accumulated manually in a

The invoice inquiry program awaits operator input

```
DISPLAY INVOICE SUMMARY                              DATE:   01/23/87

INVOICE:   _          DATE:            SUBTOTAL:
                                       DISCOUNT:
                                       SALES TAX:
                                       FREIGHT:
                                                     _ _ _ _ _ _ _ _
                                       BILLING:
                                       PMTS/ADJS:
                                                     _ _ _ _ _ _ _ _
                                       DUE:
```

Figure 3-2   Operation of an inquiry program (part 1 of 3)

batch. In contrast, terminal users in the IMS DC environment require rapid responses to the transactions they enter. As a result, the same MPP may have to run many times during a work day to meet user response time requirements.

How IMS DC programs and other kinds of interactive programs compare

Now, I want to compare IMS DC programs with other kinds of interactive programs you may have written. This section focuses on how applications appear to work to a terminal user. Typically, an IMS DC terminal user sees a screen formatted for data entry for a particular application, as in part 1 of figure 3-2. (Figure 3-2 shows the same screens I used as an example in chapter 1.) As you can see, it looks like the program is waiting for the user to enter and send data.

When the user does send an input message (by pressing the enter key after keying data into appropriate fields on the screen, as in part 2 of the figure), the program seems to respond immediately. It sends back an output message that replies to the operator's inquiry (as in part 3 of

The operator enters an invoice number

```
DISPLAY INVOICE SUMMARY                                  DATE:   01/23/87

INVOICE:  010000   DATE:              SUBTOTAL:
                                      DISCOUNT:
                                      SALES TAX:
                                      FREIGHT:
                                                   ---------
                                      BILLING:
                                      PMTS/ADJS:
                                                   ---------
                                      DUE:
```

Figure 3-2   Operation of an inquiry program (part 2 of 3)

The program retrieves the specified invoice segment and displays data from it

```
DISPLAY INVOICE SUMMARY                                  DATE:   01/23/87

INVOICE:  010000   DATE:  07/15/86   SUBTOTAL:        200.00
                                     DISCOUNT:          0.00
                                     SALES TAX:         0.00
                                     FREIGHT:          13.00
                                                    ---------
                                     BILLING:         213.00
                                     PMTS/ADJS:         0.00
                                                    ---------
                                     DUE:             213.00
```

Figure 3-2   Operation of an inquiry program (part 3 of 3) the figure) or acknowledges that the data was received and processed. At this point, the program again appears to be waiting for the user to key in the data for another input message and send it.

In short, the IMS DC program seems always to be in storage, waiting for the user to send it an input message, which it immediately processes. This impression can be reinforced because this is how other kinds of interactive programs—kinds you probably have developed—do work.

Consider, for example, typical interactive BASIC programs written for a minicomputer or a PC. Such programs, with which many of us have had programming experience (in school, on the job, or at home), often carry on continuous conversations with users. You and your program talk to one another through your screen and keyboard. When your computer is waiting for you to enter data, the program remains in storage, waiting for you to reply to it. On a PC, that's entirely reasonable because it's a *personal* computer; you don't have to share your system resources with any other users.

However, consider the computer systems at the other end of the spectrum: large mainframe systems that support thousands of users on widely dispersed telecommunications networks, the systems on which you'll find IMS DC. Obviously, a mainframe is far faster and more powerful than a PC. Even so, there's tremendous contention for system resources on mainframe systems. Because large systems have such heavy demands placed upon them, it's just not reasonable to let a single terminal user's application program remain in storage while that user keys in data, reads a screen display, or goes on an extended coffee break.

As a result, under IMS DC, an application program is in storage only when it needs to be to process an input message. So although a terminal user might enter data at a formatted display terminal, the program that will process that data probably isn't running at the time. It's invoked only when the user's entry is complete and an input message has been sent.

For this to be possible, there has to be an intermediate layer of software between your terminal and your program that isn't present when you run interactive programs on smaller systems. It's IMS itself, as figure 3-3 shows. When you enter data at a terminal for an IMS DC program, you communicate with IMS, not the application program. IMS takes care of passing the transaction to the program.

With IMS as an intermediary, a user's terminal entries and the application program that processes them are asynchronous. For example, if you enter an input message for an application program, IMS will probably have to load and execute the program before it can process

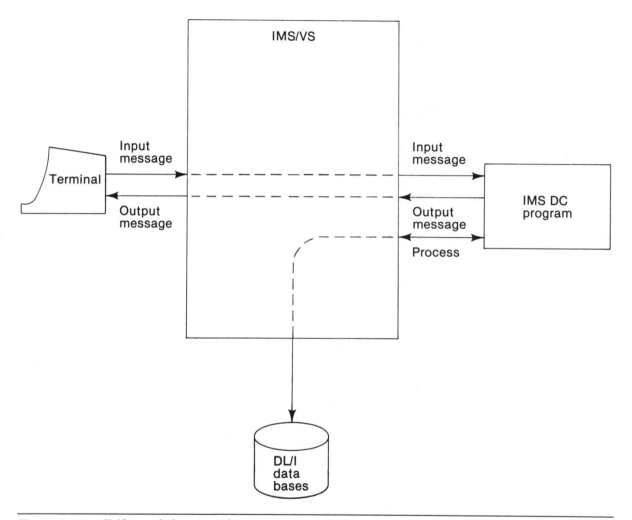

Figure 3-3   IMS stands between the terminal and the application program

your input message. And if the program happens to be in storage already, it's probably not there because it was waiting for your entry, but rather because it's processing transactions that other terminal users have already entered. (Obviously, this is likely to be the case only when many terminal users are entering transactions at the same time for the same application program.)

When the application program does process your transaction, it replies back to you, but again, not directly. The output message also passes through IMS. After the program has sent its reply, it doesn't wait for more input specifically from you the way an interactive program on a PC does. Instead, it goes on to handle another transaction of the same kind from another user. And if no other transactions are available for it, the program ends. So although a terminal user seems to have complete and unique control over an IMS DC application program, the real situation is far from that.

Another widely used IBM system software product that supports interactive applications on mainframes is *CICS/VS*, the *Customer Information Control System/Virtual Storage*. If you've developed CICS applications, you know that they're similar to IMS DC programs in that they usually don't sit idle while users enter data for them. In fact, there are other similarities between IMS DC and CICS that you'll recognize as you read on.

However, I want to warn you not to make assumptions about how you think IMS DC should work based on what you already know about CICS. As you'll see, there are many differences between IMS DC and CICS. For example, if many terminal users are running an application, the IMS system funnels all of their messages through one program. In contrast, CICS treats each terminal user separately; it considers each terminal user to be running his own copy of the program. You'll also see that IMS DC programs differ from CICS programs (1) in how directly they're tied to terminal operations, (2) in where and how they're scheduled to execute, and (3) in how they're designed and coded.

Because your application program is closely tied to IMS, you need to understand the services IMS provides for you. It's IMS that's always running, ready to pass data back and forth between your terminal and your program. But IMS serves not only you and your program, but many other terminal users on your network as well. If several other terminal users are entering data for the same program you are (in other words, if they seem to all be running the same program), all of the input messages they enter are routed to the same application program by IMS. IMS keeps track of where each input message came from and where each output message the application program sends should go.

HOW IMS FITS INTO THE MVS ENVIRONMENT

As you can imagine, IMS is complex, sophisticated, and powerful. Just think about how complicated it must be to manage networks with thousands of terminals and hundreds of application programs. This section describes how IMS uses MVS regions, then it covers the way IMS deals with terminals and security.

How IMS uses MVS regions

As you know, IMS DC executes under the control of the MVS operating system. Although it's well beyond the scope of this book to teach you the specifics of how MVS works, I do want to describe briefly how it provides storage for users. That's because IMS depends heavily on MVS to provide for the execution of multiple application programs.

Although the processor on which a given shop runs MVS has a fixed amount of real storage, MVS uses several techniques to provide a far greater amount of virtual storage for users. To make that expanded storage available for many purposes, MVS provides *multiple virtual storages* (hence the acronym *MVS*), which are called *address spaces*.

An address space is simply a range of storage addresses, from 0 up to the limit of the processor's addressing capability. For most of the processor types that support MVS, that limit is 16 megabytes. As a result, the size of an address space is usually 16 megabytes. (Newer processors and the most current versions of MVS, called MVS/XA, can handle larger addresses and, as a result, can support larger address spaces. However, for the purposes of this book, you don't need to worry about that.)

Address spaces can be created when the MVS system is initialized or dynamically after it is up and running. For example, a typical MVS system uses several address spaces to process batch jobs submitted to it. They're usually started when MVS is started, and they're always present. In contrast, when a TSO user signs on to start a terminal session, an address space is created for her; when her terminal session ends, the address space is deleted.

Each address space is divided into three main parts: the *system area*, the *common area*, and the *private area*. The system and common areas contain operating system programs and data that are shared by all of the address spaces on the system. In other words, the system area and the common area are the same for each address space. In contrast, the private area for each address space is unique.

The private area of an address space has several components. Some contain system programs and data that must be unique to the address space and, as a result, cannot be shared with other address spaces. Most of the private area, however, is available for user programs; that amounts to 10 to 12 megabytes in most cases.

The available range of addresses in the private area is either unallocated or allocated to a *user region*. It's in the user region that a program or programs execute. The actual size of the user region varies depending on the amount of storage required by the program being executed.

An IMS system uses several user regions, each in its own address space. All are managed from one user region, the *IMS control region* (also called the *CTL region*), where the *IMS control program* resides. From within the IMS control region, IMS components (called *modules*) provide a variety of services to support the rest of the system. For example, all data base processing in the system is done through the control region. As a result, comprehensive logging, also done through the control region, is possible.

The user regions in the other address spaces IMS uses are called *dependent regions*. It's in these dependent regions that DC application programs are executed. IMS can manage many dependent regions. In fact, under IMS/VS 1.3 and MVS/XA, there can be up to 255 dependent regions. Although that's the limit, the actual number is almost certain to be smaller; usually, there are just a few.

There are two kinds of dependent regions: message processing program regions and batch message processing regions. As an example, figure 3-4 presents a small IMS system that supports several terminals, three message processing program regions, and one batch message processing region.

MPP regions   As you'd expect, a *message processing program region*, or *MPP region*, is where IMS schedules and executes message processing programs, as I described in the first section of this chapter. Most of the dependent regions in an IMS DC system are MPP regions. A system has a fixed number of MPP regions (specified by the IMS system administrator); all are managed by the IMS control program running in the control region. The number of MPP regions determines the number of MPPs that can be active at any one time. For example, on the system illustrated in figure 3-4, there are three MPP regions, so no more than three message processing programs can be running at the same time.

Typically, a program that occupies an MPP region runs until it has processed all of the input messages that IMS has received for it. Then it ends, and the MPP region in which it was running is freed and made available for another application program.

When an MPP region is free, IMS schedules another MPP in it. Which program IMS schedules depends on the messages IMS has received from terminal users but hasn't been able to process yet. As you can imagine, the programs that run in a given MPP region can change rapidly. Although this seems like it might result in long waits for terminal users, that's usually not the case because the system is so much faster than operators are.

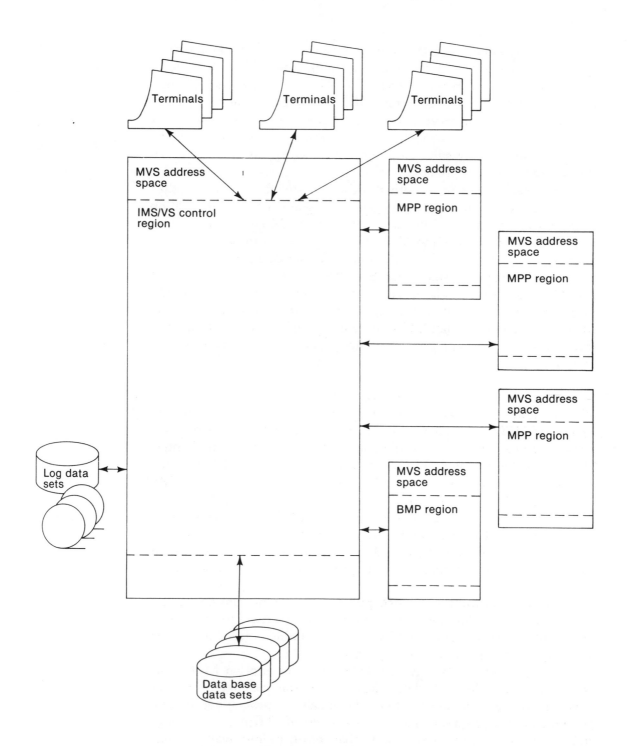

Figure 3-4   The IMS control region provides terminal control, data base management, and logging
services for application programs in dependent regions

BMP regions   The other kind of dependent region that can be part of an IMS DC system is a *batch message processing region*, or *BMP region*. A BMP region is used to run a kind of IMS DC program called a *batch message processing program*, or *BMP program*. A BMP program is much like an MPP, except terminal response is not required for each input message, and the data base processing an input message requires does not have to be done immediately.

A BMP program is even more like a typical batch program than an MPP. As terminal users enter transactions through the IMS terminal system for a BMP program, IMS accumulates them into a batch. Then, during off hours, the IMS system operator can explicitly start the BMP program.

In contrast, the basic rule for an MPP is that it's scheduled and executed automatically by IMS as rapidly as possible whenever a message for it is present. The objective is for an MPP to reply to the terminal user as quickly as it can. Although a typical IMS system will be generated to support several MPP regions, most will have only one or two BMP regions.

Why implement what's really a batch program as a BMP program? So the BMP program can access data bases that are allocated to the IMS control region for use by MPPs at the same time; a batch DL/I program running in an independent region cannot access on-line data bases. With a BMP program, it's possible for batched transactions to be posted to data bases that are used by interactive programs without disrupting the operations of the interactive programs.

Control region   As you can tell, the functions of the IMS control region are varied and complicated. Again, I want to point out that all terminal, data base, and logging operations associated with IMS DC programs are performed through the control region. As a result, IMS DC has centralized control over its data bases, terminals, and logs.

In addition to the functional modules that provide IMS services, the control region also contains a variety of control blocks that are required by the functional modules. For example, Data Management Blocks that define the characteristics of the data bases allocated to the control region are stored in the control region. Also, areas of storage that are used for buffers (for functions like terminal and data base I/O) are part of the control region address space.

Terminals and security under IMS

In the last chapter, I described the basic hardware components that make up a data communications system. Here, I just want to describe how IMS views terminals. Remember that IMS is insulated from many of the technical details of terminal use by telecommunications access methods, particularly VTAM.

One of the functional modules of IMS, the *communications control module*, does the processing necessary to remove device and TC line control information from inbound messages and to add appropriate control information to outbound messages. More important from the application programmer's point of view is that the communications control module replaces physical terminal identifiers with logical terminal names for input messages and vice versa for output messages.

Logical terminals   For application functions, IMS uses *logical terminal* (or *LTERM*) names rather than physical terminal names or addresses. Within IMS, each LTERM name is associated with one and only one physical terminal (although the same terminal can have more than one LTERM name). As a result, if IMS knows an LTERM name, it knows what physical terminal is associated with it.

Because IMS uses LTERM names for message processing, it's possible for the IMS operator to reassign logical terminals to different physical devices if some terminals are out of service. Through logical terminals, IMS insulates application programs from the organization of the terminal network.

Although the scheme varies from system to system, it's common for logical terminal names, which are limited to eight characters, to follow a standard that helps systems programmers and operators identify where a terminal is located and whether it's a display station or a printer. For example, LDPAYR01, LDPAYR02, and LDPAYR03 might be the LTERM names for three logical terminals (L in position 1 of the names) that are display stations (D in position 2) in the payroll department (PAYR in positions 3-6). Similarly, LPPAYR01 might be the LTERM name for a printer in the payroll department (P instead of D in position 2).

For simple DC programming, you don't need to be concerned with LTERM names. That's because IMS keeps track of the sources of input messages and automatically causes output messages to be routed back to the originating terminals.

However, for some applications, you may need to use an advanced DC function that lets you manipulate output message destinations in your application programs. For instance, you might be asked to design and code a program that posts an invoice transaction to a data base and also prints a copy of the invoice at a printer near the originating display station. In that case, you'd need to deal with LTERM names in your program. Or, for some unusual application, you might want the display output message to be routed to a terminal other than the one from which the input message came. Again, to do that, you'd have to deal with LTERM names.

Master terminal   One logical terminal in the IMS network is designated as the *master terminal*; it's the operational center of the system. The *master terminal operator (MTO)* can manage other terminals in the network, as well as messages and program executions in dependent regions. The MTO can also dynamically adjust resources established when the system was started. For example, if one physical terminal is disabled, the MTO can reassign the LTERM name normally associated with it to another nearby terminal so work can continue.

Security features   One of the major strong points of IMS is that it provides substantial security features. These are in effect for both data base and terminal use. This section describes security features that relate to terminals.

IMS terminal security is provided by three components: (1) IMS/VS itself, (2) features implemented through *SMU* (the *Security Maintenance Utility)*, and (3) *RACF* (the *Resource Access Control Facility*). IMS systems programmers have to be aware of which product provides which type of security. For users, however, they appear to work together.

If no security control features are specified, IMS *default terminal security* is in effect. Under IMS default terminal security, users can run any transaction and can issue a subset of the IMS commands available to the master terminal operator. However, default terminal security by itself is unusual. It's more common for one or more of these features to be used: (1) sign-on verification security, (2) LTERM security, and (3) password security.

When *sign-on verification security* is in effect, the user has to enter a sign-on command with an appropriate identification. Otherwise, the user isn't allowed to proceed.

After a user has signed on successfully, the work he can do may be restricted to certain transactions. This is called *transaction authorization*. For example, a user whose sign-on identification indicates he is from the purchasing department probably won't be authorized to run a transaction to display payroll status information, even if he is able to access a terminal in the payroll department. RACF or a user exit routine can be used to implement transaction authorization.

Authorization of transactions can also be associated with specific logical terminals. When the IMS system is started, certain transactions are authorized for certain logical terminals. This is called *LTERM security*. When this kind of security is in effect, a payroll department employee probably couldn't invoke a payroll transaction from a terminal in the purchasing department, even though the employee is authorized to run the transaction.

For additional protection, *password security* can be used. With it, an authorized user has to supply a password to run a particular transaction or issue a particular command. If this were the case, the payroll employee could run a payroll inquiry only after properly signing on at an authorized terminal and supplying the proper password to invoke the transaction.

When security violations are detected, IMS issues a message to the terminal and records the violation. As a result, it's possible for the system manager to monitor possible abuses and stop them. Again, you don't have to be thoroughly familiar with the security features IMS provides, but recognizing them can help you understand an advantage IMS offers.

The procedures terminal users have to go through to access IMS and begin data entry vary, even on the same system. Terminal users have to get these procedures from their department supervisors, who in turn get them from the data center operations staff. Fortunately, though, you don't need to worry about the layers of security that might be in place on your system to design and develop application programs.

HOW IMS PROCESSES MESSAGES

This section describes the steps IMS goes through as it processes messages. First, you'll learn about the different kinds of input messages IMS recognizes and how it handles them. Second, you'll see how IMS schedules application programs to execute and how it supports them while they're running. And third, you'll learn how IMS handles output messages produced by application programs. Finally, to summarize, this section ends by outlining the path a single transaction follows as it's worked through the system.

How IMS manages input messages

Although you don't necessarily have to deal with IMS and associated security features to create application programs, you do have to be concerned with the data the terminal user enters that is eventually passed to your program as an input message. This section describes input messages. First, it introduces the kinds of input messages IMS can handle; then it focuses specifically on one of them: the transaction (an input message that's bound for an application program).

Input message types   There are three kinds of IMS input messages: (1) transactions, (2) *terminal-to-terminal message switches* (or just *message switches*), and (3) *IMS commands*. You already know a little about the transaction, and this section will tell you much more, so I just want to mention the other two first. The second of the three types, the message switch, is an input message that's directed to another terminal. For example, the master terminal operator could use a message switch to communicate with certain terminal users. The last of the three types is the IMS command; it's an input message that's directed to IMS itself. Commands are used most by the master terminal operator to manage the IMS system, but other terminal users can use a subset of the IMS commands.

IMS uses the value in the first eight bytes of an input message to identify the message's type. If the first eight characters name an application program (identified to IMS during system definition), IMS knows that the message is a transaction. The first eight bytes of a transaction are called the *transaction code*. Similarly, if the first eight characters contain an LTERM name (also identified to IMS during system definition), IMS knows the message is a message switch. The IMS DC system administrator has be careful to avoid using the same name for an application program and a logical terminal; that's one of the reasons IMS shops follow rigid conventions for naming LTERMs and programs. Finally, if the input message begins with a slash, IMS interprets it as a command.

Figure 3-5 illustrates how IMS handles the three kinds of input messages. Here, three display stations and one printer (with the LTERM names I described earlier) are all involved in IMS operations. The terminal user at the display station associated with the LTERM name LDPAYR01 keys in the LTERM name of the printer (LPPAYR01) and some text. Because the message this user entered begins with an LTERM name, IMS routes it to the named terminal, which in this case is the local terminal printer.

The user at the second display station (LDPAYR02) has keyed in a transaction code (PAYR3410), followed by data that the associated application program will process; this is the basic form of a transaction. In this case, the data might be an employee number and the program might use it to retrieve segments for the specified employee from an employee data base. Then, the program might extract data from those

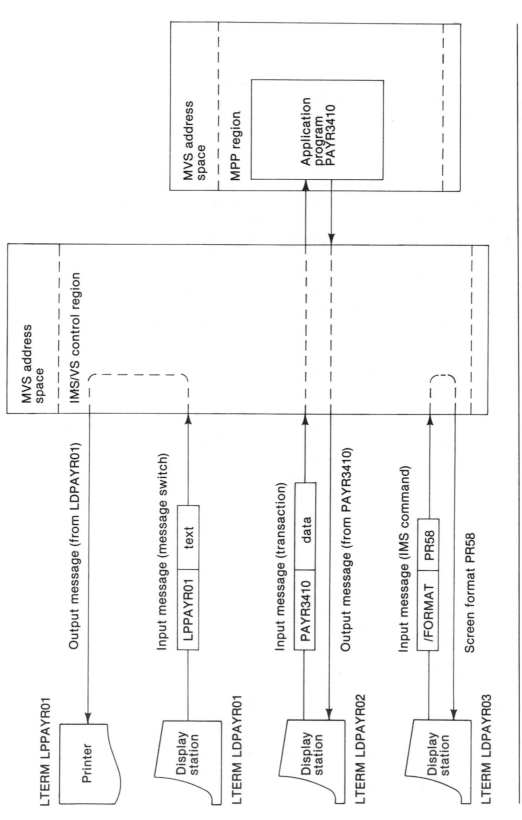

Figure 3-5   How IMS handles the three kinds of input messages

segments and use it to build an informational display for the terminal user, which it sends back to the terminal as an output message.

The user at the third display station (LDPAYR03) has keyed in an input message that begins with a slash. As a result, IMS interprets the message as a command. In this case, it's a /FORMAT command. This command, which you'll use all the time, tells IMS to format the display station screen for data entry for a particular application. To understand how a formatted entry differs from an unformatted entry like the one made by the user at the second display station in figure 3-5, you need to know more about input message editing.

Input message editing   When IMS receives a message from a terminal, it isn't passed immediately to the appropriate destination. Instead, it first undergoes editing. The editing that can occur varies, but two types are most common: IMS *basic edit* and *Message Format Service (MFS) edit*.

Basic edit does little more than remove communication control characters from input messages and add them to output messages. In contrast, *Message Format Service* provides more extensive editing functions. *MFS* modules reside in the control region and provide powerful features that let you exploit the formatted display capabilities of 3270 devices. By coding special control statements that create MFS blocks, you can define complex, formatted screens and improve processing efficiency.

An advantage of MFS is that it insulates the application program from the format of data entered from specific kinds of terminal devices. That lets users at different terminal types provide input in the same format to a program. But even more important, MFS lets you define formatted display screens that enhance the appearance and function of interactive applications. Because MFS provides such advantages, a large part of this book focuses on it, and all of the IMS DC program examples I present use messages that are processed through MFS.

To tell IMS to format a screen using the MFS specifications for a particular application, the terminal user issues the /FORMAT command, as the user at the third terminal in figure 3-5 did. The screen format can cause captions to be displayed at appropriate locations on the display screen and might guide the operator through the entry sequence for a complicated transaction.

After the operator has finished entering data and has pressed the enter key, MFS interprets the data actually on the screen and rearranges it in the format required by the application program. In essence, MFS builds the input message that the application program will receive. As part of building that message, it can insert the eight-character transaction code at the beginning of the message. As long as the terminal operator has gotten the right screen in the first place, MFS can relieve him of many of the details he would have to worry about if basic edit were in effect, such as supplying the transaction code and sequencing the input data in exactly the right order with the right spacing.

Input message queueing   Regardless of whether basic edit is in effect or MFS facilities are being used, transactions still aren't passed directly to their destination application programs after they're edited. Remember, the entry a terminal user makes to invoke a transaction and the execution of the application program with which it's associated aren't synchronous. As a result, IMS has to store the transaction temporarily. This is called *message queueing*, and it's a major IMS function.

The IMS modules that perform message queueing are collectively called the *queue manager*, and they store transactions in the *message queue*, also called the *QPOOL*. The QPOOL is an area of virtual storage within the control region that can be extended if necessary into overflow data sets on DASD. Although the virtual storage buffer and the group of data sets that contain messages are considered to be a single unit, IMS terminology associates one *input message queue* with each transaction code.

How IMS supports an application program

The presence of an input message in a transaction's queue indicates to IMS that it can schedule that program to execute in a dependent region. This section describes both scheduling and how IMS supports programs as they execute.

Scheduling   After the edited input message, beginning with the transaction code, has been queued, IMS DC's *scheduling modules* determine when to load and execute the corresponding message processing program. If an input message is queued for an MPP that isn't already running and a suitable MPP dependent region is free, IMS *schedules* the program into that region without operator intervention.

Compare this automatic program scheduling with the way a batch program is invoked. When a group of batch transactions have been gathered, the program is invoked through JCL. In contrast, IMS is always running in its control region and is ready to invoke an MPP in a dependent region whenever a transaction for the program is added to the corresponding input message queue.

However, in a typical IMS DC system, there are hundreds of terminal users who can invoke hundreds of applications. Usually, when an MPP is scheduled, it quickly processes the message (or messages) on its queue, then it ends. Because system resources are limited, IMS has to pick and choose which programs to schedule. To do that, it uses a scheduling scheme that involves classes, priorities, and processing limits.

Up to four *message classes*, numeric values between 1 and 255, are associated with each dependent region. Message classes are used to force application programs to execute in particular regions. When an application program is defined to IMS, it's assigned one message class value. Then, for IMS to be able to schedule that program for execution when an input transaction is present for it, a dependent region that has the same message class must be available.

If multiple transaction types are queued but too few dependent regions are available for all of them to be processed at the same time, IMS makes scheduling decisions. To determine what transaction to schedule in a particular region, IMS evaluates the message classes associated with that region. The order in which the systems programmer specified the classes is the order in which IMS selects associated transactions for scheduling. The higher the class, the sooner the transactions are scheduled.

It's possible that two or more different transactions with the same class may be queued for execution. When that's the case, IMS evaluates a *priority* value that is also associated with the transaction code. If two transactions with the same preferred class are available for scheduling in an available region, IMS selects the one with the higher priority value. If priorities are equal, IMS schedules the transaction that's been in the input queue the longest.

To make sure transactions don't back up and cause unacceptable waits for terminal users, IMS uses still other scheduling techniques. In addition to specifying a normal priority for a transaction, the systems programmer can also specify a *limit count* and *limit priority*. When the number of input messages for a single transaction code reaches the specified limit count, the priority of that transaction is raised to the limit priority.

For example, suppose a transaction is defined with a normal priority of 3, a limit priority of 10, and a limit count of 4. When only one, two, or three input messages for that transaction code are queued, its priority is a relatively low 3. But when a fourth input message is received, IMS increases the transaction's priority to 10. As a result, IMS will be more likely to schedule the transaction the next time an appropriate region becomes available.

As you can imagine, the systems programmer can exercise a high level of control over the scheduling functions of IMS by making proper decisions about region message classes, and transaction message class, priority, limit priority, and limit count. In a network with hundreds of users and applications, this kind of control is essential to insure optimum responses to all users.

IMS also includes features to make heavily used programs more readily available. For example, a program can be defined as a *wait-for-input (WFI) program*. When a WFI program has processed all of the input messages queued for it, it isn't replaced in its region by another program. Instead, it's retained there, waiting for another transaction. (This violates the general rule that IMS DC programs end and are removed from their region when no more input messages are available for them.)

Specifying that a program should be WFI saves the overhead of retrieving and loading a heavily used program many times during a processing period and is appropriate for very heavily used applications. However, it also reduces the number of MPP regions available for other applications. As a result, the systems programmer will be reluctant to make any but the most intensively used programs WFI. In fact, they're likely to be so heavily used that they're busy almost all of the time anyway.

Another feature that can be used for very heavily used programs is *parallel scheduling*. This allows the same transaction to be scheduled into more than one region at the same time. (In contrast, the usual technique is for an application to run in only one region at a time.) Parallel scheduling is useful for programs that have to process an especially large number of input transactions. For example, an installation's most heavily used data entry program might be set up with parallel scheduling. That way, the transactions entered by dozens or hundreds of users can be processed faster than they would be otherwise.

DL/I   Unlike the batch DL/I environment, in which DL/I modules are part of the program region, DL/I resides outside the dependent region in the DC environment. Depending on systems programming decisions, the DL/I modules may reside in the IMS control region or in a separate address space. In either case, the important point to note is that they are not in the same address spaces as the application programs that run under the control of IMS and, as a result, can be shared by all dependent regions.

Another advantage this offers is that operations that require DL/I services are centralized. All on-line data bases are allocated to the control region, not individual dependent regions. This is required because data bases are shared in the IMS DC system; several programs may need to access the same data bases at the same time. The control region insures the integrity of those data bases.

In the DC environment, application programs issue DL/I calls for data base functions, just as batch programs do. But in addition, DC programs also issue DL/I calls to request IMS functions for terminal I/O. An application program issues DL/I calls to retrieve input message segments from the message queue, much like a batch program executes a READ statement to retrieve a transaction record from a transaction file. Also, application programs issue DL/I calls to send output messages back to the originating terminals. This parallels the way a batch program prints a report line with the WRITE statement. In other words, message-processing DL/I calls take the place of some of the READ and WRITE statements you'd expect in standard batch COBOL programs. You'll learn more about these functions in the next chapter.

Logging and restart functions   In addition to providing centralized control over DL/I data base processing, logging of application program activity (both data communication and data base) is also done through the control region. Because it records program calls on a common set of log data sets, the control region can dynamically reverse the effects of application programs that abend. *Data Base Recovery Control* facilities (*DBRC*) are used in the interactive environment to support data sharing and system logging. In chapter 13, you'll learn more about the sophisticated logging and recovery facilities of IMS DC.

How IMS manages output messages

IMS manages output messages produced by application programs much as it does input messages. Specifically, IMS queues an output message and uses editing to change the format of the queued message before transmitting it to a terminal.

Output message queueing   As I mentioned when I described logical terminals, IMS keeps track of the logical terminal from which an input message came. Then, when it eventually supplies that message to an application program, it knows that it will route the output message the program produces back to the originating terminal, unless the program changes the destination. As a result, an application program usually doesn't have to figure out where a message came from or where one will go.

Output messages are queued for transmission to a terminal much like transactions are queued for retrieval by an application program. There's one *output message queue* for each logical terminal. When the logical terminal is available (and typically it's already available because it's waiting for a response), the message is edited for output, then transmitted to the terminal by IMS's communications control module.

Output message editing   As with input messages, output messages can also be edited. If IMS basic edit is in effect, the application program is responsible for all the details of formatting the output message properly for its destination device. Basic edit supplies the additional telecommunication line and device control characters required to get the message back to the terminal.

It's more likely that MFS will be used to edit the output message. Then, the application program is relieved of most device-dependent formatting responsibilities. Different MFS blocks can be used to insure that messages transmitted to different devices from the same application program appear correctly. Also, MFS can improve processing efficiency by allowing the program to send only variable data to the device, with constant data handled by MFS itself.

A summary of transaction processing

Now that I've described the major steps in processing a transaction, I want to summarize them. Again, I stress that these steps occur in *rapid* succession. To help you follow these steps, I've included figure 3-6, which illustrates an IMS system and shows some of the modules that make up IMS.

Input originates at a terminal, which as the figure shows, may or may not be under the control of the telecommunications access method VTAM. From the point of view of the application programmer, it doesn't matter if the message is from a VTAM terminal or not.

The input message is handled first within IMS by its communication control module, then it's passed to the appropriate editing modules. It's almost certain that MFS will be in use, so that's what figure 3-6 shows. After the input message has been reformatted by MFS, it's passed to the queue manager to be stored on the message queue.

The queue manager tries to store the input message in virtual storage (that is, in the QPOOL) so it can be retrieved rapidly when its

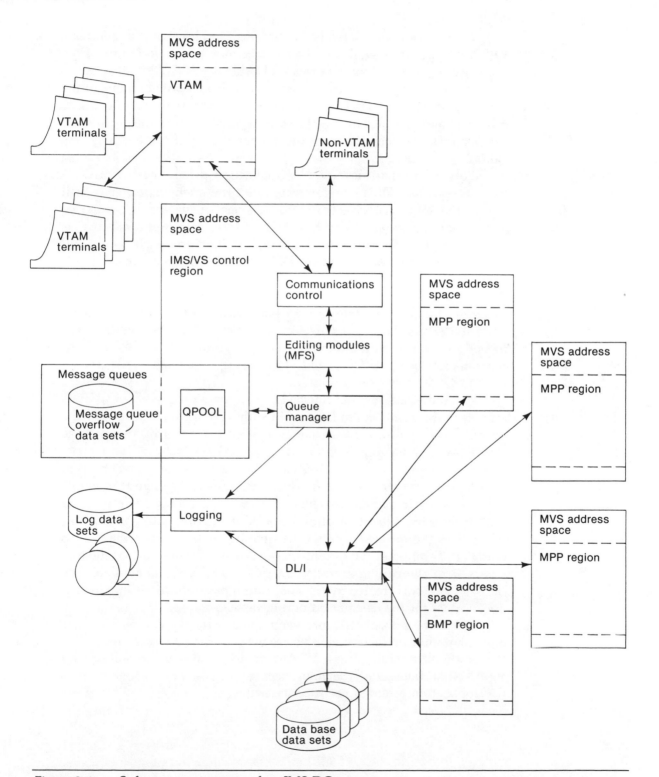

Figure 3-6   Software components of an IMS DC system

application program is ready to process it. However, if adequate QPOOL space isn't available, the message may be stored in one of the message queue overflow data sets on DASD.

When the input message is queued, it's also recorded on one of the IMS log data sets. That's what the connection between the queue manager and the logging functions in figure 3-6 indicates. After the input message is logged, it can be recovered even if there is a system failure.

To get an input message, the application program issues a DL/I call. In response, DL/I communicates with the queue manager, which passes the input message from the message queue via DL/I to the application program. After this is complete, the input message is available to the program in the I/O area specified on the DL/I call, and the program can use the data in the message however it needs to.

It's likely that part of the processing the program does will involve data base access and update using information from the input message. When the program updates a data base, it uses DL/I calls just like a batch DL/I program. In the DC environment, data base updates are logged by logging modules in the control region. That's what the connection between the DL/I and the logging functions in figure 3-6 indicates.

When the program has finished its data base processing, it formats an output message and sends it, again with a DL/I call. DL/I passes the output message to the queue manager, which stores it on the message queue. Again, logging is invoked to record the message and make restart easier in the event of a system failure. At this point, the program is probably ready to retrieve another input message and go through its processing cycle again. However, I want to continue to follow the output message it just sent until it's back at the originating terminal.

When the device that's the destination of the output message is ready, IMS retrieves the output message from the message queue and passes it to the editing modules. In figure 3-6, MFS manipulates the message as it was created by the application program so it's in a format appropriate for the destination output device.

Then, the reformatted message is passed by the communications control module to the terminal, where the user can review the output. If the destination terminal is a VTAM device, it has to be handled by VTAM first, but as with the input message, that isn't important as far as the application programmer is concerned.

DISCUSSION

All of the technical detail this chapter has presented is important because for any but the simplest of DC programs, you're going to have to deal with some elements of it. For example, you might have to design and code the MFS blocks that reformat input and output messages between the terminal and the application program. Or, you might have to contend with IMS logging functions, or write a program that causes output messages to be routed to destinations other than the terminals that originated the input messages. To use any of these features, you need to understand the underlying IMS functions.

Terminology

input message

output message

message

transaction

message processing program

MPP

CICS/VS

Customer Information Control
    System/Virtual Storage

multiple virtual storage

MVS

address space

system area

common area

private area

user region

IMS control region

CTL region

IMS control program

module

dependent region

message processing
    program region

MPP region

batch message processing region

BMP region

batch message processing program

BMP program

communications control module

logical terminal

LTERM

master terminal

master terminal operator

MTO

SMU

Security Maintenance Utility

RACF

Resource Access Control Facility

default terminal security

sign-on verification security

transaction authorization

LTERM security

password security

terminal-to-terminal
    message switch

message switch

IMS command

transaction code

basic edit

Message Format Service edit

MFS edit

Message Format Service

MFS

message queueing

queue manager

message queue

QPOOL

input message queue

scheduling module

schedule

message class

priority

limit count

limit priority

wait-for-input program

WFI program

parallel scheduling

Data Base Recovery Control

DBRC

output message queue

Objectives

1. Compare and contrast an IMS DC program with:

   a. a typical batch program.
   b. other types of interactive programs.

2. Name and describe the functions of the three main region types used under IMS DC.

3. Explain why IMS uses logical terminal names rather than physical terminal names for application program operations.

4. Describe the security features IMS offers.

5. Differentiate among the three types of input messages.

6. Describe input and output message queueing.

7. Differentiate between the two main types of message editing IMS uses.

8. Describe the scheduling techniques IMS uses.

9. Differentiate between DL/I support for batch programs and DC programs.

10. Trace the path a transaction follows from the time the terminal user sends it to the time the response is received at his terminal.

Chapter 4

COBOL basics for
message processing programs

This chapter introduces you to COBOL programming for the IMS DC environment. First, it shows you the programming elements for message processing. Then, the chapter presents a sample DC program.

PROGRAMMING ELEMENTS FOR DC PROCESSING

The elements you code in a DC program to process messages are extensions of the same elements you use to process data bases. This section describes (1) DL/I calls for DC operations, (2) the PCB mask for DC operations, (3) how to retrieve input message segments, and (4) how to send output message segments.

DL/I calls for DC operations

Just like data base calls, the basic unit of I/O for a data communication DL/I call is a *segment*. Although most messages consist of just one segment occurrence, some may contain multiple segments. However, unlike data base segments, message segments are not arranged hierarchically. Instead, they just represent parts of a message.

Figure 4-1 compares a DL/I data base call and a DL/I data communications call. Both invoke the COBOL-DL/I interface module,

A data base call

```
CALL 'CBLTDLI' USING DLI-GU
                     CR-PCB-MASK
                     RECEIVABLE-SEGMENT
                     INVOICE-NO-SSA.
```

A data communications call

```
CALL 'CBLTDLI' USING DLI-GU
                     IO-PCB-MASK
                     INPUT-MESSAGE-SEGMENT.
```

Figure 4-1   A data base call and a data communications call

CBLTDLI. And both specify a DL/I function, a PCB mask, and an I/O area. In this section, I'll describe how you use each of these three elements in a DC call. (The fourth element of a DB call, the SSA, isn't used on a DC call.)

DL/I function in a DC call   Just as in a data base call, the first argument you code on a DC call is the name of a four-character working-storage field that contains the proper function code value for the operation you want DL/I to perform. You can use the same call-function field definitions that you use for data base calls; figure 4-2 presents the ones I use.

The call functions you use for basic message processing applications are the ones that are shaded in figure 4-2: get-unique (GU), get-next (GN), and insert (ISRT). You issue a GU call to retrieve the first (and, most often, only) segment of an input message. If an input message contains multiple segments, you retrieve subsequent ones with GN calls. And to send an output message, you issue one ISRT call for each segment in the message.

PCB mask in a DC call   As with a DB call, a DC call must specify a Linkage Section PCB mask. However, the PCB mask you specify isn't a data base PCB mask, but a special one that's just for message processing. In IMS terminology, it's called the *I/O PCB*.

Just like a data base PCB, the I/O PCB resides outside your program. To provide addressability to it, your program must name its Linkage Section mask definition on the ENTRY statement at the beginning of the Procedure Division. The only restriction you need to

```
 01   DLI-FUNCTIONS.
 *
      05   DLI-GU              PIC X(4)    VALUE 'GU  '.
      05   DLI-GHU             PIC X(4)    VALUE 'GHU '.
      05   DLI-GN              PIC X(4)    VALUE 'GN  '.
      05   DLI-GHN             PIC X(4)    VALUE 'GHN '.
      05   DLI-GNP             PIC X(4)    VALUE 'GNP '.
      05   DLI-GHNP            PIC X(4)    VALUE 'GHNP'.
      05   DLI-ISRT            PIC X(4)    VALUE 'ISRT'.
      05   DLI-DLET            PIC X(4)    VALUE 'DLET'.
      05   DLI-REPL            PIC X(4)    VALUE 'REPL'.
      05   DLI-CHKP            PIC X(4)    VALUE 'CHKP'.
      05   DLI-XRST            PIC X(4)    VALUE 'XRST'.
      05   DLI-PCB             PIC X(4)    VALUE 'PCB '.
 *
```

Figure 4-2   COBOL code for DL/I call function fields

remember is that for the I/O PCB to be addressed properly, it must be the *first* PCB listed on the ENTRY statement.

The data you can access through the I/O PCB mask describes the message processing your program does. As you'd expect, that information differs from the information that describes data base processing. As a result, the format of the I/O PCB is different from a data base PCB's format. In a moment, I'll describe the format of the I/O PCB. But first, I want to describe the last argument you code on a typical DC call: the segment I/O area.

Segment I/O area in a DC call   Just like a data base call, a DC call specifies a segment I/O area that's defined in your program's Working-Storage Section. When you issue a GU or GN call to retrieve an input message segment, DL/I places the message segment data in the I/O area the call names. Similarly, when you issue an ISRT call to send an output message segment, DL/I gets the data from the I/O area you name. Of course, as with a data base ISRT call, you must first build the output data in the I/O area.

A problem you might have when you develop a DC program is deciding how to code its I/O area fields. Because message segments can vary in size, the I/O areas you use must be large enough to contain the largest segment that will be processed through them. In addition, you have to provide a prefix field in every message; the prefix contains IMS control information. As I show you how to retrieve and send messages, I'll describe the I/O area format requirements in more detail. At any

```
01   IO-PCB-MASK.
*
     05   IO-PCB-LOGICAL-TERMINAL  PIC  X(8).
     05   FILLER                   PIC  XX.
     05   IO-PCB-STATUS-CODE       PIC  XX.
     05   IO-PCB-DATE              PIC  S9(7)      COMP-3.
     05   IO-PCB-TIME              PIC  S9(6)V9    COMP-3.
     05   IO-PCB-MSG-SEQ-NUMBER    PIC  S9(5)      COMP.
     05   IO-PCB-MOD-NAME          PIC  X(8).
     05   IO-PCB-USER-ID           PIC  X(8).
*
```

Figure 4-3   COBOL code for an I/O PCB mask

rate, when you receive specifications for a DC program, they should indicate the formats of its I/O areas.

The PCB mask for DC operations

Figure 4-3 shows a complete I/O PCB mask in COBOL. For most DC applications, the only I/O PCB field you need to be concerned with is the status code field. As in a data base PCB, it's two bytes long and is located in positions 11 and 12. When I describe how to use message processing calls later in this chapter, I'll present status code values you can expect.

Most of the other fields in the I/O PCB simply contain information that identifies the message the program is processing. The first field, called IO-PCB-LOGICAL-TERMINAL in figure 4-3, contains the eight-byte LTERM name of the terminal that sent the current input message. Because IMS keeps track of the terminal that was the source of an input message, your program doesn't have to identify the source and specify the destination for an output message. All you have to do is specify the name of the I/O PCB on the ISRT call that sends an output message, and IMS takes care of routing the output message back to the terminal that originated the current input message.

It is possible to route an output message to a destination other than the terminal that originated the input message. To do that, however, you do *not* change the LTERM name in the I/O PCB. Instead, you have to use another data communications PCB, called the *alternate PCB*. This is an advanced function you'll learn about in chapter 10. For now, just remember that you shouldn't change the LTERM value in the I/O PCB.

After the name of the originating logical terminal are two bytes that are reserved for IMS (positions 9 and 10), and the two-byte status code field (positions 11 and 12). Then, the I/O PCB includes two fields that together provide time-stamp identification for the input message. Both are four-byte fields that contain packed decimal (COMP-3 usage) data. The first (in positions 13 through 16) contains the date when IMS queued the input message. It's in the format YYDDD (year and day within year). The second (in positions 17 through 20) contains the time when IMS queued the input message. Its format is HHMMSS.T (hours, minutes, seconds, assumed decimal point, and tenths of a second).

You might have reasons to use the date and time in some programs, but you'll probably never need to use the data in positions 21 through 24: the input message sequence number. This four-byte field contains a serial number assigned to the input message by IMS. The number is stored as a binary value (COMP usage).

Next in the I/O PCB is an eight-byte alphanumeric field that contains the name of the Message Format Service message definition (called a Message Output Descriptor, or MOD) currently in use. In the next chapter, you'll learn just what the MOD is. For now, I want you to realize that it's possible to change the MOD (and thus change the format of the screen displayed at the user's terminal) by using an additional argument on an ISRT call for an output message segment. You'll learn how to do that in chapter 8.

The last field in the I/O PCB is an eight-byte alphanumeric field that may contain security information. Its contents depend (1) on whether or not the security manager RACF is installed on your system, (2) on the kind of security checking in effect if RACF is installed, and (3) on the source of the message. The field may contain blanks (if RACF isn't in use), the user-id of the operator who sent the input message (if sign-on verification is in effect), or the LTERM name of the originating terminal (if sign-on verification is not in effect).

Obviously, the I/O PCB contains a variety of information that may be useful for some applications. However, I want to stress again that for most programs, all you're interested in is the status code field.

How to retrieve an input message

To retrieve an input message, an application program issues either a single GU call or a GU call followed by one or more GN calls. The technique you use depends on how many segments the input message contains. That's a decision the system designer makes and that should

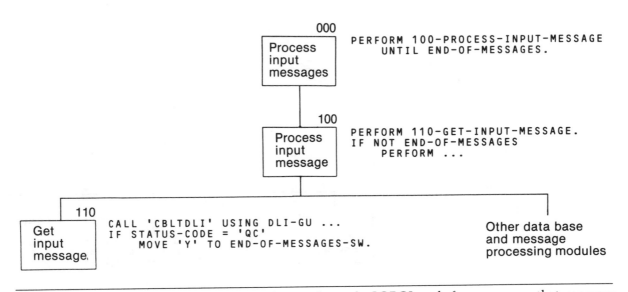

000
Process input messages

PERFORM 100-PROCESS-INPUT-MESSAGE
        UNTIL END-OF-MESSAGES.

100
Process input message

PERFORM 110-GET-INPUT-MESSAGE.
IF NOT END-OF-MESSAGES
        PERFORM ...

110
Get input message,

CALL 'CBLTDLI' USING DLI-GU ...
IF STATUS-CODE = 'QC'
        MOVE 'Y' TO END-OF-MESSAGES-SW.

Other data base and message processing modules

Figure 4-4   A partial program structure chart and sample COBOL code for a program that processes single-segment input messages

be specified in your program specifications. However, as I've already said, most programs process single-segment messages.

How to retrieve single-segment input messages   If an input message consists of just one segment occurrence, all you need to do is issue one GU call to retrieve it. When this is the case, your MPP is much like a batch transaction processing program. The batch program executes a READ statement to retrieve a transaction record from an input file, then does data base processing and reporting based upon the data in the transaction. The program repeats this cycle for each record in the transaction file. When the batch program encounters the AT END condition for the transaction file, it ends.

An MPP works similarly, but instead of being driven by transaction records in a transaction file, it's driven by messages in the message queue. Figure 4-4 presents a partial structure chart and sample COBOL source code to illustrate this. The MPP issues a DC GU call (that is, a GU call that specifies the I/O PCB) to retrieve the input message from the IMS message queue, then it does data base processing based on the input message. Usually, it sends a reply message back to the originating terminal. When the program gets a QC status code (instead of blanks) as a result of its DC GU call, it knows there are no more messages for it on the queue, and it ends.

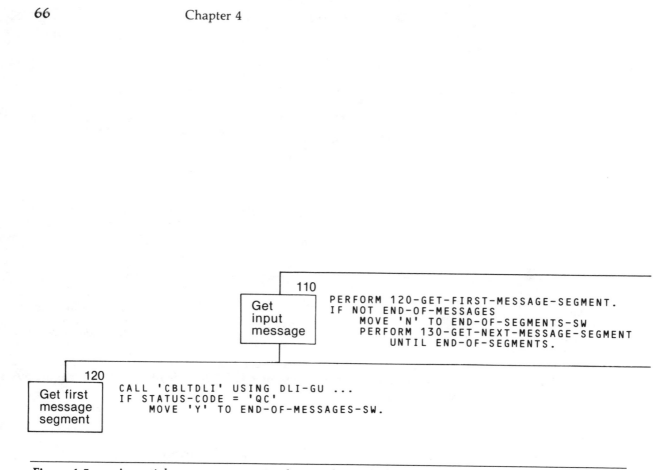

Figure 4-5   A partial program structure chart and sample COBOL code for a program that processes multiple-segment input messages

How to retrieve multiple-segment input messages   The situation is only slightly more complicated when your program processes multiple-segment input messages. Figure 4-5 illustrates that the MPP is still driven by the presence of messages on the message queue and that it ends when no more messages are present. However, the programming technique required to retrieve a complete message has more steps. To retrieve the first segment of a multiple-segment message, your program issues a GU call that specifies the I/O PCB. Then, to retrieve subsequent segments for that message, it issues GN calls repeatedly until it encounters a QD status code. (QD is the only non-blank status code you should normally expect from a data communications GN call. That's in contrast to a data base GN call, which can result in a GA, GB, or GE status code.)

There's one point you need to keep in mind: If you issue another GU call before you issue all the GN calls necessary to retrieve all the segments of a single message, those remaining segments will be lost. The GU call will return the first segment of the next message. As a result, it's

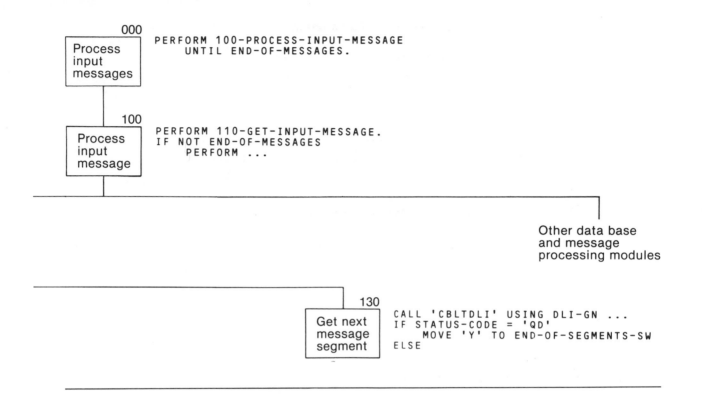

important that you're careful to retrieve all the segments associated with a multiple-segment message.

By the way, whether you're working with single- or multiple-segment input messages, getting an end-of-message status code (QD or QC) doesn't necessarily mean that there are no more input messages in your transaction's queue. IMS might supply one of these status codes to force your program to end, perhaps in response to a command issued by the master terminal operator. Fortunately, you don't need to worry about this because IMS handles program scheduling.

How to define the I/O area for an input message segment The top section of figure 4-6 shows the format of an input message segment. The input message segment IMS passes to your program begins with two two-byte fields: the *LL field* followed by the *ZZ field*. After the ZZ field comes the actual data in the message segment, which can be variable in length. The basic IMS input message format includes the transaction code immediately after the ZZ field. In multiple-segment input

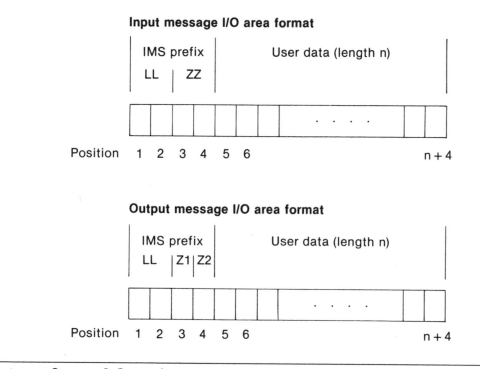

Input message I/O area format

IMS prefix | User data (length n)
LL | ZZ

Position   1   2   3   4   5   6   n + 4

Output message I/O area format

IMS prefix | User data (length n)
LL | Z1 | Z2

Position   1   2   3   4   5   6   n + 4

Figure 4-6   Segment I/O area formats

messages, the transaction code is only present in the first segment, not subsequent ones.

The LL field contains, in binary format, the length of the entire input message segment, including the LL and ZZ fields. Typically, you define the LL field with PIC S9(3) and COMP usage. The ZZ field is reserved for use by IMS, so although you define it in the segment I/O area, you don't do anything with it. You should define the ZZ field with PIC S9(3) and COMP usage or with PIC XX. The structure of the data component of the input message varies depending on the application; you're responsible for coding it correctly.

As you should remember from the last chapter, the relationship between the data that's passed to your program and the data the terminal operator entered depends on how IMS and MFS edit the message. In other words, the format of the message your program receives can be just like what the operator entered at the terminal, or it can vary significantly.

When you get specifications for a DC program, be sure they provide all the information you need about the input messages it will process. Particularly, you need to know how many segments a message can contain. That's necessary to determine how to code the calls to retrieve them. Also, you must know the segments' formats so you can code their layouts in the Working-Storage Section.

How to send an output message

As I've already mentioned, you send output message segments by issuing ISRT calls that specify the I/O PCB. Before you issue an ISRT call, you build the output message segment in the I/O area you name on the call. Although many output messages consist of just a single segment, some require more than one segment. When that's the case, your program issues a separate ISRT call for each segment. IMS considers an unbroken series of ISRT calls to make up a single message. The series is broken when your program issues a GU call against the I/O PCB; that signals to IMS that your program is ready to process a new input message. IMS holds all of the segments your program inserts in the destination terminal's output queue until the program has finished processing the input message.

In most cases, the destination of the output message is the terminal from which the input message came. When that's so, you don't have to take any special action to insure that the message is sent to the correct terminal. In some cases, though, you might need to route an output message to a destination other than the originating terminal. You use an alternate PCB to do that, as I mentioned earlier in this chapter.

How to define the I/O area for an output message segment   The bottom part of figure 4-6 shows the format of an output message segment. An output message has much the same structure as an input message: its first four bytes contain data required by IMS. An output message segment begins with a two-byte LL field that contains the length of the entire segment. Like an input segment, you usually define an output segment's LL field with PIC S9(3) and COMP usage. However, before you issue an ISRT call, you need to be sure that the LL field in the I/O area contains the actual length of the message that's to be sent, including the initial four bytes. It's your responsibility to set that length.

In an output message, the ZZ field in bytes 3 and 4 is divided into two binary fields called the *Z1 field* and the *Z2 field*. The Z1 field is reserved for the use of IMS, and you must initialize it to zero. You can use the Z2 field to control some advanced terminal operations, but for most applications, it should be set to zero too. As a result, you can code the two fields together with PIC S9(3) and COMP usage and initialize the field with VALUE ZERO. Or, you can code it as PIC XX and specify VALUE LOW-VALUE.

After the first four bytes comes the actual output message data. As with an input message, this data can vary in length, and its format depends on the application. Also, if you use MFS, the format of the data in the message can differ from what's displayed at the user's terminal. On the other hand, if you don't use MFS, the output message contains all the data that's displayed, plus whatever characters might be required to make the message display properly at the terminal. Before you code a DC program, be sure that its specifications indicate the format of its output messages. This includes the number of segments that make up an output message and the formats and lengths of those segments.

A SIMPLE INQUIRY APPLICATION

Now that you're familiar with the basics of IMS DC programming, I want to show you a simple inquiry application. First, I'll present the specifications for the application, then I'll describe the design and code of the program itself. If you've read *Part 1*, you'll recognize this program as a variation of the display invoice application it presented. Even if you're familiar with the design and code of the program in *Part 1*, I encourage you to study this one because (1) it's slightly different and (2) you'll see other versions of it later in this book.

Specifications for the display invoice application (version 1)

This program lets the terminal user display the financial status of a receivable (an invoice) from a customer data base accessed through a secondary index. If you've read *Part 1*, you're already familiar with the data base, and you can skip ahead to the heading "What the program will do." Otherwise, you should read the next section.

The customer data base   The data base view the sample program will use is based on a customer data base with the structure in figure 4-7. This is the same data base that I introduced in chapter 7 of *IMS for the COBOL Programmer, Part 1.*

However, for all the sample programs in this book, the customer data base is accessed not from its root segment, but rather through a

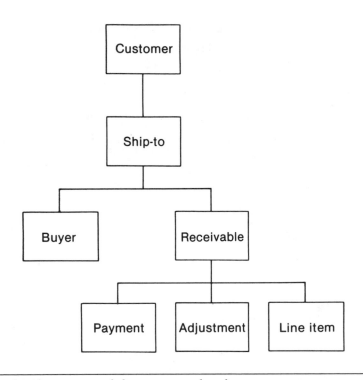

Figure 4-7   Hierarchical structure of the customer data base

secondary index built over the receivable segment type. The result is the data base view in figure 4-8. I've tried to limit the scope of the data base processing the sample programs in this book do so you can concentrate on the data communications elements they illustrate. As a result, only the segment types that are shaded in figure 4-8 are used by the programs in this book; figure 4-9 presents their segment layouts. And for the program in this chapter, only the receivable segment type is used.

The receivable segment corresponds to an invoice, or a billing. When an invoice is issued, an occurrence of the receivable segment is inserted in the data base. It contains an invoice number (the segment's sequence field), invoice date, purchase order number, and several financial fields. The invoice total (that is, the amount billed), is the sum of RS-PRODUCT-TOTAL, RS-SALES-TAX, and RS-FREIGHT, minus RS-CASH-DISCOUNT. (The billing amount isn't stored as a separate field in the segment because it can be calculated easily.) The last field in the receivable segment, RS-BALANCE-DUE, represents the total amount of money currently due on the receivable.

The difference between the total amount billed and the current balance due must be accounted for either by payments received or

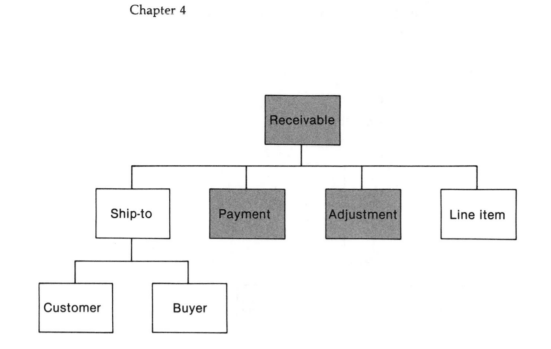

Figure 4-8   Hierarchical structure of the customer data base when accessed through a secondary index built over the receivable segment

```
01    RECEIVABLE-SEGMENT.
*
      05    RS-INVOICE-NUMBER          PIC X(6).
      05    RS-INVOICE-DATE            PIC X(6).
      05    RS-PO-NUMBER               PIC X(25).
      05    RS-PRODUCT-TOTAL           PIC S9(5)V99      COMP-3.
      05    RS-CASH-DISCOUNT           PIC S9(5)V99      COMP-3.
      05    RS-SALES-TAX               PIC S9(5)V99      COMP-3.
      05    RS-FREIGHT                 PIC S9(5)V99      COMP-3.
      05    RS-BALANCE-DUE             PIC S9(5)V99      COMP-3.
*
01    PAYMENT-SEGMENT.
*
      05    PS-CHECK-NUMBER            PIC X(16).
      05    PS-BANK-NUMBER             PIC X(25).
      05    PS-PAYMENT-DATE            PIC X(6).
      05    PS-PAYMENT-AMOUNT          PIC S9(5)V99      COMP-3.
*
01    ADJUSTMENT-SEGMENT.
*
      05    AS-REFERENCE-NUMBER        PIC X(6).
      05    AS-ADJUSTMENT-DATE         PIC X(6).
      05    AS-ADJUSTMENT-TYPE         PIC X.
      05    AS-ADJUSTMENT-AMOUNT       PIC S9(5)V99      COMP-3.
*
```

Figure 4-9   Layouts for the receivable, payment, and adjustment segment types in the customer data base adjustments made to the receivable. So subordinate to the receivable segment type are two additional segment types that correspond to these two types of transactions. The payment segment type contains the amount and date of a payment, plus its check and bank numbers. The adjustment segment type also contains an amount field, plus an identifying reference number, adjustment date, and a single-character adjustment type code.

What the program will do   The two screen layouts for the inquiry program are in figure 4-10. In part 1 of the figure, you can see how the user sends an input message. He keys in the transaction code (which in this case is DI1), followed by six spaces and the number of the invoice (receivable segment) to be retrieved.

Part 2 of figure 4-10 shows the format of the output the program will send back to the terminal. After retrieving the requested receivable segment from the customer data base, the program formats data from it, calculates the original billing total and total payments and adjustments, and sends the results to the terminal. The MFS editing in effect for the program requires that the output be displayed beginning on line 3, column 2, of the screen.

Figure 4-11 gives more specific information about the formats of the message segments the program will handle. As you can see, the input message, which consists of just one segment occurrence, has to be defined with 15 bytes for text in addition to the LL and ZZ fields. The first three characters of the text contain the transaction code DI1, and six blanks follow in positions 4 through 9. Then, in positions 10 through 15 is the invoice number. The program uses the invoice number to construct the SSA it specifies in a GU call to retrieve the requested receivable segment from the customer data base.

The output message will also consist of just one segment occurrence, with 702 bytes of text. If you count up the number of screen positions from the beginning of the output message display in line 3, column 2, and ending at line 11, column 63, you'll see that the total is 702 characters. Notice on the 3270 display that the contents of the output field wrap around from one line of the screen to the next. The program has to format both the constant and variable data on each display line. (If more sophisticated MFS editing were being used, this wouldn't necessarily be so.)

If you're familiar with the example DC program in *Part 1*, you'll recognize that its output message is handled in a different way. In that program, the output message consists of nine segments, each of which is displayed on a successive screen line, beginning with line 3. In that case,

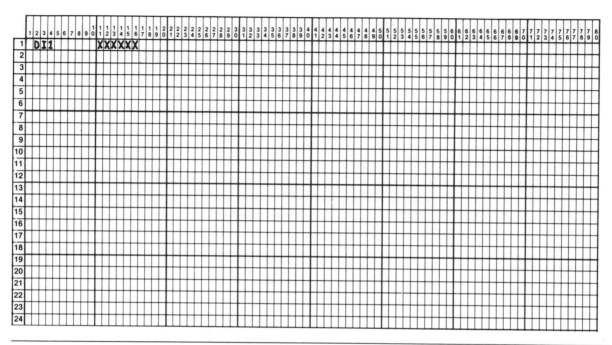

Figure 4-10   Screen layout for the display invoice application, version 1 (part 1 of 2)

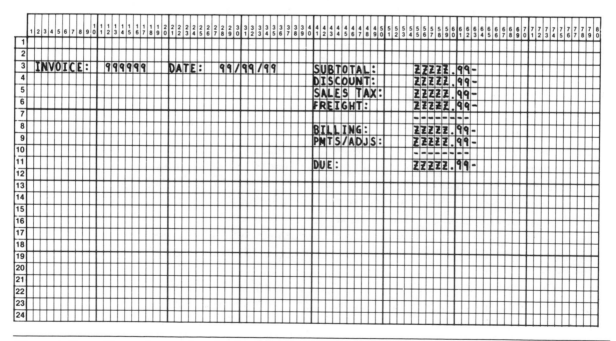

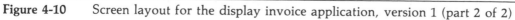

Figure 4-10   Screen layout for the display invoice application, version 1 (part 2 of 2)

Input message user data specifications

1. Contains the transaction code ' DI1   ' in positions 1-9. The trailing
    spaces are required.

2. Contains the number of the invoice (receivable) to be displayed in posi-
    tions 10-15.

3. Contains no more than 15 bytes of text.

Output message user data specifications

1. Contains one segment mapped to the screen beginning at line 3.

2. Contains no more than 702 bytes of text.

Figure 4-11   Message specifications for the display invoice application, version 1

none of the segments may be longer than 79 bytes, the length of a
display line on the 3270 screen minus one for an attribute byte in position 1. However, the program can send shorter segments if trailing positions don't contain data. The reason for the difference has to do with
the editing that's in effect. Both use MFS, but the version in the other
book uses 3270 defaults; the version in this book uses a customized MFS
format that you'll see in the next chapter.

IMS DC COBOL program for the
display invoice application (version 1)

Now that you're familiar with the requirements for the display invoice
application, you're ready to see the program itself. First, I'll show you
the program's design, then its COBOL source code.

The program's design   Figure 4-12 presents the structure chart for
the program. As you can see, it's similar to the partial structure chart in
figure 4-4. The program is driven by the presence of input messages on
the message queue. For each input message it retrieves (in module 110),
it tries to retrieve the proper receivable segment occurrence from the
customer data base (module 120). If the data base GU call is successful,
the program formats the data from the receivable segment (module 140)
and inserts the output message segment (module 150 invoked from
module 140). On the other hand, if the requested receivable segment
isn't found, the program issues an insert call to send an error message
(module 150 invoked from module 160).

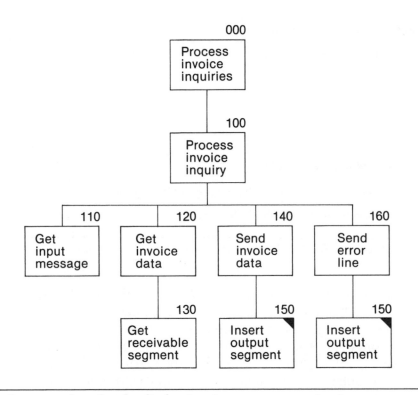

Figure 4-12   Structure chart for the display invoice program, version 1

The program's code   Now, consider figure 4-13, the complete COBOL source listing for this version of the display invoice program. I've shaded the parts of the program I particularly want you to notice.

The field INPUT-MESSAGE-IO-AREA is used by the DC GU call. It's 19 bytes long, beginning with the 2-byte LL field and the 2-byte ZZ field, followed by the 15-byte user text area. Notice that I didn't assign initial values to the LL and ZZ fields; that's because IMS stores data in them after each call. In this case, the user data part of the message is only 15 bytes long, not the full 79 bytes of the first line of the display station's screen. That's because the MFS specification I used for this program limits the input message to just what's required for the program: the transaction code and the invoice number the operator keys in to invoke the program.

Next is the field OUTPUT-MESSAGE-IO-AREA, which is the I/O area used by the DC ISRT call. It also begins with two 2-byte fields: LL and the combination of Z1 and Z2. Because IMS depends on the values stored in those fields to process an output message segment properly, I coded initial values for them. The initial value of the LL field is the length of the entire I/O area (706 bytes), and the initial value of the Z1-Z2 field is zero.

Next, the working-storage area OUTPUT-MESSAGE-LINES contains the fields the program will format to create an output message. This group item contains both literals that will be screen captions and variables that will be set by the program based on data it retrieves from the receivable segment. After this entire area has been formatted, the program moves it to OM-TEXT in the output I/O area before it issues the ISRT call to send the output message.

Notice that the items defined in OUTPUT-MESSAGE-LINES contain editing pictures (like PIC 99/99/99 for the date field and PIC Z(5).99- for dollar amounts). This makes it possible for the program to format data more meaningfully for display, and parallels the sort of formatting that's done for lines of a printed report.

The next shaded items in the program listing are the IO-PCB-MASK, which is like the one in figure 4-3, and the ENTRY statement. Notice that the first PCB name I coded in the ENTRY statement is IO-PCB-MASK. As I said earlier, the I/O PCB mask must be the first one you code on the ENTRY statement for an IMS DC program.

Next, notice in the first module in the Procedure Division that I coded a GOBACK statement to end the program, not a STOP RUN statement. That's the same as in a batch DL/I program.

The only other shaded items in the listing are the DC calls themselves and the statements related to status-code checking. You should find them easy to understand. The GU call in module 110 retrieves an input message and stores it in INPUT-MESSAGE-IO-AREA. The ISRT call in module 150 sends data stored in OUTPUT-MESSAGE-IO-AREA to be queued for output to the terminal. For most inquiries, the program will have moved the data for the formatted invoice display to OUTPUT-MESSAGE-IO-AREA before the ISRT call is issued. However, if the program was not able to retrieve the requested receivable segment, it formats an error message in the group item ERROR-LINE, then moves ERROR-LINE (not OUTPUT-MESSAGE-LINES) to OM-TEXT before it issues the ISRT call.

```
IDENTIFICATION DIVISION.
*
PROGRAM-ID.  DI1.
*
ENVIRONMENT DIVISION.
*
DATA DIVISION.
*
WORKING-STORAGE SECTION.
*
01  SWITCHES.
*
    05  INVOICE-FOUND-SW          PIC X        VALUE 'Y'.
        88  INVOICE-FOUND                      VALUE 'Y'.
    05  END-OF-MESSAGES-SW        PIC X        VALUE 'N'.
        88  END-OF-MESSAGES                    VALUE 'Y'.
*
01  INPUT-MESSAGE-IO-AREA.
*
    05  IM-LL                     PIC S9(3)    COMP.
    05  IM-ZZ                     PIC S9(3)    COMP.
    05  IM-TRANS-CODE             PIC X(9).
    05  IM-INVOICE-NO             PIC X(6).
*
01  OUTPUT-MESSAGE-IO-AREA.
*
    05  OM-LL          PIC S9(3)   COMP  VALUE +706.
    05  OM-ZZ          PIC S9(3)   COMP  VALUE ZERO.
    05  OM-TEXT        PIC X(702).
*
01  OUTPUT-MESSAGE-LINES.
*
    05  FILLER         PIC X(10)   VALUE 'INVOICE: '.
    05  OML-INV-NUMBER PIC X(6).
    05  FILLER         PIC X(10)   VALUE '   DATE: '.
    05  OML-INV-DATE   PIC 99/99/99.
    05  FILLER         PIC X(5)    VALUE SPACE.
    05  FILLER         PIC X(14)   VALUE 'SUBTOTAL:     '.
    05  OML-PROD-TOTAL PIC Z(5).99-.
    05  FILLER         PIC X(57)   VALUE SPACE.
    05  FILLER         PIC X(14)   VALUE 'DISCOUNT:     '.
    05  OML-CASH-DISC  PIC Z(5).99-.
    05  FILLER         PIC X(57)   VALUE SPACE.
    05  FILLER         PIC X(14)  .VALUE 'SALES TAX:    '.
    05  OML-SALES-TAX  PIC Z(5).99-.
    05  FILLER         PIC X(57)   VALUE SPACE.
    05  FILLER         PIC X(14)   VALUE 'FREIGHT:      '.
    05  OML-FREIGHT    PIC Z(5).99-.
    05  FILLER         PIC X(71)   VALUE SPACE.
    05  FILLER         PIC X(9)    VALUE '-------- '.
    05  FILLER         PIC X(57)   VALUE SPACE.
```

Figure 4-13   Source listing for the display invoice program, version 1 (part 1 of 4)

```
    05  FILLER              PIC X(14)   VALUE 'BILLING:      '.
    05  OML-BILLING         PIC Z(5).99-.
    05  FILLER              PIC X(57)   VALUE SPACE.
    05  FILLER              PIC X(14)   VALUE 'PMTS/ADJS:    '.
    05  OML-PMTS-ADJS       PIC Z(5).99-.
    05  FILLER              PIC X(71)   VALUE SPACE.
    05  FILLER              PIC X(9)    VALUE '-------- '.
    05  FILLER              PIC X(57)   VALUE SPACE.
    05  FILLER              PIC X(14)   VALUE 'DUE:          '.
    05  OML-BALANCE         PIC Z(5).99-.
*
01  ERROR-LINE.
*
    05  FILLER              PIC X(8)    VALUE 'INVOICE '.
    05  EL-INVOICE-NO       PIC X(6).
    05  FILLER              PIC X(10)   VALUE ' NOT FOUND'.
    05  FILLER              PIC X(55)   VALUE SPACE.
*
01  DLI-FUNCTIONS.
*
    05  DLI-GU              PIC X(4)    VALUE 'GU  '.
    05  DLI-GHU             PIC X(4)    VALUE 'GHU '.
    05  DLI-GN              PIC X(4)    VALUE 'GN  '.
    05  DLI-GHN             PIC X(4)    VALUE 'GHN '.
    05  DLI-GNP             PIC X(4)    VALUE 'GNP '.
    05  DLI-GHNP            PIC X(4)    VALUE 'GHNP'.
    05  DLI-ISRT            PIC X(4)    VALUE 'ISRT'.
    05  DLI-DLET            PIC X(4)    VALUE 'DLET'.
    05  DLI-REPL            PIC X(4)    VALUE 'REPL'.
    05  DLI-CHKP            PIC X(4)    VALUE 'CHKP'.
    05  DLI-XRST            PIC X(4)    VALUE 'XRST'.
    05  DLI-PCB             PIC X(4)    VALUE 'PCB '.
*
01  RECEIVABLE-SEGMENT.
*
    05  RS-INVOICE-NUMBER PIC X(6).
    05  RS-INVOICE-DATE   PIC X(6).
    05  RS-PO-NUMBER      PIC X(25).
    05  RS-PRODUCT-TOTAL  PIC S9(5)V99   COMP-3.
    05  RS-CASH-DISCOUNT  PIC S9(5)V99   COMP-3.
    05  RS-SALES-TAX      PIC S9(5)V99   COMP-3.
    05  RS-FREIGHT        PIC S9(5)V99   COMP-3.
    05  RS-BALANCE-DUE    PIC S9(5)V99   COMP-3.
*
01  INVOICE-NO-SSA.
*
    05  FILLER                PIC X(9)    VALUE 'CRRECSEG('.
    05  FILLER                PIC X(10)   VALUE 'CRRECXNO ='.
    05  INVOICE-NO-SSA-VALUE  PIC X(6).
    05  FILLER                PIC X       VALUE ')'.
*
```

Figure 4-13   Source listing for the display invoice program, version 1 (part 2 of 4)

```
LINKAGE SECTION.
*
01   IO-PCB-MASK.
*
     05  IO-PCB-LOGICAL-TERM    PIC X(8).
     05  FILLER                 PIC XX.
     05  IO-PCB-STATUS-CODE     PIC XX.
     05  IO-PCB-DATE            PIC S9(7)     COMP-3.
     05  IO-PCB-TIME            PIC S9(6)V9  COMP-3.
     05  IO-PCB-MSG-SEQ-NUMBER  PIC S9(5)     COMP.
     05  IO-PCB-MOD-NAME        PIC X(8).
     05  IO-PCB-USER-ID         PIC X(8).
*
01   CR-PCB-MASK.
*
     05  CR-PCB-DBD-NAME        PIC X(8).
     05  CR-PCB-SEGMENT-LEVEL   PIC XX.
     05  CR-PCB-STATUS-CODE     PIC XX.
     05  CR-PCB-PROC-OPTIONS    PIC X(4).
     05  FILLER                 PIC S9(5)     COMP.
     05  CR-PCB-SEGMENT-NAME    PIC X(8).
     05  CR-PCB-KEY-LENGTH      PIC S9(5)     COMP.
     05  CR-PCB-NUMB-SENS-SEGS  PIC S9(5)     COMP.
     05  CR-PCB-KEY             PIC X(22).
*
PROCEDURE DIVISION.
*
     ENTRY 'DLITCBL' USING IO-PCB-MASK
                           CR-PCB-MASK.
*
000-PROCESS-INVOICE-INQUIRIES.
*
    PERFORM 100-PROCESS-INVOICE-INQUIRY
        UNTIL END-OF-MESSAGES.
    GOBACK.
*
100-PROCESS-INVOICE-INQUIRY.
*
    PERFORM 110-GET-INPUT-MESSAGE.
    IF NOT END-OF-MESSAGES
        PERFORM 120-GET-INVOICE-DATA
        IF INVOICE-FOUND
            PERFORM 140-SEND-INVOICE-DATA
        ELSE
            PERFORM 160-SEND-ERROR-LINE.
*
110-GET-INPUT-MESSAGE.
*
    CALL 'CBLTDLI' USING DLI-GU
                         IO-PCB-MASK
                         INPUT-MESSAGE-IO-AREA.
    IF IO-PCB-STATUS-CODE = 'QC'
        MOVE 'Y' TO END-OF-MESSAGES-SW.
```

Figure 4-13   Source listing for the display invoice program, version 1 (part 3 of 4)

```
*
 120-GET-INVOICE-DATA.
*
     MOVE 'Y'              TO INVOICE-FOUND-SW.
     MOVE IM-INVOICE-NO TO INVOICE-NO-SSA-VALUE.
     PERFORM 130-GET-RECEIVABLE-SEGMENT.
*
 130-GET-RECEIVABLE-SEGMENT.
*
     CALL 'CBLTDLI' USING DLI-GU
                          CR-PCB-MASK
                          RECEIVABLE-SEGMENT
                          INVOICE-NO-SSA.
     IF CR-PCB-STATUS-CODE NOT = SPACE
         MOVE 'N' TO INVOICE-FOUND-SW.
*
 140-SEND-INVOICE-DATA.
*
     MOVE RS-INVOICE-NUMBER TO OML-INV-NUMBER.
     MOVE RS-INVOICE-DATE   TO OML-INV-DATE.
     MOVE RS-PRODUCT-TOTAL  TO OML-PROD-TOTAL.
     MOVE RS-CASH-DISCOUNT  TO OML-CASH-DISC.
     MOVE RS-SALES-TAX      TO OML-SALES-TAX.
     MOVE RS-FREIGHT        TO OML-FREIGHT.
     COMPUTE OML-BILLING =    RS-PRODUCT-TOTAL -
                              RS-CASH-DISCOUNT +
                              RS-SALES-TAX +
                              RS-FREIGHT.
     COMPUTE OML-PMTS-ADJS =  RS-BALANCE-DUE -
                             (RS-PRODUCT-TOTAL -
                              RS-CASH-DISCOUNT +
                              RS-SALES-TAX +
                              RS-FREIGHT).
     MOVE RS-BALANCE-DUE       TO OML-BALANCE.
     MOVE OUTPUT-MESSAGE-LINES TO OM-TEXT.
     PERFORM 150-INSERT-OUTPUT-SEGMENT.
*
 150-INSERT-OUTPUT-SEGMENT.
*
     CALL 'CBLTDLI' USING DLI-ISRT
                          IO-PCB-MASK
                          OUTPUT-MESSAGE-IO-AREA.
*
 160-SEND-ERROR-LINE.
*
     MOVE IM-INVOICE-NO TO EL-INVOICE-NO.
     MOVE ERROR-LINE    TO OM-TEXT.
     PERFORM 150-INSERT-OUTPUT-SEGMENT.
*
```

Figure 4-13   Source listing for the display invoice program, version 1 (part 4 of 4)

DISCUSSION

Although there are some rigid rules you have to follow when you develop MPPs (like coding LL and ZZ fields before user data in message segment I/O areas and naming the I/O PCB first on the ENTRY statement), I think you'll find basic MPPs easy to design and develop. They all follow essentially the same model, and, as I've said over and over, that model is like familiar batch programs. As a result, as long as you're given complete specifications, the information in this chapter is all you need to know to develop simple MPPs.

However, there are other IMS DC features and facilities you need to know. In particular, MFS is a topic you must be familiar with. So the next chapter introduces you to MFS and all of section 3 is devoted to it. Also, there are several advanced DC features that you may need to use; I mentioned one, alternate PCBs, in this chapter. You also need to know how to design and develop a batch message processing program (BMP program); this chapter just taught you how to develop an MPP. And you need to know how to use the IMS facilities for developing programs that require more than one interaction with the operator; that's called conversational programming. Section 4 presents these advanced features.

Terminology

segment
I/O PCB
alternate PCB
LL field
ZZ field
Z1 field
Z2 field

Objectives

1. List and describe the arguments you code on a DL/I data communications call.

2. Identify and describe the contents of the I/O PCB fields you might use in an application program.

3. Describe how a COBOL program retrieves both single- and multiple-segment input messages.

4. Describe how a COBOL program sends output messages.

5. Describe the format of a message segment I/O area.

6. Given specifications for a simple message processing program, design and code it using the programming elements this chapter presents.

Chapter 5

An introduction to
MFS facilities

Message Format Service, or MFS, is an IMS feature that lets you use formatted display station screens for data communications programs. Because well-designed screens can dramatically enhance operator efficiency and accuracy, the formatting MFS does is much more than just cosmetic. In addition, MFS can reduce the system resources an application uses, both in the telecommunication network and on the host system. For these reasons, you need to understand MFS editing and know how to use it.

This chapter introduces you to MFS and prepares you for the detailed MFS material the chapters in the next section present. First, this chapter describes when MFS editing occurs and the special control blocks MFS uses to perform that editing. Then, it presents two ways to use MFS for the display invoice application that I introduced in the last chapter. These examples will introduce the control statements you can use to direct MFS editing. (The chapters in the next section teach you the details you need to know to code MFS control statements.) In particular, the examples in this chapter illustrate how you coordinate MFS and your COBOL programs. Finally, this chapter describes the MFS Language Utility.

When MFS editing occurs

As figure 5-1 shows, MFS modules reside in the IMS control region, and they're invoked between IMS's communications control module

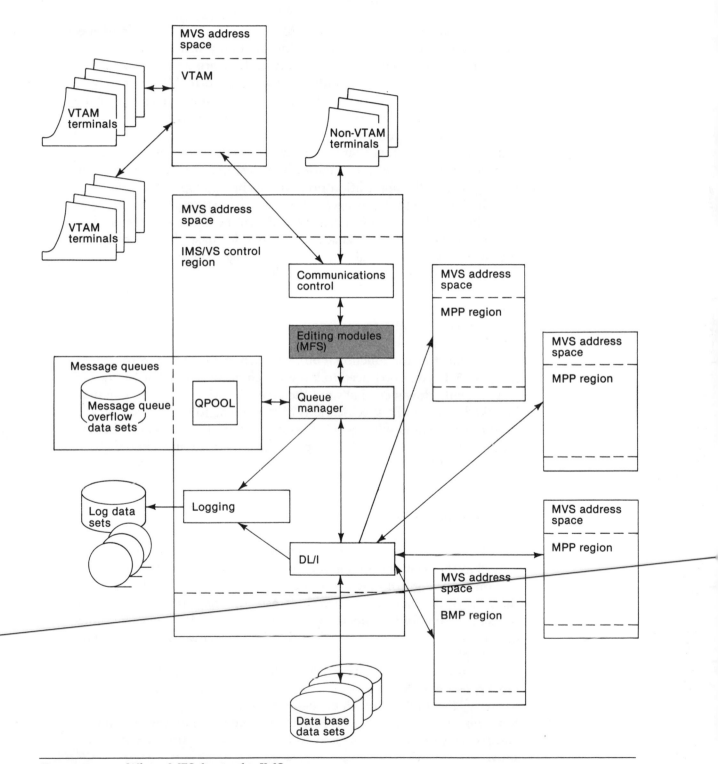

Figure 5-1   Where MFS fits in the IMS system

and its queue manager. As a result, MFS editing occurs between queueing and communications for both input and output messages.

Inbound messages from a display station are received by IMS's communications control module, then are passed to MFS. First, MFS *maps* fields from the device to fields in the input message. MFS performs that mapping according to specifications you supply to it in a series of control statements; you'll see examples of these control statements later in this chapter. After it has edited the input message, MFS passes it to the queue manager, which stores the message so it can be supplied to the application program at the appropriate time.

Similarly, output messages sent by an application program are temporarily stored by the queue manager. When the message is ready to be transferred back to the originating terminal, it's passed from the queue manager to MFS. MFS edits the output message, mapping fields from it into the positions that are appropriate for the destination terminal device. As with input editing, MFS does output editing according to specifications you supply to it via control statements. After the message has been edited, MFS passes it to the communications control module, which sends it to the terminal.

For most of the functional boxes shown in the IMS control region in figure 5-1, you don't need to know much more than what enters and leaves them. However, that's not the case with MFS. Because you may be asked to write the specifications MFS will use to edit messages, you need to understand what goes on inside the box that's labelled "Editing modules (MFS)" in figure 5-1. In particular, I want you to know about MFS control blocks.

MFS control blocks

MFS knows the formats of the screen displays and messages it handles, as well as the relationships among them, because you supply that information in the control statements you code. However, MFS does not use those control statements directly. Instead, they first have to be translated into *control blocks*, which are internal MFS representations of screens and messages. (I'll describe the translation process later in this chapter.)

To process any one transaction, MFS uses four different control blocks, as figure 5-2 shows. To make this figure (and figure 5-3) easier to study, I've omitted much of the IMS detail that figure 5-1 contains; however, don't forget that IMS functions like communications control and message queueing happen in addition to the functions these figures show.

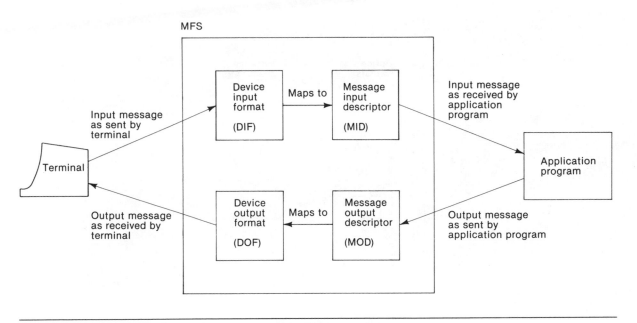

Figure 5-2   MFS blocks used to process a single transaction

For an input message, MFS uses a block called a *device input format* (or *DIF*) to interpret data as it's received from a terminal, and it uses a second block called a *message input descriptor* (or *MID*) to determine how that input data should be formatted for presentation to the application program. For an output message, MFS uses similar blocks. A *message output descriptor* (or *MOD*) is used to interpret data received from the application program, and a *device output format* (or *DOF*) is used to determine how that data should be formatted for transmission to the terminal. (By the way, although it sounds silly, it's common to use the acronyms in conversation and pronounce them as words: mid, mod, dif, and dof).

A group of related MIDs, MODs, DIFs, and DOFs is called a *format set*. The simplest format sets have four blocks, but some have more. For example, if an application can process messages from terminals with different formatting requirements, its format set must have a DIF and a DOF for each of those device types.

To understand, consider figure 5-3. It represents a format set for an application that supports two terminal types: a standard 3270 model 2 terminal with 80-character lines and a 3270 model 5 terminal with 132-character lines. Obviously, data can (and probably should) be displayed in different formats on the two different kinds of devices. However, the application program processes messages in just one format, regardless of the originating terminal type.

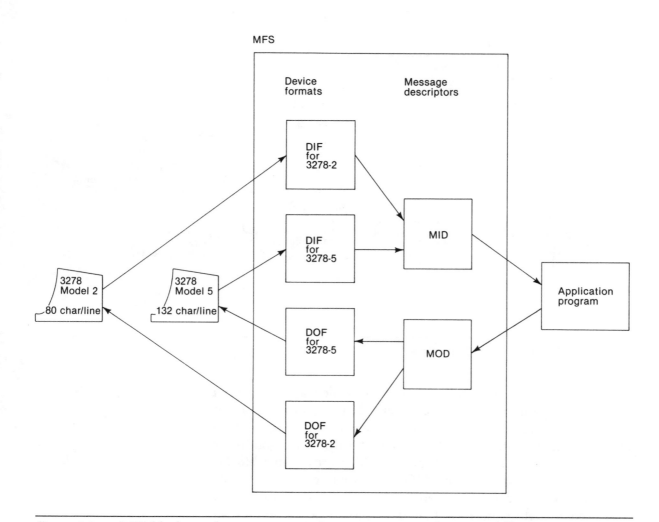

Figure 5-3   MFS blocks used to process a single transaction type from two different terminal types

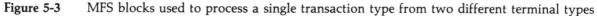

As figure 5-3 shows, MFS makes programs independent of terminal configurations by relating different device formats to the same message descriptor. In figure 5-3, either of two different DIFs can be mapped into a single MID, and a single MOD is mapped into either of two DOFs. Which DIF or DOF is selected depends on the kind of terminal that sent the input message.

With the variety of different IBM terminal types, you can imagine that a format set can contain many blocks. However, in practice, the standard 3270 model 2 display station (with a 24-line, 80-column screen) is most common. As a result, I emphasize that terminal type in this book.

```
 1          PRINT ON,NOGEN
 2 ***********************************************************************
 3 *          FORMAT SET FOR APPLICATION PROGRAM DI1.                    *
 4 ***********************************************************************
 5 DI1DF    FMT
 6          DEV    TYPE=(3270,2),FEAT=IGNORE,DSCA=X'00A0'
 7          DIV    TYPE=INOUT
 8          DPAGE  CURSOR=((1,2))
 9 TRANINV  DFLD   POS=(1,2),LTH=15
10 OUTTEXT  DFLD   POS=(3,2),LTH=702
11          FMTEND
12 ***********************************************************************
13 DI1O     MSG    TYPE=OUTPUT,SOR=(DI1DF,IGNORE),NXT=DI1I
14          SEG
15          MFLD   OUTTEXT,LTH=702
16          MSGEND
17 ***********************************************************************
18 DI1I     MSG    TYPE=INPUT,SOR=(DI1DF,IGNORE),NXT=DI1O
19          SEG
20          MFLD   TRANINV,LTH=15
21          MSGEND
22 ***********************************************************************
23          END
```

Figure 5-4   Format set for the display invoice application, version 1

MFS considerations for the display invoice application (version 1)

Now that you know about the internal blocks MFS uses to perform its editing functions, you're ready to see some examples of the control statements that define those blocks. Figure 5-4 presents the control statements for the format set used in the display invoice application I introduced in the last chapter. For your convenience, figure 5-5 repeats the screen layouts for the application.

Incidentally, it's common to use the term "format set" to refer to the MFS control statements that define a format set. So I'll use "format set" to refer both to related groups of blocks and to the control statements that define them. The specific meaning, if it matters, should be clear from context.

The statements in figure 5-4 provide all the information MFS needs to edit messages for the application. For now, I don't want you to worry about the syntax of the control statements; you'll get to that soon enough in the next chapter. Instead, I want to use this simple example to introduce the three things a format set must do.

First, a format set must define the way the screens to be used in an application will look on all supported device types. Second, it has to define the format of the input and output messages the application

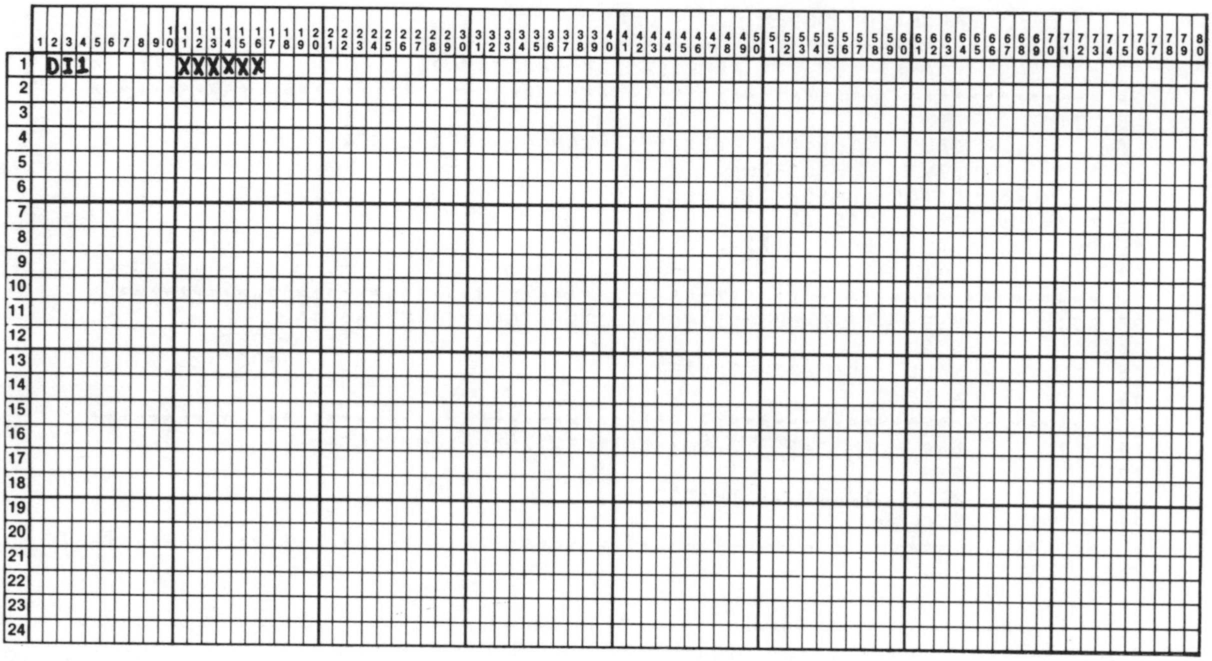

Figure 5-5 Screen layout for the display invoice application, version 1 (part 1 of 2)

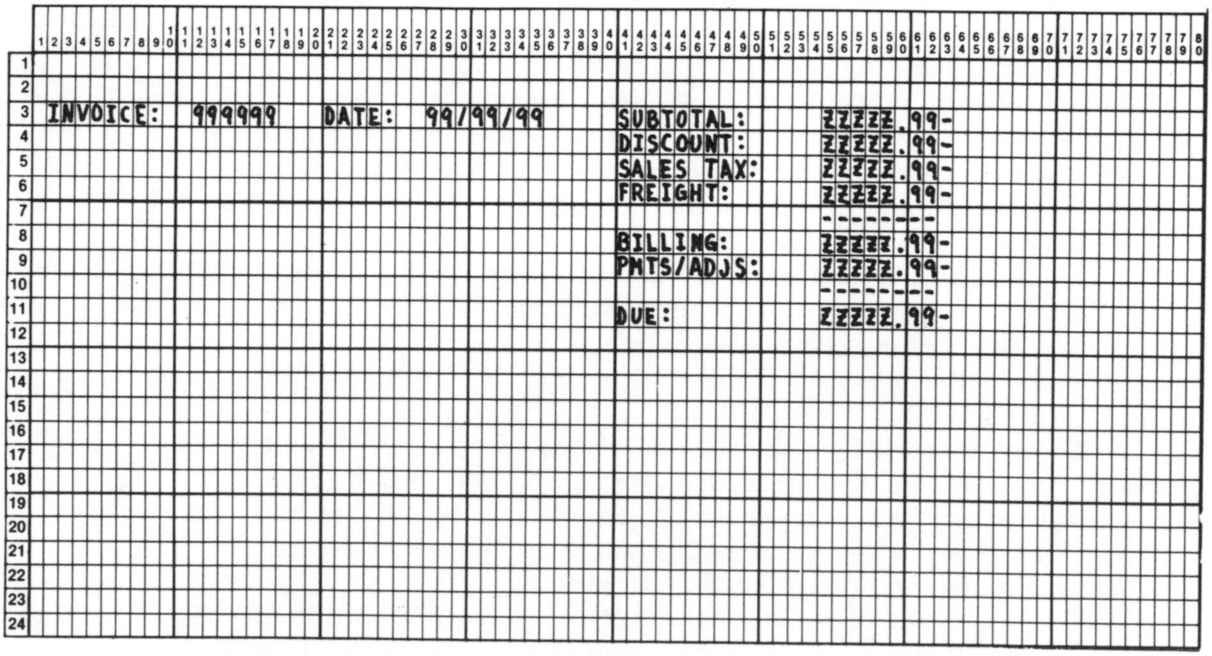

Figure 5-5 Screen layout for the display invoice application, version 1 (part 2 of 2)

program will receive and send. And third, it has to specify the relationships between data on the screen and data in a message.

How to define a screen in a format set   Although MFS requires both a DIF and a DOF to define a screen format, you only have to code one group of control statements to create both for a 3270 display station. That's because for a 3270, the same screen format must be used for both input and output; the screen that's sent for an output message becomes the format for the next input operation. Collectively, the group of statements that define the screen layout for a terminal are called a *device format*.

In figure 5-4, the statements in lines 5 through 11 are the device format. Notice that the device format begins with a FMT statement and ends with a FMTEND statement. Only one terminal device type is specified for this application, a 3270 model 2 display station, as TYPE=(3270,2) in line 6 (a DEV statement) indicates. The statements in the device format define blocks for both input (a DIF) and output (a DOF); that's what TYPE=INOUT in line 7 (a DIV statement) specifies.

I especially want you to notice how the screen fields for this application are defined. Figure 5-6 shows the complete format set again, but this time with the screen layout. I've shaded and linked corresponding elements to make the relationships among them easier to see. This application uses a simple, two-field screen: The first field (15 bytes long, starting in column 2 of line 1) is used for data entry; the second (702 bytes long, starting in column 2 of line 3) is used to display the entire output message the application program sends.

Each screen field is defined in the device format with a DFLD control statement. DFLD is easy to remember: it stands for "device field." All I had to specify on each of the two DFLD statements in figure 5-6 were the screen position (given as the line and column location of the start of the field) and the length of the field. Of course, a typical application screen will have more than two fields. Even so, this example shows you how easy it is to specify device fields.

How to define messages In a format set   Although you only have to code one group of control statements to define both a DIF and a DOF, you must code separate sets of control statements to define a MID and a MOD. As you can see in figure 5-4, the statements in lines 13-16 and 18-21 both define messages; they begin with a MSG statement and end with a MSGEND statement. The first group defines a MOD (TYPE= OUTPUT in line 13), while the second defines a MID (TYPE=INPUT in line 18).

Format set

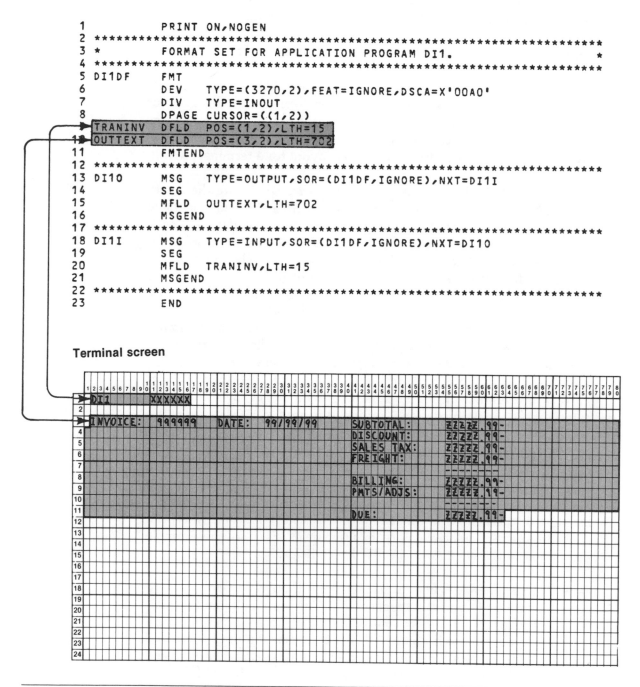

```
 1              PRINT ON,NOGEN
 2 ****************************************************************
 3 *          FORMAT SET FOR APPLICATION PROGRAM DI1.            *
 4 ****************************************************************
 5 DI1DF     FMT
 6           DEV    TYPE=(3270,2),FEAT=IGNORE,DSCA=X'00A0'
 7           DIV    TYPE=INOUT
 8           DPAGE  CURSOR=((1,2))
   TRANINV   DFLD   POS=(1,2),LTH=15
   OUTTEXT   DFLD   POS=(3,2),LTH=702
11           FMTEND
12 ****************************************************************
13 DI10      MSG    TYPE=OUTPUT,SOR=(DI1DF,IGNORE),NXT=DI1I
14           SEG
15           MFLD   OUTTEXT,LTH=702
16           MSGEND
17 ****************************************************************
18 DI1I      MSG    TYPE=INPUT,SOR=(DI1DF,IGNORE),NXT=DI10
19           SEG
20           MFLD   TRANINV,LTH=15
21           MSGEND
22 ****************************************************************
23           END
```

Terminal screen

Figure 5-6   How DFLD specifications relate to physical device fields

Format set

```
1            PRINT ON,NOGEN
2  *******************************************************************
3  *         FORMAT SET FOR APPLICATION PROGRAM DI1.                 *
4  *******************************************************************
5  DI1DF     FMT
6            DEV     TYPE=(3270,2),FEAT=IGNORE,DSCA=X'00A0'
7            DIV     TYPE=INOUT
8            DPAGE   CURSOR=((1,2))
9  TRANINV   DFLD    POS=(1,2),LTH=15
10 OUTTEXT   DFLD    POS=(3,2),LTH=702
11           FMTEND
12 *******************************************************************
13 DI10      MSG     TYPE=OUTPUT,SOR=(DI1DF,IGNORE),NXT=DI1I
14           SEG
15           MFLD    OUTTEXT,LTH=702
16           MSGEND
17 *******************************************************************
18 DI1I      MSG     TYPE=INPUT,SOR=(DI1DF,IGNORE),NXT=DI10
19           SEG
20           MFLD    TRANINV,LTH=15
21           MSGEND
22 *******************************************************************
23           END
```

COBOL source code

```
*
01  INPUT-MESSAGE-IO-AREA.
*
    05  IM-LL                           PIC S9(3)    COMP.
    05  IM-ZZ                           PIC S9(3)    COMP.
    05  IM-TRANS-CODE                   PIC X(9).
    05  IM-INVOICE-NO                   PIC X(6).
*
01  OUTPUT-MESSAGE-IO-AREA.
*
    05  OM-LL              PIC S9(3)    COMP   VALUE +706.
    05  OM-ZZ              PIC S9(3)    COMP   VALUE ZERO.
    05  OM-TEXT            PIC X(702).
*
```

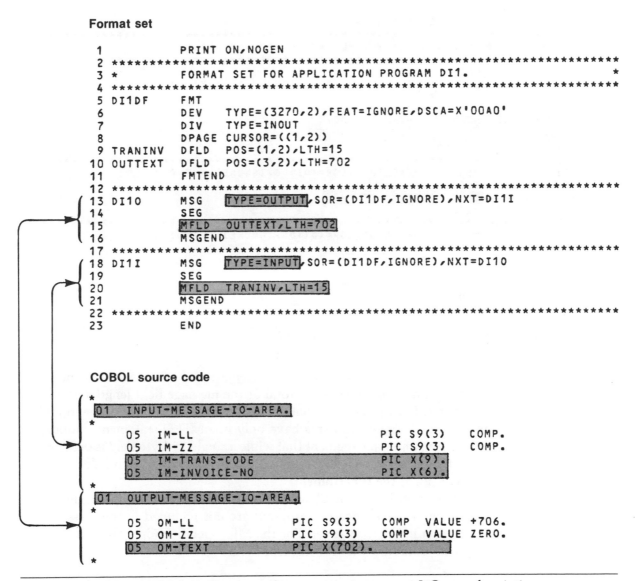

Figure 5-7   How MFLD specifications relate to program segment I/O area descriptions

Within each group of statements that defines a message, you code as many MFLD ("message field") statements as you need to identify separate fields in the message. Consider figure 5-7, which shows how the MFLD statements in the format set relate to the segment I/O area layouts in the application program. (You can look back to figure 4-13 to see the complete program listing.)

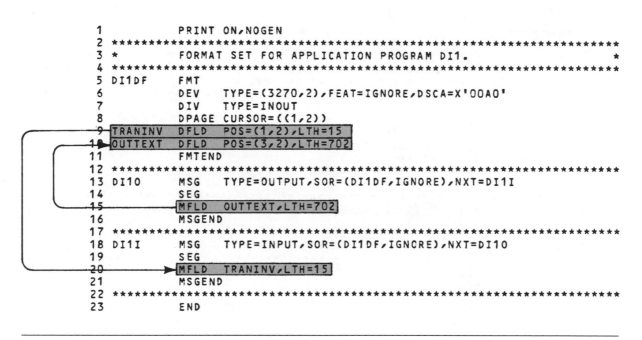

```
 1              PRINT ON,NOGEN
 2     ***************************************************************
 3     *         FORMAT SET FOR APPLICATION PROGRAM DI1.            *
 4     ***************************************************************
 5  DI1DF      FMT
 6              DEV    TYPE=(3270,2),FEAT=IGNORE,DSCA=X'00A0'
 7              DIV    TYPE=INOUT
 8              DPAGE  CURSOR=((1,2))
 9  TRANINV    DFLD   POS=(1,2),LTH=15
10  OUTTEXT    DFLD   POS=(3,2),LTH=702
11              FMTEND
12     ***************************************************************
13  DI10       MSG    TYPE=OUTPUT,SOR=(DI1DF,IGNORE),NXT=DI1I
14              SEG
15              MFLD   OUTTEXT,LTH=702
16              MSGEND
17     ***************************************************************
18  DI1I       MSG    TYPE=INPUT,SOR=(DI1DF,IGNORE),NXT=DI10
19              SEG
20              MFLD   TRANINV,LTH=15
21              MSGEND
22     ***************************************************************
23              END
```

Figure 5-8   How DFLD and MFLD specifications relate to one another

You need to be sure that the total length of the message segment in the program is the same as the total of the message field lengths in the format set. In this example, that's easy to verify because both the input and output message segments have only one MFLD statement. Notice for the input message segment that while a single 15-byte field is defined in the format set, it's viewed by the COBOL program as two fields: one six bytes long, the other nine.

Also, notice that the LL and ZZ fields that are defined in segment I/O areas in the application program are *not* included in the message description in the format set. For the MFS specification, you consider only user data, not the IMS control fields.

How to relate screen data and message data in a format set   Figures 5-6 and 5-7 have shown you how MFS control statements are related to elements outside MFS: screen displays and program views of messages. When you plan an MFS format set, you also have to be sure to coordinate the message descriptors and device format; that's what figure 5-8 illustrates.

Notice that the two MFLD statements specify the names of device fields (TRANINV and OUTTEXT). As a result, MFS knows how to map data from the DIF to the MID and from the MOD to the DOF. For example, MFS maps the device field named TRANINV into the input message field defined in line 20. In other words, the 15 bytes of data on the screen that begin in line 1, column 2, are mapped into the first (and here, the only) field in the input message segment. For output, the message field defined in line 15 is mapped into the device field with the name OUTTEXT.

In addition to linkages between fields in message descriptors and device formats like those figure 5-8 illustrates, you also have to establish the proper connections between the blocks themselves. That's what the values associated with SOR and NXT in lines 13 and 18 do. I'll describe how this works in the next chapter.

I want to stress again that this format set is simple. You can do extensive formatting with MFS, such as resequencing fields, controlling field attributes, and supplying literal values for captions. The result is that with MFS, data on the screen can appear quite differently than it does to an application program. Now, I want to present an enhancement of the display invoice application that illustrates this.

MFS considerations for the display invoice application (version 2)

This version of the display invoice application differs in that it uses MFS to (1) simplify operation for the terminal user, (2) improve telecommunication usage, and (3) simplify the application program. You'll see how all of these goals are met as I describe the application. First, I'll present the revised specifications for this version, then I'll introduce the MFS format set I created for it, and finally I'll present the simplified version of the application program.

Overview of version 2 of the display invoice application   The function of this version of the display invoice application is the same as the first version's. However, it differs in some important details. Recall how the first version of this program worked. From a blank screen, the operator keyed in a line like

```
DI1        034529
```

where DI1 and the blanks that follow it make up the transaction code, and 034529 is the number of the invoice the application will display. Both the transaction code and the variable invoice number were entered as one field, and that's how they were mapped into the input message.

Similarly, the output message was defined with just one field too. The application program had to supply the correct values for both captions and variable fields in the output message, and it had to provide

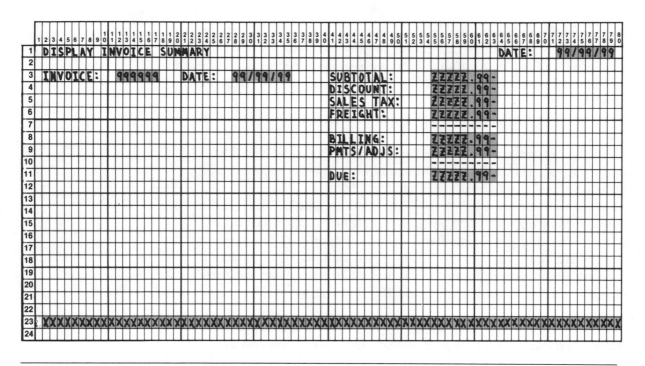

Figure 5-9   Screen layout for the display invoice application, version 2

exact spacing to insure that the data would be aligned on the screen. The result was a long output message that contained more spaces than anything else.

In the second version of the application, I used MFS more extensively. As you can see in figure 5-9, the screen looks much the same as in the first version of the application; however, it's defined differently. I formatted the screen with constant data (the data that isn't shaded in figure 5-9) through MFS, not through the application program.

The fields that *are* shaded in figure 5-9 contain variable data. The six-byte numeric field that begins in column 12 of line 3 is where the operator will key in the number of the invoice to be displayed. All of the other shaded fields will contain data that comes either from the application program (as is the case with all of the fields that follow the invoice-number entry field) or from MFS (as with the field that will contain the date, located beginning in column 72 of line 1).

Because this is a 3270 application, the same screen is used for both input and output. Remember, the data that's sent to a 3270 display station screen on an output operation becomes the format for the next input operation. For the first entry (that is, when the screen is clear), the operator has to get the terminal ready to run the application.

To do so, he enters the IMS command /FORMAT followed by the name of the MFS message output descriptor (MOD) for the application. In this case, the MOD name is DI2O. So the operator keys in

```
/FORMAT DI2O
```

to start the application. Then, MFS selects the right device output format block to format the screen for the program. The "right" DOF is the one that corresponds to the MOD you specified and to your terminal type, which IMS knows. Keep in mind that there may be several DOFs for a single MOD if the application was defined so users at several different terminal types could use it.

Format set for version 2 of the display invoice application   Figure 5-10 presents the control statements I coded to create the format set for this version of the display invoice application. As you can see, this format set is longer and more complicated than the first version. It contains 56 statements compared to the original's 23, some of those statements are more complicated, and I coded only one element per line. You'll learn all the details about the statements in this format set in the next chapter. For now, I want to use it just to illustrate basic MFS concepts.

Notice that this format set, like the one for the original version of the application, has three groups of control statements. The first (statements 5-33) defines the device format, the second (statements 35-39) describes the input message, and the third (statements 41-54) describes the output message.

I want you to think about the relationships among the fields in the device format and in the two message descriptors. Although there are more fields here than in the first version of this format set, they map back and forth in the same way. Notice that some DFLD statements (such as the one on line 9) define literals that are screen captions, while others (such as the one on line 11) define variable fields. Altogether, there are 11 variable fields in this version of the application; their DFLD statements are shaded in figure 5-10.

If you study the relationship between the variable fields in the device format and the MFLD statements, you'll see how the mapping is done. On input, only one device field (INVNO in statement 13) is mapped into the input message (in the field defined by statement 38). In contrast, all 11 variable fields are mapped back to the screen on output. For example, the output message field defined in statement 44 maps back into the device field INVNO.

```
1            PRINT ON,NOGEN
2 ********************************************************************
3 *           FORMAT SET FOR APPLICATION PROGRAM DI2.               *
4 ********************************************************************
5 DI2DF    FMT
6          DEV    TYPE=(3270,2),
                  FEAT=IGNORE,
                  SYSMSG=ERRMSG,
                  DSCA=X'00A0'
7          DIV    TYPE=INOUT
8          DPAGE  CURSOR=((3,12)),
                  FILL=PT
9          DFLD   'DISPLAY INVOICE SUMMARY',
                  POS=(1,2),
                  ATTR=(HI,PROT)
10         DFLD   'DATE:',
                  POS=(1,65),
                  ATTR=(HI,PROT)
11 CURDATE  DFLD   POS=(1,72),
                  LTH=8,
                  ATTR=(HI,PROT)
12         DFLD   'INVOICE:',
                  POS=(3,2),
                  ATTR=(HI,PROT)
13 INVNO    DFLD   POS=(3,12),
                  LTH=6,
                  ATTR=(NUM)
14         DFLD   'DATE:',
                  POS=(3,21),
                  ATTR=(HI,PROT)
15 INVDATE  DFLD   POS=(3,28),
                  LTH=8,
                  ATTR=(PROT)
16         DFLD   'SUBTOTAL:',
                  POS=(3,41),
                  ATTR=(HI,PROT)
17 SUBTOTAL DFLD   POS=(3,55),
                  LTH=9,
                  ATTR=(PROT).
18         DFLD   'DISCOUNT:',
                  POS=(4,41),
                  ATTR=(HI,PROT)
19 DISCOUNT DFLD   POS=(4,55),
                  LTH=9,
                  ATTR=(PROT)
20         DFLD   'SALES TAX:',
                  POS=(5,41),
                  ATTR=(HI,PROT)
21 SALESTAX DFLD   POS=(5,55),
                  LTH=9,
                  ATTR=(PROT)
22         DFLD   'FREIGHT:',
                  POS=(6,41),
                  ATTR=(HI,PROT)
```

Figure 5-10   Format set for the display invoice application, version 2 (part 1 of 3)

```
23 FREIGHT   DFLD    POS=(6,55),                                             X
                     LTH=9,                                                  X
                     ATTR=(PROT)
24          DFLD    '--------',                                              X
                     POS=(7,55),                                             X
                     ATTR=(HI,PROT)
25          DFLD    'BILLING:',                                              X
                     POS=(8,41),                                             X
                     ATTR=(HI,PROT)
26 BILLING   DFLD    POS=(8,55),                                             X
                     LTH=9,                                                  X
                     ATTR=(PROT)
27          DFLD    'PMTS/ADJS:',                                            X
                     POS=(9,41),                                             X
                     ATTR=(HI,PROT)
28 PMTSADJS  DFLD    POS=(9,55),                                             X
                     LTH=9,                                                  X
                     ATTR=(PROT)
29          DFLD    '--------',                                              X
                     POS=(10,55),                                            X
                     ATTR=(HI,PROT)
30          DFLD    'DUE:',                                                  X
                     POS=(11,41),                                            X
                     ATTR=(HI,PROT)
31 DUE       DFLD    POS=(11,55),                                            X
                     LTH=9,                                                  X
                     ATTR=(PROT)
32 ERRMSG    DFLD    POS=(23,2),                                             X
                     LTH=79,                                                 X
                     ATTR=(PROT)
33          FMTEND
34 ********************************************************************************
35 DI2I      MSG     TYPE=INPUT,                                             X
                     SOR=(DI2DF,IGNORE),                                     X
                     NXT=DI2O
36          SEG
37          MFLD    'DI2     ',                                              X
                     LTH=8
38          MFLD    INVNO,                                                   X
                     LTH=6,                                                  X
                     JUST=R,                                                 X
                     FILL=C'0'
39          MSGEND
40 ********************************************************************************
41 DI2O      MSG     TYPE=OUTPUT,                                            X
                     SOR=(DI2DF,IGNORE),                                     X
                     NXT=DI2I
42          SEG
43          MFLD    (CURDATE,DATE2)
44          MFLD    INVNO,                                                   X
                     LTH=6
45          MFLD    INVDATE,                                                 X
                     LTH=8
```

Figure 5-10   Format set for the display invoice application, version 2 (part 2 of 3)

```
46           MFLD    SUBTOTAL,                                                          X
                     LTH=9
47          .MFLD    DISCOUNT,                                                          X
                     LTH=9
48           MFLD    SALESTAX,                                                          X
                     LTH=9
49           MFLD    FREIGHT,                                                           X
                     LTH=9
50           MFLD    BILLING,                                                           X
                     LTH=9
51           MFLD    PMTSADJS,                                                          X
                     LTH=9
52           MFLD    DUE,                                                               X
                     LTH=9
53           MFLD    ERRMSG,                                                            X
                     LTH=79
54           MSGEND
55 ***************************************************************************
56           END
```

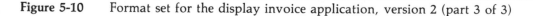

Figure 5-10   Format set for the display invoice application, version 2 (part 3 of 3)

As for the second input message field in figure 5-10, it contains the transaction code for the application (DI2). Because it's supplied as a literal in the format set, the operator doesn't have to key it in with each transaction.

COBOL source code for version 2 of the display invoice application
Although the purpose of this chapter isn't to teach you COBOL elements, I want you to consider the program that's part of this version of the application anyway. Figure 5-11 presents it. This program is much like the first version, but differs slightly to accommodate the enhanced message and screen formats of the second version.

The segment layout for the input message in this program is basically the same as in the first version. However, the output message format is different. In the output message segment layout in figure 5-11, I coded only the variable data fields that the program will have to supply to MFS for each transaction. As a result, the output message segment here is smaller than in the first version, where it included not only variable data but also all the literals required to present a meaningful display.

This produces a twofold benefit. First, the application program is simpler because the literals (which had to be coded with exact spacing to insure the display column would be aligned) aren't necessary any more. And second, telecommunications efficiency is improved because the output message size is reduced from over 700 bytes to about 150.

```
IDENTIFICATION DIVISION.
*
PROGRAM-ID.  DI2.
*
ENVIRONMENT DIVISION.
*
DATA DIVISION.
*
WORKING-STORAGE SECTION.
*
01  SWITCHES.
*
    05  INVOICE-FOUND-SW        PIC X       VALUE 'Y'.
        88  INVOICE-FOUND                   VALUE 'Y'.
    05  END-OF-MESSAGES-SW      PIC X       VALUE 'N'.
        88  END-OF-MESSAGES                 VALUE 'Y'.
*
01  INPUT-MESSAGE-IO-AREA.
*
    05  IM-LL                   PIC S9(3)   COMP.
    05  IM-ZZ                   PIC S9(3)   COMP.
    05  IM-TRANSACTION-CODE     PIC X(8).
    05  IM-INVOICE-NO           PIC X(6).

01  OUTPUT-MESSAGE-IO-AREA.
*
    05  OM-LL                   PIC S9(3)   COMP VALUE +160.
    05  OM-Z1-Z2                PIC S9(3)   COMP VALUE ZERO.
    05  OM-INVOICE-NO           PIC X(6).
    05  OM-INVOICE-DATE         PIC 99/99/99.
    05  OM-PROD-TOTAL           PIC Z(5).99-.
    05  OM-CASH-DISC            PIC Z(5).99-.
    05  OM-SALES-TAX            PIC Z(5).99-.
    05  OM-FREIGHT              PIC Z(5).99-.
    05  OM-BILLING              PIC Z(5).99-.
    05  OM-PMTS-ADJS            PIC Z(5).99-.
    05  OM-BALANCE              PIC Z(5).99-.
    05  OM-ERROR-LINE           PIC X(79).
*
01  ERROR-LINE.
*
    05  FILLER                  PIC X(8)    VALUE 'INVOICE '.
    05  EL-INVOICE-NO           PIC X(6).
    05  FILLER                  PIC X(10)   VALUE ' NOT FOUND'.
    05  FILLER                  PIC X(55)   VALUE SPACE.
*
01  DLI-FUNCTIONS.
*
    05  DLI-GU                  PIC X(4)    VALUE 'GU  '.
    05  DLI-GHU                 PIC X(4)    VALUE 'GHU '.
    05  DLI-GN                  PIC X(4)    VALUE 'GN  '.
    05  DLI-GHN                 PIC X(4)    VALUE 'GHN '.
    05  DLI-GNP                 PIC X(4)    VALUE 'GNP '.
    05  DLI-GHNP                PIC X(4)    VALUE 'GHNP'.
```

Figure 5-11   Source listing for the display invoice program, version 2 (part 1 of 4)

```
       05   DLI-ISRT                  PIC X(4)       VALUE 'ISRT'.
       05   DLI-DLET                  PIC X(4)       VALUE 'DLET'.
       05   DLI-REPL                  PIC X(4)       VALUE 'REPL'.
       05   DLI-CHKP                  PIC X(4)       VALUE 'CHKP'.
       05   DLI-XRST                  PIC X(4)       VALUE 'XRST'.
       05   DLI-PCB                   PIC X(4)       VALUE 'PCB '.
  *
  01   RECEIVABLE-SEGMENT.
  *
       05   RS-INVOICE-NUMBER         PIC X(6).
       05   RS-INVOICE-DATE           PIC X(6).
       05   RS-PO-NUMBER              PIC X(25).
       05   RS-PRODUCT-TOTAL          PIC S9(5)V99       COMP-3.
       05   RS-CASH-DISCOUNT          PIC S9(5)V99       COMP-3.
       05   RS-SALES-TAX              PIC S9(5)V99       COMP-3.
       05   RS-FREIGHT                PIC S9(5)V99       COMP-3.
       05   RS-BALANCE-DUE            PIC S9(5)V99       COMP-3.
  *
  01   INVOICE-NO-SSA.
  *
       05   FILLER                    PIC X(9)       VALUE 'CRRECSEG('.
       05   FILLER                    PIC X(10)      VALUE 'CRRECXNO ='.
       05   INVOICE-NO-SSA-VALUE      PIC X(6).
       05   FILLER                    PIC X          VALUE ')'.
  *
  LINKAGE SECTION.
  *
  01   IO-PCB-MASK.
  *
       05   IO-PCB-LOGICAL-TERMINAL PIC X(8).
       05   FILLER                    PIC XX.
       05   IO-PCB-STATUS-CODE        PIC XX.
       05   IO-PCB-DATE               PIC S9(7)      COMP-3.
       05   IO-PCB-TIME               PIC S9(6)V9    COMP-3.
       05   IO-PCB-MSG-SEQ-NUMBER     PIC S9(5)      COMP.
       05   IO-PCB-MOD-NAME           PIC X(8).
       05   IO-PCB-USER-ID            PIC X(8).
  *
  01   CR-PCB-MASK.
  *
       05   CR-PCB-DBD-NAME           PIC X(8).
       05   CR-PCB-SEGMENT-LEVEL      PIC XX.
       05   CR-PCB-STATUS-CODE        PIC XX.
       05   CR-PCB-PROC-OPTIONS       PIC X(4).
       05   FILLER                    PIC S9(5)      COMP.
       05   CR-PCB-SEGMENT-NAME       PIC X(8).
       05   CR-PCB-KEY-LENGTH         PIC S9(5)      COMP.
       05   CR-PCB-NUMB-SENS-SEGS     PIC S9(5)      COMP.
       05   CR-PCB-KEY                PIC X(22).
  *
  PROCEDURE DIVISION.
  *
       ENTRY 'DLITCBL' USING IO-PCB-MASK
                             CR-PCB-MASK.
```

Figure 5-11   Source listing for the display invoice program, version 2 (part 2 of 4)

```
*
 000-PROCESS-INVOICE-INQUIRIES.
*
     PERFORM 100-PROCESS-INVOICE-INQUIRY
         UNTIL END-OF-MESSAGES.
     GOBACK.
*
 100-PROCESS-INVOICE-INQUIRY.
*
     PERFORM 110-GET-INPUT-MESSAGE.
     IF NOT END-OF-MESSAGES
         PERFORM 120-GET-INVOICE-DATA
         MOVE IM-INVOICE-NO TO OM-INVOICE-NO
         IF INVOICE-FOUND
             MOVE SPACE TO OM-ERROR-LINE
             PERFORM 140-SEND-INVOICE-DATA
         ELSE
             PERFORM 160-SEND-ERROR-LINE.
*
 110-GET-INPUT-MESSAGE.
*
     CALL 'CBLTDLI' USING DLI-GU
                         IO-PCB-MASK
                         INPUT-MESSAGE-IO-AREA.
     IF IO-PCB-STATUS-CODE = 'QC'
         MOVE 'Y' TO END-OF-MESSAGES-SW.
*
 120-GET-INVOICE-DATA.
*
     MOVE 'Y'           TO INVOICE-FOUND-SW.
     MOVE IM-INVOICE-NO TO INVOICE-NO-SSA-VALUE.
     PERFORM 130-GET-RECEIVABLE-SEGMENT.
*
 130-GET-RECEIVABLE-SEGMENT.
*
     CALL 'CBLTDLI' USING DLI-GU
                         CR-PCB-MASK
                         RECEIVABLE-SEGMENT
                         INVOICE-NO-SSA.
     IF CR-PCB-STATUS-CODE NOT = SPACE
         MOVE 'N' TO INVOICE-FOUND-SW.
*
 140-SEND-INVOICE-DATA.
*
     MOVE RS-INVOICE-DATE  TO OM-INVOICE-DATE.
     MOVE RS-PRODUCT-TOTAL TO OM-PROD-TOTAL.
     MOVE RS-CASH-DISCOUNT TO OM-CASH-DISC.
     MOVE RS-SALES-TAX     TO OM-SALES-TAX.
     MOVE RS-FREIGHT       TO OM-FREIGHT.
     COMPUTE OM-BILLING =      RS-PRODUCT-TOTAL -
                               RS-CASH-DISCOUNT +
                               RS-SALES-TAX +
                               RS-FREIGHT.
```

Figure 5-11   Source listing for the display invoice program, version 2 (part 3 of 4)

```
        COMPUTE OM-PMTS-ADJS =    RS-BALANCE-DUE -
                                 (RS-PRODUCT-TOTAL -
                                  RS-CASH-DISCOUNT +
                                  RS-SALES-TAX +
                                  RS-FREIGHT).
        MOVE RS-BALANCE-DUE    TO OM-BALANCE.
        PERFORM 150-INSERT-OUTPUT-SEGMENT.
   *
    150-INSERT-OUTPUT-SEGMENT.
   *
        CALL 'CBLTDLI' USING DLI-ISRT
                             IO-PCB-MASK
                             OUTPUT-MESSAGE-IO-AREA.
   *
    160-SEND-ERROR-LINE.
   *
        MOVE ZERO           TO OM-INVOICE-DATE
                               OM-PROD-TOTAL
                               OM-CASH-DISC
                               OM-SALES-TAX
                               OM-FREIGHT
                               OM-BILLING
                               OM-PMTS-ADJS
                               OM-BALANCE.
        MOVE IM-INVOICE-NO TO EL-INVOICE-NO.
        MOVE ERROR-LINE    TO OM-ERROR-LINE.
        PERFORM 150-INSERT-OUTPUT-SEGMENT.
   *
```

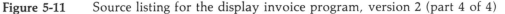

Figure 5-11   Source listing for the display invoice program, version 2 (part 4 of 4)

I want you to notice the one-to-one relationship between the individual fields I defined in the format set output message descriptor and the fields I defined in the output message I/O area in the COBOL program. Also, for the fields in the COBOL program, I used editing PICTURE clauses to format the data properly before it's passed to MFS. For example, the field OM-BALANCE, which I defined with

```
PIC Z(5).99-
```

is mapped into the output message field defined in statement 52, which is simply defined with

```
LTH=9
```

For the data to be displayed properly in those nine bytes, the COBOL program has to edit it before it inserts the message.

The program elements that follow the output segment in the Data Division are like those in the original version of the program, so I'm not going to describe them. The Procedure Division is straightforward too; the structure chart for the program is the same as the first version's.

For each transaction, the program retrieves an input message segment (module 110 invoked from module 100) and issues a GU call to retrieve the specified invoice from the customer data base (module 120, also invoked from module 100). If the program retrieves the specified invoice segment successfully, it clears the value in the error message field of the output message, then invokes module 140 to send the invoice data. Module 140 formats the output message either by moving a field directly from the receivable segment to the output message or by calculating an output message field value based on other data from the receivable segment. After it has completely formatted the output message, module 140 invokes module 150, which issues an ISRT call to send the output message.

However, if the program can't retrieve the receivable segment the operator requested, it formats the output message in a different way. Module 160 moves zeros to all the data fields in the output message except the invoice number field. That way, the user won't accidentally think data from the previous display is for an invoice that the program really didn't find. Then module 160 formats an error line with the number of the invoice that couldn't be found, moves the error line to the error line field in the output message, and invokes module 150 to send the message.

I think you'll agree that this version of the application is a better implementation than the first one. However, to develop a format set like the one in figure 5-10, you need to learn the details of the control statements it contains. That's what the chapters in the next section teach you. But first, I want to tell you a little about the MFS Language Utility.

The MFS Language Utility

After you've coded a format set like the one in figure 5-4 or 5-10, you have to translate it into control blocks before MFS can use it. To do that, you use the *MFS Language Utility*.

The MFS Language Utility performs several functions. Basically, it makes sure your specifications are syntactically correct and that they are complete. Recall that the format set in figure 5-4 has three parts; one defines the screen format, one the input message format, and one the output message format. It's possible to process these groups separately and at different times with the MFS Language Utility.

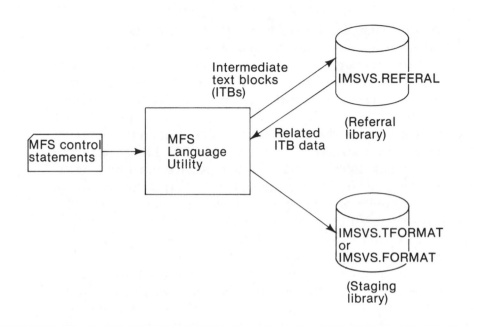

Figure 5-12   Translating MFS control statements

As figure 5-12 shows, the MFS Language Utility stores all the syntactically correct specifications it receives as *intermediate text blocks*, or *ITBs*, in a library called the *referral library* (its default data set name is IMSVS.REFERAL). The utility doesn't create final-form blocks until it can construct a complete format set, either entirely from the control statements it receives in a particular run or from the control statements combined with data stored in ITBs.

Because the MFS Language Utility uses ITBs, it's possible to update a format set by changing only a part of it. For example, you could change the location of the output field in the sample format set in figure 5-4 by simply changing the DFLD statement with the label OUTTEXT and translating only the statements in the group that defines the screen. Although this seems unnecessary for such a simple format set, it becomes practical when a format set contains complicated specifications for many terminal types, and only one needs to be changed.

If the control statements for a format set are complete and correct, the MFS Language Utility translates them into blocks that it stores in a partitioned data set called the *staging library*. Its data set name in the production environment is usually IMSVS.FORMAT; in the testing environment, it's usually IMSVS.TFORMAT.

The staging library is not the MFS library used by the on-line system. To make a format set from the staging library available for use in the production environment requires some additional system programming work for which you probably won't be responsible.

To help you execute the MFS Language Utility, IMS supplies several cataloged procedures. However, you probably won't be able to use them. Instead, it's more likely that your shop has installed customized procedures for application programmers to translate format sets in a testing environment. Check with your supervisor to find out if this is the case.

Discussion

In the chapters that follow, I present MFS features and facilities in terms of integrated application development. In other words, I assume that the same programmer will develop both parts of a typical application: the application program and the format set. However, that isn't the case in all shops.

Some installations have a DC system administrator whose staff is responsible, among other things, for creating new MFS blocks and maintaining old ones. The systems administration group performs the same sort of functions for the DC elements of IMS that the data base administration group performs for its DB elements. Because the systems administration group is independent of the application programming group, you may never have to code MFS blocks yourself.

Even if that's the case, you must still be familiar with MFS. Obviously, your programs have to handle messages processed through MFS, so you need to understand the processing MFS does. In addition, if the design of your MFS application calls for some special MFS features, your program has to be compatible with them. As a result, you need a thorough understanding of MFS, even if you won't be coding format sets yourself. That's what the four chapters in the next section provide.

Terminology

map
control block
device input format
DIF
message input descriptor
MID
message output descriptor
MOD
device output format
DOF
format set
device format
MFS Language Utility
intermediate text block
ITB
referral library
staging library

Objectives

1. Describe message flow within IMS when MFS is in use.

2. Name the four types of MFS control blocks and briefly describe the purpose of each.

3. Explain why a typical format set contains only one group of control statements to define a screen, but two groups to describe messages.

4. Describe how screen fields are defined in a format set.

5. Describe how message fields are defined in a format set.

6. Describe how screen fields are related to message fields in a format set.

7. Explain why you don't have to supply all the control statements required for a complete format set when you invoke the MFS Language Utility.

Using MFS facilities

This section contains four chapters that, combined with the introduction to MFS in chapter 5, present a complete subset of MFS. The first chapter in this section, chapter 6, presents the syntax of the MFS control statements and shows you how to code them to define format sets. Chapter 7 shows you how to control field attributes and the cursor, chapter 8 describes complex screen flows, and chapter 9 introduces physical and logical paging.

In contrast to IBM's MFS manual, these chapters focus specifically on 3270 devices. That's because the MFS applications you work on will almost certainly be for 3270s. After you've finished the chapters in this section, it should be easy for you to extract what you need to know about unusual terminals and features from the *MFS User's Guide*.

Chapter 6

How to code
MFS control statements

In this chapter, I'll teach you the syntax of MFS control statements. First, I'll describe the general syntax rules that apply to all MFS control statements; then I'll discuss the statements individually. I've divided them into three groups which I'll cover separately: (1) device format control statements, (2) message descriptor control statements, and (3) compilation control statements.

The material in this chapter can seem overwhelming. Frankly, I don't expect you to memorize all the details it presents. Instead, I encourage you to read through the chapter to get a feeling for the facilities MFS offers. After you've finished this chapter, you can refer back to it as often as necessary to refresh your memory on details.

SYNTAX RULES FOR MFS CONTROL STATEMENTS

It's easy to code MFS control statements, as long as you remember a few simple rules. This section describes the general format of MFS control statements; then it shows you how to use continuation statements and comments.

Statement format

MFS control statements look like assembler language statements, and they're coded the same way. That means each has the format shown in figure 6-1.

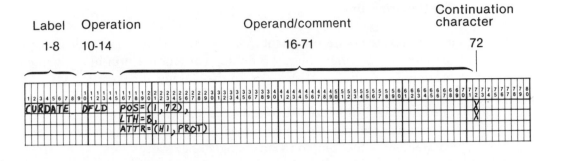

Figure 6-1 Format of an MFS control statement

Columns 1 through 8 make up the *label field*. For some statements, you must code a label value in this field; for other statements, it's optional. If you do code a label value, it must begin in column 1, and the first character must be alphabetic.

In figure 6-1, the value of the label field (CURDATE) meets these requirements. In most cases, the maximum length of a label is eight characters. However, there are two exceptions, which I'll point out later in this chapter. (In both of those cases, the maximum length of the label field value is six characters instead of eight.)

The second field of an MFS control statement begins in column 10. It's the *operation field*, and it contains the name of the control statement you're coding, like FMT, DFLD, MSG, DEV, and so on. These values are called *operation codes*. I'll present the operation codes in the sections on the device format, message descriptor, and compilation control statements.

After the operation field, you usually code the *operand field*, which contains one or more *parameters* that indicate what the statement is to do. When you code the operand field, it must be separated from the operation field by one or more spaces. Because most of the operation codes are five or fewer characters long, they end in or before column 14. If you leave column 15 blank, that means the operand field can begin in column 16.

Most of the time, the parameters you code in the operand field won't fill the line. When the MFS Language Utility encounters a space after a parameter, it considers the operand field to have ended, and it ignores any data that follows up through column 71. As a result, you can code brief comments in this *comment field*. I'll have more to say about the comment field in a moment. First, I want to describe how to handle a statement that's too long to fit on a single line.

Continuation lines

If you need to code a statement that's too long to fit on a single line, you can use *continuation lines*. To do so, you code a non-blank value in column 72 of all lines that make up the statement except the last. You must begin each line of the statement (except the first) in column 16. The statement in figure 6-1 follows this pattern.

Frankly, you'll seldom be forced to use continuation lines because a statement is too long to fit on a single line. More often, you'll choose to use continuation lines to make your format sets more readable. It's easier to read a format set when you code just one parameter per line. Probably, your shop's standards will require you to code format sets one way or another, so find out what the standards are and follow them.

Figure 6-2 shows how a format set looks when you code one parameter per line. Each continued line has an X in column 72, and the line that follows begins in column 16. This is the same format set I showed you in the last chapter for the second version of the display invoice application. Throughout this chapter, I'll use the format set in figure 6-2 as a source of examples.

Comments

You can include comments in your MFS format sets in two ways: (1) as *comment lines* or (2) as *embedded comments*. A comment line is any line that has an asterisk in column 1. I use comment lines to separate parts of a format set; the lines of asterisks in figure 6-2 are comment lines. I recommend you use comment lines in this way; it's all too easy to get lost in a complex format set without them.

Embedded comments are text you code after the operand field on a non-comment line. As I described above, the end of a series of parameters in the operand field is marked by a space. After that space, any data that appears on the line, up to but not including column 72, is ignored by the MFS Language Utility. As a result, you can code brief comments on most lines in a format set.

Generally, I don't like embedded comments. Most statements are complicated enough with just the parameters you have to code. The extra clutter introduced by embedded comments makes the format set harder to read. And usually, there isn't enough space in the comment field to make a useful comment anyway. As a result, if you want to include documentation in your format set, I recommend you use comment lines instead of embedded comments.

```
1          PRINT ON,NOGEN
2 *******************************************************************
3 *          FORMAT SET FOR APPLICATION PROGRAM DI2.               *
4 *******************************************************************
5 DI2DF     FMT
6          DEV   TYPE=(3270,2),                                     X
                 FEAT=IGNORE,                                       X
                 SYSMSG=ERRMSG,                                     X
                 DSCA=X'00A0'
7          DIV   TYPE=INOUT
8          DPAGE CURSOR=((3,12)),                                   X
                 FILL=PT
9          DFLD  'DISPLAY INVOICE SUMMARY',                         X
                 POS=(1,2),                                         X
                 ATTR=(HI,PROT)
10         DFLD  'DATE:',                                           X
                 POS=(1,65),                                        X
                 ATTR=(HI,PROT)
11 CURDATE DFLD  POS=(1,72),                                        X
                 LTH=8,                                             X
                 ATTR=(HI,PROT)
12         DFLD  'INVOICE:',                                        X
                 POS=(3,2),                                         X
                 ATTR=(HI,PROT)
13 INVNO   DFLD  POS=(3,12),                                        X
                 LTH=6,                                             X
                 ATTR=(NUM)
14         DFLD  'DATE:',                                           X
                 POS=(3,21),                                        X
                 ATTR=(HI,PROT)
15 INVDATE DFLD  POS=(3,28),                                        X
                 LTH=8,                                             X
                 ATTR=(PROT)
16         DFLD  'SUBTOTAL:',                                       X
                 POS=(3,41),                                        X
                 ATTR=(HI,PROT)
17 SUBTOTAL DFLD POS=(3,55),                                        X
                 LTH=9,                                             X
                 ATTR=(PROT)
18         DFLD  'DISCOUNT:',                                       X
                 POS=(4,41),                                        X
                 ATTR=(HI,PROT)
19 DISCOUNT DFLD POS=(4,55),                                        X
                 LTH=9,                                             X
                 ATTR=(PROT)
20         DFLD  'SALES TAX:',                                      X
                 POS=(5,41),                                        X
                 ATTR=(HI,PROT)
21 SALESTAX DFLD POS=(5,55),                                        X
                 LTH=9,                                             X
                 ATTR=(PROT)
22         DFLD  'FREIGHT:',                                        X
                 POS=(6,41),                                        X
                 ATTR=(HI,PROT)
```

Figure 6-2   Format set for the display invoice application, version 2 (part 1 of 3)

```
23 FREIGHT  DFLD   POS=(6,55),                                          X
                   LTH=9,                                               X
                   ATTR=(PROT)
24          DFLD   '---------',                                         X
                   POS=(7,55),                                          X
                   ATTR=(HI,PROT)
25          DFLD   'BILLING:',                                          X
                   POS=(8,41),                                          X
                   ATTR=(HI,PROT)
26 BILLING  DFLD   POS=(8,55),                                          X
                   LTH=9,                                               X
                   ATTR=(PROT)
27          DFLD   'PMTS/ADJS:',                                        X
                   POS=(9,41),                                          X
                   ATTR=(HI,PROT)
28 PMTSADJS DFLD   POS=(9,55),                                          X
                   LTH=9,                                               X
                   ATTR=(PROT)
29          DFLD   '---------',                                         X
                   POS=(10,55),                                         X
                   ATTR=(HI,PROT)
30          DFLD   'DUE:',                                              X
                   POS=(11,41),                                         X
                   ATTR=(HI,PROT)
31 DUE      DFLD   POS=(11,55),                                         X
                   LTH=9,                                               X
                   ATTR=(PROT)
32 ERRMSG   DFLD   POS=(23,2),                                         X
                   LTH=79,                                              X
                   ATTR=(PROT)
33          FMTEND
34 ******************************************************************
35 DI2I     MSG    TYPE=INPUT,                                         X
                   SOR=(DI2DF,IGNORE),                                 X
                   NXT=DI2O
36          SEG
37          MFLD   'DI2     ',                                         X
                   LTH=8
38          MFLD   INVNO,                                              X
                   LTH=6,                                              X
                   JUST=R,                                             X
                   FILL=C'0'
39          MSGEND
40 ******************************************************************
41 DI2O     MSG    TYPE=OUTPUT,                                        X
                   SOR=(DI2DF,IGNORE),                                 X
                   NXT=DI2I
42          SEG
43          MFLD   (CURDATE,DATE2)
44          MFLD   INVNO,                                              X
                   LTH=6
45          MFLD   INVDATE,                                            X
                   LTH=8
```

Figure 6-2   Format set for the display invoice application, version 2 (part 2 of 3)

```
46          MFLD    SUBTOTAL,                                               X
                    LTH=9
47          MFLD    DISCOUNT,                                               X
                    LTH=9
48          MFLD    SALESTAX,                                               X
                    LTH=9
49          MFLD    FREIGHT,                                                X
                    LTH=9
50          MFLD    BILLING,                                                X
                    LTH=9
51          MFLD    PMTSADJS,                                               X
                    LTH=9
52          MFLD    DUE,                                                    X
                    LTH=9
53          MFLD    ERRMSG,                                                 X
                    LTH=79
54          MSGEND
55  ************************************************************************
56          END
```

Figure 6-2   Format set for the display invoice application, version 2 (part 3 of 3)

HOW TO CODE THE DEVICE FORMAT CONTROL STATEMENTS

The control statements in the first group I'm going to describe are the ones you use to define screen images. Figure 6-3 shows the operation codes for these device format control statements. As you can see in the bottom section of the figure, you code the device format control statements in a hierarchical arrangement; this will become clearer to you as you read the descriptions of the statements. This section describes each of the device format control statements, beginning with the ones that delimit a device format: FMT and FMTEND.

The FMT and FMTEND control statements

As figure 6-3 shows, the control statements for a device format always begin with a FMT statement and always end with a FMTEND statement. Figure 6-4 presents the syntax of these two statements. They're simple; neither requires parameters. All you have to remember when you code these statements is to provide an appropriate label on the FMT statement.

The label you code on the FMT statement can be no more than six characters long. (This is the first of the two exceptions to the rule that a label can be eight characters long.) For example, the FMT statement I

The device format control statements

FMT   Identifies the beginning of a device format.

DEV   Identifies the beginning of a series of control statements for a particular device type; you may code multiple DEV statements within a device format.

DIV   Identifies the beginning of a series of control statements for a particular format type subordinate to a DEV statement; for 3270 display stations, you code only one DIV statement subordinate to the DEV statement.

DPAGE   Identifies the beginning of a series of control statements for a device page subordinate to a DIV statement.

DFLD   Identifies a device field within a device page.

FMTEND   Identifies the end of a device format.

The device format control statements are arranged hierarchically

```
FMT
  DEV
    DIV
      DPAGE
        DFLD
           .
        DFLD
      DPAGE
        DFLD
           .
        DFLD
  DEV
    DIV
      DPAGE
        DFLD
           .
        DFLD
      DPAGE
        DFLD
           .
        DFLD
FMTEND
```

Figure 6-3   The device format control statements

The FMT and FMTEND control statements

```
label     FMT

          FMTEND
```

Explanation

label   The one- to six-character name that will become part of the names of the DIFs and DOFs created as a result of this device format specification.

Figure 6-4   The FMT and FMTEND control statements

coded in statement 5 of figure 6-2,

```
    DI2DF     FMT
```

has a five-character label. MFS uses the label you supply as part of the DIF and DOF names it creates from the control statements you code between the FMT and FMTEND statements. The other parts of the block names come from specifications you make on subordinate DEV statements.

The DEV control statement

For each different device type for which you want MFS support for a given application, you code a DEV statement. For instance, if three different device types were to be used for the same application, you'd code three DEV statements, one for each. Subordinate to each of these three DEV statements, you'd code a set of DIV, DPAGE, and DFLD statements to define the screen format for each device type.

A DEV statement not only identifies a particular kind of device, but it specifies its characteristics as well. Fortunately, most of the applications for which you'll develop format sets will be used on only one terminal type: the 3270 model 2 display station. As a result, most format definitions will contain a single DEV statement that names that terminal type.

Figure 6-5 presents the format of the DEV statement for 3270 display stations. The complete syntax of the DEV statement is far more complex than figure 6-5. For example, you can code DEV statements for 3270s with unusual features like the selector light pen or magnetic card reader, and you can specify a variety of terminal types other than 3270s. If you need to develop a format set that uses unusual features or devices, refer to the *MFS User's Guide*.

The DEV control statement

```
DEV          TYPE= ⎧(3270,1)⎫
                   ⎨(3270,2)⎬
                   ⎩3270-An ⎭

             ,FEAT=IGNORE

                                        ⎧'literal'⎫
                                        ⎪NEXTPP   ⎪
             [,PFK=(pfkeyfield,[integer=]⎨NEXTMSGP⎬ [, ...])]
                                        ⎪NEXTLP   ⎪
                                        ⎩ENDMPPI  ⎭

             [,DSCA=X'nnnn']

             [,SYSMSG=msgfield]
```

Explanation

The TYPE parameter

The various TYPE values specify the device models for which device format blocks should be created. The values are:

(3270,1)   3270 model 1 display station (12-line screen).

(3270,2)   3270 model 2 display station (24-line screen).

3270-An   3270 display station symbolic name. The symbolic name must be defined in the IMS device characteristics table. IBM recommends these names for terminals with the indicated screen sizes:

> 3270-A1   12-line, 80-column display
>
> 3270-A2   24-line, 80-column display
>
> 3270-A3   32-line, 80-column display
>
> 3270-A4   43-line, 80-column display
>
> 3270-A5   12-line, 40-column display
>
> 3270-A7   27-line, 132-column display

Although these are the recommended names, your shop's symbolic names may differ.

Figure 6-5   The DEV control statement (part 1 of 2)

The FEAT parameter

IGNORE   Specifies that the DIF and DOF generated for this DEV statement will work
                      with the indicated 3270 terminal type, regardless of any special features
                      installed on it. This is the usual value you code for the FEAT parameter.

The PFK parameter

pfkeyfield   Specifies a name that can be referred to by the MFLD statement that defines
                      the input message field that will receive literal data as a result of a PF key
                      operation; this should **not** be the name of a device field.

integer   An integer value from 1 to 36 that identifies the PF key that will be associated
                      with the value that follows. For example, if you code 4 = '/FORMAT DI2O', the
                      literal string /FORMAT DI2O is associated with PF key 4. If you use the integer
                      keyword format for one PF key assignment, you should use it for all
                      assignments you make on the DEV statement.

                      If you do not use the integer keyword to identify PF key assignments, the
                      assignments are positional. In other words, the first value you specify is
                      associated with PF1, the second with PF2, and so on.

'literal'   Specifies the text string you want to associate with the PF key you've
                      indicated (in the keyword format) or implied (in the positional format).

NEXTPP   These are keywords you can specify instead of literals to associate PF keys
NEXTMSGP   with MFS paging functions. The NEXTPP function causes MFS to display the
NEXTLP   next physical page of a message; it's the same as the default PA1 action.
ENDMPPI   NEXTMSGP requests the next message, bypassing remaining pages of the
                      current message; it's the same as the default PA2 action. ENDMPPI is used to
                      signal to MFS that no more physical pages are left to be entered for a multi-
                      page input message. NEXTLP requests the next logical page of an output
                      message. Chapter 9 presents more information on these functions.

The DSCA parameter

X'nnnn'   'nnnn' is a hexadecimal value for the two-byte default system control area for
                      the terminal. The value of this field determines default terminal actions when
                      output messages are received. You're most likely to code X'00A0'; this
                      causes unprotected fields on the screen to be erased before new data is
                      written to it. You might also want to code X'00C0'; this causes the entire
                      device buffer to be cleared before output is written to the screen.

The SYSMSG parameter

msgfield   Specifies the name of a device field (that is, the label of a DFLD statement)
                      that can be used to display messages from IMS. The field should be at least 79
                      bytes long.

Figure 6-5   The DEV control statement (part 2 of 2)

The TYPE parameter of the DEV statement   You code the first parameter of the DEV statement, TYPE, to identify the terminal type to which the control statements that follow apply. Figure 6-5 lists the TYPE parameter values for 3270s. For example, to identify a basic 3270 model 2 display station, you might code

```
TYPE=(3270,2)
```

However, most IMS shops use a *device characteristics table* that relates symbolic terminal names to particular 3270 models. Those symbolic names have the format 3270-An, where n is a digit between 1 and 9. Figure 6-5 shows the assignments IBM recommends. If your shop uses the recommended names, you could also code

```
TYPE=3270-A2
```

to refer to a standard 3270 model 2 display station.

The FEAT parameter of the DEV statement   You code the FEAT parameter to specify the exact configuration of optional features on the 3270 device for which you're coding the DEV statement. These features include the selector light pen, the operator identification magnetic card reader, the special data entry keyboard, and program function keys.

Although the complete syntax of the FEAT parameter includes a variety of values for different option combinations, figure 6-5 shows only one: IGNORE. I recommend you always code

```
FEAT=IGNORE
```

unless you receive specifications that explicitly require you to name the features. Strangely, when you code IGNORE, your blocks work with *any* combination of device features. However, if you do specify individual features on the FEAT parameter, the blocks that result work only for devices with those exact combinations.

How MFS uses TYPE and FEAT parameter values to create block names   MFS combines the specifications you provide on the TYPE and FEAT parameters of the DEV statement with the label you coded on the FMT statement to build unique names for the DIFs and DOFs it generates. Figure 6-6 illustrates the structure of DIF and DOF names. The device type (specified with the TYPE parameter of the DEV statement) for which a particular block will be used is recorded in the first byte of the block name with a unique hexadecimal value. The combination of device features the block supports (specified on the FEAT

Byte	Contents
1	Hexadecimal value indicating device type; some examples are:

        X'00'   3270 model 1
        X'02'   3270 model 2
        X'41'   3270-A1
        X'42'   3270-A2
        X'45'   3270-A5

Byte	Contents
2	Hexadecimal value indicating features on the device; the only value you should see is:

        X'7F'   Ignore features

Other values are used if you specify a particular configuration of features.

Byte	Contents
3-8	Label from the FMT statement. If the block is a DIF, character 3 is a lowercase letter; if it's a DOF, character 3 is an uppercase letter.

Figure 6-6   The structure of DIF and DOF names

---

parameter of the DEV statement) is identified by a unique hexadecimal value in the second byte of the block name.

The six-character FMT statement label is stored in positions 3-8 of the block name. If the block is a DIF, the first character of the FMT label is a lowercase letter; if the block is a DOF, the first character of the FMT label is an uppercase letter.

In the format set in figure 6-2, I coded

```
DI2DF      FMT
           DEV     TYPE=(3270,2),
                   FEAT=IGNORE,...
```

to specify that blocks should be created for a 3270 model 2 display station and that special features should be ignored. (This is the way you'll usually code the DEV statement.) As a result of these two statements, the MFS Language Utility creates a DOF with a name that looks like " DI2DF " and a DIF with a name that looks like " dI2DF ". In each case, the last character of the name is a space because the label I coded on the FMT statement had a space in its sixth position.

The first two positions of these block names look like they also contain spaces. Actually, they contain appropriate hex values for the device type and feature configuration I specified. Byte 1 of each name contains hex 02 (for a 3270 model 2 terminal) and byte 2 contains hex 7F (for IGNORE).

You don't have to be concerned with the exact block names MFS generates as a result of your specifications. However, this information will help you understand that there's nothing magical about the way MFS supports a variety of device types with multiple feature configurations.

The PFK parameter of the DEV statement   The third parameter of the DEV statement, PFK, lets you specify how MFS should support program function keys. When you press a PF key, an input message is formatted and sent, just like when you press the enter key. However, if the PF key you press is specified in the PFK parameter of the DEV statement, MFS moves literal data that you've specified for that PF key to a field in the input message before it passes it to IMS for queueing.

If the message field is at the beginning of the message, the literal data specifies the destination of the message: a program, a terminal, or IMS (as a command). As a result, a properly defined PF key can be used to request programs or IMS functions. On the other hand, if the field is embedded in the message, the literal data is passed along with the rest of the message to its destination, which is probably an application program. Then, the application program can use the PF key data as control information. You'll see examples of both techniques in chapter 8.

Although the PFK parameter in figure 6-5 looks complicated, it has only two main parts, and it's easy to code. The first part of the PFK parameter names the target input message field; I'll describe it in a moment. The second part, which can have many components, specifies the literals that are associated with particular PF keys. You can code the second part of the parameter in either keyword or positional format.

To understand, consider figure 6-7, which presents parts of two format sets; both use PF keys in the same way. In fact, the only difference between the two is that the first uses the keyword format of the PFK parameter and the second uses the positional format.

In each example, the first value I coded on the PFK parameter is PFKTEXT. That's the name of the message field into which the PF key literal data will be moved. What I want you to notice now is the difference in how I coded the PF key literal data in the two examples.

In both, I specified that text strings should be associated with five PF keys: PF1, PF2, PF3, PF4, and PF10. Notice that you don't have to

Using the keyword format of the PFK parameter

```
PFKEX     FMT
          DEV    TYPE=(3270,2),
                 FEAT=IGNORE,
                 PFK=(PFKTEXT,1='01',2='02',3='03',4='04',10='10')
          .
          .
          .
          FMTEND
PFKEXI    MSG    TYPE=INPUT,
                 SOR=(PFKEX,IGNORE),
                 NXT=PFKEXO
          SEG
          .
          .
          .
          MFLD   PFKTEXT,
                 LTH=2
          .
          .
          .
          MSGEND
```

Using the positional format of the PFK parameter

```
PFKEX     FMT
          DEV    TYPE=(3270,2),
                 FEAT=IGNORE,
                 PFK=(PFKTEXT,'01','02','03','04',,,,,,'10')
          .
          .
          .
          FMTEND
PFKEXI    MSG    TYPE=INPUT,
                 SOR=(PFKEX,IGNORE),
                 NXT=PFKEXO
          SEG
          .
          .
          .
          MFLD   PFKTEXT,
                 LTH=2
          .
          .
          .
          MSGEND
```

Figure 6-7   How to specify PF key functions

supply a text string for all the PF keys that might be present on a terminal. If you don't specify a text string for a particular PF key and the operator uses it, the message field is filled with spaces, as long as you didn't specify another fill option for the field. (I'll describe field fill later in this chapter.)

To use the keyword format, illustrated in the top section of figure 6-7, you code an integer that corresponds to the PF key you're defining, an equals sign, then the literal you want to specify; the literal is enclosed between apostrophes. You repeat this for each PF key you want to enable, and you separate each PF key specification from the others with commas.

To use the positional format, illustrated in the bottom section of figure 6-7, you don't need to code the identifying integers for enabled PF keys. Instead, you just code the literal values you want to assign to the keys. The first value you code is for PF1, the second is for PF2, and so on. Again, you separate the values from one another with commas. However, unlike the keyword format, the positional format requires you to account for unassigned keys with commas. That's why the parameter looks so strange in the second part of figure 6-7: The series of commas indicates that PF5 through PF9 do not have literals associated with them.

In both examples in figure 6-7, the literal data associated with enabled keys is moved to a field named PFKTEXT when a particular PF key is selected. MFS uses the same message field for all PF key operations, even though many PF keys may have literals associated with them. That makes sense, because in a single input operation, only one PF key can be detected; pressing the PF key causes the input data to be sent from the terminal, just like the enter key does.

The input message field that will receive the PF key literals is shown in both examples in figure 6-7. The MFLD statement is coded as if it referred to a device field named PFKTEXT, the name I specified in the PFK parameter of the DEV statement. However, there is no actual device field named PFKTEXT. Here, PFKTEXT is the name of a *pseudofield* that's used as a mechanism to connect the literal specification in the PFK parameter of the DEV statement and the message field. (By the way, there's nothing special about the name PFKTEXT; I selected it because it's meaningful to me. You can use any name you like in the PFK parameter.)

Also, notice that I specified that the length of the target field for PF key data is two bytes (LTH=2). That's because each of the text strings I associated with a PF key is two bytes long. However, for some applications, you'll need to use longer text strings. Just be sure that the length you specify for the target message field is as long as the longest text string associated with a PF key. The maximum size is 256 bytes.

Figure 6-5 also lists four keyword values (NEXTPP, NEXTMSGP, NEXTLP, and ENDMPPI) that you can associate with PF keys. These correspond to MFS functions for paging operations. I'll describe them in chapter 9 when I present paging. So don't worry about them for now.

In fact, don't worry about understanding any of the paging elements I mention in this chapter. I'll explain them all in detail in chapter 9. I've just included them in the command formats in this chapter so that the formats will be more complete references for you later on.

The DSCA parameter of the DEV statement   The DSCA parameter lets you specify a default terminal action that's performed when an output message is sent to a 3270 device. Usually, you'll code

```
DSCA=X'00A0'
```

which causes unprotected fields on the screen to be erased before the output message is displayed. Protected fields, which contain constant data like captions, are not sent to the terminal with each output operation, and, as a result, should not be erased. Although you can code a variety of values for this parameter, you're not likely to need them.

The SYSMSG parameter of the DEV statement   The SYSMSG parameter names a device field in which messages that come to the terminal from IMS will be displayed; that field should be 79 bytes long. In figure 6-2,

```
SYSMSG=ERRMSG
```

specifies that IMS messages should be displayed in the device field ERRMSG.

It's not a requirement that you code a SYSMSG field. However, if you don't, any messages from IMS are displayed at the top of the screen; that destroys the format of the display. As a result, it's sensible to provide a SYSMSG field. The chances are that your shop has a screen design standard that dictates where the SYSMSG field should be located.

It's quite all right to use the SYSMSG field for application messages too. For example, you can see in figure 6-2 that the output message field defined in statement 53 also refers to the device field ERRMSG. This technique can help you make better use of space on crowded screens.

The DIV control statement

```
DIV        TYPE=INOUT
```

Explanation

The TYPE parameter

INOUT   Specifies that the same device format specification should be used to
                       generate both a DIF and a DOF. Always code TYPE = INOUT for 3270 display
                       stations.

Figure 6-8   The DIV control statement

The DIV control statement

After the DEV statement, you code a DIV statement, illustrated in figure 6-8. For a 3270 display station, you always code

```
DIV    TYPE=INOUT
```

to indicate that the same device format specifications should be used to generate both a DIF and a DOF. (That's the value I coded in statement 7 of the format set in figure 6-2.) You code INOUT for a 3270 display station because an output format becomes the input format for the next message.

The DPAGE control statement

The primary function of the DPAGE control statement (illustrated in figure 6-9) is to let you specify a device format that will handle multiple logical pages, which I'll cover in chapter 9. Although you won't need to use logical paging for most format sets, you may need to use two secondary functions provided by the DPAGE statement: initial cursor positioning and field fill.

The CURSOR parameter of the DPAGE statement   To specify a default location where the cursor should be positioned each time a screen is displayed, you code the CURSOR parameter of the DPAGE statement. In figure 6-2, I coded

```
CURSOR=((3,12))
```

The DPAGE control statement

```
label      DPAGE    [CURSOR=((line,column[,cfield])...)]

                    [,FILL=fillchar]

                    [,MULT=YES]
```

Explanation

label   The name of the logical device page. Optional for format sets that do not use the logical paging feature.

The CURSOR parameter

line   The line number of the default cursor position.

column   The column number of the default cursor position.

cfield   The name of a pseudofield referred to in an MFLD statement that will be used to pass cursor control information between MFS and the application program. You'll learn how to use it in chapter 7.

The FILL parameter

fillchar   The fill character to be used for output device fields. Values you can specify for 3270 display stations are:

          PT   Specifies the program tab (the default); output fields that do not fill the device field are followed by a program tab character to erase the remainder of the device field.

          C'c'   Specifies a character to be used as a fill character.

          X'hh'   Specifies a hexadecimal value to be used as a fill character.

The MULT parameter

YES   Specifies that multiple physical pages within this device page can be used to generate an input message. Chapter 9 presents more information.

Figure 6-9   The DPAGE control statement

to specify that the cursor should be located at column 12 of line 3 each time an output message is mapped to the screen. For this application, that means that the cursor is located where the operator begins to key in the number of the invoice the program is to display.

The syntax of the CURSOR parameter lets you specify multiple cursor locations. You do that when you're defining multiple physical pages; I'll describe physical paging in chapter 9. For now, just realize that you usually code two pairs of parentheses around the line and column values.

The FILL parameter of the DPAGE statement   The FILL parameter specifies what character should be used to pad device fields when output data sent to them doesn't fill them. The default for 3270 terminals is a special character called the *program tab*. In figure 6-2, I explicitly requested the default by coding

```
FILL=PT
```

on the DPAGE statement. The program tab character lets MFS avoid transmitting blanks to fill partially full fields, but at the same time it erases previously displayed data that would otherwise be left in the unused parts of those fields.

Don't be overwhelmed by the amount of detail involved in the DEV, DIV, and DPAGE statements. For almost all of the format sets you define, you'll code these statements as they appear in figure 6-2. Although there is more to learn about these statements, the way I coded them in figure 6-2 can serve as a model for your format sets.

The DFLD control statement

The statement you'll code most often in device formats is the DFLD statement; figure 6-10 presents its syntax. As you can see in figure 6-2, most of the statements in the device format specification group (24 out of 29) are DFLD statements that identify individual fields on the screen. As you should remember from chapter 5, the DFLD statement specifies where on the screen a field is located (with the POS parameter) and how large the field is (with the LTH parameter). Although the syntax of the DFLD statement might look imposing, there's little that's difficult about it.

When to use labels on DFLD statements   If you look down the DFLD statements in figure 6-2, you'll see that some are labelled, and others aren't. You need to code a label on a DFLD statement only when the device field it defines has to be related to a message field (for input, output, or both).

Device fields that are not related to message fields are captions. For example, the first DFLD statement in figure 6-2,

```
DFLD  'DISPLAY INVOICE SUMMARY',
      POS=(1,2),
      ATTR=(HI,PROT)
```

provides the screen title. Because this field contains the same value throughout the execution of the application, there's no need for it to be sent to the program with each input message or back to the screen with each output message. As a result, I didn't need to code a label for it.

In contrast, the labelled DFLD statements all contain variable data, and they're referred to in the message descriptor statements that follow in the format set. As you should remember from chapter 5, that's how MFS is able to map screen fields to and from message fields.

For example,

```
CURDATE   DFLD   POS=(1,72),
                 LTH=8,
                 ATTR=(HI,PROT)
```

defines the device field that will contain the current date. In the message descriptor code for the output message segment, an MFLD statement, statement 43, refers to this device field.

The 'literal' parameter of the DFLD statement   To create a caption on the screen, you assign a literal value to a device field. All you do is code the literal value between apostrophes as the first parameter of the DFLD statement. For example,

```
DFLD  'DISPLAY INVOICE SUMMARY',
      POS=(1,2),
      ATTR=(HI,PROT)
```

tells MFS to display the text string DISPLAY INVOICE SUMMARY at the indicated screen location and with the specified attributes. If you code the value I suggested for the DEV statement's DSCA parameter, literals are sent to the screen only when the screen is initially formatted for your application. After that, only variable data is sent.

The POS parameter of the DFLD statement   The POS parameter tells MFS where a device field is located. On it, you specify the line and column position of the first byte of a display field. For instance, the DFLD statement I just showed you displays the screen title in line 1, beginning in column 2.

The DFLD control statement

```
label     DFLD      ['literal']

                    ,POS=(line,column[,page])

                    [,LTH=length]
```

$$[,\text{ATTR}=(\ \left[\begin{Bmatrix}\underline{\text{ALPHA}}\\ \text{NUM}\end{Bmatrix}\right]\left[,\begin{Bmatrix}\underline{\text{NOPROT}}\\ \text{PROT}\end{Bmatrix}\right]\left[,\begin{Bmatrix}\underline{\text{NORM}}\\ \text{NODISP}\\ \text{HI}\end{Bmatrix}\right]\left[,\begin{Bmatrix}\underline{\text{NOMOD}}\\ \text{MOD}\end{Bmatrix}\right])\ ]$$

$$[,\text{EATTR}=(\ \left[\begin{Bmatrix}\text{HD}\\ \text{HBLINK}\\ \text{HREV}\\ \text{HUL}\end{Bmatrix}\right]\left[,\begin{Bmatrix}\text{CD}\\ \text{BLUE}\\ \text{RED}\\ \text{PINK}\\ \text{GREEN}\\ \text{TURQ}\\ \text{YELLOW}\\ \text{NEUTRAL}\end{Bmatrix}\right])\ ]$$

Explanation

label   The one- to eight-character name of the device field. If you specify 'literal', you must **not** code a label on the DFLD statement.

The 'literal' parameter

literal   Specifies a constant value for the device field. If you specify 'literal', it must be the first parameter on the DFLD statement. For 3270s, the value cannot be longer than 256 characters.

The POS parameter

line   Specifies the line that contains the first character of the device field.

column   Specifies the column that contains the first character of the device field (not its preceding attribute byte).

page   Specifies the physical page where the field in located. (Optional; the default is 1.)

Figure 6-10   The DFLD control statement (part 1 of 2)

Remember, a 3270 attribute byte must precede all display fields. Keep that in mind when you code format sets; don't code POS parameter values that will cause fields or attribute bytes to overlap.

The LTH parameter

length   Specifies the length, in bytes, of the device field. If you code 'literal' on the DFLD statement, you do not code the LTH parameter; otherwise, it's required.

The ATTR and EATTR parameters

For these parameters, you can code one or more keyword values for attribute or extended attribute characteristics. You only need to code the values you want to change from the defaults. These values are described in the text.

Figure 6-10   The DFLD control statement (part 2 of 2)

In addition to the line and column subparameters, there is a third POS subparameter you can code when you use physical paging. I'll describe it in chapter 9.

The LTH parameter of the DFLD statement   To define a device field completely, you also have to specify how long it is. You provide that information with the LTH parameter of the DFLD statement. For example,

```
CURDATE    DFLD   POS=(1,72),
                  LTH=8,
                  ATTR=(HI,PROT)
```

tells MFS that the device field that begins in column 72 of line 1 is eight bytes long; in other words, the field occupies columns 72-79. (MFS automatically supplies the required ending attribute byte after each field.)

If you code a literal for a device field, you don't have to code the LTH parameter. That's because MFS counts the number of characters in the literal and uses that value as the field length. As a result, it's usual for a DFLD statement to have either a literal value or the LTH parameter, but not both.

The ATTR parameter of the DFLD statement   The ATTR parameter of the DFLD statement lets you specify default values for the basic attributes of a device field. Figure 6-10 shows the values you can code for the ATTR parameter; they correspond to the field characteristics I described in chapter 2. The underlined values are the defaults for data entry fields (that is, fields for which you do not specify a literal value). So if you define a data entry field and do not code the ATTR parameter on its DFLD statement, the field will have alphanumeric shift (ALPHA), will be unprotected (NOPROT), and will be displayed in normal intensity (NORM). (I'll describe the fourth attribute, indicated by NOMOD and MOD, in a moment.)

For a literal field, the default attributes MFS uses are different: shift is numeric, and the field is protected and displayed with normal intensity. Remember from chapter 2 that a protected numeric field is an auto-skip field, which the cursor skips over automatically during data entry. That's just how you want the terminal to treat caption fields.

Often, you can depend on the default attributes for a device field and not code the ATTR parameter at all. However, I usually code the parameter, even if I don't have to. For instance, in the format set in figure 6-2, I coded

```
ATTR=(HI,PROT)
```

for all the caption fields on the screen. As a result, they're displayed with high intensity. Strictly speaking, I didn't have to code PROT because that's the default for literals. However, when I look at a format set, I like to see immediately whether a field is protected or not, and coding PROT on the ATTR parameter makes that easy. On the other hand, I didn't code a shift attribute for the caption fields. As a result, the default value NUM remains in effect for them.

There are several variable fields in the format set in figure 6-2. For example, consider the data entry field into which the operator keys the number of the invoice he wants the program to retrieve. I defined it with this statement:

```
INVNO      DFLD   POS=(3,12),
                  LTH=6,
                  ATTR=(NUM)
```

Because there is no literal for this field, its default attributes would be alphanumeric, unprotected, and normal intensity. However, since the value that will be entered through this field must be numeric, I changed the field's shift from alphanumeric to numeric with the ATTR parameter; I left the other attributes unchanged.

You should realize that although coding NUM on a field's ATTR parameter keeps the user from entering non-numeric characters into it, it does not insure that the operator enters a valid numeric value. For example, the period is considered to be a valid numeric character because it's used as the decimal point, but

. . . . . .

is not a valid numeric value.

For the display-only variable fields (that is, those in which data from the requested invoice is displayed), I coded

```
ATTR=(PROT)
```

Here, PROT overrides the default protection attribute for a non-literal field: unprotected. I left the defaults for shift (alphanumeric) and intensity (normal) in effect for these device fields.

The last two keywords for the ATTR parameter, MOD and NOMOD, let you set a field's *modified data tag (MDT)*. The MDT, which is part of the attribute byte, indicates whether or not the data in the field has been changed by the terminal user since the last screen was sent to the device.

When a screen is displayed on a 3270 terminal, the MDTs of all fields are normally set to off. Then, as the terminal operator keys in data, the 3270 sets the MDTs of modified fields to on. When the entry is complete and the operator presses enter (or one of the other attention keys), only fields whose MDTs are on are transmitted back to the host. Fields that really don't need to be transmitted, like captions and fields into which the operator did not enter data, are bypassed. The result is improved telecommunications efficiency.

Although transmitting only modified fields yields this benefit, it also has a drawback. Suppose a value is present in a data entry field from the previous transaction and the operator wants to use the same value for the current transaction. With the 3270 default in effect, the operator would have to change the field in some way to insure that it's included in the next transmission, even though the data it contains is correct. That means that the terminal user has to make more keystrokes than should be necessary.

Fortunately, you can get around this by coding MOD in the ATTR parameter for a data entry field. This indicates that a field is "premodified," and the 3270 transmits it to the host even if the operator doesn't change its contents. In the next chapter, you'll see how you can use this technique. For now, though, realize that you'll often code the MOD keyword on the ATTR parameter for data entry fields.

The EATTR parameter of the DFLD statement   The EATTR
parameter of the DFLD statement lets you specify default values for the
extended attributes of a device field. As you should remember from
chapter 2, extended attributes are optional 3270 features, and can
include underlining, reverse video, blinking, and color.

Although I'm not going to describe the EATTR keywords in detail,
they're relatively easy to understand. Those in the first group control
extended highlighting. HD means use default highlighting, HBLINK
means make the field blink, HREV means display the field in reverse
video, and HUL means underline the field. Keywords in the second
group let you control field colors; the color values should be self-
explanatory, except for CD and NEUTRAL. CD means use default
color, and NEUTRAL depends on the device; usually, NEUTRAL
results in a white field.

HOW TO CODE
THE MESSAGE DESCRIPTOR CONTROL STATEMENTS

Figure 6-11 shows the hierarchical relationships among the statements
you code to produce a message descriptor, either a MID or a MOD.
This section presents the syntax of each. Unlike the situation for a DIF
and a DOF, you must code separate groups of statements to define a
MID and a MOD. As a result, a typical format set includes one device
format code group, but two message descriptor code groups.

The MSG and MSGEND control statements

Each segment of code that describes a message, whether it's an input
message or an output message, begins with a MSG statement and ends
with a MSGEND statement. Figure 6-12 presents the formats of these
two statements. As you can see, the MSGEND statement has no
parameters.

You must code a label on each MSG statement. MFS uses the label
as the full name of the block it generates from the statements that follow
the MSG statement. That's unlike the situation with the FMT statement, whose label is only a part of the DIF and DOF names MFS
creates. In figure 6-2, I used the names DI2I for the input message
descriptor and DI2O for the output message descriptor. Your shop certainly has standards for block names; find out what they are and follow
them when you code message descriptor statements.

The message descriptor device format control statements

MSG   Identifies the beginning of a message descriptor.

LPAGE   Identifies the beginning of a series of control statements for a logical page subordinate to a MSG statement.

PASSWORD   Identifies the beginning of a series of MFLD statements that are used to construct the password for an input message. You may code only one PASSWORD statement subordinate to an LPAGE statement.

SEG   Identifies the beginning of a series of MFLD statements that make up a message segment. You may code multiple SEG statements subordinate to an LPAGE statement.

MFLD   Identifies a message field subordinate to either a PASSWORD statement or a SEG statement.

MSGEND   Identifies the end of a message descriptor.

The message descriptor control statements are arranged hierarchically

```
MSG
  LPAGE
    PASSWORD
      MFLD
         .
      MFLD
    SEG
      MFLD
         .
      MFLD
    SEG
      MFLD
         .
      MFLD
  LPAGE
    PASSWORD
      MFLD
         .
      MFLD
    SEG
      MFLD
         .
      MFLD
    SEG
      MFLD
         .
      MFLD
MSGEND
```

Figure 6-11   The message descriptor control statements

The MSG and MSGEND control statements

```
msgname      MSG    TYPE= {INPUT }
                          {OUTPUT}

             ,SOR=(dfname,IGNORE)

             [,NXT=nextmsgname]

             [,PAGE=YES]


       MSGEND
```

Explanation

msgname   The name to be used for the MID (if TYPE = INPUT) or MOD (if TYPE = OUTPUT).

The TYPE parameter

INPUT   Specifies that the message descriptor control statements that follow will be used to generate a MID.

OUTPUT   Specifies that the message descriptor control statements that follow will be used to generate a MOD.

The SOR parameter

dfname   The device format to which this message descriptor is related.

IGNORE   Indicates that the device format coded with FEAT = IGNORE should be used with this message descriptor. As a general rule, all 3270 format sets should specify IGNORE on both MSG and DEV statements.

The NXT parameter

nextmsgname   If TYPE = INPUT, the name of the next MOD to be used; if TYPE = OUTPUT, the name of the next MID to be used.

The PAGE parameter

YES   Valid only if TYPE = OUTPUT. Specifies that operator logical paging should be supported for this output message. See chapter 9 for more information.

Figure 6-12   The MSG and MSGEND control statements

The TYPE parameter of the MSG statement   To specify whether to generate a MID or a MOD from the statements that follow, you code the TYPE parameter on the MSG statement. For example,

```
TYPE=INPUT
```

causes MFS to create a MID, while

```
TYPE=OUTPUT
```

causes MFS to create a MOD. The TYPE parameter is required on each MSG statement.

The SOR parameter of the MSG statement   The SOR parameter is required on each MSG statement too. On it, you code the name of the device format (that is, the label of the FMT statement) that's associated with the message this group of statements defines.

In figure 6-2, the SOR parameter for both the MID and MOD specifications is

```
SOR=(DI2DF,IGNORE)
```

DI2DF is the name I specified on the FMT statement in the format set. If you specify IGNORE on the FEAT parameter(s) of the DEV statement(s) in the related device format, be sure you also code IGNORE on the SOR parameter; you'll almost always do so.

In a complete group of control statements for one format set, it might seem unnecessary to name the device format on the SOR parameter of a MSG statement. However, you should remember that the MFS Language Utility doesn't require that all parts of a complete format set be processed together. It uses the value you specify on the SOR parameter to retrieve the associated ITB (intermediate text block) from the referral library when you don't code the control statements for the device format along with those for the message descriptors.

The NXT parameter of the MSG statement   The NXT parameter specifies the message descriptor MFS will use during execution after it uses the one defined by the statements associated with this MSG statement. As figure 6-12 shows, in a MSG statement that defines a MID, you code the name of a MOD, and in a MSG statement that defines a MOD, you code the name of a MID. MFS uses the names you code on NXT parameters to anticipate what blocks will be needed next; this is an MFS performance feature.

The PAGE parameter of the MSG statement   You code the PAGE parameter on the MSG statement that defines an output message descriptor when you want to be able to use operator logical paging. For now, don't worry about this; I'll describe it in chapter 9.

The LPAGE control statement

The next statement in the hierarchy of message descriptor statements is LPAGE. As with its format set counterpart, the DPAGE statement, its primary function is for applications that do logical paging. However, unlike the DPAGE statement, it does not include parameters that you'll need to use for basic format sets. As a result, I'm not going to cover it here. Chapter 9 presents the information you need to know about the LPAGE statement to code format sets for applications that will do logical paging.

The PASSWORD control statement

As you should remember from chapter 3, some IMS transactions are password-protected to prevent unauthorized users from invoking them. To be able to invoke a password-protected transaction, the message sent to IMS has to contain the password. However, IMS removes the password from the message before it sends it to the application program. In this flow, MFS gets the message before IMS checks and removes the password. As a result, MFS facilities can be used to build or format the password.

    If you're coding the format set for an application that is password-protected, you provide for the password in the input message. Before you code the control statements that define the text of the message, you code the PASSWORD statement, which has neither a label nor parameters. After it, you code from one to eight MFLD statements that identify the fields that make up the password. The total length of the fields that make up the password can be no longer than eight characters.

    To understand this, consider figure 6-13. Here, I present two segments of code for an input message that will include a password. In the first segment of code, the password is entered directly by the user in a single device field called PWFIELD. As you can see, I coded one MFLD statement that refers to that device field right after the PASSWORD statement.

Supplying an operator-entered password in an input message

Device format statements

```
PWFIELD  DFLD   POS=...,LTH=8,ATTR=(NODISP...)
```

Message descriptor statements

```
INMSG    MSG    TYPE=INPUT,...
         PASSWORD
         MFLD   PWFIELD,LTH=8
         SEG
         MFLD . . .
           .
           .
           .
```

Supplying a literal as part of a password in an input message

Device format statements

```
PWFIELD  DFLD   POS=...,LTH=3,ATTR=(NODISP...)
```

Message descriptor statements

```
INMSG    MSG    TYPE=INPUT,...
         PASSWORD
         MFLD   PWFIELD,LTH=3
         MFLD   'PSWRD',LTH=5
         SEG
         MFLD . . .
           .
           .
           .
```

Figure 6-13   How to use the PASSWORD statement to specify the IMS password in an input message

When MFS constructs the input message, it uses the data the operator entered in PWFIELD as the password. Notice that the message field(s) that make up the password are *not* part of the text of the message, which is specified by statements that follow the SEG statement. As a result, the application program does not get the password in the input message segment it receives as a result of a get call.

All of the data that is used to construct the password need not come from the display station. It's possible to supply part of the data as a literal, as in the second example in figure 6-13. Here, I coded the literal 'PSWRD' as the value for bytes 4 through 8 of the eight-character password. The first three bytes come from an operator entry.

The most complex password you can specify would be built from eight one-character device fields, all entered by the operator on different parts of the screen. This would be unusual, though. When you receive program specifications, they should indicate how to generate the password. Typically, applications at an installation all use a similar password entry technique.

The SEG control statement

The SEG control statement lets you identify the segments that make up messages. It has no parameters that you'll need to code for typical format sets, so I don't present a syntax figure for it. Most applications use single-segment messages, both for input and output. When that's the case, you code one SEG statement before the MFLD statements that define the message fields, as I did in statements 36 and 42 in figure 6-2. When a message descriptor includes multiple segment types, you code a SEG statement followed by one or more MFLD statements for each message segment. The application program must insert or retrieve those segments in the sequence in which they're coded in the format set.

The MFLD control statement

Most of the statements you code that define messages will be MFLD statements; you code one for each field in a message segment. Figure 6-14 presents the format of the MFLD statement. Remember, there's typically a one-to-one relationship between fields in the message segment descriptor and fields in the application program's I/O area.

The content parameter of the MFLD statement   For each MFLD statement, you must code the first parameter. For an input message, the first parameter specifies the contents or source of the field. For an output message, the first parameter specifies the destination for the data the field contains.

For a field in an input message, you can code this parameter in three ways. First, you can specify a literal value for the input field, as in

```
MFLD    'DI2
        LTH=8
```

in statement 37 in the format set in figure 6-2. This statement specifies that the eight-byte field will *always* contain the value DI2, followed by five spaces. This is a typical way to specify a transaction code in an input message.

When you supply the transaction code like this (as a literal in the first position of an input message), the terminal user doesn't have to enter it for each transaction. MFS always includes the transaction code when it constructs an input message. The result is that the correct value is always supplied in the right position and the number of keystrokes the operator has to make is reduced.

The second way to specify what an input message field contains is to indicate that its contents should be taken from a device field, as in statement 38 in the format set in figure 6-2:

```
MFLD   INVNO,
       LTH=6,...
```

This statement means that the value the operator keyed into the device field INVNO should be mapped into this message field.

Third, you can specify a source field from a device format *and* provide an optional default value to be used for the message field if the operator doesn't make an entry into the source field. For example,

```
MFLD   (INVNO,'000000'),
       LTH=6
```

will cause the value 000000 to be used for this message field if the operator doesn't key any data into the device field INVNO. (I didn't specify a default value for the invoice number field in the input message descriptor in figure 6-2. You'll see why I didn't need to in a moment. However, for other applications, it might be appropriate to supply default values for input fields.)

For an output message field, the first parameter specifies the destination of the field. Most often you'll code the name of the field in the device format into which the output message field should be mapped. For instance,

```
MFLD   INVNO,
       LTH=6
```

in the output message description means that the six bytes in the indicated position in the output message should be mapped into the device field with the name INVNO.

The MFLD control statement

```
MFLD    {source      }
        {destination }

   [,LTH=length]

   [,JUST=  {L}  ]
            {R}

   [,FILL=fillchar]

   [,ATTR=(YES)]
```

Explanation

The source parameter (in input messages only)

Specifies the source of the data MFS will map into this field; you can code this parameter in three ways:

'literal'   A literal value that's to be a part of every input message sent to the application program; this bears no relation to a device field.

devfield   The label of the device field from which data for this message field will be mapped.

(devfield,'literal')   The first subparameter, devfield, is the label of the device field from which data for this message field will be mapped. If that device field contains no data, the value specified for 'literal' will be used instead.

The destination parameter (in output messages only)

Specifies the destination of the data MFS will map from this field; you can code this parameter in two ways:

devfield   The label of the device field into which data from this message field will be mapped.

(devfield,syslit)   The first subparameter, devfield, is the label of the device field into which data from this message field will be mapped. The data is specified by syslit, which can be one of the system literals in figure 6-15. If you use this option, you must not provide space for this field in the application program's view of the output message.

Figure 6-14   The MFLD control statement (part 1 of 2)

The LTH parameter

length

The length in bytes of the field. The parameter is optional if you specify 'literal' for an input message field. You must not code LTH if you name a system literal on an MFLD statement.

The JUST parameter

L
R

Specify R to cause data to be right justified in the message field. You can code L to specify left justification, but you don't have to because it's the default.

The FILL parameter

fillchar

Valid only for fields defined for an input message. This value specifies the character to be used to pad data from the device when it's shorter than the field size. Possible values are:

X'hh'   Any specified hex value.

C'c'   Any specified character value.

NULL   Do not use fill.

The ATTR parameter

YES

Specifies that dynamic attribute modification by the application program is allowed. See chapter 7 for more information.

Figure 6-14   The MFLD control statement (part 2 of 2)

There's one other way you can code the first parameter of the MFLD statement for an output message field that I want you to know about. Statement 43 of the format set in figure 6-2 illustrates it:

```
MFLD    (CURDATE,DATE2)
```

This statement specifies that the contents of a special MFS field called DATE2 should be mapped to the device field CURDATE. DATE2 contains the current IMS system date and is one of several IMS *system literals* you can specify on MFLD statements. Figure 6-15 lists the most useful system literals and describes their formats and contents.

Name	Length	Description
DATE1	6	System date in the format YY.DDD.
DATE2	8	System date in the format MM/DD/YY.
DATE3	8	System date in the format DD/MM/YY.
DATE4	8	System date in the format YY/MM/DD.
TIME	8	System time in the format HH:MM:SS.
LTNAME	8	Logical terminal name of the device that will receive the current output message.

Figure 6-15   System literals

When you use a system literal in an MFLD statement, you have to remember two rules. First, do not specify the LTH parameter on the MFLD statement. And second, do not code the field in your application program's view of the output message segment. Because MFS supplies the value of a system literal, your program doesn't even know it's part of the message. As a result, if a program needs to use the current date, for example, you'll have to code an ACCEPT statement in the program itself.

The LTH parameter of the MFLD statement   The second parameter of the MFLD statement, LTH, is required most of the time. For an input message, you can omit it if you code **'literal'** for the contents of the field. For an output field, you *must* omit the LTH parameter if you use a system literal.

The JUST parameter of the MFLD statement   The JUST parameter lets you specify how MFS should position data in a message field. Unless you specify otherwise, MFS maps data into a field with *left justification*. In other words, it places the leftmost character of the data in the leftmost position of the field and fills the field from there toward the right. That's what you want for most fields, so you usually don't need to specify the JUST parameter.

However, there may be times when you'll want to define a numeric field with *right justification*. Then, MFS places the rightmost character of the data in the rightmost position of the field, and fills the field toward the left. To request right justification, code

        JUST=R

on the MFLD statement as in statement 38 in figure 6-2. If you use right justification for a numeric field, you should also consider specifying that MFS fill unused positions in the field with zeros. To do that, you code the FILL parameter on the MFLD statement.

The FILL parameter of the MFLD statement   The FILL parameter lets you specify what *pad character* MFS should use to complete a field when the data that's mapped into it doesn't fill it. Figure 6-14 shows the options you can use. The space (C' ' or X'40') is the default. For a numeric field,

```
FILL=C'0'
```

is what you're likely to request.

For some input message fields, you might not want MFS to pad the data from the corresponding device field if it's shorter than the message field. When that's the case, you can code

```
FILL=NULL
```

on the MFLD statement for the message field. However, using null fill means your COBOL program will have to deal with variable-length fields in the input message, and that can be a nightmare. As a result, it's unusual to use null fill for data entry fields. Even so, in some applications it's desirable to use input message fields with null fill; you'll see some examples later in this book.

The ATTR parameter of the MFLD statement   The last parameter of MFLD, ATTR, lets you specify that an application program can dynamically change the attributes of the device field associated with this message field. I'll describe how you use this parameter in the next chapter.

HOW TO CODE THE COMPILATION CONTROL STATEMENTS

In addition to the control statements that define message descriptors and device formats, you can also code several statements to control the way the MFS Language Utility works. These are called *compilation control statements*, and they're listed in figure 6-16. As you can see, I've broken them into two groups: basic and advanced compilation control statements.

Basic compilation control statements

The top section of figure 6-16 lists the five compilation control statements I call "basic." They're all easy to use. I recommend you always code two of these statements: PRINT and END.

If you look at figure 6-2, you'll see that I started my format set with the statement

```
PRINT ON,NOGEN
```

By default, the MFS Language Utility produces a printed listing and includes the hexadecimal code generated for each intermediate text block (ITB). I don't want my listings to include the ITB code, so I disabled that function with the NOGEN parameter of the PRINT statement. If I wanted to suppress the print listing altogether, I'd code

```
PRINT OFF
```

The last statement in the format set in figure 6-2 is

```
END
```

If you omit the END statement, the MFS Language Utility will supply one and translate your control statements properly. However, because the MFS Language Utility generates an error message as a result of the missing END statement, you should always code END.

Two of the other basic compilation control statements let you exercise more control over the format of the output listing the MFS Language Utility produces. The EJECT statement causes the listing to advance to a new page. You might want to use this statement to cause control statements for different blocks to be printed on different pages of the output listing. The TITLE statement lets you specify a literal that's printed at the top of each page of the output listing.

The last of the basic compilation control statements is COPY. It lets you name a member in a partitioned data set that's copied into the control statement stream at translation time. For example, if most of the format sets you code contain the lines

```
DEV     TYPE=(3270,2),
        FEAT=IGNORE,
        SYSMSG=ERRMSG,
        DSCA=X'00A0'
DIV     TYPE=INOUT
```

Basic compilation control statements

```
PRINT  [{ON  }] [{GEN   }]
        [{OFF}] [{NOGEN}]

END

EJECT

TITLE 'literal'

COPY   membername
```

Advanced compilation control statements

```
symbol   EQU   'literal'

         DO    count

         ENDDO
```

Figure 6-16   The MFS Language Utility compilation control statements

you might store these statements in a member named DEVDIV in a partitioned data set. Then, instead of going to the trouble to enter that text each time you code a format set, you could code simply

```
COPY   DEVDIV
```

Frankly, it's often just as easy to use your text editor to copy the lines you want from a format set you've already coded. But you should be aware of the COPY control statement in case you ever want to use it.

Advanced compilation control statements

The compilation control statements that I classify as "advanced" help you save time as you write device format and message descriptor control statements. The EQU statement lets you create your own shorthand by equating abbreviations with longer text strings you use often. And the DO and ENDDO statements let you easily code MFLD or DFLD statements for groups of repeating fields.

The EQU statement matches a symbol you specify as the label of the statement with a literal value. For example, if you set the characters

APA equal to an attribute parameter, like this:

```
APA        EQU    'ATTR=(PROT,ALPHA)'
```

you could then code the symbol APA any place in the format set where you'd otherwise need to code the complete attribute parameter. In others words, the statements

```
SUBTOTAL DFLD   POS=(3,55),LTH=9,ATTR=(PROT,ALPHA)
```

and

```
SUBTOTAL DFLD   POS=(3,55),LTH=9,APA
```

would be treated the same way by the MFS Language Utility.

The EQU statement can be a time-saver. However, when you use it, be careful to pick symbols that are both meaningful and that can't possibly conflict with actual values you might code in the format set.

The last two of the advanced compilation control statements, DO and ENDDO, work together. You code the DO statement to indicate that the statements that follow, up to the ENDDO statement, are to be duplicated the number times indicated by the count parameter. For example, consider figure 6-17. Here, I've coded a single DFLD statement to define a device field, but I've bracketed it with a DO and an ENDDO statement to cause the field to be duplicated. In this case, the field will be duplicated eight times, since that's the count value I specified on the DO statement.

The statements in the bottom part of the figure show what MFS generated. Notice that each field has a name that's based on the name of the original field, plus a two-character numeric suffix. Because MFS appends the suffix to the label you supply on the original statement, the label may be no longer than six characters. (This is the second of the two exceptions to the rule that the length of a label can be up to eight characters.) Also, notice that MFS increased the line number in each POS parameter by one as it generated each DFLD statement. Otherwise, the generated statements are the same for each of the eight fields.

The output you see on the MFS listing for duplicated fields looks slightly different from what figure 6-17 shows. For example, the attribute parameter looks like

```
ATTR=(...)
```

Don't worry, though. The original attributes that you specified will be in effect, even though the listing looks unusual.

Statements as coded

```
           DO    8
MSGTXT     DFLD  POS=(14,2),LTH=79,ATTR=(PROT,ALPHA)
           ENDDO
```

Statements generated and processed by the MFS Language Utility

```
MSGTXT01  DFLD   POS=(14,2),LTH=79,ATTR=(PROT,ALPHA)
MSGTXT02  DFLD   POS=(15,2),LTH=79,ATTR=(PROT,ALPHA)
MSGTXT03  DFLD   POS=(16,2),LTH=79,ATTR=(PROT,ALPHA)
MSGTXT04  DFLD   POS=(17,2),LTH=79,ATTR=(PROT,ALPHA)
MSGTXT05  DFLD   POS=(18,2),LTH=79,ATTR=(PROT,ALPHA)
MSGTXT06  DFLD   POS=(19,2),LTH=79,ATTR=(PROT,ALPHA)
MSGTXT07  DFLD   POS=(20,2),LTH=79,ATTR=(PROT,ALPHA)
MSGTXT08  DFLD   POS=(21,2),LTH=79,ATTR=(PROT,ALPHA)
```

Figure 6-17   How the DO and ENDDO statements work

DISCUSSION

As I said at the beginning of this chapter, don't let yourself be over-whelmed by the amount of detail involved with the MFS control statements. You can always refer back to this chapter when you have questions. In the next three chapters, I'll present some specific techniques you can use when you develop MFS applications. Like this chapter, chapters 7, 8, and 9 all present MFS details. However, they also emphasize application programming considerations, which this chapter did not do.

Terminology

label field
operation field
operation code
operand field
parameter
comment field
continuation line
comment line
embedded comment
device characteristics table

pseudofield
program tab
modified data tag
MDT
system literal
left justification
right justification
pad character
compilation control statements

Objectives

1. Describe the format of an MFS control statement.

2. Describe how MFS is able to support the same application from multiple terminal types.

3. Explain why you should nearly always code IGNORE on the FEAT parameter of the DEV statement for 3270 devices.

4. Describe how MFS forms the names of DIFs, DOFs, MIDs, and MODs.

5. Describe how MFS provides support for program function keys.

6. Describe how to provide literal caption fields on a screen.

7. Describe the coding elements that relate device format blocks to message descriptor blocks.

8. Describe how to include a password in an input message segment.

9. Describe how to code the control statements you'd use to duplicate lines in a format set.

10. Given complete specifications for an application that uses the MFS features this chapter presents, code a format set and application program for it.

Chapter 7

How to control field attributes and cursor position

In the last chapter you learned how to specify field attribute values (with the ATTR parameter of the DFLD statement) and cursor position (with the CURSOR parameter of the DPAGE statement). In this chapter, I'll show you how you can change ATTR and CURSOR parameter specifications dynamically (that is, while an application is running) through application programs. In the first section of this chapter, you'll learn the MFS and COBOL considerations for dynamically modifying field attributes, and in the second, you'll learn the considerations for cursor control.

As you'll see, these techniques are typically used to call attention to data entry errors. Changing a field's attributes can make the field easier to see, and moving the cursor to the field can save entry time for the terminal user. The third section of this chapter presents a sample data entry application that illustrates how to use the techniques the first two sections introduce.

How to control field attributes

To change attributes dynamically, your COBOL program passes control information to MFS, which formats its output messages accordingly. To use this feature, you have to know three things. First, you must be able to identify and define fields that are eligible for dynamic attribute modification. You identify those eligible fields within your MFS format sets. Second, you have to know the format and content of the control information your program will pass to MFS to request dynamic attribute modification. And third, you have to code your COBOL program so it can pass the correct control information to MFS. This section shows you how to do these three things.

How to identify and define fields that are eligible for dynamic attribute modification   Although it's a device field that's ultimately affected when you change an attribute, you don't identify a device field directly when you request dynamic attribute modification. Instead, you identify the related output message field. If that seems peculiar to you, remember that it's the application program that requests attribute changes, and the only way the application program can communicate with MFS is through an output message.

On the MFLD statement that describes the message field that's related to the device field whose attribute you want to be able to change, you code

```
ATTR=YES
```

(Do not confuse this with the ATTR parameter of the DFLD statement, which you code in a device format to specify a field's initial attributes.) When you code ATTR=YES for a message field, MFS assumes that the first two bytes of the message field will contain control information that specifies what the overriding attributes will be. The user data that's actually mapped from the message field to the device field starts in the third byte of the message field, not the first.

Although the two-byte prefix isn't displayed, it is part of the data sent to MFS by the application program. As a result, you have to account for it by adding two to the value you code on the LTH parameter of the MFLD statement.

For example, suppose a device format includes a six-byte field used to display an invoice number. If you don't plan to use dynamic attribute modification for the field, you might code

```
MFLD     INVNO,
         LTH=6
```

for its related output message field. On the other hand, if you do want to be able to use dynamic attribute modification for the device field

INVNO, you define the output message field like this:

```
MFLD    INVNO,
        LTH=8,
        ATTR=YES
```

Here, I've coded the ATTR parameter and added two to the field length.

The format and content of the control bytes you use for dynamic attribute modification   The two-byte field prefixes you use to control dynamic attribute modification are packed with information. As a result, you have to understand them at the bit level. For the description that follows, you might like to refer to the table in appendix D, which presents all possible combinations of bits and their hexadecimal equivalents. And, if a bit combination has a character equivalent, the appendix shows it too.

Figure 7-1 shows what the bit positions in each two-byte prefix indicate. The first byte is for cursor control; I'll describe it later in this chapter. For now, assume that cursor positioning is not required. When that's the case, all of the bits in the first control byte should be off:

```
0000 0000
```

In COBOL, you can refer to a value of all binary zeros as LOW-VALUE.

The second control byte is more complicated. As figure 7-1 shows, the value of bit 0 should always be 1; it isn't used by your programs. Bit 1 has a special function that I'll describe in a moment.

In bits 2 through 7, you specify the overriding attribute values. The value of bit 2 determines the field's protection attribute, and the value of bit 3 determines its shift attribute. Bits 4 and 5 together determine field intensity. Bit 6 is used to specify whether or not a field is detectable by the selector light pen; its value should be 0 for all non-light-pen applications. The last bit, bit 7, sets the modified data tag. (By the way, these bit settings are the same as those in the actual 3270 display screen attribute byte.)

Now, back to bit 1. If bit 1 is on (that is, has a value of 1), the attribute specifications that follow in bits 2 through 7 override the device field's current attributes. However, the situation is a little less clear cut if bit 1 is off. When that's the case, the overriding values in bits 2-7 don't necessarily replace the corresponding bits in the attribute byte. Instead, if a particular bit is on in *either* the field's current

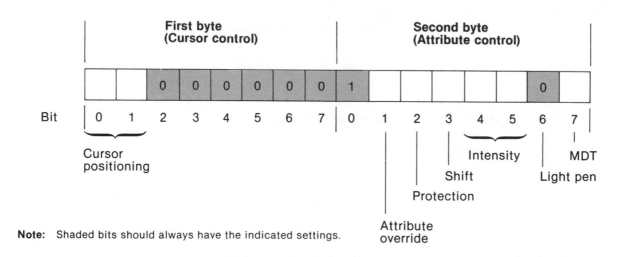

Note: Shaded bits should always have the indicated settings.

Byte	Bits	Function	Values	
1	0-1	Cursor positioning	00	Cursor positioning not requested.
			11	Position the cursor at this field. (Bits 0 and 1 must have the same value; values 01 and 10 are invalid.)
	2-7		000000	(Always)
2	0		1	(Always)
	1	Attribute override type	0	Use the attribute specifications that follow to activate only specified attributes (that is, attributes whose corresponding override bit is on).
			1	Use the attribute specifications that follow to replace all device field attributes.
	2	Protection attribute	0	Unprotected.
			1	Protected.
	3	Shift attribute	0	Alphanumeric shift.
			1	Numeric shift.
	4-5	Intensity attribute	00	Normal intensity.
			01	Normal intensity. (If bit 4 is off, bit 5 is ignored.)
			10	Bright intensity.
			11	No-display.
	6	Light-pen detectability attribute	0	Should always be 0 for non-light-pen applications.
	7	Modified data tag	0	MDT off.
			1	MDT on.

Figure 7-1   The format and content of the cursor and attribute control bytes

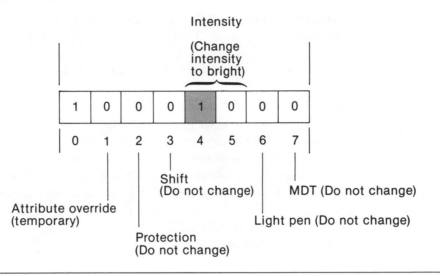

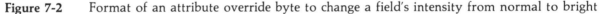

Figure 7-2   Format of an attribute override byte to change a field's intensity from normal to bright

attribute or the overriding value you supply, MFS turns that bit on for the current output message. (This is a logical OR operation.)

The advantage of supplying an override byte with bit 1 off is that you can activate only the attributes you want, and leave others unchanged. For example, consider figure 7-2. It illustrates the bit combination required to change the display intensity of a field to bright:

      1000 1000

Because bits 1-3 and 5-7 are all off, no attributes other than intensity are affected. However, if the override byte's bit configuration were

      1100 1000

(with bit 1 on) the attributes of the device field would be changed to unprotected, alphanumeric, bright intensity, no light pen, and MDT off, regardless of what they were to begin with.

A disadvantage of providing an override byte with bit 1 off is that you can't deactivate an attribute. For instance, you can't change a field already displayed with bright intensity to normal intensity. That's because if *either* the attribute byte or the override byte contains a 1 in a particular bit position, the corresponding attribute is activated. You also are unable to turn the MDT off or to change a numeric field to alphanumeric. In contrast, if the override value you supply has a 1 in bit 1, you can activate or deactivate any attribute.

How to specify field attribute overrides from an application program   In your COBOL programs, you have to keep three things in mind when you override attributes. First, you have to code working storage fields that contain values that have the combinations of bits for the attributes you want. Second, you have to code the two-byte prefix for each output message field defined to MFS with ATTR=YES. And third, you have to code Procedure Division statements that insure those prefix fields have the proper values before the program inserts the output message segment.

To code the fields that contain attribute overrides, you first determine the bit combinations that you need. For example, a common function is changing a field's intensity from normal to bright without changing other attributes. To do that, you use the bit combination I described in figure 7-2:

```
1000 1000
```

After you've determined the bit settings for attribute overrides you expect you'll need, you find out what their character or hexadecimal equivalents are. For example, if you look to appendix D, you'll find that the character equivalent of the bit combination 1000 1000 is the letter *h*. So in my COBOL program, I can code a field definition like

```
05  ATTR-CHANGE-TO-BRIGHT  PIC X  VALUE 'h'.
```

for the override byte. (When you do this, be sure that your terminal and editor are set properly so they don't translate lowercase letters to uppercase.)

Another attribute value you'll use often specifies that a field's default attribute value should be used. Its binary value is

```
1000 0000
```

which does not have a character equivalent. However, its hexadecimal equivalent is 80, so I can use the hex feature of my text editor to enter hex 80 in the field's VALUE clause:

```
05  ATTR-RESET-TO-DEFAULT       PIC X      VALUE ' '.
```

The value between the single quotes isn't a space, but the non-printable character whose value is hex 80.

Also in your program's Working-Storage Section, either in the output segment layout or in the area used to format the output message, you have to code the two-byte prefixes for all fields defined to MFS with ATTR = YES. Then, to request dynamic attribute modification for a field, all you do is move a value like ATTR-CHANGE-TO-BRIGHT to the second byte of the appropriate field's prefix.

For example, suppose an invoice number field that contains six bytes of data is part of an output message. If the field is not eligible for dynamic attribute modification, you might code it like this in your program's Working-Storage Section:

```
05  OM-INVOICE-NO    PIC X(6).
```

However, if the field is defined with ATTR = YES in the MFS output message descriptor, its COBOL definition must contain the two-byte MFS prefix. You can code it like this:

```
05  OM-INVOICE-NO.
    10  OM-INVOICE-NO-PREFIX.
        15  OM-INVOICE-NO-CURSOR    PIC X
                                    VALUE LOW-VALUE.
        15  OM-INVOICE-NO-ATTR      PIC X.
    10  OM-INVOICE-NO-DATA          PIC X(6).
```

Here, I've defined the two bytes for the prefix and assigned a literal value (LOW-VALUE) to the first (the cursor-positioning byte).

Now, suppose the device field into which the operator enters the invoice number is defined as an unprotected field with numeric shift that's displayed with normal intensity. If the operator makes an entry error in this field, the program moves the invoice number value the operator entered to OM-INVOICE-NO-DATA and a one-byte predefined value, like ATTR-CHANGE-TO-BRIGHT, to OM-INVOICE-NO-ATTR. Then, when the output message is sent, MFS changes the display intensity of the invoice number field from normal to bright. As a result, the application calls the operator's attention to the invalid field.

In addition to marking the invalid field, the program probably formats an error message that's displayed elsewhere on the screen. Also, the cursor should be positioned at the invalid field; you'll learn how to do that in the next section.

On the other hand, suppose the invoice number value the operator entered was, along with the rest of the entry, acceptable. In that case, the program would probably move space or zeros to the OM-INVOICE-NO-DATA field and move another predefined attribute value, like ATTR-RESET-TO-DEFAULT, to OM-INVOICE-NO-ATTR to cause the device field's default attributes to be used for the next output message.

How to control the cursor

As you should remember, the cursor is a mark on the terminal screen
that identifies where the next data the operator enters will be displayed.
This section describes how you can specify where the cursor should be
positioned when an output message is displayed.

As a general rule, you should at least position the cursor at the first
data entry field on the screen. That saves the operator the trouble of
having to tab to that field to start an entry. To supply a default cursor
position, you code the CURSOR parameter on the DPAGE statement,
as I described in the last chapter. For example, to specify that the
default position for the cursor is in column 17 of line 3, you'd code

```
DPAGE   CURSOR=((3,17))
```

This cursor positioning technique is performed entirely through MFS
and requires no interaction with the application program.

Even if your application program uses the cursor control features
this section describes to position the cursor each time it sends an output
message, you should still specify a default cursor position on the
DPAGE statement. Otherwise, when the operator initially invokes the
format set using the /FORMAT command, the cursor won't be positioned properly.

To position the cursor from an application program, you can use
either of two techniques: *field-oriented cursor control* or *absolute
cursor control*. In most cases, field-oriented cursor control is a better
choice.

How to use field-oriented cursor control   When you use field-
oriented cursor control, your program marks a particular field in its
output message. Then, when MFS maps that message field to its corresponding device field, the cursor is positioned at that device field.

Field-oriented cursor control is closely related to attribute byte
control. In fact, you have to provide for attribute byte control in your
application to be able to use field-oriented cursor control. When you
code ATTR=YES on MFLD statements, you identify the fields that are
eligible for dynamic attribute modification. But at the same time,
ATTR=YES makes them possible targets for dynamic cursor positioning.

The first of the two bytes of control information MFS expects for a
message field defined with ATTR=YES lets you specify that the cursor
should be positioned at the related device field. To request cursor posi-

tioning at a field, move the left brace (**⦃** , hex C0, binary 1100 0000) to the first of the two control bytes. The second byte must also contain a proper attribute byte override value; hex 80 (binary 1000 0000) in the second byte causes the default attributes for the field to be used. If you don't want the cursor to be positioned at a field, be sure the first byte of the prefix contains COBOL LOW-VALUE (hex 00, binary 0000 0000).

If you mark more than one field for field-oriented cursor positioning, MFS locates the cursor at the first marked field on the screen. This is convenient; if your program marks several screen fields found to be in error for cursor positioning, the cursor will appear at the first of them, and that's what you want.

How to use absolute cursor control   The other technique you can use to position the cursor is absolute cursor control. With absolute cursor control, your program specifies the exact column and line position where the cursor will be located. Although this technique is fairly simple, it ties your program to the format of the terminal and the particular screen layout used on it. That means the same program may not be able to process the same transaction from 3270 models with different screen sizes. Another problem is that if you change a screen format, you might also have to change the application program so its line and column references for cursor positioning remain correct.

Because of these problems, I don't recommend absolute cursor control for most applications. However, absolute cursor control does offer a function that field-oriented cursor control does not: It lets your program determine where the cursor was located when an input message was sent from the terminal. For most applications, this information isn't useful, but for a few (perhaps some menu-type applications), it can be.

To use absolute cursor positioning, you specify the name of a pseudofield in the CURSOR parameter of the DPAGE statement in this format:

```
CURSOR=((line,column,cfield))
```

Because it's a pseudofield, cfield may *not* be the name of an actual device field (that is, the name associated with a DFLD statement). Instead, you code that field name on an MFLD statement that will be used to pass cursor location information back and forth between MFS and your application program.

The message field that refers to the cursor-positioning pseudofield should be four bytes long. As a result, you'll typically code the DPAGE statement and the related MFLD statement like this:

```
DPAGE CURSOR=((3,17,CFIELD))
     .
     .
     .
MFLD   CFIELD,
       LTH=4
```

If you code an MFLD statement that refers to the cursor pseudofield in an input message descriptor, the data that's passed to the application program in it is the position of the cursor when the user pressed the enter key. On the other hand, if you code an MFLD statement that refers to the cursor pseudofield in an output message descriptor, MFS uses the data in that field (put there by the application program) to determine where to locate the cursor when it sends the output message to the terminal.

Although you code the cursor pseudofield as one field in your MFS specifications, it actually has two parts; the first specifies the cursor's line position, while the second specifies its column position. Both parts are binary halfwords. As a result, you should define the field like this in your COBOL programs:

```
05   IM-CURSOR-LOCATION.
     10   IM-CURSOR-LINE      PIC S9(3)   COMP.
     10   IM-CURSOR-COLUMN    PIC S9(3)   COMP.
```

Again, I want to stress that field-oriented cursor control is almost always a better choice than absolute cursor control. Unless your application must be able to find out where the cursor was located when an input message was sent, you should avoid absolute cursor control.

The cash receipts application

Now, I want to illustrate the essential features this chapter has presented with an application example. The application is an MPP that accepts user entries for cash receipts that are posted against the customer-receivables data base I've already described. (You can look back to chapter 4 to refresh your memory about this data base). In this section, I'll present the specifications for the application, its MFS format set, and its COBOL program.

Specifications for the cash receipts application   For this application, the user makes one entry for each payment received from a customer

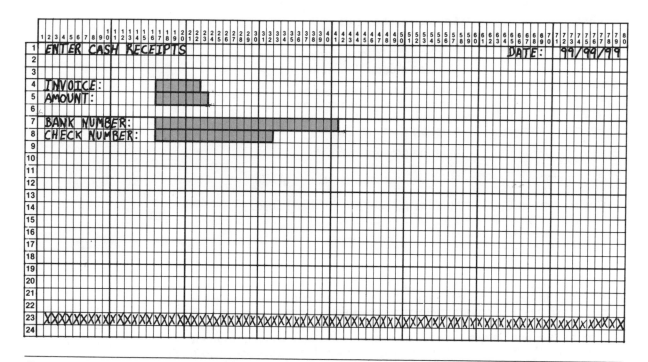

Figure 7-3   Screen layout for the cash receipts application

for an open invoice. Figure 7-3 shows the screen layout for the application. As you can see, it's simple and straightforward. Only four data entry fields are provided; they're shaded in figure 7-3. The first data entry field, identified by the caption "INVOICE," is for the key of the invoice to which the payment is to be applied. The other three data entry fields come directly from the customer's check: payment amount, bank number, and check number.

Figure 7-4 presents the editing specifications for the cash receipts application. As you can see, there's an editing requirement for each field. For the invoice number field, the operator must supply an invoice number that's numeric and greater than zero. In addition, that number must be the key of an existing receivable segment in the customer data base. The editing for the other three fields is simpler. The second field, payment amount, must have a numeric value greater than zero. And the last two fields (bank number and check number) simply must be present.

The application specifications in figure 7-4 also describe how the application should indicate entry errors to the terminal user. If either the invoice number or payment amount field is invalid, it should be

Field	Editing requirements
Invoice number	Must be numeric.
	Must be greater than zero.
	Must match the key field of an existing receivable segment in the customer data base.
Payment amount	Must be numeric.
	Must be greater than zero.
Bank number	Must be present (that is, non-blank).
Check number	Must be present (that is, non-blank).

Indicating an error

Fields found to be in error should be marked for the operator. If a single field is in error, move the cursor to the first byte of that field and display an error message in line 23 that describes the error. If the field in error is the invoice number or payment amount field, redisplay the invalid entry in bright intensity.

If more than one field is found to be in error, position the cursor to the first of the invalid fields and display an error message that corresponds to it. For example, if both the invoice number and payment amount fields are invalid, move the cursor to the invoice number field and display an error message for the invoice number field. In that case, display both the invoice number and payment amount fields in bright intensity.

Processing specifications

If an entry is valid, use the data in the input message to update the customer data base. Replace the receivable segment after subtracting the payment amount from the balance due field. Insert a new occurrence of the payment segment type using the data in the input message. For the payment date field in the payment segment, use the current date.

Figure 7-4   Specifications for the cash receipts application

redisplayed in bright intensity to call the operator's attention to it. Errors in the bank number and check number fields are not indicated by a change in display intensity. That's because the only thing that can be wrong with either of them is that the user didn't enter a value; changing the display intensity of an empty field wouldn't produce any visible result.

If any one of the four fields is invalid, the cursor should be positioned at the first byte of the field, and a descriptive message should be displayed for the operator. If two or more fields are invalid, the cursor should be placed at the first one on the screen, and the error message should relate to it.

If the program doesn't detect any errors in the input message, it uses data from the message to update the customer-receivables data base. The receivable segment is replaced, after the program has subtracted the payment amount from the balance due field. And a new payment segment occurrence is inserted to record the transaction.

Frankly, this is a simple application, both because it involves so few fields and because its editing requirements are rudimentary. It's likely that applications you develop will be more complex. However, I'm using a simple illustration so you can concentrate on the programming techniques instead of a complicated application problem. Even though the cash receipts application is simple, it shows you what you need to know about dynamic modification of field attributes and cursor position.

Format set for the cash receipts application   Figure 7-5 presents the format set for the cash receipts application. Most of its elements should be familiar to you. For example, a single set of control statements defines both a DIF and a DOF, while separate sets define a MID and a MOD. However, this format set does present some elements I particularly want you to notice; they're shaded in figure 7-5.

In the device format description, I coded complete attribute specifications for all fields, both caption and data entry, even though some of my specifications are the same as the defaults. To implement the screen layout in figure 7-3, I coded

    ATTR=(PROT,ALPHA,HI,NOMOD)

for all headings and captions to specify that they're protected, bright, alphanumeric fields, with their MDTs set to off. (The NOMOD keyword isn't required to specify that a field's MDT should be set to off, but I coded it anyway in figure 7-5.)

For the invoice-number and payment-amount data entry fields (INVNO in statement 13 and AMOUNT in statement 15) I coded

    ATTR=(NOPROT,NUM,NORM,MOD)

Obviously, the fields have to be unprotected for the operator to be able to key data into them. I specified numeric shift to keep the operator from accidentally entering non-numeric characters; this helps to minimize the number of invalid input messages that the application program has to process.

```
1              PRINT ON,NOGEN
2  **********************************************************************
3              TITLE 'FORMAT SET FOR APPLICATION CR'
4  **********************************************************************
5  CRDF    FMT
6          DEV   TYPE=(3270,2),                                          X
                 FEAT=IGNORE,                                            X
                 SYSMSG=ERRMSG,                                          X
                 DSCA=X'00A0'
7          DIV   TYPE=INOUT
8          DPAGE CURSOR=((4,17)),                                        X
                 FILL=PT
9          DFLD  'ENTER CASH RECEIPTS',                                  X
                 POS=(1,2),                                              X
                 ATTR=(PROT,ALPHA,HI,NOMOD)
10         DFLD  'DATE:',                                                X
                 POS=(1,65),                                             X
                 ATTR=(PROT,ALPHA,HI,NOMOD)
11 CURDATE DFLD  POS=(1,72),                                             X
                 LTH=8,                                                  X
                 ATTR=(PROT,ALPHA,HI,NOMOD)
12         DFLD  'INVOICE:',                                             X
                 POS=(4,2),                                              X
                 ATTR=(PROT,ALPHA,HI,NOMOD)
13 INVNO   DFLD  POS=(4,17),                                             X
                 LTH=6,                                                  X
                 ATTR=(NOPROT,NUM,NORM,MOD)
14         DFLD  'AMOUNT:',                                              X
                 POS=(5,2),                                              X
                 ATTR=(PROT,ALPHA,HI,NOMOD)
15 AMOUNT  DFLD  POS=(5,17),                                             X
                 LTH=7,                                                  X
                 ATTR=(NOPROT,NUM,NORM,MOD)
16         DFLD  'BANK NUMBER:',                                         X
                 POS=(7,2),                                              X
                 ATTR=(PROT,ALPHA,HI,NOMOD)
17 BANKNO  DFLD  POS=(7,17),                                             X
                 LTH=25,                                                 X
                 ATTR=(NOPROT,ALPHA,NORM,MOD)
18         DFLD  'CHECK NUMBER:',                                        X
                 POS=(8,2),                                              X
                 ATTR=(PROT,ALPHA,HI,NOMOD)
19 CHECKNO DFLD  POS=(8,17),                                             X
                 LTH=16,                                                 X
                 ATTR=(NOPROT,ALPHA,NORM,MOD)
20 ERRMSG  DFLD  POS=(23,2),                                             X
                 LTH=79,                                                 X
                 ATTR=(PROT,ALPHA,NORM,NOMOD)
21         FMTEND
```

Figure 7-5   Format set for the cash receipts application (part 1 of 2)

```
22 **********************************************************************
23 CRI      MSG     TYPE=INPUT,                                          X
                    SOR=(CRDF,IGNORE),                                   X
                    NXT=CRO
24          SEG
25          MFLD    'CR       ',                                        X
                    LTH=8
26          MFLD    INVNO,                                              X
                    LTH=6,                                              X
                    JUST=R,                                             X
                    FILL=C'0'
27          MFLD    AMOUNT,                                             X
                    LTH=7,                                              X
                    JUST=R,                                             X
                    FILL=C'0'
28          MFLD    BANKNO,                                             X
                    LTH=25
29          MFLD    CHECKNO,                                            X
                    LTH=16
30          MSGEND
31 **********************************************************************
32 CRO      MSG     TYPE=OUTPUT,                                         X
                    SOR=(CRDF,IGNORE),                                   X
                    NXT=CRI
33          SEG
34          MFLD    (CURDATE,DATE2)
35          MFLD    INVNO,                                              X
                    LTH=8,                                              X
                    ATTR=YES
36          MFLD    AMOUNT,                                             X
                    LTH=9,                                              X
                    ATTR=YES
37          MFLD    BANKNO,                                             X
                    LTH=27,                                             X
                    ATTR=YES
38          MFLD    CHECKNO,                                            X
                    LTH=18,                                             X
                    ATTR=YES
39          MFLD    ERRMSG,                                             X
                    LTH=79
40          MSGEND
41 **********************************************************************
42          END
```

Figure 7-5   Format set for the cash receipts application (part 2 of 2)

For all four data entry fields, I specified normal intensity to distinguish operator-entered data from screen captions, which are all displayed with high intensity. However, as the application specifications indicate, the program may change the display intensity of the invoice number or amount field if it detects an entry error in either.

Finally, I specified the MOD attribute for all four data entry fields. That insures that the data they contain will always be transmitted to MFS, even if the operator does not change it. This makes error correction efficient; the operator doesn't have to re-enter data if it's OK.

The last field in the device format description, the error message field, is defined with

```
ATTR=(PROT,ALPHA,NORM,NOMOD)
```

This field cannot be modified, but is unlike the other protected fields on the screen because its contents can vary from entry to entry. As a result, I specified that it should be displayed with normal intensity to make it stand out from the caption and heading data on the screen. And since the message never needs to be transmitted back to MFS, I specified the NOMOD attribute for it.

The next section of the format set is the input message descriptor. It's straightforward. The first field is an eight-byte literal that contains the transaction code for the application: CR. Then, four fields that correspond to each of the data entry fields are defined. As you can see, the invoice number can be 6 bytes long, the payment amount can be 7 bytes long, the bank number can be 25 bytes long, and the check number can be 16 bytes long. Those are the exact lengths of the device fields and of the data fields in the data base description of the payment segment.

For the two numeric fields, I specified

```
JUST=R,
FILL=C'0'
```

to help insure that numeric data is treated properly. For example, the operator can enter the value 12030 in the amount field, and it will be passed to the application program as 0012030: MFS justifies the data to the right, then fills the input message field with zeros. Note, however, that the operator does not key in the decimal point.

Now look at the output message descriptor section of the format set; I want you to notice two points. First, for the four fields in the output message descriptor that will be mapped to the device data entry fields, I coded

```
ATTR=YES
```

to enable dynamic attribute modification. Then, for each of those fields, I provided for the two-byte prefix that dynamic attribute modification requires. As a result, the LTH parameter for each of these fields specifies a value that's two greater than the value for the corresponding input message field.

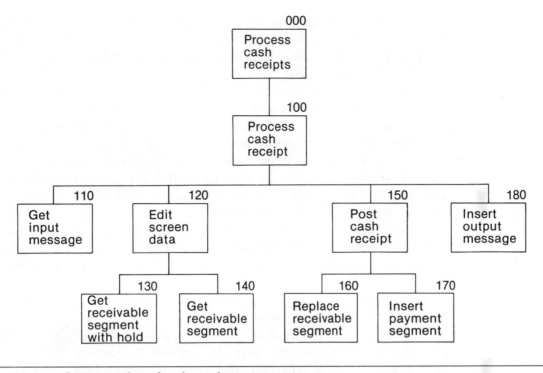

Figure 7-6 Structure chart for the cash receipts program

COBOL program for the cash receipts application Figure 7-6 presents the structure chart for the cash receipts application program and figure 7-7 presents its COBOL source code. The structure of this program is what you'd expect. Like a typical MPP, the program goes through the same steps for each input transaction; they're reflected in the subordinates to module 100. First, the program retrieves the input message (module 110). Then, it edits the message (module 120) and, if no errors are detected, uses the input data to update its data base (module 150). Finally, it sends an output message back to the originating terminal (module 180).

The points I want to stress in this example are illustrated in the source code, so look now at figure 7-7. In the Data Division, I particularly want you to notice the output message description (OUTPUT-MESSAGE-IO-AREA) and the control character literals (CONTROL-CHARACTER-DEFINITIONS) I supplied.

In the output message description, I defined not only the data component of each field, but also each field's prefix. Remember that you define the prefix only when you've specified

ATTR=YES

on the MFLD statement for the field in the MOD code. In this case, I didn't request dynamic attribute modification for the last output message field (OM-USER-MESSAGE), so I didn't define a prefix for it in my COBOL source code.

After the description of the output message, I coded several control character definitions. The first is a two-byte field I called CC-RESET. The value of this field is such that when it is moved to the prefix of an output message field, it will not cause the cursor to be positioned at that field (because its first byte contains binary zeros), but it will cause the default attributes for the field to be used (because its second byte contains hex 80). I define the two bytes of CC-RESET separately so I can use them individually if I need to.

The other two control character definitions are for individual bytes. I use the CURSOR-ON field, whose value is hex C0, to request cursor positioning at a device field. To do that, the program simply moves CURSOR-ON to the first byte of a field's prefix. The last control character definition I coded is for an attribute override. It's the same as the value I described in figure 7-2.

In the Procedure Division, I especially want you to study module 120 and its subordinates modules 130 and 140. It's these modules that implement the error checking the program specifications call for. Module 120 checks each field in the input message to make sure it meets the editing criteria in the specifications. If any errors are detected, the module turns off a program switch called VALID-ENTRY-SW. (Module 100 uses the value of VALID-ENTRY-SW to determine whether it should invoke module 150 to update the data base.)

Module 120 begins under the assumption that there are no errors in the input message. First, it moves space to the user message field (OM-USER-MESSAGE); then it moves the two byte field CC-RESET to each field prefix in the output message description. As I described above, the value of CC-RESET specifies that neither attribute byte modification nor cursor positioning is requested.

After it moves proper values to the message and prefix fields, module 120 begins to edit the data entry fields. It works from the bottom of the screen to the top. That way, if error messages have to be moved to the user message field, the one moved last will actually be for the invalid field that's closest to the top of the screen, as the program specifications require.

The editing the module does for the check number and bank number fields is simple. If either field is blank, the program requests cursor positioning by moving CURSOR-ON to the first byte of the field's prefix. Then, it moves an appropriate message to the user message field.

```
IDENTIFICATION DIVISION.
*
PROGRAM-ID.  CR.
*
ENVIRONMENT DIVISION.
*
DATA DIVISION.
*
WORKING-STORAGE SECTION.
*
01  SWITCHES.
*
    05  VALID-INVOICE-NO-SW          PIC X         VALUE 'Y'.
        88  VALID-INVOICE-NO                       VALUE 'Y'.
    05  VALID-ENTRY-SW               PIC X         VALUE 'Y'.
        88  VALID-ENTRY                            VALUE 'Y'.
    05  END-OF-MESSAGES-SW           PIC X         VALUE 'N'.
        88  END-OF-MESSAGES                        VALUE 'Y'.
*
01  INPUT-MESSAGE-IO-AREA.
*
    05  IM-LL                        PIC S9(3)     COMP.
    05  IM-ZZ                        PIC S9(3)     COMP.
    05  IM-TRANSACTION-CODE          PIC X(8).
    05  IM-INVOICE-NO                PIC X(6).
    05  IM-INVOICE-NO-NUM            REDEFINES IM-INVOICE-NO
                                     PIC 9(6).
    05  IM-AMOUNT                    PIC X(7).
    05  IM-AMOUNT-NUM                REDEFINES IM-AMOUNT
                                     PIC 9(5)V99.
    05  IM-BANK-NUMBER               PIC X(25).
    05  IM-CHECK-NUMBER              PIC X(16).
*
01  OUTPUT-MESSAGE-IO-AREA.
*
    05  OM-LL                        PIC S9(3)     COMP
                                                   VALUE +145.
    05  OM-Z1-Z2                     PIC S9(3)     COMP
                                                   VALUE ZERO.
    05  OM-INVOICE-NO.
        10  OM-INVOICE-NO-PREFIX.
            15  OM-INVOICE-NO-CURSOR PIC X.
            15  OM-INVOICE-NO-ATTR   PIC X.
        10  OM-INVOICE-NO-DATA       PIC X(6).
    05  OM-AMOUNT.
        10  OM-AMOUNT-PREFIX.
            15  OM-AMOUNT-CURSOR     PIC X.
            15  OM-AMOUNT-ATTR       PIC X.
        10  OM-AMOUNT-DATA           PIC X(7).
    05  OM-BANK-NUMBER.
        10  OM-BANK-NUMBER-PREFIX.
            15  OM-BANK-NUMBER-CURSOR PIC X.
            15  OM-BANK-NUMBER-ATTR   PIC X.
        10  OM-BANK-NUMBER-DATA      PIC X(25).
```

Figure 7-7   Source listing for the cash receipts program (part 1 of 7)

```
      05   OM-CHECK-NUMBER.
           10   OM-CHECK-NUMBER-PREFIX.
                15   OM-CHECK-NUMBER-CURSOR   PIC X.
                15   OM-CHECK-NUMBER-ATTR     PIC X.
           10   OM-CHECK-NUMBER-DATA          PIC X(16).
      05   OM-USER-MESSAGE                    PIC X(79).
*
 01  CONTROL-CHARACTER-DEFINITIONS.
*
      05   CC-RESET.
           10   CC-RESET-CURSOR               PIC X     VALUE LOW-VALUE.
           10   CC-RESET-ATTR                 PIC X     VALUE ' '.
*
*                                                       BINARY VALUE:
*                                                       1000 0000
*                                                       (X'80')
*
      05   CURSOR-ON                          PIC X     VALUE ' '.
*
*                                                       BINARY VALUE:
*                                                       1100 0000
*                                                       (X'C0')
*
      05   ATTR-CHANGE-TO-BRIGHT              PIC X     VALUE ' '.
*
*                                                       BINARY VALUE:
*                                                       1000 1000
*                                                       (X'88')
*
 01  WORK-FIELDS.
*
      05   PRESENT-DATE.
           10   PRESENT-YEAR      PIC 99.
           10   PRESENT-MONTH     PIC 99.
           10   PRESENT-DAY       PIC 99.
      05   ERROR-MESSAGE-TEXT.
           10   FILLER            PIC X(8)     VALUE 'INVOICE '.
           10   EMT-INVOICE-NO    PIC X(6).
           10   FILLER            PIC X(11)    VALUE ' NOT FOUND.'.
           10   FILLER            PIC X(54)    VALUE SPACE.
      05   VALID-MESSAGE-TEXT.
           10   VMT-AMOUNT        PIC $$$,$$$.99-.
           10   FILLER            PIC X(15)
                                  VALUE ' PAYMENT POSTED'.
           10   FILLER            PIC X(12)
                                  VALUE ' TO INVOICE '.
           10   VMT-INVOICE-NO    PIC X(6).
           10   FILLER            PIC X        VALUE '.'.
           10   FILLER            PIC X(34)    VALUE SPACE.
      05   DIVISION-FIELDS.
           10   GOOD-NUMERATOR    PIC S9       COMP-3
                                               VALUE +1.
           10   BAD-DENOMINATOR   PIC S9       COMP-3
                                               VALUE ZERO.
```

Figure 7-7   Source listing for the cash receipts program (part 2 of 7)

```
*
01   DLI-FUNCTIONS.
*
     05   DLI-GU                 PIC X(4)      VALUE 'GU  '.
     05   DLI-GHU                PIC X(4)      VALUE 'GHU '.
     05   DLI-GN                 PIC X(4)      VALUE 'GN  '.
     05   DLI-GHN                PIC X(4)      VALUE 'GHN '.
     05   DLI-GNP                PIC X(4)      VALUE 'GNP '.
     05   DLI-GHNP               PIC X(4)      VALUE 'GHNP'.
     05   DLI-ISRT               PIC X(4)      VALUE 'ISRT'.
     05   DLI-DLET               PIC X(4)      VALUE 'DLET'.
     05   DLI-REPL               PIC X(4)      VALUE 'REPL'.
     05   DLI-CHKP               PIC X(4)      VALUE 'CHKP'.
     05   DLI-XRST               PIC X(4)      VALUE 'XRST'.
     05   DLI-PCB                PIC X(4)      VALUE 'PCB '.
*
01   RECEIVABLE-SEGMENT.
*
     05   RS-INVOICE-NUMBER      PIC X(6).
     05   RS-INVOICE-DATE        PIC X(6).
     05   RS-PO-NUMBER           PIC X(25).
     05   RS-PRODUCT-TOTAL       PIC S9(5)V99     COMP-3.
     05   RS-CASH-DISCOUNT       PIC S9(5)V99     COMP-3.
     05   RS-SALES-TAX           PIC S9(5)V99     COMP-3.
     05   RS-FREIGHT             PIC S9(5)V99     COMP-3.
     05   RS-BALANCE-DUE         PIC S9(5)V99     COMP-3.
*
01   PAYMENT-SEGMENT.
*
     05   PS-CHECK-NUMBER        PIC X(16).
     05   PS-BANK-NUMBER         PIC X(25).
     05   PS-PAYMENT-DATE.
          10   PS-PAYMENT-MONTH  PIC XX.
          10   PS-PAYMENT-DAY    PIC XX.
          10   PS-PAYMENT-YEAR   PIC XX.
     05   PS-PAYMENT-AMOUNT      PIC S9(5)V99     COMP-3.
*
01   INVOICE-NO-SSA.
*
     05   FILLER                 PIC X(9)      VALUE 'CRRECSEG('.
     05   FILLER                 PIC X(10)     VALUE 'CRRECXNO ='.
     05   INVOICE-NO-SSA-VALUE   PIC X(6).
     05   FILLER                 PIC X         VALUE ')'.
*
01   UNQUALIFIED-SSA            PIC X(9)      VALUE 'CRPAYSEG '.
*
LINKAGE SECTION.
*
01   IO-PCB-MASK.
*
     05   IO-PCB-LOGICAL-TERMINAL PIC X(8).
     05   FILLER                 PIC XX.
     05   IO-PCB-STATUS-CODE     PIC XX.
     05   IO-PCB-DATE            PIC S9(7)        COMP-3.
     05   IO-PCB-TIME            PIC S9(6)V9      COMP-3.
```

Figure 7-7   Source listing for the cash receipts program (part 3 of 7)

```
     05  IO-PCB-MSG-SEQ-NUMBER    PIC S9(5)        COMP.
     05  IO-PCB-MOD-NAME          PIC X(8).
     05  IO-PCB-USER-ID           PIC X(8).
*
 01  CR-PCB-MASK.
*
     05  CR-PCB-DBD-NAME          PIC X(8).
     05  CR-PCB-SEGMENT-LEVEL     PIC XX.
     05  CR-PCB-STATUS-CODE       PIC XX.
     05  CR-PCB-PROC-OPTIONS      PIC X(4).
     05  FILLER                   PIC S9(5)        COMP.
     05  CR-PCB-SEGMENT-NAME      PIC X(8).
     05  CR-PCB-KEY-LENGTH        PIC S9(5)        COMP.
     05  CR-PCB-NUMB-SENS-SEGS    PIC S9(5)        COMP.
     05  CR-PCB-KEY               PIC X(22).
*
 PROCEDURE DIVISION.
*
     ENTRY 'DLITCBL' USING IO-PCB-MASK
                           CR-PCB-MASK.
*
 000-PROCESS-CASH-RECEIPTS.
*
     ACCEPT PRESENT-DATE FROM DATE.
     PERFORM 100-PROCESS-CASH-RECEIPT
         UNTIL END-OF-MESSAGES.
     GOBACK.
*
 100-PROCESS-CASH-RECEIPT.
*
     PERFORM 110-GET-INPUT-MESSAGE.
     IF NOT END-OF-MESSAGES
         MOVE 'Y' TO VALID-ENTRY-SW
         PERFORM 120-EDIT-SCREEN-DATA
         IF VALID-ENTRY
             PERFORM 150-POST-CASH-RECEIPT.
     IF NOT END-OF-MESSAGES
         PERFORM 180-INSERT-OUTPUT-MESSAGE.
*
 110-GET-INPUT-MESSAGE.
*
     CALL 'CBLTDLI' USING DLI-GU
                          IO-PCB-MASK
                          INPUT-MESSAGE-IO-AREA.
     IF IO-PCB-STATUS-CODE = 'QC'
         MOVE 'Y' TO END-OF-MESSAGES-SW.
*
 120-EDIT-SCREEN-DATA.
*
     MOVE SPACE    TO OM-USER-MESSAGE.
     MOVE CC-RESET TO OM-INVOICE-NO-PREFIX
                      OM-AMOUNT-PREFIX
                      OM-BANK-NUMBER-PREFIX
                      OM-CHECK-NUMBER-PREFIX.
*
```

Figure 7-7   Source listing for the cash receipts program (part 4 of 7)

```
        IF IM-CHECK-NUMBER = SPACE
            MOVE CURSOR-ON TO OM-CHECK-NUMBER-CURSOR
            MOVE 'ENTER A CHECK NUMBER.'
                TO OM-USER-MESSAGE.
*
        IF IM-BANK-NUMBER = SPACE

            MOVE CURSOR-ON TO OM-BANK-NUMBER-CURSOR
            MOVE 'ENTER A BANK NUMBER.'
                TO OM-USER-MESSAGE.
*
        IF IM-AMOUNT NOT NUMERIC
            MOVE ATTR-CHANGE-TO-BRIGHT TO OM-AMOUNT-ATTR
            MOVE CURSOR-ON TO OM-AMOUNT-CURSOR
            MOVE 'ENTER A NUMERIC AMOUNT.'
                TO OM-USER-MESSAGE
        ELSE
            IF IM-AMOUNT-NUM NOT > 0
                MOVE ATTR-CHANGE-TO-BRIGHT TO OM-AMOUNT-ATTR
                MOVE CURSOR-ON TO OM-AMOUNT-CURSOR
                MOVE 'ENTER AN AMOUNT GREATER THAN ZERO.'
                    TO OM-USER-MESSAGE.
*
        IF IM-INVOICE-NO NOT NUMERIC
            MOVE ATTR-CHANGE-TO-BRIGHT TO OM-INVOICE-NO-ATTR
            MOVE CURSOR-ON                TO OM-INVOICE-NO-CURSOR
            MOVE 'ENTER A NUMERIC INVOICE NUMBER.'
                TO OM-USER-MESSAGE
        ELSE
            IF IM-INVOICE-NO-NUM NOT > 0
                MOVE ATTR-CHANGE-TO-BRIGHT TO OM-INVOICE-NO-ATTR
                MOVE CURSOR-ON                TO OM-INVOICE-NO-CURSOR
                MOVE 'ENTER AN INVOICE NUMBER GREATER THAN ZERO.'
                    TO OM-USER-MESSAGE
            ELSE
                MOVE IM-INVOICE-NO TO INVOICE-NO-SSA-VALUE
                IF OM-USER-MESSAGE = SPACE
                    PERFORM 130-GET-REC-SEG-WITH-HOLD
                ELSE
                    PERFORM 140-GET-RECEIVABLE-SEGMENT.
*
        IF OM-USER-MESSAGE = SPACE
            MOVE CURSOR-ON                TO OM-INVOICE-NO-CURSOR
            MOVE SPACE                    TO OM-INVOICE-NO-DATA
                                             OM-AMOUNT-DATA
                                             OM-BANK-NUMBER-DATA
                                             OM-CHECK-NUMBER-DATA
            MOVE IM-AMOUNT-NUM       TO VMT-AMOUNT
            MOVE IM-INVOICE-NO       TO VMT-INVOICE-NO
            MOVE VALID-MESSAGE-TEXT TO OM-USER-MESSAGE
        ELSE
            MOVE IM-INVOICE-NO     TO OM-INVOICE-NO-DATA
            MOVE IM-AMOUNT         TO OM-AMOUNT-DATA
            MOVE IM-BANK-NUMBER    TO OM-BANK-NUMBER-DATA
            MOVE IM-CHECK-NUMBER TO OM-CHECK-NUMBER-DATA
            MOVE 'N'                TO VALID-ENTRY-SW.
```

Figure 7-7   Source listing for the cash receipts program (part 5 of 7)

```
*
 130-GET-REC-SEG-WITH-HOLD.
*
     CALL 'CBLTDLI' USING DLI-GHU
                          CR-PCB-MASK
                          RECEIVABLE-SEGMENT
                          INVOICE-NO-SSA.
     IF CR-PCB-STATUS-CODE NOT = SPACE
         MOVE ATTR-CHANGE-TO-BRIGHT TO OM-INVOICE-NO-ATTR
         MOVE CURSOR-ON             TO OM-INVOICE-NO-CURSOR
         MOVE IM-INVOICE-NO         TO EMT-INVOICE-NO
         MOVE ERROR-MESSAGE-TEXT    TO OM-USER-MESSAGE.
*
 140-GET-RECEIVABLE-SEGMENT.
*
     CALL 'CBLTDLI' USING DLI-GU
                          CR-PCB-MASK
                          RECEIVABLE-SEGMENT
                          INVOICE-NO-SSA.
     IF CR-PCB-STATUS-CODE NOT = SPACE
         MOVE ATTR-CHANGE-TO-BRIGHT TO OM-INVOICE-NO-ATTR
         MOVE CURSOR-ON             TO OM-INVOICE-NO-CURSOR
         MOVE IM-INVOICE-NO         TO EMT-INVOICE-NO
         MOVE ERROR-MESSAGE-TEXT    TO OM-USER-MESSAGE.
*
 150-POST-CASH-RECEIPT.
*
     SUBTRACT IM-AMOUNT-NUM FROM RS-BALANCE-DUE.
     PERFORM 160-REPLACE-RECEIVABLE-SEG.
     MOVE IM-CHECK-NUMBER TO PS-CHECK-NUMBER.
     MOVE IM-BANK-NUMBER  TO PS-BANK-NUMBER.
     MOVE IM-AMOUNT-NUM   TO PS-PAYMENT-AMOUNT.
     MOVE PRESENT-MONTH   TO PS-PAYMENT-MONTH.
     MOVE PRESENT-DAY     TO PS-PAYMENT-DAY.
     MOVE PRESENT-YEAR    TO PS-PAYMENT-YEAR.
     PERFORM 170-INSERT-PAYMENT-SEGMENT.
*
 160-REPLACE-RECEIVABLE-SEG.
*
     CALL 'CBLTDLI' USING DLI-REPL
                          CR-PCB-MASK
                          RECEIVABLE-SEGMENT.
     IF CR-PCB-STATUS-CODE NOT = SPACE
         DIVIDE BAD-DENOMINATOR INTO GOOD-NUMERATOR.
*
 170-INSERT-PAYMENT-SEGMENT.
*
     CALL 'CBLTDLI' USING DLI-ISRT
                          CR-PCB-MASK
                          PAYMENT-SEGMENT
                          INVOICE-NO-SSA
                          UNQUALIFIED-SSA.
     IF CR-PCB-STATUS-CODE NOT = SPACE
         DIVIDE BAD-DENOMINATOR INTO GOOD-NUMERATOR.
*
```

Figure 7-7   Source listing for the cash receipts program (part 6 of 7)

```
180-INSERT-OUTPUT-MESSAGE.
*
     CALL 'CBLTDLI' USING DLI-ISRT
                          IO-PCB-MASK
                          OUTPUT-MESSAGE-IO-AREA.
*
```

Figure 7-7   Source listing for the cash receipts program (part 7 of 7)

Next, the program edits the payment amount field. Here, the editing requires two tests. The first determines whether the field contains numeric data. If it does, the second test determines whether the value is greater than zero. If either test detects an error, an appropriate message is moved to OM-USER-MESSAGE, and cursor positioning is requested for the field.

In addition, if the payment amount field is found to be in error, its default attribute byte is overridden. The statement

```
MOVE ATTR-CHANGE-TO-BRIGHT TO OM-AMOUNT-ATTR
```

changes the field's intensity attribute from normal to bright. I described the details of this technique earlier in this chapter.

The last field to be edited, invoice number, presents the most complex problem. First, it's edited to insure that its value is numeric and greater than zero, just like the payment amount field. Then, if the value the user entered is OK, the program uses it to retrieve the related receivable segment from the customer data base. The statement

```
MOVE IM-INVOICE-NO TO INVOICE-NO-SSA-VALUE
```

formats the segment search argument that will be used in the retrieval call.

What the program does after it has formatted the SSA depends on whether any errors were detected by previous editing. If any were, the program performs module 140 to retrieve the receivable segment without hold. Because errors were found elsewhere in the input message, the data will not be posted to the data base, and, as a result, there's no reason to hold the segment for update; to do so would waste IMS resources. However, the data base still needs to be accessed to verify the invoice number value the operator entered.

If no errors have been found in the input message, the program performs module 130 to issue a get-hold call for the receivable segment. If that call is successful, the program is ready to update the segment.

Modules 130 and 140 do similar editing. If either the GU call or the GHU call returns a status code other than space, the invoice number is considered to be invalid. Then, the program moves an appropriate message to the user message field, requests cursor positioning at the invoice number field, and changes the intensity attribute of the invoice number field from normal to bright.

Module 120 ends by completing the formatting of the output message. If no errors were detected for the input message, the value of OM-USER-MESSAGE will be space. If that's the case, module 120 clears the data entry fields in the output message, formats a message that indicates the data was posted, and specifies cursor positioning at the invoice number field (the right place for a new entry to begin). On the other hand, if errors were detected, the input data entry field values are moved to the output message and VALID-ENTRY-SW is set to N to indicate to module 100 that the data should not be used to update the data base.

You shouldn't have any trouble understanding the rest of the code in this program, but I want you to note the DIVIDE statements in modules 160 and 170, the modules that update the customer data base by replacing and inserting segments. If either type of call returns a status code other than space, it means a serious error has occurred. In that case, the DIVIDE statement will execute, resulting in a divide by zero that will cause the program to end abnormally. I coded the program this way because, when an MPP abends, IMS reverses any data base changes made during the run so that the data bases are intact even though a serious error has occurred. In addition, IMS won't schedule the program again until the master terminal operator specifically enables it. That way, a program with a bug won't be invoked over and over. You'll learn more about the IMS facilities for error handling in chapter 13.

Terminology

field-oriented cursor control
absolute cursor control

Objectives

1. Describe the mechanisms MFS uses to let programs override the default attributes of device fields.

2. Describe the mechanisms MFS uses to let programs override the default location of the cursor.

3. Explain why field-oriented cursor control is usually preferable to absolute cursor control.

4. Given complete specifications, develop the format set and COBOL program for a data entry application that requires dynamic attribute modification and cursor control.

Chapter 8

How to use
complex screen flows

As you know, the output message MFS sends to a 3270 terminal determines what the next input message will be. On first thought, that might
seem like an application can use only one display screen format.
However, that's not the case: Nothing forces you to use a particular
output format just because a particular input format was used. When
you change output formats, you can develop applications that use
complex screen flows, that is, a series of two or more different screen
displays. In this chapter, I'll show you how to control what output
formats are used, both from application programs and entirely within
MFS.

Complex screen flow concepts

As you'll see in this section, there's nothing particularly difficult about
using complex screen flows. However, you do need to understand the
linkages between control blocks. And you also need to know when you
should and should not use complex screen flows.

Control block linkages   Figure 8-1 represents the MFS control block
linkages you're already familiar with. Here, a single device format (a
DIF and DOF) and its two related message descriptors (a MID and a
MOD) are used. The same screen format is used for each entry.

/FORMAT MOD

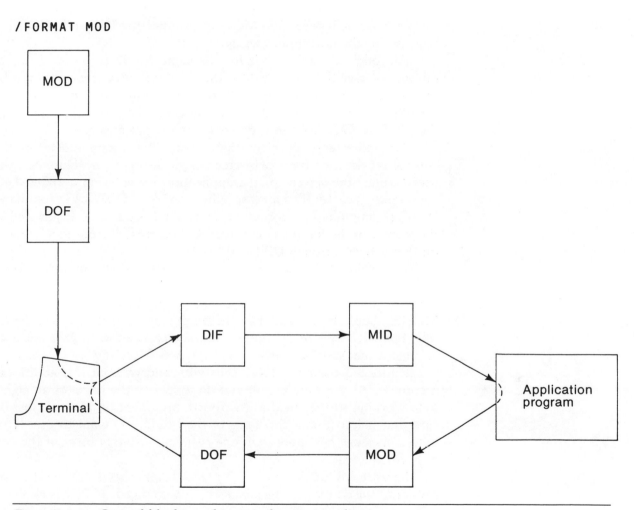

Figure 8-1   Control blocks used in a single-screen application

The user formats the screen by entering the /FORMAT command followed by the name of the MOD to be used. That MOD points to a particular DOF, which MFS uses to format the screen. After the screen has been formatted, the user can key in data and transmit the message by pressing the enter key. Then, MFS maps the device fields, identified in the DIF, to the input message, according to specifications recorded in the MID.

The application program processes the input message and formats and sends a return output message. *By default*, MFS uses the MOD from the current format set to map the output message fields back to the device. This, in turn, starts another entry sequence which will use the same blocks as before: The MOD determines the DIF and MID MFS will use for the next input message.

Although it's the default for the same MOD to be used for an output message that was used for the previous entry, that need not be the case. If an application program needs to use different screen formats for different parts of a single entry sequence, the program can change the MOD MFS uses when it processes an output message.

To understand, consider figure 8-2. This figure illustrates the control blocks used for a two-screen application. As in figure 8-1, the user formats the screen for the application by entering a /FORMAT command. The MOD name specified on the /FORMAT command (MOD1) determines the format of the screen (through DOF1) as well as the format of the input message that will be created from data entered on that screen (through DIF1 and MID1).

When the application program receives the input message format according to MID1, it processes it. However, when the program is ready to send its return output message, it specifies that another MOD, MOD2, should be used to map the output fields to the device. To do this, the ISRT call for the output message is coded with an additional argument that specifies the name of the new MOD.

Figure 8-3 compares ISRT calls with and without this additional argument. As you can see, all you do is specify the name of an eight-byte working storage field as the fourth argument on the call. Just be sure that field contains the name of the MOD you want to use. If an output message has more than one segment, use this form of the call only for the first.

Because MOD2 in figure 8-2 points to another DOF, DOF2, the format of the data on the terminal screen is changed. MOD2 is part of a different format set altogether. That means not only that a different DOF is used to format the screen for the output message, but also that a different DIF and MID (DIF2 and MID2) are used to map the next entry to an input message. When the application program receives an input message mapped according to the specifications in MID2, it processes it and sends an output message whose ISRT call specifies that MOD1 should be used. As a result, the program alternates between using MOD1 and MOD2 as it processes the input messages from a particular terminal. The terminal user sees two different screens, one after the other.

Of course, you have to provide some mechanism for the program to figure out if it's processing an input message from the first or second screen. An easy way to do that is to code a literal MFLD in the MID; that field's value can uniquely identify the message type. The program evaluates the field to determine which screen the message came from.

/ FORMAT MOD1

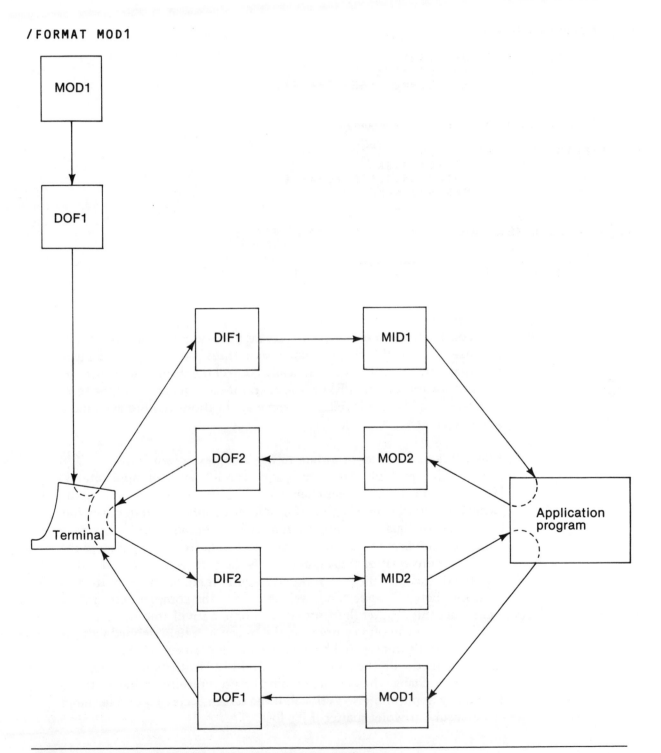

Figure 8-2   Control blocks used in a two-screen application

Basic format of the ISRT call

```
CALL 'CBLTDLI' USING DLI-ISRT
                     IO-PCB-MASK
                     OUTPUT-MESSAGE-IO-AREA.
```

Format of the ISRT call with the MOD name argument

```
CALL 'CBLTDLI' USING DLI-ISRT
                     IO-PCB-MASK
                     OUTPUT-MESSAGE-IO-AREA
                     MFS-MOD-NAME.
```

Note: MFS-MOD-NAME is a working storage field defined with PIC X(8).

Figure 8-3   Formats of the data communications ISRT call

Although figure 8-2 illustrates a two-screen application that alternates back and forth between two screens unvaryingly, that need not be
the case. Later in this chapter, you'll see a three-screen inquiry application that lets the operator dynamically control the display sequence. By
pressing an appropriate PF key, the operator requests which of the three
screens should be displayed. And some applications require even more
screen formats.

When it is and isn't appropriate to use complex screen flows   You
can use this multiple-screen technique for all sorts of applications.
However, until you're familiar with conversational programming
(which I describe in chapter 12), you probably shouldn't use this
technique for data entry applications. That's because multiple-screen
data entry applications almost always store data from one screen to the
next, and conversational programming is the best technique to do that.

In contrast, inquiries that do not require large amounts of data to
be stored between screens are well suited for the complex screen flow
techniques this chapter illustrates. When only a small amount of data is
involved, you can often store it on the screen in a field defined with its
MDT on so it's transmitted back to MFS with each entry. (Such a field
can be defined with the NODISPLAY and PROT attributes so the user
can't see or change the data it contains.) And typically, stored data for
an inquiry application isn't critical; if the screen is cleared or a terminal
error occurs, it won't matter if it's lost.

Although using complex screen flows is appropriate for a variety of applications, you should also be aware that it can present some performance problems. Each time you change a MOD, clear the screen, or issue a /FORMAT command, MFS has to do a *full-format operation* to send not only variable data, but also screen literals and 3270 device orders. Full-format operations are relatively inefficient, and MFS was designed to keep them to a minimum.

Not only will telecommunications performance be reduced when you use complex screen flows because of the larger number of full-format operations required, but MFS internal performance will be reduced too. That's because MFS will have to retrieve and store more blocks. That can require more storage for MFS in the IMS control region, and it means more DASD accesses will have to be done to fetch the necessary blocks. Although the MFS administrator can use a variety of techniques to optimize performance, there is still a cost to using complex screen flows.

Because of the inefficiencies involved in full-format operations, you should use the complex screen flow techniques in this chapter sparingly. Generally, it's a good idea to limit your applications to single-screen formats, as long as you don't reduce operator efficiency. In fact, the *MFS User's Guide* even recommends using the same device format for as many applications as possible, with a device field into which the operator can enter a transaction code. This seems like an extreme recommendation to me, but in heavily used systems on inadequate hardware configurations, it might be necessary to insure acceptable performance.

How to control screen flows from within MFS: A menu application

It's easy to control screen flows from within MFS without involving an application program. All you do is provide a way for the operator to cause an input message that begins with

```
/FORMAT mod-name
```

to be transmitted. The user can always do this by clearing the screen and entering the command directly, but a more sophisticated and less error-prone approach is to provide a menu facility implemented with an MFS format set. In this section, I'll present a simple menu application that illustrates this technique.

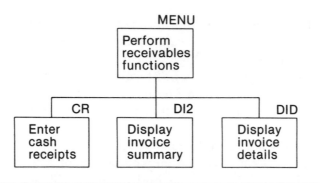

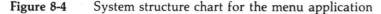

Figure 8-4   System structure chart for the menu application

Specifications for the menu application   Figure 8-4 is a partial system structure chart for a receivables application subsystem. As you can see, the application consists of a menu (the box at the top of the chart) and three subordinate applications. To enter the application, the operator keys in

```
/FORMAT MENUO
```

(MENUO is the MOD name for the MENU application.) After the user has done that, he doesn't have to enter the /FORMAT command again. The menu format set will generate appropriate /FORMAT commands, based on selections the operator makes with PF keys.

Figure 8-5 presents the screen layout for the menu application. Three PF keys (PF1, PF2, and PF3) are enabled. Each is associated with one of the functions shown subordinate to the menu in figure 8-4. (By the way, figure 8-5 is output of the MFS Language Utility; a screen layout like this is printed when the MFS control statements for a format set are translated. This screen image is useful because it lets you quickly check the accuracy of your control statements, particularly field length and position and literal values.)

Format set for the menu application   Figure 8-6 presents the MFS control statements for the menu format set. I want you to notice the PFK parameter of the DEV statement (statement 6), which assigns literal values to the enabled PF keys:

```
PFK=(PFKFIELD,
'/FOR CRO  ',
'/FOR DI2O ',
'/FOR DIDSO')
```

```
*---------------------------------------------------------------------*
[ RECEIVABLES MENU                                      DATE:  :::::::::[
[                                                                      [
[                                                                      [
[                                                                      [
[       PF1   ENTER CASH RECEIPTS                                      [
[       PF2   DISPLAY INVOICE SUMMARY                                  [
[       PF3   DISPLAY INVOICE DETAILS                                  [
[                                                                      [
[                                                                      [
[       PRESS THE INDICATED PF KEY FOR THE                             [
[       FUNCTION YOU WANT TO PERFORM.                                  [
[                                                                      [
[                                                                      [
[                                                                      [
[                                                                      [
[                                                                      [
[                                                                      [
[                                                                      [
[                                                                      [
[  :::::::::::::::::::::::::::::::::::::::::::::::::::::::::::::::::::::[
[                                                                      [
*---------------------------------------------------------------------*
```

Figure 8-5   Screen layout for the menu application

I selected these MOD names because they're relatively descriptive. (You should recognize the name CRO from the format set in chapter 7 and the name DI2O from the format set in chapters 5 and 6; you'll see DIDSO in a moment.) In practice, the chances are that your shop's standards will dictate MOD names that are less obvious.

Only two of the device fields can contain variable data: CURDATE and ERRMSG. However, neither is a data entry field; data that's displayed in these fields comes from MFS. CURDATE contains the date, and ERRMSG (specified on the SYSMSG parameter of the DEV statement) is used for IMS system messages. All of the other device fields are captions.

Now, take a look at the two message descriptors. The MSG statements establish the sort of one-screen linkages you're familiar with. (Although MENUO won't be the MOD used after MENUI, I specified it on the NXT parameter to complete the format set.) What I want you to notice are the MFLD statements.

The only message field in the input message descriptor is the one associated with the pseudofield PFKFIELD. When the user presses one of the enabled PF keys, the literal associated with it by the PFK parameter of the DEV statement is moved to this message field. Because

```
 1              PRINT ON,NOGEN
 2  **************************************************************
 3              TITLE 'FORMAT SET FOR APPLICATION MENU'
 4  **************************************************************
 5  MENUDF    FMT
 6              DEV    TYPE=(3270,2),                                 X
                       FEAT=IGNORE,                                   X
                       SYSMSG=ERRMSG,                                 X
                       DSCA=X'00A0',                                  X
                       PFK=(PFKFIELD,                                 X
                       '/FOR CRO   ',                                 X
                       '/FOR DI2O ',                                  X
                       '/FOR DIDSO')
 7              DIV    TYPE=INOUT
 8              DPAGE  CURSOR=((1,2)),                                X
                       FILL=PT
 9              DFLD   'RECEIVABLES MENU',                            X
                       POS=(1,2),                                     X
                       ATTR=(PROT,ALPHA,HI,NOMOD)
10              DFLD   'DATE:',                                       X
                       POS=(1,65),                                    X
                       ATTR=(PROT,ALPHA,HI,NOMOD)
11 CURDATE     DFLD   POS=(1,72),                                    X
                       LTH=9,                                         X
                       ATTR=(PROT,ALPHA,HI,NOMOD)
12              DFLD   'PF1',                                         X
                       POS=(5,10),                                    X
                       ATTR=(PROT,ALPHA,HI,NOMOD)
13              DFLD   'ENTER CASH RECEIPTS',                         X
                       POS=(5,15),                                    X
                       ATTR=(PROT,ALPHA,NORM,NOMOD)
14              DFLD   'PF2',                                         X
                       POS=(6,10),                                    X
                       ATTR=(PROT,ALPHA,HI,NOMOD)
15              DFLD   'DISPLAY INVOICE SUMMARY',                     X
                       POS=(6,15),                                    X
                       ATTR=(PROT,ALPHA,NORM,NOMOD)
16              DFLD   'PF3',                                         X
                       POS=(7,10),                                    X
                       ATTR=(PROT,ALPHA,HI,NOMOD)
17              DFLD   'DISPLAY INVOICE DETAILS',                     X
                       POS=(7,15),                                    X
                       ATTR=(PROT,ALPHA,NORM,NOMOD)
18              DFLD   'PRESS THE INDICATED PF KEY FOR THE',          X
                       POS=(10,10),                                   X
                       ATTR=(PROT,ALPHA,NORM,NOMOD)
19              DFLD   'FUNCTION YOU WANT TO PERFORM.',               X
                       POS=(11,10),                                   X
                       ATTR=(PROT,ALPHA,NORM,NOMCD)
20 ERRMSG      DFLD   POS=(23,2),                                    X
                       LTH=79,                                        X
                       ATTR=(PROT,ALPHA,NORM,NOMOD)
21              FMTEND
22  **************************************************************
23              EJECT
```

Figure 8-6   Format set for the menu application (part 1 of 2)

```
24 *******************************************************************
25 MENUI     MSG     TYPE=INPUT,                                       X
                     SOR=(MENUDF,IGNORE),                              X
                     NXT=MENUO
26         SEG
27         MFLD    PFKFIELD,                                           X
                   LTH=10
28         MSGEND
29 *******************************************************************
30 MENUO     MSG     TYPE=OUTPUT,                                      X
                     SOR=(MENUDF,IGNORE),                              X
                     NXT=MENUI
31         SEG
32         MFLD    (CURDATE,DATE2)
33         MFLD    LTH=1
34         MSGEND
35 *******************************************************************
36         END
```

Figure 8-6   Format set for the menu application (part 2 of 2)

this field is at the beginning of the input message and because all of the literal values I specified begin with /FOR (an accepted abbreviation for /FORMAT), any input message generated from this format set is an IMS command that invokes one of the three applications listed in the menu.

In the output message descriptor, I coded two MFLD statements. The first names the system literal DATE2 and associates it with the device field CURDATE; its only purpose is to provide the current date for the menu screen. The other message field is a one-byte filler field that isn't associated with a device field. It's required simply because MFS doesn't allow an output message with length zero.

For this sort of menu structure to work effectively, it's necessary not only for the menu to format the screen properly for the selected application, but also for each application to return properly to the menu. Returning to a menu is easy, as you'll see as I describe the display invoice details application, the third choice on the sample menu.

How to control screen flows from an application program: The display invoice details application

This section describes the application the user can invoke by pressing PF3 from the menu in figure 8-5. It's a more complicated version of the display invoice application you've already seen in chapters 4, 5, and 6.

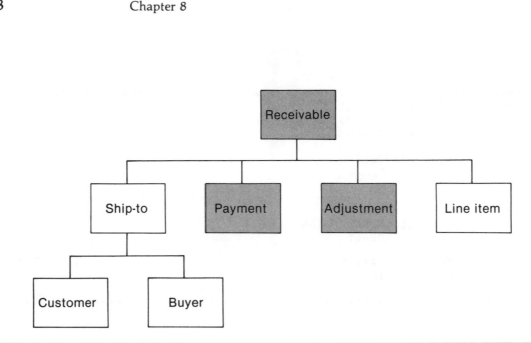

Figure 8-7   Hierarchical structure of the customer data base when accessed through a secondary index
built over the receivable segment

After I've shown you the screen layouts for this application, I'll present
the MFS format sets that implement them. Finally, I'll describe the
application's COBOL program.

Specifications for the display invoice details application (version 1)
As you should recall from chapter 4, the application programs in this
book all use the data structure shown in figure 8-7. The data base is
accessed through a secondary index built over the receivable segment of
the customer data base. Subordinate to the receivable segment can be
multiple occurrences of the payment and adjustment segment types.

The application in this section lets the user display data from all
three of the shaded segment types in figure 8-7, as the three screen
layouts in figure 8-8 indicate. The first screen, in part 1 of the figure,
displays data extracted from an occurrence of the receivable segment
type, much like the simpler version of the display invoice application
you've already seen. However, notice the operator instructions at the
bottom of the screen. The user can specify what the application should
do by pressing an enabled PF key.

If the user presses PF3, the application ends and returns to the
menu. However, if the user selects one of the other enabled PF keys,
particular invoice information is displayed: PF5 displays the invoice
summary, PF7 displays payments applied to the specified invoice, and
PF9 displays financial adjustments made to the invoice. Although the

```
*-------------------------------------------------------------------------------------*
[ DISPLAY INVOICE DETAILS -- SUMMARY                              DATE:  ::::::::  [
[                                                                                  [
[ INVOICE:  _____   DATE:  ::::::::       SUBTOTAL:     ::::::::::                 [
[                                          DISCOUNT:     ::::::::::                 [
[                                          SALES TAX:    ::::::::::                 [
[                                          FREIGHT:      ::::::::::                 [
[                                                        ----------                [
[                                          BILLING:      ::::::::::                 [
[                                          PMTS/ADJS:    ::::::::::                 [
[                                                        ----------                [
[                                          DUE:          ::::::::::                 [
[                                                                                  [
[                                                                                  [
[                                                                                  [
[                                                                                  [
[                                                                                  [
[                                                                                  [
[                                                                                  [
[ PF3=MENU; PF5=SUMMARY; PF7=PAYMENTS; PF9=ADJUSTMENTS                             [
[ :::::::::::::::::::::::::::::::::::::::::::::::::::::::::::::::::::::::::::::::::::[
[                                                                                  [
*-------------------------------------------------------------------------------------*
```

Figure 8-8   Screen layouts for the display invoice details application, version 1 (part 1 of 3)

```
*-------------------------------------------------------------------------------------*
[ DISPLAY INVOICE DETAILS -- PAYMENTS                             DATE:  ::::::::  [
[                                                                                  [
[ INVOICE:  _____    DATE:  ::::::::      CURRENT BALANCE DUE: ::::::::::          [
[                                                                                  [
[ DATE       BANK NUMBER                   CHECK NUMBER          AMOUNT            [
[ ::::::::   ::::::::::::::::::::::::::::    :::::::::::::::::     ::::::::::         [
[ ::::::::   ::::::::::::::::::::::::::::    :::::::::::::::::     ::::::::::         [
[ ::::::::   ::::::::::::::::::::::::::::    :::::::::::::::::     ::::::::::         [
[ ::::::::   ::::::::::::::::::::::::::::    :::::::::::::::::     ::::::::::         [
[ ::::::::   ::::::::::::::::::::::::::::    :::::::::::::::::     ::::::::::         [
[ ::::::::   ::::::::::::::::::::::::::::    :::::::::::::::::     ::::::::::         [
[ ::::::::   ::::::::::::::::::::::::::::    :::::::::::::::::     ::::::::::         [
[ ::::::::   ::::::::::::::::::::::::::::    :::::::::::::::::     ::::::::::         [
[ ::::::::   ::::::::::::::::::::::::::::    :::::::::::::::::     ::::::::::         [
[ ::::::::   ::::::::::::::::::::::::::::    :::::::::::::::::     ::::::::::         [
[ ::::::::   ::::::::::::::::::::::::::::    :::::::::::::::::     ::::::::::         [
[ ::::::::::::::::::::::::::                                      ::::::::::         [
[                                                               ----------         [
[                                                                ::::::::::         [
[                                                                                  [
[ PF3=MENU; PF5=SUMMARY; PF7=PAYMENTS; PF9=ADJUSTMENTS                             [
[ :::::::::::::::::::::::::::::::::::::::::::::::::::::::::::::::::::::::::::::::::::[
[                                                                                  [
*-------------------------------------------------------------------------------------*
```

Figure 8-8   Screen layouts for the display invoice details application, version 1 (part 2 of 3)

```
*-------------------------------------------------------------------------------*
[ DISPLAY INVOICE DETAILS -- ADJUSTMENTS                          DATE: ::::::::: [
[                                                                                [
[ INVOICE:  _____   DATE: ::::::::   CURRENT BALANCE DUE: :::::::::              [
[                                                                                [
[ DATE       TYPE   NUMBER    AMOUNT                                             [
[ :::::::::    :    ::::::  :::::::::                                             [
[ :::::::::    :    ::::::  :::::::::                                             [
[ :::::::::    :    ::::::  :::::::::                                             [
[ :::::::::    :    ::::::  :::::::::                                             [
[ :::::::::    :    ::::::  :::::::::                                             [
[ :::::::::    :    ::::::  :::::::::                                             [
[ :::::::::    :    ::::::  :::::::::                                             [
[ :::::::::    :    ::::::  :::::::::                                             [
[ :::::::::    :    ::::::  :::::::::                                             [
[ :::::::::    :    ::::::  :::::::::                                             [
[ :::::::::    :    ::::::  :::::::::                                             [
[ :::::::::::::::::::::     :::::::::                                             [
[                          ---------                                             [
[                          :::::::::                                             [
[                                                                                [
[ PF3=MENU; PF5=SUMMARY; PF7=PAYMENTS; PF9=ADJUSTMENTS                           [
[ :::::::::::::::::::::::::::::::::::::::::::::::::::::::::::::::::::::::::::::::::[
[                                                                                [
*-------------------------------------------------------------------------------*
```

Figure 8-8   Screen layouts for the display invoice details application, version 1 (part 3 of 3)

user should select one of the specified PF keys, you can't depend on that. As a result, the application will treat the enter key and any of the other PF keys as if the user had selected PF5.

The application is entered through the invoice summary screen (part 1 of figure 8-8). Here, only one field on the screen is unprotected: invoice number. (You can tell that the field is unprotected on the MFS-produced screen images because it's indicated with underscores; in contrast, protected fields are indicated with colons.) The operator keys in the invoice number, then presses one of the enabled PF keys.

PF5 causes the program to perform the same processing as the simpler version of the display invoice application. Essentially, the program retrieves the specified receivable segment from the customer data base and displays its contents on the screen. PF7 and PF9, on the other hand, cause more extensive processing to be done.

PF7 requests a display of payments applied to the specified invoice. For this function, the program also retrieves the specified receivable segment with a GU call, but then it retrieves all of its subordinate payment segments using a series of GNP calls. As you can see in part 2 of the figure, a different screen format is used to display payment data.

The top of the screen contains a descriptive heading, followed by a redisplay of critical information about the invoice for which payment data is being presented: invoice number, invoice date, and current balance due. Next, the screen layout includes one line for each of the first 12 payment segments subordinate to the specified invoice. The display shows the payment date, the bank and check numbers associated with the payment, and, of course, the payment amount. At the bottom of the amount column, the application displays the total of all payments received.

In almost all cases, the screen in part 2 of figure 8-8 allows enough space for all of an invoice's payments. But although it's unlikely an invoice would have more than 12 payments, it's not impossible. As a result, the application has to be able to provide for this special case.

Although there are a variety of ways you can handle this special case, I selected a simple approach for this example. After the 12 detail lines the screen provides, I allowed a 13th in which a simple message is displayed that shows the number of payments over 12 received and, in the amount column, their total.

For example, if 15 payment segments are retrieved for the specified invoice, the first 12 are displayed. Then, the application displays the message

    3 OTHERS TOTALING

in the field beginning in column 2 of line 18. And in column 55 of the same line, the application displays the payment total for payments 13, 14, and 15.

The third screen of the application displays adjustment transactions. It, like the payments screen, displays details for up to 12 adjustment segments. And if more than 12 adjustment segments are present for the specified invoice, it summarizes them in a 13th line.

On each of the three screens, the invoice number field is unprotected, and its MDT is on. As a result, the data in that field is transmitted back to the application program. The program always receives an invoice number as part of its input message, regardless of the screen the message came from and whether or not the operator keyed in a new value.

Format sets for the the display invoice details application (version 1)
Figure 8-9 presents the MFS code for the three format sets required for this application. As you can see, these format sets are long. However, don't let that intimidate you. You're already familiar with the first one from the simpler display invoice application you've already seen. And the other two are the payment detail and adjustment detail format sets, which are similar.

In addition, the key points that I want you to learn from this example are limited. Specifically, I want to stress how to use PF keys to generate messages that control screen flows. In addition, two of the format sets illustrate repetitive processing with the DO and ENDDO statements. I've shaded the elements I particularly want you to notice in the format sets.

I started this block of MFS code with a sort of "table of contents" that lists the names I used for the parts of the format sets that follow and their functions. It's not necessary to use comments like this, but they can help others understand your code.

If you take a moment to review this part of the listing, you'll see that I used a simple naming convention for this application. All block names start with the characters DID, which stands for Display Invoice Details. The fourth character of each name identifies the screen to which it's related: S for the summary screen, P for the payment detail screen, and A for the adjustment detail screen. The last characters of the name identify a segment of code as a device format definition (DF), an input descriptor (I), or an output descriptor (O).

In the DEV statement in each of the three format sets, I coded the same PFK parameter:

```
PFK=(PFKIN,
3='/FOR MENUO',
5='DID      05',
7='DID      07',
9='DID      09')
```

And, in each MID, the first MFLD statement is

```
MFLD   PFKIN,
       LTH=10,
       FILL=NULL
```

As a result, when the operator presses one of the enabled PF keys, the specified literal is stored in the first 10 bytes of the input message. If the user presses PF3, that value is

```
/FOR MENUO
```

which is an IMS command that causes the terminal screen to be reformatted with the menu display; this is how the user exits the application. Note that this value is handled completely within MFS. It's not passed to the application program, so the program doesn't have to provide for it.

On the other hand, if the user presses PF5, PF7, or PF9, the input message begins with the characters DID followed by five blanks, then by 05, 07, or 09. The result is a transaction that will invoke the DID program. The data in positions 9 and 10 of the PF key literals is passed

```
 1            PRINT ON,NOGEN
 2   *****************************************************************
 3            TITLE 'FORMAT SET FOR APPLICATION DID'
 4   *****************************************************************
 5   *        NAME            FUNCTION                               *
 6   *        ----------      -------------------------------------  *
 7   *        DIDSDF          SUMMARY SCREEN DEVICE FORMAT           *
 8   *        DIDPDF          PAYMENTS SCREEN DEVICE FORMAT          *
 9   *        DIDADF          ADJUSTMENTS SCREEN DEVICE FORMAT       *
10   *        DIDSI           SUMMARY SCREEN MID                     *
11   *        DIDPI           PAYMENTS SCREEN MID                    *
12   *        DIDAI           ADJUSTMENTS SCREEN MID                 *
13   *        DIDSO           SUMMARY SCREEN MOD                     *
14   *        DIDPO           PAYMENTS SCREEN MOD                    *
15   *        DIDAO           ADJUSTMENTS SCREEN MOD                 *
16   *                                                               *
17   *****************************************************************
18            EJECT
```

Figure 8-9   Format sets for the display invoice details application, version 1 (part 1 of 10)

to the application program. The program evaluates that data to determine which of the three screens it should format and display.

I specified

```
FILL=NULL
```

on the MFLD statement for the PF key data so if the terminal user presses enter or one of the PF keys that is not enabled, the field will remain empty. In contrast, if I hadn't coded the FILL parameter, the default fill character (the space) would have been used. Then, when the operator pressed enter or a PF key other than 3, 5, 7, or 9, the first ten bytes of the input message would have contained spaces, and that's not a valid message format. (Remember, an input message must begin with a transaction code, an LTERM name, or an IMS command code.)

To make sure the first ten bytes of the message contain an acceptable value even if the user does accidentally press a "bad" key, I coded

```
MFLD    'DID
        LTH=10
```

right after the PF key message field. Then, if the user presses a "bad" key, the ten bytes left empty because of the FILL=NULL parameter are formatted with the correct transaction code in positions 1-8, followed by two spaces. On the other hand, if the user presses an acceptable PF key, this ten-byte field follows the ten-byte value from PFKIN. As you'll see in a moment, that means that the application program will have to deal with input messages in two formats.

```
19 **************************************************************
20 DIDSDF    FMT
21          DEV    TYPE=(3270,2),                                    X
                   FEAT=IGNORE,                                      X
                   SYSMSG=ERRMSG,                                    X
                   DSCA=X'00A0',                                     X
                   PFK=(PFKIN,                                       X
                   3='/FOR MENU0',                                  X
                   5='DID      05',                                  X
                   7='DID      07',                                  X
                   9='DID      09')
22          DIV    TYPE=INOUT
23          DPAGE  CURSOR=((3,12)),                                  X
                   FILL=PT
24          DFLD   'DISPLAY INVOICE DETAILS -- SUMMARY',             X
                   POS=(1,2),                                        X
                   ATTR=(PROT,ALPHA,HI,NOMOD)
25          DFLD   'DATE:',                                          X
                   POS=(1,65),                                       X
                   ATTR=(PROT,ALPHA,HI,NOMOD)
26 CURDATE  DFLD   POS=(1,72),                                       X
                   LTH=8,                                            X
                   ATTR=(PROT,ALPHA,HI,NOMOD)
27          DFLD   'INVOICE:',                                       X
                   POS=(3,2),                                        X
                   ATTR=(PROT,ALPHA,HI,NOMOD)
28 INVNO    DFLD   POS=(3,12),                                       X
                   LTH=6,                                            X
                   ATTR=(NOPROT,NUM,NORM,MOD)
29          DFLD   'DATE:',                                          X
                   POS=(3,21),                                       X
                   ATTR=(PROT,ALPHA,HI,NOMOD)
30 INVDATE  DFLD   POS=(3,28),                                       X
                   LTH=8,                                            X
                   ATTR=(PROT,ALPHA,NORM,NOMOD)
31          DFLD   'SUBTOTAL:',                                      X
                   POS=(3,41),                                       X
                   ATTR=(PROT,ALPHA,HI,NOMOD)
32 SUBTOTAL DFLD   POS=(3,55),                                       X
                   LTH=9,                                            X
                   ATTR=(PROT,ALPHA,NORM,NOMCD)
33          DFLD   'DISCOUNT:',                                      X
                   POS=(4,41),                                       X
                   ATTR=(PROT,ALPHA,HI,NOMOD)
34 DISCOUNT DFLD   POS=(4,55),                                       X
                   LTH=9,                                            X
                   ATTR=(PROT,ALPHA,NORM,NOMOD)
35          DFLD   'SALES TAX:',                                     X
```

Figure 8-9   Format sets for the display invoice details application, version 1 (part 2 of 10)

Next, each input message descriptor also contains a six-byte field associated with the device field INVNO. In each case, it contains the number of the invoice for which data should be displayed.

```
                              POS=(5,41),                                        X
                              ATTR=(PROT,ALPHA,HI,NOMOD)
36 SALESTAX DFLD              POS=(5,55),                                        X
                              LTH=9,                                             X
                              ATTR=(PROT,ALPHA,NORM,NOMOD)
37          DFLD              'FREIGHT:',                                        X
                              POS=(6,41),                                        X
                              ATTR=(PROT,ALPHA,HI,NOMOD)
38 FREIGHT  DFLD              POS=(6,55),                                        X
                              LTH=9,                                             X
                              ATTR=(PROT,ALPHA,NORM,NOMCD)
39          DFLD              '----------',                                      X
                              POS=(7,55),                                        X
                              ATTR=(PROT,ALPHA,HI,NOMOD)
40          DFLD              'BILLING:',                                        X
                              POS=(8,41),                                        X
                              ATTR=(PROT,ALPHA,HI,NOMOD)
41 BILLING  DFLD              POS=(8,55),                                        X
                              LTH=9,                                             X
                              ATTR=(PROT,ALPHA,NORM,NOMCD)
42          DFLD              'PMTS/ADJS:',                                      X.
                              POS=(9,41),                                        X
                              ATTR=(PROT,ALPHA,HI,NOMOD)
43 PMTSADJS DFLD              POS=(9,55),                                        X
                              LTH=9,                                             X
                              ATTR=(PROT,ALPHA,NORM,NOMOD)
44          DFLD              '----------',                                      X
                              POS=(10,55),                                       X
                              ATTR=(PROT,ALPHA,HI,NOMOD)
45          DFLD              'DUE:',                                            X
                              POS=(11,41),                                       X
                              ATTR=(PROT,ALPHA,HI,NOMOD)
46 DUE      DFLD              POS=(11,55),                                       X
                              LTH=9,                                             X
                              ATTR=(PROT,ALPHA,NORM,NOMOD)
47          DFLD              'PF3=MENU; PF5=SUMMARY; PF7=PAYMENTS; PF9=ADJUSTMENTS', X
                              POS=(22,2),                                        X
                              ATTR=(PROT,ALPHA,HI,NOMOD)
48 ERRMSG   DFLD              POS=(23,2),                                        X
                              LTH=79,                                            X
                              ATTR=(PROT,ALPHA,NORM,NOMOD)
49          FMTEND
50 **********************************************************************
51          EJECT
```

Figure 8-9   Format sets for the display invoice details application, version 1 (part 3 of 10)

Before I present the application program, I want to describe another MFS feature figure 8-9 illustrates. The device format and message descriptor definitions for both the payment detail and the adjustment detail screens show how you can use the DO and ENDDO statements to generate similar fields repeatedly.

```
52 *************************************************************************
53 DIDPDF    FMT
54            DEV    TYPE=(3270,2),                                          X
                     FEAT=IGNORE,                                            X
                     SYSMSG=ERRMSG,                                          X
                     DSCA=X'00A0',                                          X
                     PFK=(PFKIN,                                             X
                     3='/FOR MENU0',                                         X
                     5='DID      05',                                        X
                     7='DID      07',                                        X
                     9='DID      09')
55            DIV    TYPE=INOUT
56            DPAGE  CURSOR=((3,12)),                                        X
                     FILL=PT
57            DFLD   'DISPLAY INVOICE DETAILS -- PAYMENTS',                 X
                     POS=(1,2),                                             X
                     ATTR=(PROT,ALPHA,HI,NOMOD)
58            DFLD   'DATE:',                                                X
                     POS=(1,65),                                            X
                     ATTR=(PROT,ALPHA,HI,NOMOD)
59 CURDATE    DFLD   POS=(1,72),                                            X
                     LTH=8,                                                 X
                     ATTR=(PROT,ALPHA,HI,NOMOD)
60            DFLD   'INVOICE:',                                            X
                     POS=(3,2),                                             X
                     ATTR=(PROT,ALPHA,HI,NOMOD)
61 INVNO      DFLD   POS=(3,12),                                           X
                     LTH=6,                                                 X
                     ATTR=(NOPROT,ALPHA,NORM,MOD)
62            DFLD   'DATE:',                                                X
                     POS=(3,21),                                            X
                     ATTR=(PROT,ALPHA,HI,NOMOD)
63 INVDATE    DFLD   POS=(3,28),                                           X
                     LTH=8,                                                 X
                     ATTR=(PROT,ALPHA,NORM,NOMOD)
64            DFLD   'CURRENT BALANCE DUE:',                                X
                     POS=(3,41),                                            X
                     ATTR=(PROT,ALPHA,HI,NOMOD)
65 DUE        DFLD   POS=(3,62),                                           X
                     LTH=9,                                                 X
                     ATTR=(PROT,ALPHA,NORM,NOMOD)
66            DFLD   'DATE      BANK NUMBER',                               X
                     POS=(5,2),                                             X
                     ATTR=(PROT,ALPHA,HI,NOMOD)
67            DFLD   'CHECK NUMBER          AMOUNT',                        X
                     POS=(5,38),                                            X
                     ATTR=(PROT,ALPHA,HI,NOMOD)
68            DO     12
```

Figure 8-9   Format sets for the display invoice details application, version 1 (part 4 of 10)

```
 69 PDATE     DFLD    POS=(6,2),                                              X
                      LTH=8,                                                  X
                      ATTR=(PROT,ALPHA,NORM,NOMOD)
 70 PBNKNO    DFLD    POS=(6,12),                                             X
                      LTH=25,                                                 X
                      ATTR=(PROT,ALPHA,NORM,NOMOD)
 71 PCHKNO    DFLD    POS=(6,38),                                             X
                      LTH=16,                                                 X
                      ATTR=(PROT,ALPHA,NORM,NOMOD)
 72 PAMT      DFLD    POS=(6,55),                                             X
                      LTH=9,                                                  X
                      ATTR=(PROT,ALPHA,NORM,NOMOD)
 73           ENDDO
122 OV12MSG   DFLD    POS=(18,2),                                             X
                      LTH=19,                                                 X
                      ATTR=(PROT,ALPHA,NORM,NOMOD)
123 OV12TOT   DFLD    POS=(18,55),                                            X
                      LTH=9,                                                  X
                      ATTR=(PROT,ALPHA,NORM,NOMOD)
124           DFLD    '----------',                                           X
                      POS=(19,55),                                            X
                      ATTR=(PROT,ALPHA,HI,NOMOD)
125 TOTALPMT  DFLD    POS=(20,55),                                            X
                      LTH=9,                                                  X
                      ATTR=(PROT,ALPHA,NORM,NOMOD)
126           DFLD    'PF3=MENU; PF5=SUMMARY; PF7=PAYMENTS; PF9=ADJUSTMENTS', X
                      POS=(22,2),                                             X
                      ATTR=(PROT,ALPHA,HI,NOMOD)
127 ERRMSG    DFLD    POS=(23,2),                                             X
                      LTH=79,                                                 X
                      ATTR=(PROT,ALPHA,NORM,NOMOD)
128           FMTEND
129 ***********************************************************************
130           EJECT
```

Figure 8-9   Format sets for the display invoice details application, version 1 (part 5 of 10)

To understand, consider the payment detail screen (parts 4 and 5 of figure 8-9). I coded definitions for the device fields PDATE, PBNKNO, PCHKNO, and PAMT between DO and ENDDO statements (statements 68 through 73). Because I specified 12 on the DO statement, those four fields are repeated 12 times in the same column positions, but on different lines.

```
131 ********************************************************************
132 DIDADF   FMT
133          DEV    TYPE=(3270,2),                                        X
                    FEAT=IGNORE,                                          X
                    SYSMSG=ERRMSG,                                        X
                    DSCA=X'00A0',                                         X
                    PFK=(PFKIN,                                           X
                    3='/FOR MENU0',                                       X
                    5='DID      05',                                      X
                    7='DID      07',                                      X
                    9='DID      09')
134          DIV'   TYPE=INOUT
135          DPAGE  CURSOR=((3,12)),                                      X
                    FILL=PT
136          DFLD   'DISPLAY INVOICE DETAILS -- ADJUSTMENTS',            X
                    POS=(1,2),                                            X
                    ATTR=(PROT,ALPHA,HI,NOMOD)
137          DFLD   'DATE:',                                              X
                    POS=(1,65),                                           X
                    ATTR=(PROT,ALPHA,HI,NOMOD)
138 CURDATE  DFLD   POS=(1,72),                                           X
                    LTH=8,                                                X
                    ATTR=(PROT,ALPHA,HI,NOMOD)
139          DFLD   'INVOICE:',                                           X
                    POS=(3,2),                                            X
                    ATTR=(PROT,ALPHA,HI,NOMOD)
140 INVNO    DFLD   POS=(3,12),                                           X
                    LTH=6,                                                X
                    ATTR=(NOPROT,ALPHA,NORM,MOD)
141          DFLD   'DATE:',                                              X
                    POS=(3,21),                                           X
                    ATTR=(PROT,ALPHA,HI,NOMOD)
142 INVDATE  DFLD   POS=(3,28),                                           X
                    LTH=8,                                                X
                    ATTR=(PROT,ALPHA,NORM,NOMOD)
143          DFLD   'CURRENT BALANCE DUE:',                               X
                    POS=(3,41),                                           X
                    ATTR=(PROT,ALPHA,HI,NOMOD)
144 DUE      DFLD   POS=(3,62),                                           X
                    LTH=9,                                                X
                    ATTR=(PROT,ALPHA,NORM,NOMOD)
145          DFLD   'DATE      TYPE   NUMBER      AMOUNT',                X
                    POS=(5,2),                                            X
                    ATTR=(PROT,ALPHA,HI,NOMOD)
146          DO     12
147 ADATE    DFLD   POS=(6,2),                                            X
                    LTH=8,                                                X
                    ATTR=(PROT,ALPHA,NORM,NOMOD)
```

Figure 8-9   Format sets for the display invoice details application, version 1 (part 6 of 10)

```
148 ATYPE     DFLD    POS=(6,14),                                                    X
                      LTH=1,                                                         X
                      ATTR=(PROT,ALPHA,NORM,NOMOD)
149 ANO       DFLD    POS=(6,18),                                                    X
                      LTH=6,                                                         X
                      ATTR=(PROT,ALPHA,NORM,NOMCD)
150 AAMT      DFLD    POS=(6,26),                                                    X
                      LTH=9,                                                         X
                      ATTR=(PROT,ALPHA,NORM,NOMOD)
151           ENDDO
200 OV12MSG   DFLD    POS=(18,2),                                                    X
                      LTH=19,                                                        X
                      ATTR=(PROT,ALPHA,NORM,NOMOD)
201 OV12TOT   DFLD    POS=(18,26),                                                   X
                      LTH=9,                                                         X
                      ATTR=(PROT,ALPHA,NORM,NOMCD)
202           DFLD    '----------',                                                 X
                      POS=(19,26),                                                   X
                      ATTR=(PROT,ALPHA,HI,NOMOD)
203 TOTALADJ  DFLD    POS=(20,26),                                                   X
                      LTH=9,                                                         X
                      ATTR=(PROT,ALPHA,NORM,NOMOD)
204           DFLD    'PF3=MENU; PF5=SUMMARY; PF7=PAYMENTS; PF9=ADJUSTMENTS',        X
                      POS=(22,2),                                                    X
                      ATTR=(PROT,ALPHA,HI,NOMOD)
205 ERRMSG    DFLD    POS=(23,2),                                                    X
                      LTH=79,                                                        X
                      ATTR=(PROT,ALPHA,NORM,NOMOD)
206           FMTEND
207 *************************************************************************
208           EJECT
```

Figure 8-9   Format sets for the display invoice details application, version 1 (part 7 of 10)

```
209  *************************************************************************
210  DIDSI    MSG     TYPE=INPUT,                                              X
                      SOR=(DIDSDF,IGNORE),                                     X
                      NXT=DIDSO
211           SEG
212           MFLD    PFKIN,                                                   X
                      LTH=10,                                                  X
                      FILL=NULL
213           MFLD    'DID        ',                                           X
                      LTH=10
214           MFLD    INVNO,                                                   X
                      LTH=6
215           MSGEND
216  *************************************************************************
217  DIDSO    MSG     TYPE=OUTPUT,                                             X
                      SOR=(DIDSDF,IGNORE),                                     X
                      NXT=DIDSI
218           SEG
219           MFLD    (CURDATE,DATE2)
220           MFLD    INVNO,                                                   X
                      LTH=6
221           MFLD    INVDATE,                                                 X
                      LTH=8
222           MFLD    SUBTOTAL,                                                X
                      LTH=9
223           MFLD    DISCOUNT,                                                X
                      LTH=9
224           MFLD    SALESTAX,                                                X
                      LTH=9
225           MFLD    FREIGHT,                                                 X
                      LTH=9
226           MFLD    BILLING,                                                 X
                      LTH=9
227           MFLD    PMTSADJS,                                                X
                      LTH=9
228           MFLD    DUE,                                                     X
                      LTH=9
229           MFLD    ERRMSG,                                                  X
                      LTH=79
230           MSGEND
231  *************************************************************************
232           EJECT
```

Figure 8-9   Format sets for the display invoice details application, version 1 (part 8 of 10)

```
233 ***********************************************************************
234 DIDPI     MSG     TYPE=INPUT,                                         X
                      SOR=(DIDPDF,IGNORE),                               X
                      NXT=DIDPO
235           SEG
236           MFLD    PFKIN,                                             X
                      LTH=10,                                            X
                      FILL=NULL
237           MFLD    'DID                                               X
                      LTH=10
238           MFLD    INVNO,                                             X
                      LTH=6
239           MSGEND
240 ***********************************************************************
241 DIDPO     MSG     TYPE=OUTPUT,                                       X
                      SOR=(DIDPDF,IGNORE),                              X
                      NXT=DIDPI
242           SEG
243           MFLD    (CURDATE,DATE2)
244           MFLD    INVNO,                                             X
                      LTH=6
245           MFLD    INVDATE,                                           X
                      LTH=8
246           MFLD    DUE,                                               X
                      LTH=9
247           DO      12
248           MFLD    PDATE,                                             X
                      LTH=8
249           MFLD    PBNKNO,                                            X
                      LTH=25
250           MFLD    PCHKNO,                                            X
                      LTH=16
251           MFLD    PAMT,                                              X
                      LTH=9
252           ENDDO
301           MFLD    OV12MSG,                                           X
                      LTH=19
302           MFLD    OV12TOT,                                           X
                      LTH=9
303           MFLD    TOTALPMT,                                          X
                      LTH=9
304           MFLD    ERRMSG,                                            X
                      LTH=79
305           MSGEND
306 ***********************************************************************
307           EJECT
```

Figure 8-9   Format sets for the display invoice details application, version 1 (part 9 of 10)

```
308 ***************************************************************
309 DIDAI     MSG     TYPE=INPUT,                               X
                      SOR=(DIDADF,IGNORE),                      X
                      NXT=DIDAO
310           SEG
311           MFLD    PFKIN,                                    X
                      LTH=10,                                   X
                      FILL=NULL
312           MFLD    'DID                                      X
                      LTH=10
313           MFLD    INVNO,                                    X
                      LTH=6
314           MSGEND
315 ***************************************************************
316 DIDAO     MSG     TYPE=OUTPUT,                              X
                      SOR=(DIDADF,IGNORE),                      X
                      NXT=DIDAI
317           SEG
318           MFLD    (CURDATE,DATE2)
319           MFLD    INVNO,                                    X
                      LTH=6
320           MFLD    INVDATE,                                  X
                      LTH=8
321           MFLD    DUE,                                      X
                      LTH=9
322           DO      12
323           MFLD    ADATE,                                    X
                      LTH=8
324           MFLD    ATYPE,                                    X
                      LTH=1
325           MFLD    ANO,                                      X
                      LTH=6
326           MFLD    AAMT,                                     X
                      LTH=9
327           ENDDO
376           MFLD    OV12MSG,                                  X
                      LTH=19
377           MFLD    OV12TOT,                                  X
                      LTH=9
378           MFLD    TOTALADJ,                                 X
                      LTH=9
379           MFLD    ERRMSG,                                   X
                      LTH=79
380           MSGEND
381 ***************************************************************
382           END
```

Figure 8-9   Format sets for the display invoice details application, version 1 (part 10 of 10)

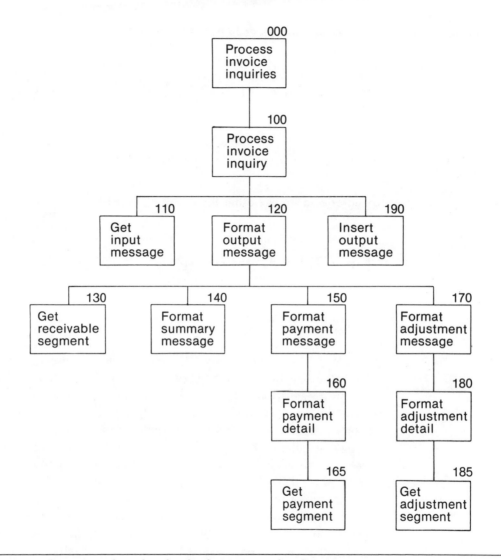

Figure 8-10   Structure chart for the display invoice details program, version 1

The program for the display invoice details application (version 1)
Figure 8-10 presents the structure chart for this application's program.
The structure chart is much like those for the programs you're already
familiar with: the program is driven by the presence of input messages
on its input queue. It repeatedly retrieves an input message (module
110), formats an appropriate output message (module 120), and inserts
an output message (module 190).

Input message format when the operator presses PF5, PF7, or PF9

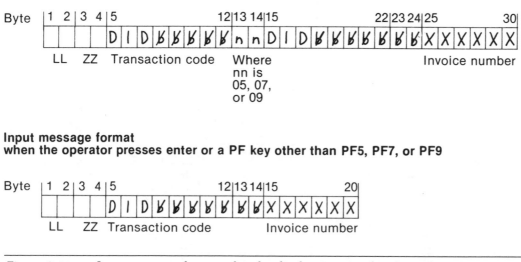

**Input message format
when the operator presses enter or a PF key other than PF5, PF7, or PF9**

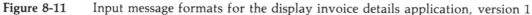

Figure 8-11   Input message formats for the display invoice details application, version 1

After the program has retrieved the input message, it must determine whether the operator pressed a valid PF key. Figure 8-11 shows the two message formats the program must be able to handle. The program evaluates the data in bytes 13 and 14; if that field contains spaces, the program assumes the summary screen should be displayed and gets the invoice number from the six-byte field that begins in position 15. Otherwise, the program uses the data in bytes 13 and 14 to determine which screen should be displayed and gets the invoice number from the field that begins in position 25.

The subsequent processing the program does for an input message depends on which of the three displays the operator requested. In any case, the program retrieves the specified receivable segment from the customer data base (module 130). Then, the program performs module 140 (to format a summary screen), module 150 (to format a payment detail screen), or module 170 (to format an adjustment detail screen). If either of the detail displays is requested, the program has to do additional formatting and data base retrieval (represented on the chart by modules 160, 165, 180, and 185).

Now, take a look at the source code in figure 8-12. I've shaded the portions I want you to pay attention to. First, in the input message description, I coded a flag field named IM-PFKEY-SELECTION. Subordinate to it, I coded four condition names; the condition names I used and the values I related to them should be obvious. In addition, I defined the data that follows the flag field in two ways to correspond to the message layouts in figure 8-11.

Next, notice how I coded the output segment description. All I did was provide a single field that's long enough to contain the longest output message the program will send. Depending on the function selected, the program will send one of three different output text strings, whose lengths are 156 bytes (for the summary display), 427 bytes (for the adjustment detail display), and 835 bytes (for the payment detail display). After the proper message has been formatted, the program moves it to OM-TEXT, then moves the length of the complete output message to OM-LL. The complete length includes the two-byte LL and two-byte ZZ fields, so it will be 160, 431, or 839, depending on the particular output message to be sent.

The formatting areas used by the program to prepare the output message text are next. I coded three groups of fields which correspond exactly to the output message descriptor fields I specified in the format sets. Notice in the definitions for the payment detail and adjustment detail messages that I used a table with 12 occurrences to contain detail data. These tables correspond to the message fields generated by MFS as a result of the DO and ENDDO statements I coded in the format sets. Take a moment to compare the way I defined the fields in the program with the way I defined them in the MOD specifications in figure 8-9.

The last Data Division field I want to point out is MFS-MOD-NAME. It's an eight-byte field that's specified as the fourth argument on the ISRT call that will send the output message back to the terminal. Before the ISRT call is issued, the program moves the correct MOD name for the screen to be displayed to this field. Those names are DIDSO for the summary screen, DIDPO for the payment detail screen, and DIDAO for the adjustment detail screen.

Now, consider the Procedure Division. I only need to point out three details here. First, in module 100, I coded an IF statement to evaluate and reformat the data in the input message so the statements that follow can handle all input messages in the same way.

Second, notice the last three statements in modules 140, 150, and 170. In each of these three modules, the last three statements prepare the output message segment I/O area and assign a proper value to the MOD name field.

Finally, take a look at module 190 at the end of the listing. Here, you can see that I specified the MOD name argument on the ISRT statement. By changing the value of MFS-MOD-NAME, the program controls the MODs MFS uses to format the messages the program sends.

```
       IDENTIFICATION DIVISION.
       *
       PROGRAM-ID.  DID.
       *
       ENVIRONMENT DIVISION.
       *
       DATA DIVISION.
       *
       WORKING-STORAGE SECTION.
       *
       01  SWITCHES.
       *
           05  INVOICE-FOUND-SW            PIC X         VALUE 'Y'.
               88  INVOICE-FOUND                         VALUE 'Y'.
           05  END-OF-MESSAGES-SW          PIC X         VALUE 'N'.
               88  END-OF-MESSAGES                       VALUE 'Y'.
           05  ALL-DETAILS-PROCESSED-SW    PIC X         VALUE 'N'.
               88  ALL-DETAILS-PROCESSED                 VALUE 'Y'.
       *
       01  INPUT-MESSAGE-IO-AREA.
       *
           05  IM-LL                       PIC S9(3)     COMP.
           05  IM-ZZ                       PIC S9(3)     COMP.
           05  IM-TRANSACTION-CODE         PIC X(8).
           05  IM-PFKEY-SELECTION          PIC XX.
               88  IM-DISPLAY-SUMMARY                    VALUE '05'.
               88  IM-DISPLAY-PAYMENTS                   VALUE '07'.
               88  IM-DISPLAY-ADJUSTMENTS                VALUE '09'.
               88  IM-NO-PFKEY-SELECTED                  VALUE '  '.
           05  IM-MSG-DATA.
               10  IM-MSG-DATA-SHORT.
                   15  IM-INVOICE-NO       PIC X(6).
                   15  FILLER              PIC X(10).
               10  IM-MSG-DATA-LONG        REDEFINES
                                           IM-MSG-DATA-SHORT.
                   15  FILLER              PIC X(10).
                   15  IM-INVOICE-NO-LONG  PIC X(6).
       *
       01  OUTPUT-MESSAGE-IO-AREA.
       *
           05  OM-LL                       PIC S9(3)     COMP.
           05  OM-Z1-Z2                    PIC S9(3)     COMP
                                                         VALUE ZERO.
           05  OM-TEXT                     PIC X(835).
       *
       01  OUTPUT-MESSAGE-TEXT-BLOCKS.
       *
           05  OMTB-SUMMARY-TEXT.
               10  OMTB-S-INVOICE-NO       PIC X(6).
               10  OMTB-S-INVOICE-DATE     PIC 99/99/99.
               10  OMTB-S-PROD-TOTAL       PIC Z(5).99-.
               10  OMTB-S-CASH-DISC        PIC Z(5).99-.
               10  OMTB-S-SALES-TAX        PIC Z(5).99-.
               10  OMTB-S-FREIGHT          PIC Z(5).99-.
```

Figure 8-12   Source listing for the display invoice details program, version 1 (part 1 of 8)

```
           10  OMTB-S-BILLING            PIC Z(5).99-.
           10  OMTB-S-PMTS-ADJS          PIC Z(5).99-.
           10  OMTB-S-BALANCE            PIC Z(5).99-.
           10  OMTB-S-ERROR-LINE         PIC X(79).
*
       05  OMTB-PAYMENT-TEXT.
           10  OMTB-P-INVOICE-NO         PIC X(6).
           10  OMTB-P-INVOICE-DATE       PIC 99/99/99.
           10  OMTB-P-BALANCE            PIC Z(5).99-.
           10  OMTB-P-DETAIL-LINES.
               15  OMTB-P-DETAIL-LINE    OCCURS 12 TIMES.
                   20  OMTB-P-DATE       PIC 99/99/99.
                   20  OMTB-P-BANK       PIC X(25).
                   20  OMTB-P-CHECK      PIC X(16).
                   20  OMTB-P-AMT        PIC Z(5).99-.
           10  OMTB-P-DETAIL-TABLE       REDEFINES OMTB-P-DETAIL-LINES
                                         PIC X(696).
           10  OMTB-P-OVER-12-MSG.
               15  OMTB-P-OVER-12-TITLE PIC X(19).
               15  OMTB-P-OVER-12-TOTAL PIC Z(5).99-.
           10  OMTB-P-PMT-TOTAL          PIC Z(5).99-.
           10  OMTB-P-ERROR-LINE         PIC X(79).
*
       05  OMTB-ADJUSTMENT-TEXT.
           10  OMTB-A-INVOICE-NO         PIC X(6).
           10  OMTB-A-INVOICE-DATE       PIC 99/99/99.
           10  OMTB-A-BALANCE            PIC Z(5).99-.
           10  OMTB-A-DETAIL-LINES.
               15  OMTB-A-DETAIL-LINE    OCCURS 12 TIMES.
                   20  OMTB-A-DATE       PIC 99/99/99.
                   20  OMTB-A-TYPE       PIC X.
                   20  OMTB-A-NO         PIC X(6).
                   20  OMTB-A-AMT        PIC Z(5).99-.
           10  OMTB-A-DETAIL-TABLE       REDEFINES OMTB-A-DETAIL-LINES
                                         PIC X(288).
           10  OMTB-A-OVER-12-MSG.
               15  OMTB-A-OVER-12-TITLE PIC X(19).
               15  OMTB-A-OVER-12-TOTAL PIC Z(5).99-.
           10  OMTB-A-ADJ-TOTAL          PIC Z(5).99-.
           10  OMTB-A-ERROR-LINE         PIC X(79).
*
 01  ERROR-LINE.
*
     05  FILLER                  PIC X(8)      VALUE 'INVOICE '.
     05  EL-INVOICE-NO           PIC X(6).
     05  FILLER                  PIC X(10)     VALUE ' NOT FOUND'.
     05  FILLER                  PIC X(55)     VALUE SPACE.
*
 01  OVER-12-TITLE.
*
     05  OVER-12-TITLE-COUNT     PIC ZZ9.
     05  FILLER                  PIC X(16)
                                 VALUE ' OTHERS TOTALING'.
*
```

Figure 8-12   Source listing for the display invoice details program, version 1 (part 2 of 8)

```
01    SUBSCRIPTS.
*
      05   DETAIL-COUNT             PIC S9(3)           COMP.
*
01    TOTAL-FIELDS.
*
      05   DETAIL-TOTAL-OVER-12     PIC S9(5)V99        COMP-3.
      05   DETAIL-TOTAL             PIC S9(5)V99        COMP-3.
*
01    DLI-FUNCTIONS.
*
      05   DLI-GU                   PIC X(4)       VALUE 'GU  '.
      05   DLI-GHU                  PIC X(4)       VALUE 'GHU '.
      05   DLI-GN                   PIC X(4)       VALUE 'GN  '.
      05   DLI-GHN                  PIC X(4)       VALUE 'GHN '.
      05   DLI-GNP                  PIC X(4)       VALUE 'GNP '.
      05   DLI-GHNP                 PIC X(4)       VALUE 'GHNP'.
      05   DLI-ISRT                 PIC X(4)       VALUE 'ISRT'.
      05   DLI-DLET                 PIC X(4)       VALUE 'DLET'.
      05   DLI-REPL                 PIC X(4)       VALUE 'REPL'.
      05   DLI-CHKP                 PIC X(4)       VALUE 'CHKP'.
      05   DLI-XRST                 PIC X(4)       VALUE 'XRST'.
      05   DLI-PCB                  PIC X(4)       VALUE 'PCB '.
*
01    MFS-FIELDS.
*
      05   MFS-MOD-NAME             PIC X(8).
*
01    RECEIVABLE-SEGMENT.
*
      05   RS-INVOICE-NUMBER        PIC X(6).
      05   RS-INVOICE-DATE          PIC X(6).
      05   RS-PO-NUMBER             PIC X(25).
      05   RS-PRODUCT-TOTAL         PIC S9(5)V99        COMP-3.
      05   RS-CASH-DISCOUNT         PIC S9(5)V99        COMP-3.
      05   RS-SALES-TAX             PIC S9(5)V99        COMP-3.
      05   RS-FREIGHT               PIC S9(5)V99        COMP-3.
      05   RS-BALANCE-DUE           PIC S9(5)V99        COMP-3.
*
01    PAYMENT-SEGMENT.
*
      05   PS-CHECK-NUMBER          PIC X(16).
      05   PS-BANK-NUMBER           PIC X(25).
      05   PS-PAYMENT-DATE          PIC X(6).
      05   PS-PAYMENT-AMOUNT        PIC S9(5)V99        COMP-3.
*
01    ADJUSTMENT-SEGMENT.
*
      05   AS-REFERENCE-NUMBER      PIC X(6).
      05   AS-ADJUSTMENT-DATE       PIC X(6).
      05   AS-ADJUSTMENT-TYPE       PIC X.
      05   AS-ADJUSTMENT-AMOUNT     PIC S9(5)V99        COMP-3.
*
```

Figure 8-12   Source listing for the display invoice details program, version 1 (part 3 of 8)

```
01   INVOICE-NO-SSA.
*
     05   FILLER                    PIC X(9)      VALUE 'CRRECSEG('.
     05   FILLER                    PIC X(10)     VALUE 'CRRECXNO ='.
     05   INVOICE-NO-SSA-VALUE      PIC X(6).
     05   FILLER                    PIC X         VALUE ')'.
*
 01   UNQUALIFIED-SSA.
*
     05   UNQUAL-SSA-SEGMENT-NAME PIC X(8).
     05   FILLER                    PIC X         VALUE SPACE.
*
 LINKAGE SECTION.
*
 01   IO-PCB-MASK.
*
     05   IO-PCB-LOGICAL-TERMINAL PIC X(8).
     05   FILLER                    PIC XX.
     05   IO-PCB-STATUS-CODE        PIC XX.
     05   IO-PCB-DATE               PIC S9(7)     COMP-3.
     05   IO-PCB-TIME               PIC S9(6)V9   COMP-3.
     05   IO-PCB-MSG-SEQ-NUMBER     PIC S9(5)     COMP.
     05   IO-PCB-MOD-NAME           PIC X(8).
     05   IO-PCB-USER-ID            PIC X(8).
*
 01   CR-PCB-MASK.
*
     05   CR-PCB-DBD-NAME           PIC X(8).
     05   CR-PCB-SEGMENT-LEVEL      PIC XX.
     05   CR-PCB-STATUS-CODE        PIC XX.
     05   CR-PCB-PROC-OPTIONS       PIC X(4).
     05   FILLER                    PIC S9(5)     COMP.
     05   CR-PCB-SEGMENT-NAME       PIC X(8).
     05   CR-PCB-KEY-LENGTH         PIC S9(5)     COMP.
     05   CR-PCB-NUMB-SENS-SEGS     PIC S9(5)     COMP.
     05   CR-PCB-KEY                PIC X(22).
*
 PROCEDURE DIVISION.
*
     ENTRY 'DLITCBL' USING IO-PCB-MASK
                           CR-PCB-MASK.
*
 000-PROCESS-INVOICE-INQUIRIES.
*
     PERFORM 100-PROCESS-INVOICE-INQUIRY
         UNTIL END-OF-MESSAGES.
     GOBACK.
*
 100-PROCESS-INVOICE-INQUIRY.
*
     PERFORM 110-GET-INPUT-MESSAGE.
     IF NOT END-OF-MESSAGES
         IF IM-NO-PFKEY-SELECTED
             MOVE '05' TO IM-PFKEY-SELECTION
         ELSE
```

Figure 8-12   Source listing for the display invoice details program, version 1 (part 4 of 8)

```
            MOVE IM-INVOICE-NO-LONG TO IM-INVOICE-NO.
    IF NOT END-OF-MESSAGES
        PERFORM 120-FORMAT-OUTPUT-MESSAGE
        PERFORM 190-INSERT-OUTPUT-MESSAGE.
*
 110-GET-INPUT-MESSAGE.
*
    CALL 'CBLTDLI' USING DLI-GU
                         IO-PCB-MASK
                         INPUT-MESSAGE-IO-AREA.
    IF IO-PCB-STATUS-CODE = 'QC'
        MOVE 'Y' TO END-OF-MESSAGES-SW.
*
 120-FORMAT-OUTPUT-MESSAGE.
*
    MOVE 'Y'            TO INVOICE-FOUND-SW.
    MOVE IM-INVOICE-NO TO INVOICE-NO-SSA-VALUE.
    PERFORM 130-GET-RECEIVABLE-SEGMENT.
    IF NOT INVOICE-FOUND
        PERFORM 140-FORMAT-SUMMARY-MESSAGE
    ELSE
        IF IM-DISPLAY-PAYMENTS
            PERFORM 150-FORMAT-PAYMENT-MESSAGE
        ELSE
            IF IM-DISPLAY-ADJUSTMENTS
                PERFORM 170-FORMAT-ADJUSTMENT-MESSAGE
            ELSE
                PERFORM 140-FORMAT-SUMMARY-MESSAGE.
*
 130-GET-RECEIVABLE-SEGMENT.
*
    CALL 'CBLTDLI' USING DLI-GU
                         CR-PCB-MASK
                         RECEIVABLE-SEGMENT
                         INVOICE-NO-SSA.
    IF CR-PCB-STATUS-CODE NOT = SPACE
        MOVE 'N' TO INVOICE-FOUND-SW.
*
 140-FORMAT-SUMMARY-MESSAGE.
*
    MOVE IM-INVOICE-NO TO OMTB-S-INVOICE-NO.
    IF INVOICE-FOUND
        MOVE SPACE            TO OMTB-S-ERROR-LINE
        MOVE RS-INVOICE-DATE  TO OMTB-S-INVOICE-DATE
        MOVE RS-PRODUCT-TOTAL TO OMTB-S-PROD-TOTAL
        MOVE RS-CASH-DISCOUNT TO OMTB-S-CASH-DISC
        MOVE RS-SALES-TAX     TO OMTB-S-SALES-TAX
        MOVE RS-FREIGHT       TO OMTB-S-FREIGHT
        COMPUTE OMTB-S-BILLING =   RS-PRODUCT-TOTAL -
                                   RS-CASH-DISCOUNT +
                                   RS-SALES-TAX +
                                   RS-FREIGHT
```

Figure 8-12   Source listing for the display invoice details program, version 1 (part 5 of 8)

```
            COMPUTE OMTB-S-PMTS-ADJS = RS-BALANCE-DUE -
                                      (RS-PRODUCT-TOTAL -
                                      RS-CASH-DISCOUNT +
                                      RS-SALES-TAX +
                                      RS-FREIGHT)
            MOVE RS-BALANCE-DUE TO OMTB-S-BALANCE
        ELSE
            MOVE ZERO              TO OMTB-S-INVOICE-DATE
                                      OMTB-S-PROD-TOTAL
                                      OMTB-S-CASH-DISC
                                      OMTB-S-SALES-TAX
                                      OMTB-S-FREIGHT
                                      OMTB-S-BILLING
                                      OMTB-S-PMTS-ADJS
                                      OMTB-S-BALANCE
            MOVE IM-INVOICE-NO TO EL-INVOICE-NO
            MOVE ERROR-LINE       TO OMTB-S-ERROR-LINE.
        MOVE OMTB-SUMMARY-TEXT TO OM-TEXT.
        MOVE 160               TO OM-LL.
        MOVE 'DIDSO    '       TO MFS-MOD-NAME.
*
    150-FORMAT-PAYMENT-MESSAGE.
*
        MOVE IM-INVOICE-NO    TO OMTB-P-INVOICE-NO.
        MOVE SPACE            TO OMTB-P-DETAIL-TABLE
                                OMTB-P-ERROR-LINE.
        MOVE RS-INVOICE-DATE  TO OMTB-P-INVOICE-DATE.
        MOVE RS-BALANCE-DUE   TO OMTB-P-BALANCE.
        MOVE ZERO            TO DETAIL-COUNT
                                DETAIL-TOTAL
                                DETAIL-TOTAL-OVER-12.
        MOVE 'N'             TO ALL-DETAILS-PROCESSED-SW.
        MOVE 'CRPAYSEG'      TO UNQUAL-SSA-SEGMENT-NAME.
        PERFORM 160-FORMAT-PAYMENT-DETAIL
            UNTIL ALL-DETAILS-PROCESSED.
        MOVE DETAIL-TOTAL TO OMTB-P-PMT-TOTAL.
        IF DETAIL-COUNT > 12
            SUBTRACT 12 FROM DETAIL-COUNT
                GIVING OVER-12-TITLE-COUNT
            MOVE OVER-12-TITLE        TO OMTB-P-OVER-12-TITLE
            MOVE DETAIL-TOTAL-OVER-12 TO OMTB-P-OVER-12-TOTAL
        ELSE
            MOVE SPACE               TO OMTB-P-OVER-12-MSG.
        MOVE OMTB-PAYMENT-TEXT TO OM-TEXT.
        MOVE 839               TO OM-LL.
        MOVE 'DIDPO    '       TO MFS-MOD-NAME.
*
    160-FORMAT-PAYMENT-DETAIL.
*
        PERFORM 165-GET-PAYMENT-SEGMENT.
        IF NOT ALL-DETAILS-PROCESSED
            ADD 1                    TO DETAIL-COUNT
            ADD PS-PAYMENT-AMOUNT    TO DETAIL-TOTAL
```

Figure 8-12   Source listing for the display invoice details program, version 1 (part 6 of 8)

```
     IF DETAIL-COUNT < 13
         MOVE PS-CHECK-NUMBER   TO OMTB-P-CHECK (DETAIL-COUNT)
         MOVE PS-BANK-NUMBER    TO OMTB-P-BANK  (DETAIL-COUNT)
         MOVE PS-PAYMENT-DATE   TO OMTB-P-DATE  (DETAIL-COUNT)
         MOVE PS-PAYMENT-AMOUNT TO OMTB-P-AMT   (DETAIL-COUNT)
     ELSE
         ADD PS-PAYMENT-AMOUNT  TO DETAIL-TOTAL-OVER-12.
*
 165-GET-PAYMENT-SEGMENT.
*
     CALL 'CBLTDLI' USING DLI-GNP
                         CR-PCB-MASK
                         PAYMENT-SEGMENT
                         UNQUALIFIED-SSA.
     IF CR-PCB-STATUS-CODE NOT = SPACE
         MOVE 'Y' TO ALL-DETAILS-PROCESSED-SW.
*
 170-FORMAT-ADJUSTMENT-MESSAGE.
*
     MOVE IM-INVOICE-NO    TO OMTB-A-INVOICE-NO.
     MOVE SPACE            TO OMTB-A-DETAIL-TABLE
                             OMTB-A-ERROR-LINE.
     MOVE RS-INVOICE-DATE TO OMTB-A-INVOICE-DATE.
     MOVE RS-BALANCE-DUE  TO OMTB-A-BALANCE.
     MOVE ZERO            TO DETAIL-COUNT
                             DETAIL-TOTAL
                             DETAIL-TOTAL-OVER-12.
     MOVE 'N'             TO ALL-DETAILS-PROCESSED-SW.
     MOVE 'CRADJSEG'      TO UNQUAL-SSA-SEGMENT-NAME.
     PERFORM 180-FORMAT-ADJUSTMENT-DETAIL
         UNTIL ALL-DETAILS-PROCESSED.
     MOVE DETAIL-TOTAL TO OMTB-A-ADJ-TOTAL.
     IF DETAIL-COUNT > 12
         SUBTRACT 12 FROM DETAIL-COUNT
             GIVING OVER-12-TITLE-COUNT
         MOVE OVER-12-TITLE        TO OMTB-A-OVER-12-TITLE
         MOVE DETAIL-TOTAL-OVER-12 TO OMTB-A-OVER-12-TOTAL
     ELSE
         MOVE SPACE               TO OMTB-A-OVER-12-MSG.
     MOVE OMTB-ADJUSTMENT-TEXT  TO OM-TEXT.
     MOVE 431                   TO OM-LL.
     MOVE 'DIDAO   '            TO MFS-MOD-NAME.
*
 180-FORMAT-ADJUSTMENT-DETAIL.
*
     PERFORM 185-GET-ADJUSTMENT-SEGMENT.
     IF NOT ALL-DETAILS-PROCESSED
         ADD 1                 TO DETAIL-COUNT
         ADD AS-ADJUSTMENT-AMOUNT TO DETAIL-TOTAL
         IF DETAIL-COUNT < 13
             MOVE AS-ADJUSTMENT-DATE
                 TO OMTB-A-DATE (DETAIL-COUNT)
             MOVE AS-ADJUSTMENT-TYPE
                 TO OMTB-A-TYPE (DETAIL-COUNT)
             MOVE AS-REFERENCE-NUMBER
                 TO OMTB-A-NO  (DETAIL-COUNT)
```

Figure 8-12   Source listing for the display invoice details program, version 1 (part 7 of 8)

```
            MOVE AS-ADJUSTMENT-AMOUNT
                 TO OMTB-A-AMT  (DETAIL-COUNT)
        ELSE
            ADD AS-ADJUSTMENT-AMOUNT
                 TO DETAIL-TOTAL-OVER-12.
*
 185-GET-ADJUSTMENT-SEGMENT.
*
    CALL 'CBLTDLI' USING DLI-GNP
                         CR-PCB-MASK
                         ADJUSTMENT-SEGMENT
                         UNQUALIFIED-SSA.
    IF CR-PCB-STATUS-CODE NOT = SPACE
        MOVE 'Y' TO ALL-DETAILS-PROCESSED-SW.
*
 190-INSERT-OUTPUT-MESSAGE.
*
    CALL 'CBLTDLI' USING DLI-ISRT
                         IO-PCB-MASK
                         OUTPUT-MESSAGE-IO-AREA
                         MFS-MOD-NAME.
```

Figure 8-12   Source listing for the display invoice details program, version 1 (part 8 of 8)

Discussion

Although this application illustrates programming techniques with which you should be familiar, there are other ways to implement the same functions. For example, the technique I used to return to the menu from the application can be done through the application program. If the format set is coded so it invokes the program when PF3 is pressed, just as when PF5, PF7, or PF9 is pressed, the program can supply the MOD name MENUO through its ISRT call and send an output message with only one byte. However, because this involves an extra execution of the program (which probably has to be scheduled in a dependent region just for this execution), it's inefficient. It makes more sense to use the /FORMAT command within MFS. Then, the program is not involved.

However, if you try to test an application that uses the /FORMAT command like this under Batch Terminal Simulator with Full Screen Support (TSO), it may not work all the time. I'll have plenty more to say about BTS in section 5. For now, just be aware that the /FORMAT command can produce "unpredictable" results when issued under BTS FSS from a formatted screen.

As you'll see, there are a number of ways to approach and solve most application problems under IMS DC with MFS. To illustrate, chapters 9 and 12 present other ways to implement the display invoice details application. Usually, there are trade-offs, and often the price you have to pay is increased program complexity or reduced efficiency. However, as long as you understand the IMS DC and MFS concepts upon which your applications are based, those problems are relatively easy to solve when taken individually.

Terminology

complex screen flow
full-format operation

Objectives

1. Identify the point in processing a transaction at which an application can change the format of the screen.

2. Describe the performance problems involved with using complex screen flows.

3. Given complete specifications, develop a menu using MFS facilities.

4. Given complete specifications, develop an application (format set and program) that uses multiple screen formats.

Chapter 9

How to use
physical and logical paging

Paging is a facility that lets messages be broken down into components for display, for processing, or for both. When you use paging facilities, you can create long and complex output messages more easily than you can otherwise. MFS provides two kinds of paging: physical and logical. This chapter presents both.

PHYSICAL PAGING

With *physical paging*, a message with a fixed number of segments is further divided into parts that are sized properly for a particular device. Suppose an application is designed to send an output message that fills a single standard 3270 model 2 terminal screen (24 lines by 80 columns). Although most of the users who will run the application will work at standard size 3270s, a few may have 3270 model 1 terminals with smaller 12-line screens. In this case, the device format has to be coded so the output can be mapped to a single *physical page* (screen) of the larger terminal or two physical pages of the smaller terminal.

You implement physical paging through the DFLD statement. To specify the physical page on which a particular field is displayed, you code the third subparameter of the DFLD statement's POS parameter. If you omit it, the default is 1. As a result,

```
POS=(8,12)
```

and

        POS=(8,12,1)

are equivalent.

To help you understand physical paging, figure 9-1 shows two sets of partial DFLD statements. Both sets define the same fields, but those on the left are for a terminal with a 24-line screen and those on the right are for a terminal with a 12-line screen. Notice that I coded the physical page number (1 or 2) as the third subparameter of the POS parameters in the group of DFLD statements on the right. As a result, FIELD9 through FIELD16 will be displayed on a second screen at a 12-line terminal.

When the application program sends an output message that will be mapped according to one of these device formats, it doesn't need to know which will be used. MFS selects the correct device format depending on the device to which the message is sent.

Although a basic function of physical paging is to let you use the same message format with terminals that have different screen sizes, you can use physical paging in other ways, too. For example, you can use it to implement multiple-screen display applications that use a single format set.

For example, consider the three-screen display invoice details application the last chapter introduced. As you should recall, I implemented that application with three different format sets: one for the invoice summary screen, one for the payments screen, and a third for the adjustments screen. Another approach would have been to define each screen as a separate physical page in one device format, then send a single message from the application program that contains all the data necessary to format all three physical pages.

However, if I had implemented the display invoice details application with physical paging, I wouldn't have been able to request a particular screen for display. Instead, the output message sent to the terminal would always have consisted of all three screens, and the terminal user would have had to use operator physical paging to move from one to the next.

Operator physical paging

When an output message consists of multiple physical pages, MFS first sends the first physical page (that is, DFLDs with 1 as the third subparameter of POS). The operator reviews that page of the output, then

Possible DFLD statements   **Possible DFLD statements**
for a 24-line terminal   **for a 12-line terminal**

```
FIELD1    DFLD   POS=(3,12)  . . .    FIELD1    DFLD   POS=(3,12,1)  . . .
FIELD2    DFLD   POS=(4,12)  . . .    FIELD2    DFLD   POS=(4,12,1)  . . .
FIELD3    DFLD   POS=(5,12)  . . .    FIELD3    DFLD   POS=(5,12,1)  . . .
FIELD4    DFLD   POS=(6,12)  . . .    FIELD4    DFLD   POS=(6,12,1)  . . .
FIELD5    DFLD   POS=(7,12)  . . .    FIELD5    DFLD   POS=(7,12,1)  . . .
FIELD6    DFLD   POS=(8,12)  . . .    FIELD6    DFLD   POS=(8,12,1)  . . .
FIELD7    DFLD   POS=(9,12)  . . .    FIELD7    DFLD   POS=(9,12,1)  . . .
FIELD8    DFLD   POS=(10,12)  . . .   FIELD8    DFLD   POS=(10,12,1)  . . .
FIELD9    DFLD   POS=(11,12)  . . .   FIELD9    DFLD   POS=(3,12,2)  . . .
FIELD10   DFLD   POS=(12,12)  . . .   FIELD10   DFLD   POS=(4,12,2)  . . .
FIELD11   DFLD   POS=(13,12)  . . .   FIELD11   DFLD   POS=(5,12,2)  . . .
FIELD12   DFLD   POS=(14,12)  . . .   FIELD12   DFLD   POS=(6,12,2)  . . .
FIELD13   DFLD   POS=(15,12)  . . .   FIELD13   DFLD   POS=(7,12,2)  . . .
FIELD14   DFLD   POS=(16,12)  . . .   FIELD14   DFLD   POS=(8,12,2)  . . .
FIELD15   DFLD   POS=(17,12)  . . .   FIELD15   DFLD   POS=(9,12,2)  . . .
FIELD16   DFLD   POS=(18,12)  . . .   FIELD16   DFLD   POS=(10,12,2)  . . .
```

Figure 9-1   Corresponding DFLD statements for two devices with different screen sizes

requests the next page by pressing the PA1 key. This is called *operator physical paging*. To bypass all the remaining physical pages of the current message and continue with the next message, the operator can press the PA2 key. (Note that with operator physical paging, the terminal user cannot back up in the output.)

You can also use PF keys to perform these operator physical paging functions. Remember, you enable PF keys by coding the PFK parameter of the DEV statement. To associate PF keys with operator physical paging functions, you can use the keywords in figure 6-5. For example,

```
PFK=(PFKIN,08=NEXTPP,10=NEXTMSGP)
```

enables the terminal user to press either PA1 or PF8 to move forward to the next physical page and PA2 or PF10 to move to the next message. Notice that NEXTPP and NEXTMSGP are not enclosed in apostrophes on the PFK parameter; that's because they're MFS keywords, not literals.

Multiple physical page input

MFS also lets you generate a single input message from multiple physical pages. To do so, you have to code the DPAGE statement in the format set and specify MULT=YES on it. Then, as each output physical page is displayed, the operator can change unprotected fields on it. The operator presses the enter key for each screen on which entries are made or uses the PA1 key to skip over a screen without making an entry. Also, the operator can use a PF key associated with the MFS operator command ENDMPPI to signal to MFS that multiple physical page input is over and that the complete input message can be constructed and queued.

To position the cursor at specific locations for data entry on multiple input pages, all you have to do is code multiple subparameters of the CURSOR parameter of the DPAGE statement. For example

```
CURSOR=((3,12),(3,17)),MULT=YES
```

specifies that multiple physical pages are to be used for input and that the cursor should be positioned in column 12 of line 3 on physical page 1 and in column 17 of line 3 on physical page 2.

Using multiple physical pages for input can be confusing and error-prone because the operator has to alternate between reviewing part of an output message and entering data for the next transaction. As a result, multiple physical page input is uncommon, and I don't encourage you to use it.

LOGICAL PAGING

The other kind of paging MFS supports is *logical paging*. A logical page is usually associated with a single screen image, just like a physical page. However, with logical paging, you can send multiple occurrences of the same screen, but with different data, as part of one output message. As a result, logical paging is often used for applications that produce relatively large amounts of output.

Logical paging is a little more difficult to understand than physical paging. A *logical page* is simply a group of related fields, either on the terminal screen or in a message. A group of fields as seen at a device is called a *device page*; as I said, a device page is usually a single screen image. The data that's received from or sent to a device page by an application program is called a *message page*.

If you want to use logical paging support, you have to be sure the MFS format set properly defines both device and message pages. You code the DPAGE statement to define a device page and the LPAGE statement to define a message page. In fact, it's common to call a device page a "DPAGE" and to call a message page an "LPAGE." In a moment,

Command	Action
=	Move forward one logical page.
=nnn	Move to logical page nnn.
=L	Move to the last logical page.
=-nnn	Move backward nnn logical pages.
=+nnn	Move forward nnn logical pages.

Figure 9-2   Operator logical paging commands

I'll show you how you code the control statements to define logical pages.

Operator logical paging

Because an application that uses logical paging can produce a large amount of output, the terminal user needs to be able to view it efficiently. To display logical pages, the terminal user *can* use the operator physical paging techniques I described earlier in this chapter; PA1 causes the next screen to be displayed, and PA2 bypasses the rest of the message. However, with operator physical paging, the terminal user can only move forward. There's no facility to back up.

With *operator logical paging*, the terminal user has more control over which logical pages of a message are displayed. The user can enter paging commands, illustrated in figure 9-2, to tell MFS which page to display next.

To end logical paging output and delete the current output message, the terminal user can press PA2. And, depending on how the user's terminal is defined to IMS, pressing enter to send a new input message from any screen may cause the current output message to be deleted.

For the operator to be able to use operator logical paging, you have to enable it, provide a device field into which he can enter paging commands, and insure that the paging command is presented properly to MFS. I'll describe how you meet these requirements as I show you how to define logical pages.

How to define logical pages

To define logical pages, you need to know the proper coding considerations for the DPAGE and LPAGE statements. As you'll see, they're easy to learn.

How to define device pages   To define a logical page as it's displayed on a terminal (a device page), you use the DPAGE statement. Each device page represents a complete screen image that MFS can select when it sends output to a terminal. Subordinate to each DPAGE statement, you code all the DFLD statements necessary to define a complete screen image.

As you already know, when you develop format sets that define a single device page, you still have to code the DPAGE statement if you want to specify an initial cursor position on the screen. Also, you can code the FILL parameter on the DPAGE statement, even if the format set contains just one DPAGE.

When you code multiple DPAGE statements to define multiple device pages within one format set, you don't have to code any parameters other than the ones you've already seen. However, you must supply a one- to eight-character label for each DPAGE statement so it can be linked to a message page. MFS uses the names you assign to DPAGE statements to determine which device page to use when it maps an output message to a terminal.

How to define message pages   To define a message page, you code the LPAGE statement in a message descriptor. Unlike the DPAGE statement, the LPAGE statement has no function other than to delimit multiple message pages. As a result, you don't code it in format sets that don't use logical paging.

However, when you do define a message that has multiple logical pages, you identify each with an LPAGE statement. Subordinate to each LPAGE statement, you code MFLD statements to define the fields that make up that message page. You can specify LPAGEs for both input and output messages.

Figure 9-3 presents the syntax of the LPAGE statement. To relate the message page an LPAGE statement defines to its corresponding device page, you code the SOR parameter and specify the label of the related DPAGE statement. For example, the output LPAGE statement

```
SUMLPAGE LPAGE SOR=SUMDPAGE,...
```

relates a message page named SUMLPAGE to a device format logical page named SUMDPAGE. As a result of this code, the MFLD

The LPAGE statement for output messages

```
[label]    LPAGE    SOR=dpagename,
```

$$COND=(mfldname, \left\{ \begin{array}{c} = \\ \lnot \\ < \\ > \\ <= \\ >= \end{array} \right\} , 'comparison-value')$$

The LPAGE statement for input messages

```
[label]    LPAGE    SOR=(dpagename,...)
```

Explanation

label	The one- to eight-character name for this logical page (optional).
dpagename	The label of the DPAGE statement that defines the device page to which this logical page is related.
mfldname	The label of the message field that will be used by MFS to check whether this LPAGE should be used to format an output message.
comparison-value	The value that is compared with the contents of the specified output message field to determine if this output LPAGE should be used to format the current message.

Figure 9-3   The LPAGE control statement

statements that follow the SUMLPAGE LPAGE statement are mapped into DFLDs that are part of SUMDPAGE.

When a program inserts a message for a MOD that contains more than one message page, MFS has to decide which LPAGE to select for formatting. As a result of that selection, the appropriate device page is automatically selected because it was specified in the SOR parameter of the output LPAGE statement.

But how does MFS know which LPAGE to select? Your program has to tell it by moving an identifying value to a particular field in the output message segment. What that field is and the values it can have are up to you. You just need to be sure that MFS and your program are coordinated.

In MFS, you identify the message field that will contain the logical page selection indicator in the COND parameter of the LPAGE statement. The COND parameter has three parts; the first is the name of the field in the output message segment, and the other two (a relational operator and a comparison value) specify a condition test that's applied to the field. If the specified condition tests true, the LPAGE is selected for formatting.

For example, suppose you code a message descriptor that includes these statements:

```
SUMLPAGE  LPAGE  SOR=SUMDPAGE,
                 COND=(LPAGEID,=,'S')
          SEG
LPAGEID   MFLD   LTH=1
            .
            .
            .
```

If the application program stores the letter *S* in the first byte of the output message (after the IMS prefix, of course), the message page SUMLPAGE is selected for formatting and, as a result, so is the device page SUMDPAGE.

If a message descriptor has multiple LPAGE statements and none of the selection conditions they specify is true, then the last LPAGE in the MOD is selected. As a result, you don't have to code the COND parameter on the last LPAGE statement in a message descriptor, although you may.

Logical paging also works for input. For any input message, only one message page can be used, even if several are defined. If you explicitly define just one input LPAGE, it's used for all of the application's input messages. (The same is true by default if you don't code any LPAGE statements in the MID; then, MFS assumes that all the fields in the MID are part of the same message page.)

In contrast, if you *do* specify different logical pages for the MID by coding two or more LPAGE statements, MFS selects one of them to format an input message. The one it picks is determined by the device page that was used to format the screen from which the terminal user sent the input (that is, pressed the enter key).

On the LPAGE statement that defines a message page in a MID, you name the device pages that are related to it on the SOR parameter. Although you code only one related DPAGE on the SOR parameter for an output message page, you may code more than one for an input message page. Just code the labels of the related DPAGE statements within parentheses and separate them from one another with commas. Then, that message page will be selected to format the input message when input is sent from any of the device pages listed.

How to provide support for operator logical paging   As I've already mentioned, operator physical paging is always automatically provided for output messages that consist of multiple logical pages. However, if you're going to develop an application that creates output messages that have multiple logical pages, you'll probably also want to enable operator logical paging so the terminal user can exercise more control over the screens that are displayed.

To enable operator logical paging, you code

```
PAGE=YES
```

on the MSG statement that marks the beginning of the output message descriptor. This tells MFS to examine related input messages to see if they begin with an operator logical paging command (one of those listed in figure 9-2). If so, MFS performs the requested paging function without involving the application program. Otherwise, MFS routes the input message to the transaction specified in the first bytes of the message.

As you can imagine, you have to be careful when you define an input message that can contain an operator logical paging command. The command field must be at the beginning of the input message segment, and it must be five characters long. However, if the operator does not enter a paging command, the first characters of the input message must contain another valid value, like a transaction code. As a result, you need to define the page command field in the input message with null fill.

Here's how you can provide for a page field in an input message descriptor:

```
SEG
MFLD   PAGECMD,
       LTH=5,
       FILL=NULL
MFLD   'DIL        ',
       LTH=8
```

PAGECMD is the name of a device field into which the operator can enter logical paging commands. You code a DFLD statement like this:

```
PAGECMD   DFLD    POS=(22,17),
                  LTH=5,
                  ATTR=(NOPROT,ALPHA,NORM,NOMOD)
```

to define the device field into which the user can enter logical paging requests.

I want you to notice three points in this example. First, I specified that the device field is five bytes long. And second, I specified NOMOD on the ATTR parameter so the field's MDT will be set to off. As a result, if the operator doesn't enter a paging command, no data for this field will be transmitted. And third, if no data is transmitted, the FILL=NULL specification on the related MFLD statement will insure that the next message field, the literal transaction code, will appear at the beginning of the input message segment.

The logical paging version of the display invoice details application

This section presents another version of the display invoice details application the last chapter introduced. You can look back to the last chapter to review the specifications for it.

In the logical paging version, the operator will not select the particular screen he wants to see next with a PF key. Instead, the application formats all three types of screens as separate logical pages. Then, MFS sends them to the terminal one after another as the operator requests. Although PF key support isn't necessary, the application does have to provide for operator logical paging. If you examine the screen layouts in figure 9-4, you'll see that each screen includes a data entry field on line 22 into which the operator can key paging commands. The format set also provides PF key support for two commonly used operator logical paging operations: PF7 is associated with the command to back up one logical page (=−1   ) and PF8 is associated with the command to move forward one logical page (=   ).

Also, in the logical paging version, the application is not restricted to displaying just one payment or adjustment screen. If more than 12 payment or adjustment segment occurrences are present in the customer data base for the specified invoice, the program displays as many screens as are necessary to show them all. It does that by inserting two or more segments for the same logical page type. MFS takes care of providing them to the operator. As a result, if a particular invoice has 30 payments (very unlikely, but possible), the application program inserts three segments for the payment screen logical page; two have 12 detail lines, and the third has 6.

Now, take a look at the format set in figure 9-5. Notice that unlike the one in chapter 8, it contains just one device format. However, it includes three device pages. Each DPAGE statement and the DFLD statements that follow it define a complete screen image. Notice in each device page that I provided for a page command data entry field.

```
DEVICE MAPPING FOR FMT=DILDF  DEVICE=3270 - 2 TYPE=INOUT  DPAGE=01 PHYSICAL PAGE=01
*-------------------------------------------------------------------------------*
[ DISPLAY INVOICE DETAILS -- SUMMARY                            DATE:  ::::::::: [
[                                                                               [
[ INVOICE:  _____   DATE:  ::::::::       SUBTOTAL:    :::::::::                [
[                                          DISCOUNT:    :::::::::                [
[                                          SALES TAX:   :::::::::                [
[                                          FREIGHT:     :::::::::                [
[                                                       ---------                [
[                                          BILLING:     :::::::::                [
[                                          PMTS/ADJS:   :::::::::                [
[                                                       ---------                [
[                                          DUE:         :::::::::                [
[                                                                               [
[                                                                               [
[                                                                               [
[                                                                               [
[                                                                               [
[                                                                               [
[                                                                               [
[ PAGE COMMAND:  _____                                                          [
[ PF3=RETURN TO MENU; PF8=NEXT                                                  [
[ :::::::::::::::::::::::::::::::::::::::::::::::::::::::::::::::::::::::::::::::::[
[                                                                               [
*-------------------------------------------------------------------------------*
```

Figure 9-4   Screen layouts for the display invoice details application, version 2 (part 1 of 3)

```
DEVICE MAPPING FOR FMT=DILDF  DEVICE=3270 - 2 TYPE=INOUT  DPAGE=02 PHYSICAL PAGE=01
*-------------------------------------------------------------------------------*
[ DISPLAY INVOICE DETAILS -- PAYMENTS                           DATE:  ::::::::: [
[                                                                               [
[ INVOICE:  _____    DATE:  ::::::::     CURRENT BALANCE DUE: ::::::::::        [
[                                                                               [
[ DATE       BANK NUMBER                  CHECK NUMBER        AMOUNT             [
[ :::::::    :::::::::::::::::::::::::::    :::::::::::::::::   :::::::::          [
[ :::::::    :::::::::::::::::::::::::::    :::::::::::::::::   :::::::::          [
[ :::::::    :::::::::::::::::::::::::::    :::::::::::::::::   :::::::::          [
[ :::::::    :::::::::::::::::::::::::::    :::::::::::::::::   :::::::::          [
[ :::::::    :::::::::::::::::::::::::::    :::::::::::::::::   :::::::::          [
[ :::::::    :::::::::::::::::::::::::::    :::::::::::::::::   :::::::::          [
[ :::::::    :::::::::::::::::::::::::::    :::::::::::::::::   :::::::::          [
[ :::::::    :::::::::::::::::::::::::::    :::::::::::::::::   :::::::::          [
[ :::::::    :::::::::::::::::::::::::::    :::::::::::::::::   :::::::::          [
[ :::::::    :::::::::::::::::::::::::::    :::::::::::::::::   :::::::::          [
[ :::::::    :::::::::::::::::::::::::::    :::::::::::::::::   :::::::::          [
[                                                            ---------           [
[                                                            :::::::::           [
[ PAGE COMMAND:  _____                                                          [
[ PF3=RETURN TO MENU; PF7=PREVIOUS; PF8=NEXT                                    [
[ :::::::::::::::::::::::::::::::::::::::::::::::::::::::::::::::::::::::::::::::::[
[                                                                               [
*-------------------------------------------------------------------------------*
```

Figure 9-4   Screen layouts for the display invoice details application, version 2 (part 2 of 3)

```
DEVICE MAPPING FOR FMT=DILDF  DEVICE=3270 - 2 TYPE=INOUT  DPAGE=03 PHYSICAL PAGE=01
*-------------------------------------------------------------------------------*
[ DISPLAY INVOICE DETAILS -- ADJUSTMENTS                        DATE:  ::::::::: [
[                                                                                [
[ INVOICE:  _____     DATE:  :::::::::    CURRENT BALANCE DUE: ::::::::::        [
[                                                                                [
[ DATE        TYPE   NUMBER      AMOUNT                                          [
[ :::::::::    :    ::::::  :::::::::                                            [
[ :::::::::    :    ::::::  :::::::::                                            [
[ :::::::::    :    ::::::  :::::::::                                            [
[ :::::::::    :    ::::::  :::::::::                                            [
[ :::::::::    :    ::::::  :::::::::                                            [
[ :::::::::    :    ::::::  :::::::::                                            [
[ :::::::::    :    ::::::  :::::::::                                            [
[ :::::::::    :    ::::::  :::::::::                                            [
[ :::::::::    :    ::::::  :::::::::                                            [
[ :::::::::    :    ::::::  :::::::::                                            [
[ :::::::::    :    ::::::  :::::::::                                            [
[                                                                                [
[                             ---------                                          [
[                            :::::::::                                           [
[ PAGE COMMAND:  _____                                                          [
[ PF3=RETURN TO MENU; PF7=PREVIOUS; PF8=NEXT                                    [
[ ::::::::::::::::::::::::::::::::::::::::::::::::::::::::::::::::::::::::::::::::::[
[                                                                                [
*-------------------------------------------------------------------------------*
```

Figure 9-4   Screen layouts for the display invoice details application, version 2 (part 3 of 3)

The MID for this application contains only one message page, defined with the statement

```
LPAGE   SOR=(SUMDPAGE,PAYDPAGE,ADJDPAGE)
```

The SOR parameter specifies that input sent from any of the three device pages in the device format is to be mapped using this input message page. (Because this MID contains only one message page, I really didn't need to code this LPAGE statement.)

The first field defined in the MID for this application is for the operator-entered logical paging command, as I described a moment ago. Because I defined it with null fill, it isn't present if the operator does not enter a paging command manually (I'll get to the paging commands that are associated with PF keys in a minute). You can look back to the device format to see that I defined the PAGECMD field with its MDT off (the NOMOD keyword of the ATTR parameter) in each device page.

The next MFLD in the MID is for PF key data. If the operator doesn't enter a logical paging command but does press an enabled PF key, this will be the first field in the input message. Since I defined it too with null fill, if the user doesn't press a PF key or enter a paging command, the message begins with the literal data I specified in the third MFLD statement in the MID. It and the invoice number data field that follows make up a transaction.

In the MOD for the application, I requested operator logical paging by coding the PAGE parameter on the MSG statement. As a result, MFS will look for a paging command in the first five bytes of each input message and perform the requested paging function if there is one; the application program won't be executed at all. If there isn't a paging command, MFS will go back to the menu (if the message begins with /FOR MENUO) or send the message to the application program (if the message starts with the transaction code). In contrast to the program in chapter 8, then, the program for this application will only have to deal with one input message format.

After the MSG statement in the MOD, I coded definitions for three message pages. Each of the three LPAGE statements points to one of the DPAGEs in the device format (through its SOR parameter).

Also, each LPAGE statement contains a COND parameter that names a particular message field that MFS will check to select the LPAGE to be used to format each output message. In each case, that field is in the first byte of the user data component of the message segment that's inserted by the application program. If that field's value is S, the program formats the output using the message page SUMLPAGE and the associated device page SUMDPAGE; if its value is P, the program formats the output using PAYLPAGE and PAYDPAGE; and if its value is A, the program uses ADJLPAGE and ADJDPAGE.

Notice that I coded the message page SUMLPAGE last instead of first as you might expect. That enables MFS to use it to format a message if no selection value is specified in the output message. That doesn't happen during execution of the program, but it's necessary when the screen is prepared for the application with the command

```
/FORMAT DILO
```

(It is possible to send a data string to MFS from the /FORMAT command that MFS can use to select the appropriate LPAGE for formatting. For this to work, the MFLD named in the LPAGE statement's COND parameter must be within the first eight bytes of the message. You can refer to *IMS/VS Operator's Reference* for more information on this technique.)

```
1              PRINT ON,NOGEN
2  *****************************************************************
3              TITLE 'FORMAT SET FOR APPLICATION DIL'
4  *****************************************************************
5  DILDF    FMT
6          DEV    TYPE=(3270,2),                                      X
                  FEAT=IGNORE,                                        X
                  SYSMSG=ERRMSG,                                      X
                  DSCA=X'00A0',                                       X
                  PFK=(PFKIN,                                         X
                  03='/FCR MENUO',                                    X
                  07='=-1   ',                                        X
                  08='=      ')
7          DIV    TYPE=INOUT
8  * - - - - - - - - - - - - - - - - - - - - - - - - - - - - - - - *
9  SUMDPAGE DPAGE CURSOR=((3,12)),                                    X
                  FILL=PT
10         DFLD   'DISPLAY INVOICE DETAILS -- SUMMARY',               X
                  POS=(1,2),                                          X
                  ATTR=(PROT,ALPHA,HI,NOMOD)
11         DFLD   'DATE:',                                            X
                  POS=(1,65),                                         X
                  ATTR=(PROT,ALPHA,HI,NOMOD)
12 CURDATE DFLD   POS=(1,72),                                         X
                  LTH=8,                                              X
                  ATTR=(PROT,ALPHA,HI,NOMOD)
13         DFLD   'INVOICE:',                                         X
                  POS=(3,2),                                          X
                  ATTR=(PROT,ALPHA,HI,NOMOD)
14 INVNO   DFLD   POS=(3,12),                                         X
                  LTH=6,                                              X
                  ATTR=(NOPROT,NUM,NORM,MOD)
15         DFLD   'DATE:',                                            X
                  POS=(3,21),                                         X
                  ATTR=(PROT,ALPHA,HI,NOMOD)
16 INVDATE DFLD   POS=(3,28),                                         X
                  LTH=8,                                              X
                  ATTR=(PROT,ALPHA,NORM,NOMCD)
17         DFLD   'SUBTOTAL:',                                        X
                  POS=(3,41),                                         X
                  ATTR=(PROT,ALPHA,HI,NOMOD)
18 SUBTOTAL DFLD  POS=(3,55),                                         X
                  LTH=9,                                              X
                  ATTR=(PROT,ALPHA,NORM,NOMCD)
19         DFLD   'DISCOUNT:',                                        X
                  POS=(4,41),                                         X
                  ATTR=(PROT,ALPHA,HI,NOMOD)
20 DISCOUNT DFLD  POS=(4,55),                                         X
                  LTH=9,                                              X
                  ATTR=(PROT,ALPHA,NORM,NOMCD)
```

Figure 9-5   Format set for the display invoice details application, version 2 (part 1 of 8)

```
21          DFLD    'SALES TAX:',                                      X
                    POS=(5,41),                                        X
                    ATTR=(PROT,ALPHA,HI,NOMOD)
22 SALESTAX DFLD    POS=(5,55),                                        X
                    LTH=9,                                             X
                    ATTR=(PROT,ALPHA,NORM,NOMOD)
23          DFLD    'FREIGHT:',                                        X
                    POS=(6,41),                                        X
                    ATTR=(PROT,ALPHA,HI,NOMOD)
24 FREIGHT  DFLD    POS=(6,55),                                        X
                    LTH=9,                                             X
                    ATTR=(PROT,ALPHA,NORM,NOMOD)
25          DFLD    '---------',                                       X
                    POS=(7,55),                                        X
                    ATTR=(PROT,ALPHA,HI,NOMOD)
26          DFLD    'BILLING:',                                        X
                    POS=(8,41),                                        X
                    ATTR=(PROT,ALPHA,HI,NOMOD)
27 BILLING  DFLD    POS=(8,55),                                        X
                    LTH=9,                                             X
                    ATTR=(PROT,ALPHA,NORM,NOMOD)
28          DFLD    'PMTS/ADJS:',                                      X
                    POS=(9,41),                                        X
                    ATTR=(PROT,ALPHA,HI,NOMOD)
29 PMTSADJS DFLD    POS=(9,55),                                        X
                    LTH=9,                                             X
                    ATTR=(PROT,ALPHA,NORM,NOMOD)
30          DFLD    '---------',                                       X
                    POS=(10,55),                                       X
                    ATTR=(PROT,ALPHA,HI,NOMOD)
31          DFLD    'DUE:',                                            X
                    POS=(11,41),                                       X
                    ATTR=(PROT,ALPHA,HI,NOMOD)
32 DUE      DFLD    POS=(11,55),                                       X
                    LTH=9,                                             X
                    ATTR=(PROT,ALPHA,NORM,NOMOD)
33          DFLD    'PAGE COMMAND: ',                                  X
                    POS=(21,2),                                        X
                    ATTR=(PROT,ALPHA,HI,NOMOD)
34 PAGECMD  DFLD    POS=(21,17),                                       X
                    LTH=5,                                             X
                    ATTR=(NOPROT,ALPHA,NORM,NCMOD)
35          DFLD    'PF3=RETURN TO MENU; PF8=NEXT',                    X
                    POS=(22,2),                                        X
                    ATTR=(PROT,ALPHA,HI,NOMOD)
36 ERRMSG   DFLD    POS=(23,2),                                        X
                    LTH=79,                                            X
                    ATTR=(PROT,ALPHA,NORM,NCMOD)
```

Figure 9-5   Format set for the display invoice details application, version 2 (part 2 of 8)

```
37 * - - - - - - - - - - - - - - - - - - - - - - - *
38 PAYDPAGE DPAGE CURSOR=((21,17)),                              X
                 FILL=PT
39          DFLD  'DISPLAY INVOICE DETAILS -- PAYMENTS',          X
                  POS=(1,2),                                      X
                  ATTR=(PROT,ALPHA,HI,NOMOD)
40          DFLD  'DATE:',                                        X
                  POS=(1,65),                                     X
                  ATTR=(PROT,ALPHA,HI,NOMOD)
41 CURDATE  DFLD  POS=(1,72),                                     X
                  LTH=8,                                          X
                  ATTR=(PROT,ALPHA,HI,NOMOD)
42          DFLD  'INVOICE:',                                     X
                  POS=(3,2),                                      X
                  ATTR=(PROT,ALPHA,HI,NOMOD)
43 INVNO    DFLD  POS=(3,12),                                     X
                  LTH=6,                                          X
                  ATTR=(NOPROT,NUM,NORM,MOD)
44          DFLD  'DATE:',                                        X
                  POS=(3,21),                                     X
                  ATTR=(PROT,ALPHA,HI,NOMOD)
45 INVDATE  DFLD  POS=(3,28),                                     X
                  LTH=8,                                          X
                  ATTR=(PROT,ALPHA,NORM,NOMOD)
46          DFLD  'CURRENT BALANCE DUE:',                         X
                  POS=(3,41),                                     X
                  ATTR=(PROT,ALPHA,HI,NOMOD)
47 DUE      DFLD  POS=(3,62),                                     X
                  LTH=9,                                          X
                  ATTR=(PROT,ALPHA,NORM,NOMOD)
48          DFLD  'DATE      BANK NUMBER',                        X
                  POS=(5,2),                                      X
                  ATTR=(PROT,ALPHA,HI,NOMOD)
49          DFLD  'CHECK NUMBER        AMOUNT',                   X
                  POS=(5,38),                                     X
                  ATTR=(PROT,ALPHA,HI,NOMOD)
50          DO    12
51 PDATE    DFLD  POS=(6,2),                                      X
                  LTH=8,                                          X
                  ATTR=(PROT,ALPHA,NORM,NOMOD)
52 PBNKNO   DFLD  POS=(6,12),                                     X
                  LTH=25,                                         X
                  ATTR=(PROT,ALPHA,NORM,NOMOD)
53 PCHKNO   DFLD  POS=(6,38),                                     X
                  LTH=16,                                         X
                  ATTR=(PROT,ALPHA,NORM,NOMOD)
54 PAMT     DFLD  POS=(6,55),                                     X
                  LTH=9,                                          X
                  ATTR=(PROT,ALPHA,NORM,NOMOD)
55          ENDDO
```

Figure 9-5   Format set for the display invoice details application, version 2 (part 3 of 8)

```
104        DFLD   '--------',                                        X
                  POS=(19,55),                                       X
                  ATTR=(PROT,ALPHA,HI,NOMOD)
105 TOTALPMT DFLD POS=(20,55),                                       X
                  LTH=9,                                             X
                  ATTR=(PROT,ALPHA,NORM,NOMOD)
106        DFLD   'PAGE COMMAND: ',                                  X
                  POS=(21,2),                                        X
                  ATTR=(PROT,ALPHA,HI,NOMOD)
107 PAGECMD DFLD  POS=(21,17),                                       X
                  LTH=5,                                             X
                  ATTR=(NOPROT,ALPHA,NORM,NOMOD)
108        DFLD   'PF3=RETURN TO MENU; PF7=PREVIOUS; PF8=NEXT',      X
                  POS=(22,2),                                        X
                  ATTR=(PROT,ALPHA,HI,NOMOD)
109 ERRMSG DFLD   POS=(23,2),                                        X
                  LTH=79,                                            X
                  ATTR=(PROT,ALPHA,NORM,NOMOD)
```

Figure 9-5   Format set for the display invoice details application, version 2 (part 4 of 8)

```
110 * - - - - - - - - - - - - - - - - - - - - - *
111 ADJDPAGE DPAGE CURSOR=((21,17)),                              X
                   FILL=PT
112          DFLD  'DISPLAY INVOICE DETAILS -- ADJUSTMENTS',      X
                   POS=(1,2),                                     X
                   ATTR=(PROT,ALPHA,HI,NOMOD)
113          DFLD  'DATE:',                                       X
                   POS=(1,65),                                    X
                   ATTR=(PROT,ALPHA,HI,NOMOD)
114 CURDATE  DFLD  POS=(1,72),                                   X
                   LTH=8,                                         X
                   ATTR=(PROT,ALPHA,HI,NOMOD)
115          DFLD  'INVOICE:',                                    X
                   POS=(3,2),                                     X
                   ATTR=(PROT,ALPHA,HI,NOMOD)
116 INVNO    DFLD  POS=(3,12),                                   X
                   LTH=6,                                         X
                   ATTR=(NOPROT,NUM,NORM,MOD)
117          DFLD  'DATE:',                                       X
                   POS=(3,21),                                    X
                   ATTR=(PROT,ALPHA,HI,NOMOD)
118 INVDATE  DFLD  POS=(3,28),                                   X
                   LTH=8,                                         X
                   ATTR=(PROT,ALPHA,NORM,NOMOD)
119          DFLD  'CURRENT BALANCE DUE:',                        X
                   POS=(3,41),                                    X
                   ATTR=(PROT,ALPHA,HI,NOMOD)
120 DUE      DFLD  POS=(3,62),                                   X
                   LTH=9,                                         X
                   ATTR=(PROT,ALPHA,NORM,NOMOD)
121          DFLD  'DATE      TYPE   NUMBER      AMOUNT',         X
                   POS=(5,2),                                     X
                   ATTR=(PROT,ALPHA,HI,NOMOD)
122          DO    12
123 ADATE    DFLD  POS=(6,2),                                    X
                   LTH=8,                                         X
                   ATTR=(PROT,ALPHA,NORM,NOMOD)
124 ATYPE    DFLD  POS=(6,14),                                   X
                   LTH=1,                                         X
                   ATTR=(PROT,ALPHA,NORM,NOMOD)
125 ANO      DFLD  POS=(6,18),                                   X
                   LTH=6,                                         X
                   ATTR=(PROT,ALPHA,NORM,NOMOD)
126 AAMT     DFLD  POS=(6,26),                                   X
                   LTH=9,                                         X
                   ATTR=(PROT,ALPHA,NORM,NOMOD)
127          ENDDO
176          DFLD  '----------',                                 X
                   POS=(19,26),                                   X
                   ATTR=(PROT,ALPHA,HI,NOMOD)
```

Figure 9-5   Format set for the display invoice details application, version 2 (part 5 of 8)

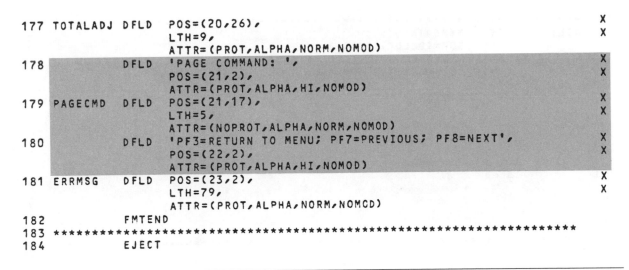

```
177 TOTALADJ DFLD    POS=(20,26),                                                X
                     LTH=9,                                                      X
                     ATTR=(PROT,ALPHA,NORM,NOMOD)
178          DFLD    'PAGE COMMAND: ',                                           X
                     POS=(21,2),                                                 X
                     ATTR=(PROT,ALPHA,HI,NOMOD)
179 PAGECMD  DFLD    POS=(21,17),                                               X
                     LTH=5,                                                      X
                     ATTR=(NOPROT,ALPHA,NORM,NOMOD)
180          DFLD    'PF3=RETURN TO MENU; PF7=PREVIOUS; PF8=NEXT',               X
                     POS=(22,2),                                                 X
                     ATTR=(PROT,ALPHA,HI,NOMOD)
181 ERRMSG   DFLD    POS=(23,2),                                                X
                     LTH=79,                                                     X
                     ATTR=(PROT,ALPHA,NORM,NOMOD)
182          FMTEND
183 ********************************************************************
184          EJECT
```

Figure 9-5   Format set for the display invoice details application, version 2 (part 6 of 8)

```
185 ******************************************************************
186 DILI     MSG    TYPE=INPUT,                                        X
                    SOR=(DILDF,IGNORE),                                X
                    NXT=DILO
187          LPAGE  SOR=(SUMDPAGE,PAYDPAGE,ADJDPAGE)
188          SEG
189          MFLD   PAGECMD,                                           X
                    LTH=5,                                             X
                    FILL=NULL
190          MFLD   PFKIN,                                             X
                    LTH=10,                                            X
                    FILL=NULL
191          MFLD   'DIL     ',                                        X
                    LTH=8
192          MFLD   INVNO,                                             X
                    LTH=6
193          MSGEND
194 ******************************************************************
195 DILO     MSG    TYPE=OUTPUT,                                       X
                    SOR=(DILDF,IGNORE),                                X
                    NXT=DILI,                                          X
                    PAGE=YES
196 * - - - - - - - - - - - - - - - - - - - - - - - - - - - - - - *
197 PAYLPAGE LPAGE  SOR=PAYDPAGE,                                      X
                    COND=(LPAGEID,=,'P')
198          SEG
199          MFLD   (CURDATE,DATE2)
200 LPAGEID  MFLD   LTH=1
201          MFLD   INVNO,                                             X
                    LTH=6
202          MFLD   INVDATE,                                           X
                    LTH=8
203          MFLD   DUE,                                               X
                    LTH=9
204          DO     12
205          MFLD   PDATE,                                             X
                    LTH=8
206          MFLD   PBNKNO,                                            X
                    LTH=25
207          MFLD   PCHKNO,                                            X
                    LTH=16
208          MFLD   PAMT,                                              X
                    LTH=9
209          ENDDO
258          MFLD   TOTALPMT,                                          X
                    LTH=9
259          MFLD   ERRMSG,                                            X
                    LTH=79
```

Figure 9-5   Format set for the display invoice details application, version 2 (part 7 of 8)

```
260  *  -  -  -  -  -  -  -  -  -  -  -  -  -  -  -  -  -  *
261  ADJLPAGE LPAGE  SOR=ADJDPAGE,                              X
                    COND=(LPAGEID,=,'A')
262           SEG
263           MFLD   (CURDATE,DATE2)
264  LPAGEID  MFLD   LTH=1
265           MFLD   INVNO,                                    X
                    LTH=6
266           MFLD   INVDATE,                                  X
                    LTH=8
267           MFLD   DUE,                                      X
                    LTH=9
268           DO     12
269           MFLD   ADATE,                                    X
                    LTH=8
270           MFLD   ATYPE,                                    X
                    LTH=1
271           MFLD   ANO,                                      X
                    LTH=6
272           MFLD   AAMT,                                     X
                    LTH=9
273           ENDDO
322           MFLD   TOTALADJ,                                 X
                    LTH=9
323           MFLD   ERRMSG,                                   X
                    LTH=79
324  *  -  -  -  -  -  -  -  -  -  -  -  -  -  -  -  -  -  *
325  SUMLPAGE LPAGE  SOR=SUMDPAGE,                              X
                    COND=(LPAGEID,=,'S')
326           SEG
327           MFLD   (CURDATE,DATE2)
328  LPAGEID  MFLD   LTH=1
329           MFLD   INVNO,                                    X
                    LTH=6
330           MFLD   INVDATE,                                  X
                    LTH=8
331           MFLD   SUBTOTAL,                                 X
                    LTH=9
332           MFLD   DISCOUNT,                                 X
                    LTH=9
333           MFLD   SALESTAX,                                 X
                    LTH=9
334           MFLD   FREIGHT,                                  X
                    LTH=9
335           MFLD   BILLING,                                  X
                    LTH=9
336           MFLD   PMTSADJS,                                 X
                    LTH=9
337           MFLD   DUE,                                      X
                    LTH=9
338           MFLD   ERRMSG,                                   X
                    LTH=79
339           MSGEND
340  *********************************************************
341           END
```

Figure 9-5   Format set for the display invoice details application, version 2 (part 8 of 8)

Figures 9-6 and 9-7 present the structure chart and source code for this application's program. I've shaded the parts of the program I want you to pay attention to. First, in the description of each output message type (summary, payment, or adjustment) I coded a one-byte field to contain the page type indicator (OMTB-S-PAGE-TYPE, OMTB-P-PAGE-TYPE, and OMTB-A-PAGE-TYPE). This will be the first byte of data in the user component of each output message the program inserts, and MFS will use it to select the proper LPAGE (and, as a result, DPAGE) for a particular output message.

In the Procedure Division, notice in module 120 that the program does not prepare just one output screen for a given input message. Instead, if the invoice the operator specified is found, the program prepares all three screen types.

The logic of the modules that produce the payment and adjustment detail displays is somewhat different than in the version of the program in chapter 8. That's because the program can format as many screens as are necessary to display all the details for the requested invoice.

In each of the three modules that formats an output screen (140, 150, and 170), the program moves the right value to the page type field as part of formatting the output message segment. Then, module 190 is invoked to insert each output message segment. In module 190, I did not code the MOD name argument on the call because the same MOD is used for each output message.

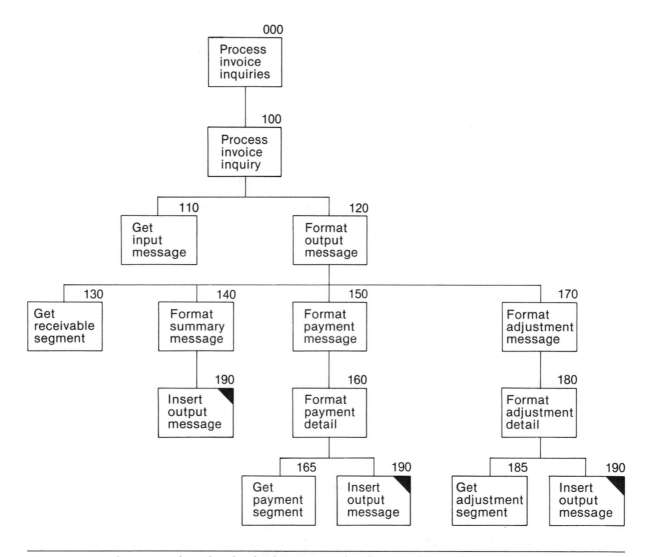

Figure 9-6   Structure chart for the display invoice details program, version 2

```
IDENTIFICATION DIVISION.
*
PROGRAM-ID.  DIL.
*
ENVIRONMENT DIVISION.
*
DATA DIVISION.
*
WORKING-STORAGE SECTION.
*
 01   SWITCHES.
*
      05   INVOICE-FOUND-SW         PIC X         VALUE 'Y'.
           88   INVOICE-FOUND                     VALUE 'Y'.
      05   END-OF-MESSAGES-SW       PIC X         VALUE 'N'.
           88   END-OF-MESSAGES                   VALUE 'Y'.
      05   ALL-DETAILS-PROCESSED-SW PIC X         VALUE 'N'.
           88   ALL-DETAILS-PROCESSED             VALUE 'Y'.
*
 01   INPUT-MESSAGE-IO-AREA.
*
      05   IM-LL                    PIC S9(3)     COMP.
      05   IM-ZZ                    PIC S9(3)     COMP.
      05   IM-TRANSACTION-CODE      PIC X(8).
      05   IM-INVOICE-NO            PIC X(6).
*
 01   OUTPUT-MESSAGE-IO-AREA.
*
      05   OM-LL                    PIC S9(3)     COMP.
      05   OM-Z1-Z2                 PIC S9(3)     COMP
                                                  VALUE ZERO.
      05   OM-TEXT                  PIC X(808).
*
 01   OUTPUT-MESSAGE-TEXT-BLOCKS.
*
      05   OMTB-SUMMARY-TEXT.
           10   OMTB-S-PAGE-TYPE        PIC X.
           10   OMTB-S-INVOICE-NO       PIC X(6).
           10   OMTB-S-INVOICE-DATE     PIC 99/99/99.
           10   OMTB-S-PROD-TOTAL       PIC Z(5).99-.
           10   OMTB-S-CASH-DISC        PIC Z(5).99-.
           10   OMTB-S-SALES-TAX        PIC Z(5).99-.
           10   OMTB-S-FREIGHT          PIC Z(5).99-.
           10   OMTB-S-BILLING          PIC Z(5).99-.
           10   OMTB-S-PMTS-ADJS        PIC Z(5).99-.
           10   OMTB-S-BALANCE          PIC Z(5).99-.
           10   OMTB-S-ERROR-LINE       PIC X(79).
*
```

Figure 9-7   Source listing for the display invoice details program, version 2 (part 1 of 8)

```
05   OMTB-PAYMENT-TEXT.
     10   OMTB-P-PAGE-TYPE          PIC X.
     10   OMTB-P-INVOICE-NO         PIC X(6).
     10   OMTB-P-INVOICE-DATE       PIC 99/99/99.
     10   OMTB-P-BALANCE            PIC Z(5).99-.
     10   OMTB-P-DETAIL-LINES.
          15   OMTB-P-DETAIL-LINE   OCCURS 12 TIMES.
               20   OMTB-P-DATE     PIC 99/99/99.
               20   OMTB-P-BANK     PIC X(25).
               20   OMTB-P-CHECK    PIC X(16).
               20   OMTB-P-AMT      PIC Z(5).99-.
     10   OMTB-P-DETAIL-TABLE       REDEFINES OMTB-P-DETAIL-LINES
                                    PIC X(696).
     10   OMTB-P-PMT-TOTAL          PIC Z(5).99-.
     10   OMTB-P-PMT-TOTAL-MORE     REDEFINES OMTB-P-PMT-TOTAL
                                    PIC X(9).
     10   OMTB-P-ERROR-LINE         PIC X(79).
*
05   OMTB-ADJUSTMENT-TEXT.
     10   OMTB-A-PAGE-TYPE          PIC X.
     10   OMTB-A-INVOICE-NO         PIC X(6).
     10   OMTB-A-INVOICE-DATE       PIC 99/99/99.
     10   OMTB-A-BALANCE            PIC Z(5).99-.
     10   OMTB-A-DETAIL-LINES.
          15   OMTB-A-DETAIL-LINE   OCCURS 12 TIMES.
               20   OMTB-A-DATE     PIC 99/99/99.
               20   OMTB-A-TYPE     PIC X.
               20   OMTB-A-NO       PIC X(6).
               20   OMTB-A-AMT      PIC Z(5).99-.
     10   OMTB-A-DETAIL-TABLE       REDEFINES OMTB-A-DETAIL-LINES
                                    PIC X(288).
     10   OMTB-A-ADJ-TOTAL          PIC Z(5).99-.
     10   OMTB-A-ADJ-TOTAL-MORE     REDEFINES OMTB-A-ADJ-TOTAL
                                    PIC X(9).
     10   OMTB-A-ERROR-LINE         PIC X(79).
*
01 ERROR-LINE.
*
   05   FILLER                 PIC X(8)     VALUE 'INVOICE '.
   05   EL-INVOICE-NO          PIC X(6).
   05   FILLER                 PIC X(10)    VALUE ' NOT FOUND'.
   05   FILLER                 PIC X(55)    VALUE SPACE.
*
01 SUBSCRIPTS.
*
   05   DETAIL-COUNT               PIC S9(3)    COMP.
*
01 TOTAL-FIELDS.
*
   05   DETAIL-TOTAL               PIC S9(5)V99    COMP-3.
*
```

Figure 9-7   Source listing for the display invoice details program, version 2 (part 2 of 8)

```
01   DLI-FUNCTIONS.
*
     05   DLI-GU                   PIC X(4)       VALUE 'GU  '.
     05   DLI-GHU                  PIC X(4)       VALUE 'GHU '.
     05   DLI-GN                   PIC X(4)       VALUE 'GN  '.
     05   DLI-GHN                  PIC X(4)       VALUE 'GHN '.
     05   DLI-GNP                  PIC X(4)       VALUE 'GNP '.
     05   DLI-GHNP                 PIC X(4)       VALUE 'GHNP'.
     05   DLI-ISRT                 PIC X(4)       VALUE 'ISRT'.
     05   DLI-DLET                 PIC X(4)       VALUE 'DLET'.
     05   DLI-REPL                 PIC X(4)       VALUE 'REPL'.
     05   DLI-CHKP                 PIC X(4)       VALUE 'CHKP'.
     05   DLI-XRST                 PIC X(4)       VALUE 'XRST'.
     05   DLI-PCB                  PIC X(4)       VALUE 'PCB '.
*
01   RECEIVABLE-SEGMENT.
*
     05   RS-INVOICE-NUMBER        PIC X(6).
     05   RS-INVOICE-DATE          PIC X(6).
     05   RS-PO-NUMBER             PIC X(25).
     05   RS-PRODUCT-TOTAL         PIC S9(5)V99   COMP-3.
     05   RS-CASH-DISCOUNT         PIC S9(5)V99   COMP-3.
     05   RS-SALES-TAX             PIC S9(5)V99   COMP-3.
     05   RS-FREIGHT               PIC S9(5)V99   COMP-3.
     05   RS-BALANCE-DUE           PIC S9(5)V99   COMP-3.
*
01   PAYMENT-SEGMENT.
*
     05   PS-CHECK-NUMBER          PIC X(16).
     05   PS-BANK-NUMBER           PIC X(25).
     05   PS-PAYMENT-DATE          PIC X(6).
     05   PS-PAYMENT-AMOUNT        PIC S9(5)V99   COMP-3.
*
01   ADJUSTMENT-SEGMENT.
*
     05   AS-REFERENCE-NUMBER      PIC X(6).
     05   AS-ADJUSTMENT-DATE       PIC X(6).
     05   AS-ADJUSTMENT-TYPE       PIC X.
     05   AS-ADJUSTMENT-AMOUNT     PIC S9(5)V99   COMP-3.
*
01   INVOICE-NO-SSA.
*
     05   FILLER                   PIC X(9)       VALUE 'CRRECSEG('.
     05   FILLER                   PIC X(10)      VALUE 'CRRECXNO ='.
     05   INVOICE-NO-SSA-VALUE     PIC X(6).
     05   FILLER                   PIC X          VALUE ')'.
*
01   UNQUALIFIED-SSA.
*
     05   UNQUAL-SSA-SEGMENT-NAME  PIC X(8).
     05   FILLER                   PIC X          VALUE SPACE.
*
```

Figure 9-7   Source listing for the display invoice details program, version 2 (part 3 of 8)

```
LINKAGE SECTION.
*
01  IO-PCB-MASK.
*
    05   IO-PCB-LOGICAL-TERMINAL  PIC X(8).
    05   FILLER                   PIC XX.
    05   IO-PCB-STATUS-CODE       PIC XX.
    05   IO-PCB-DATE              PIC S9(7)        COMP-3.
    05   IO-PCB-TIME              PIC S9(6)V9      COMP-3.
    05   IO-PCB-MSG-SEQ-NUMBER    PIC S9(5)        COMP.
    05   IO-PCB-MOD-NAME          PIC X(8).
    05   IO-PCB-USER-ID           PIC X(8).
*
01  CR-PCB-MASK.
*
    05   CR-PCB-DBD-NAME          PIC X(8).
    05   CR-PCB-SEGMENT-LEVEL     PIC XX.
    05   CR-PCB-STATUS-CODE       PIC XX.
    05   CR-PCB-PROC-OPTIONS      PIC X(4).
    05   FILLER                   PIC S9(5)        COMP.
    05   CR-PCB-SEGMENT-NAME      PIC X(8).
    05   CR-PCB-KEY-LENGTH        PIC S9(5)        COMP.
    05   CR-PCB-NUMB-SENS-SEGS    PIC S9(5)        COMP.
    05   CR-PCB-KEY               PIC X(22).
*
PROCEDURE DIVISION.
*
    ENTRY 'DLITCBL' USING IO-PCB-MASK
                          CR-PCB-MASK.
*
000-PROCESS-INVOICE-INQUIRIES.
*
    PERFORM 100-PROCESS-INVOICE-INQUIRY
        UNTIL END-OF-MESSAGES.
    GOBACK.
*
100-PROCESS-INVOICE-INQUIRY.
*
    PERFORM 110-GET-INPUT-MESSAGE.
    IF NOT END-OF-MESSAGES
        PERFORM 120-FORMAT-OUTPUT-MESSAGE.
*
110-GET-INPUT-MESSAGE.
*
    CALL 'CBLTDLI' USING DLI-GU
                         IO-PCB-MASK
                         INPUT-MESSAGE-IO-AREA.
    IF IO-PCB-STATUS-CODE = 'QC'
        MOVE 'Y' TO END-OF-MESSAGES-SW.
*
```

Figure 9-7   Source listing for the display invoice details program, version 2 (part 4 of 8)

```
120-FORMAT-OUTPUT-MESSAGE.
*
    MOVE 'Y'            TO INVOICE-FOUND-SW.
    MOVE IM-INVOICE-NO TO INVOICE-NO-SSA-VALUE.
    PERFORM 130-GET-RECEIVABLE-SEGMENT.
    PERFORM 140-FORMAT-SUMMARY-MESSAGE.
    IF INVOICE-FOUND
        PERFORM 150-FORMAT-PAYMENT-MESSAGE
        PERFORM 170-FORMAT-ADJUSTMENT-MESSAGE.
*
130-GET-RECEIVABLE-SEGMENT.
*
    CALL 'CBLTDLI' USING DLI-GU
                         CR-PCB-MASK
                         RECEIVABLE-SEGMENT
                         INVOICE-NO-SSA.
    IF CR-PCB-STATUS-CODE NOT = SPACE
        MOVE 'N' TO INVOICE-FOUND-SW.
*
140-FORMAT-SUMMARY-MESSAGE.
*
    MOVE IM-INVOICE-NO TO OMTB-S-INVOICE-NO.
    IF INVOICE-FOUND
        MOVE SPACE             TO OMTB-S-ERROR-LINE
        MOVE RS-INVOICE-DATE   TO OMTB-S-INVOICE-DATE
        MOVE RS-PRODUCT-TOTAL  TO OMTB-S-PROD-TOTAL
        MOVE RS-CASH-DISCOUNT  TO OMTB-S-CASH-DISC
        MOVE RS-SALES-TAX      TO OMTB-S-SALES-TAX
        MOVE RS-FREIGHT        TO OMTB-S-FREIGHT
        COMPUTE OMTB-S-BILLING =  RS-PRODUCT-TOTAL -
                                  RS-CASH-DISCOUNT +
                                  RS-SALES-TAX +
                                  RS-FREIGHT
        COMPUTE OMTB-S-PMTS-ADJS = RS-BALANCE-DUE -
                                  (RS-PRODUCT-TOTAL -
                                  RS-CASH-DISCOUNT +
                                  RS-SALES-TAX +
                                  RS-FREIGHT)
        MOVE RS-BALANCE-DUE TO OMTB-S-BALANCE
    ELSE
        MOVE ZERO              TO OMTB-S-INVOICE-DATE
                                  OMTB-S-PROD-TOTAL
                                  OMTB-S-CASH-DISC
                                  OMTB-S-SALES-TAX
                                  OMTB-S-FREIGHT
                                  OMTB-S-BILLING
                                  OMTB-S-PMTS-ADJS
                                  OMTB-S-BALANCE
        MOVE IM-INVOICE-NO TO EL-INVOICE-NO
        MOVE ERROR-LINE    TO OMTB-S-ERROR-LINE.
    MOVE 'S'               TO OMTB-S-PAGE-TYPE.
    MOVE OMTB-SUMMARY-TEXT TO OM-TEXT.
    MOVE 161               TO OM-LL.
    PERFORM 190-INSERT-OUTPUT-MESSAGE.
```

Figure 9-7   Source listing for the display invoice details program, version 2 (part 5 of 8)

```
*
 150-FORMAT-PAYMENT-MESSAGE.
*
     MOVE IM-INVOICE-NO     TO OMTB-P-INVOICE-NO.
     MOVE SPACE             TO OMTB-P-DETAIL-TABLE.
     MOVE SPACE             TO OMTB-P-ERROR-LINE.
     MOVE RS-INVOICE-DATE   TO OMTB-P-INVOICE-DATE.
     MOVE RS-BALANCE-DUE    TO OMTB-P-BALANCE.
     MOVE ZERO              TO DETAIL-COUNT
                               DETAIL-TOTAL.
     MOVE 'P'               TO OMTB-P-PAGE-TYPE.
     MOVE 812               TO OM-LL.
     MOVE 'N'               TO ALL-DETAILS-PROCESSED-SW.
     MOVE 'CRPAYSEG'        TO UNQUAL-SSA-SEGMENT-NAME.
     PERFORM 160-FORMAT-PAYMENT-DETAIL
         UNTIL ALL-DETAILS-PROCESSED.
*
 160-FORMAT-PAYMENT-DETAIL.
*
     PERFORM 165-GET-PAYMENT-SEGMENT.
     IF ALL-DETAILS-PROCESSED
         IF DETAIL-COUNT > 0
             MOVE DETAIL-TOTAL     TO OMTB-P-PMT-TOTAL
             MOVE OMTB-PAYMENT-TEXT TO OM-TEXT
             PERFORM 190-INSERT-OUTPUT-MESSAGE.
     IF NOT ALL-DETAILS-PROCESSED
         ADD 1                     TO DETAIL-COUNT
         ADD PS-PAYMENT-AMOUNT     TO DETAIL-TOTAL
         IF DETAIL-COUNT < 13
             MOVE PS-CHECK-NUMBER  TO OMTB-P-CHECK (DETAIL-COUNT)
             MOVE PS-BANK-NUMBER   TO OMTB-P-BANK  (DETAIL-COUNT)
             MOVE PS-PAYMENT-DATE  TO OMTB-P-DATE  (DETAIL-COUNT)
             MOVE PS-PAYMENT-AMOUNT TO OMTB-P-AMT  (DETAIL-COUNT)
         ELSE
             MOVE 'MORE.....'      TO OMTB-P-PMT-TOTAL-MORE
             MOVE OMTB-PAYMENT-TEXT TO OM-TEXT
             PERFORM 190-INSERT-OUTPUT-MESSAGE
             MOVE 1                TO DETAIL-COUNT
             MOVE PS-CHECK-NUMBER  TO OMTB-P-CHECK (DETAIL-COUNT)
             MOVE PS-BANK-NUMBER   TO OMTB-P-BANK  (DETAIL-COUNT)
             MOVE PS-PAYMENT-DATE  TO OMTB-P-DATE  (DETAIL-COUNT)
             MOVE PS-PAYMENT-AMOUNT TO OMTB-P-AMT  (DETAIL-COUNT).
*
 165-GET-PAYMENT-SEGMENT.
*
     CALL 'CBLTDLI' USING DLI-GNP
                          CR-PCB-MASK
                          PAYMENT-SEGMENT
                          UNQUALIFIED-SSA.
     IF CR-PCB-STATUS-CODE NOT = SPACE
         MOVE 'Y' TO ALL-DETAILS-PROCESSED-SW.
*
```

Figure 9-7   Source listing for the display invoice details program, version 2 (part 6 of 8)

```
170-FORMAT-ADJUSTMENT-MESSAGE.
*
    MOVE IM-INVOICE-NO     TO OMTB-A-INVOICE-NO.
    MOVE SPACE             TO OMTB-A-DETAIL-TABLE.
    MOVE SPACE             TO OMTB-A-ERROR-LINE.
    MOVE RS-INVOICE-DATE   TO OMTB-A-INVOICE-DATE.
    MOVE RS-BALANCE-DUE    TO OMTB-A-BALANCE.
    MOVE ZERO              TO DETAIL-COUNT
                             DETAIL-TOTAL.
    MOVE 'A'               TO OMTB-A-PAGE-TYPE.
    MOVE 404               TO OM-LL.
    MOVE 'N'               TO ALL-DETAILS-PROCESSED-SW.
    MOVE 'CRADJSEG'        TO UNQUAL-SSA-SEGMENT-NAME.
    PERFORM 180-FORMAT-ADJUSTMENT-DETAIL
        UNTIL ALL-DETAILS-PROCESSED.
*
180-FORMAT-ADJUSTMENT-DETAIL.
*
    PERFORM 185-GET-ADJUSTMENT-SEGMENT.
    IF ALL-DETAILS-PROCESSED
        IF DETAIL-COUNT > 0
            MOVE DETAIL-TOTAL         TO OMTB-A-ADJ-TOTAL
            MOVE OMTB-ADJUSTMENT-TEXT TO OM-TEXT
            PERFORM 190-INSERT-OUTPUT-MESSAGE.
    IF NOT ALL-DETAILS-PROCESSED
        ADD 1                  TO DETAIL-COUNT
        ADD AS-ADJUSTMENT-AMOUNT TO DETAIL-TOTAL
        IF DETAIL-COUNT < 13
            MOVE AS-ADJUSTMENT-DATE
                TO OMTB-A-DATE (DETAIL-COUNT)
            MOVE AS-ADJUSTMENT-TYPE
                TO OMTB-A-TYPE (DETAIL-COUNT)
            MOVE AS-REFERENCE-NUMBER
                TO OMTB-A-NO   (DETAIL-COUNT)
            MOVE AS-ADJUSTMENT-AMOUNT
                TO OMTB-A-AMT  (DETAIL-COUNT)
        ELSE
            MOVE 'MORE.....' TO OMTB-A-ADJ-TOTAL-MORE
            MOVE OMTB-ADJUSTMENT-TEXT TO OM-TEXT
            PERFORM 190-INSERT-OUTPUT-MESSAGE
            MOVE 1 TO DETAIL-COUNT
            MOVE AS-ADJUSTMENT-DATE
                TO OMTB-A-DATE (DETAIL-COUNT)
            MOVE AS-ADJUSTMENT-TYPE
                TO OMTB-A-TYPE (DETAIL-COUNT)
            MOVE AS-REFERENCE-NUMBER
                TO OMTB-A-NO   (DETAIL-COUNT)
            MOVE AS-ADJUSTMENT-AMOUNT
                TO OMTB-A-AMT  (DETAIL-COUNT).
*
```

Figure 9-7   Source listing for the display invoice details program, version 2 (part 7 of 8)

```
 185-GET-ADJUSTMENT-SEGMENT.
*
     CALL 'CBLTDLI' USING DLI-GNP
                          CR-PCB-MASK
                          ADJUSTMENT-SEGMENT
                          UNQUALIFIED-SSA.
     IF CR-PCB-STATUS-CODE NOT = SPACE
        MOVE 'Y' TO ALL-DETAILS-PROCESSED-SW.
*
 190-INSERT-OUTPUT-MESSAGE.
*
     CALL 'CBLTDLI' USING DLI-ISRT
                          IO-PCB-MASK
                          OUTPUT-MESSAGE-IO-AREA.
*
```

Figure 9-7   Source listing for the display invoice details program, version 2 (part 8 of 8)

Advanced logical paging topics

This section covers two other logical paging topics I want you to know about. First, it shows you how to handle complex logical pages that have multiple segments. And second, it describes how to deal with logical pages that map to multiple physical pages.

How to handle output logical pages that contain multiple segments

Although it's typical for an output logical page to consist of just one segment which your program sends with a single ISRT call, that's not a requirement. You might have to develop an application in which a logical page consists of several segments. When that's the case, your format set contains multiple SEG statements and their subordinate MFLD statements, all subordinate to the LPAGE statement that delimits the page. To send a logical page that consists of multiple segments, your program issues one ISRT call for each segment.

As long as the program issues the calls in the same sequence as the segments were defined in the format set, there shouldn't be a problem. However, you can run into difficulties if your program needs to send an incomplete page. If the program doesn't insert all of the segments that make up a logical page, but skips ahead to send the first segment of the next page, MFS assumes that segment is part of the previous page.

To get around this, your program has to signal to MFS that it has finished with a page (even though it's incomplete), and is starting a new page. To do so, the program moves hex 40 (a space) to the Z2 field in the prefix of the first segment of the new page. (Remember, the Z2 field is the fourth of the four bytes of the IMS segment prefix.) This is one of the rare times an application program should change the contents of one of the Z fields.

There is one other detail you should keep in mind when you use multiple-segment output logical pages. Be sure that the page identifier field (the MFLD you name on the COND parameter of the LPAGE statement) is in the first segment of the logical page. If it isn't, MFS probably won't use the right logical page to format the message.

How to handle logical pages that map to multiple physical pages   As if logical paging by itself weren't confusing enough, you can use it in combination with physical paging. Fortunately, that's easy to deal with. Within the specifications for device pages for a small terminal type, all you do is code DFLD statement POS parameters to specify which physical pages fields belong to. MFS takes care of mapping the device page data to the correct physical page.

For example, if the version of the display invoice details application this chapter presented had to be used with both the standard 3270 model 2 and the smaller model 1, the format set would contain two device formats. The first would be just like the one in figure 9-5. The second would define the same fields and device pages. However, each device page would be divided into two physical pages, just like the example in figure 9-1.

Within a logical page that has multiple physical pages, the terminal user presses the PA1 key to advance from one physical page to the next. As an alternative, a PF key associated with the keyword NEXTPP can be used.

Terminology

paging
physical paging
physical page
operator physical paging
logical paging
logical page
device page
message page
operator logical paging

Objectives

1. Given complete specifications, develop an application that uses physical paging.

2. Describe how operator physical paging functions are requested by a terminal user.

3. Describe how operator logical paging functions are requested by a terminal user.

4. Describe how logical paging differs from physical paging.

5. Given complete specifications, develop an application that uses logical paging, with or without support for operator logical paging commands.

Section 4

Advanced IMS DC programming

This section contains four chapters that expand the IMS DC programming information you learned in section 2. Chapter 10 shows you how to develop a program that uses an IMS alternate destination to route an output message to another program or to a terminal other than the one from which the input message came. Chapter 11 teaches you how to design and code a BMP (batch message processing) program. Chapter 12 introduces conversational programming, a technique that lets you develop applications that save data between terminal interactions. Finally, chapter 13 describes error handling in the IMS DC environment.

Chapter 10

How to route output to alternate destinations

All of the application examples you've seen so far in this book have had one feature in common: when they receive an input message, they process it and send an output message that IMS automatically routes back to the originating terminal. Most of the MPPs you develop will work this way. And fortunately, IMS is designed to make that easy.

Sometimes, though, you may need to send output to *alternate destinations*, either instead of or in addition to the originating terminal. An alternate destination can be another terminal device (a display station or terminal printer) or another transaction.

In this chapter, you'll learn how to develop applications that send output to alternate destinations. After I present some concepts you need to understand, I'll describe the basic programming techniques you use. Then, I'll present a simple application that demonstrates those techniques.

Alternate destination concepts

The alternate destination facility of IMS is flexible. An application program that's processing a single input message can send multiple output messages (in the same or different formats) to multiple destinations. To send an output message to an alternate destination, the application program issues an ISRT call just as it does for a message that's bound for the originating terminal. The difference is that the ISRT call doesn't specify the name of the I/O PCB, but rather of an *alternate PCB*.

As you should remember, a PCB is an IMS control block that specifies a program's interface to (1) a data base or (2) the source and/or destination of a message. The I/O PCB, which is required in all message processing programs, specifies the primary terminal from which messages are received and to which messages are sent. Alternate PCBs, which are specified in a program's PSBGEN job, name the other terminals or transactions to which the program can send messages. To help you understand alternate PCBs, I want to show you two application examples that use them.

Application examples of alternate destinations   Figures 10-1 and 10-2 show the message flow in a pair of simple order entry applications; the first does not use an alternate destination, while the second does. In both cases, the terminal user enters an order transaction, which the application program posts to the appropriate data bases. Then, the program sends an acknowledgment message back to the originating terminal. In the second example, the program also sends a message to a printer at the terminal user's site; that printer is an alternate destination. In this case, the message that goes to the printer is an invoice, which is probably printed on multi-part paper. The format of the invoice that's produced on the printer differs from the output message that's displayed on the operator's terminal.

Figure 10-2 is about the simplest possible use of an alternate destination; figure 10-3 presents a more extensive order entry application. This shows that alternate destinations need not be near the terminal that initiated a transaction; instead, they can be widely dispersed. In concept, though, an alternate destination is the same whether it's across your desk or across the country.

In figure 10-3, a terminal user in Sacramento, California, enters a transaction that's sent to the host system located in Palo Alto. The application program, running on the host system, processes the transaction and sends output back to the originating terminal (via the I/O PCB) and to three alternate destinations (via three alternate PCBs).

One of the alternate destinations, a printer located in the accounting department in Los Angeles, receives a copy of the invoice produced from the entry. This is just like the invoice copy that's printed in figure 10-2, only the destination isn't at the site where the entry was made.

The second alternate destination in figure 10-3 is another printer, but this one is located in a warehouse across the country. The output

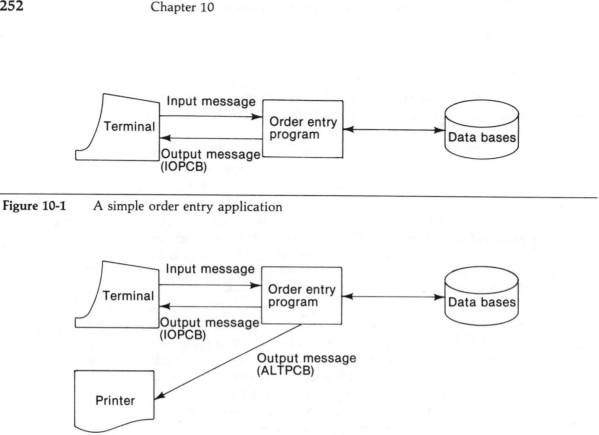

Figure 10-1   A simple order entry application

Figure 10-2   An order entry application with one alternate destination

that's printed here is the same as that printed in the accounting department, only it's used as a packing list. This illustrates that the same message can be sent to more than one alternate destination.

The third alternate destination in figure 10-3 isn't a terminal device, but an application program; the output routed to it is a transaction. Sending a transaction to another program can reduce the amount of data base processing the first program has to do and, as a result, can improve its performance.

The post orders program in figure 10-3 is likely to be a batch message processing (BMP) program. As you know, a transaction for a BMP program isn't processed as rapidly as possible. Instead, BMP transactions are queued like MPP transactions, but are held until the BMP program is invoked through JCL. In figure 10-3, it's likely that BMP transactions are accumulated throughout the day, then processed at night when system activity is at a lower level.

As you can imagine, the number of ways alternate destinations can be used in IMS DC applications is limitless. Just how you'll be called

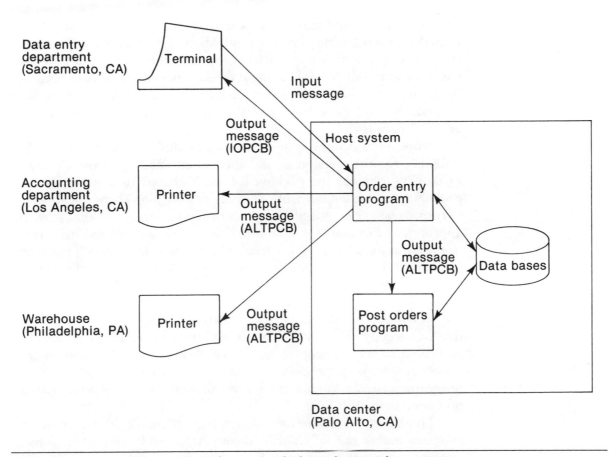

Figure 10-3   An order entry application with three alternate destinations

upon to use alternate destinations depends on your system designers, your network's hardware, and your users' needs. In any event, the alternate PCBs you'll use for an application have to be defined in the application's PSBGEN job. (If you work in a typical IMS shop, it's the data base administrator, not you, who is responsible for PSBGENs.)

Modifiable and fixed alternate PCBs   When the system administrator defines an application's alternate PCBs, she specifies whether each is a *modifiable alternate PCB* or a *fixed alternate PCB*. If a PCB is modifiable, the application program can change the terminal or program to which associated output messages are sent; such a destination is called a *modifiable alternate destination*. In contrast, a program cannot change the terminal or program associated with a fixed alternate PCB; that terminal or program is called a *fixed alternate destination*.

For example, in figure 10-2, the output sent to the printer would be routed to a modifiable alternate destination. That's necessary because the copy of the invoice that will be produced at the alternate destination has to be at the site where the input message was entered. And because operators from many sites can probably invoke this application, the program has to be able to change alternate destinations for each transaction it handles.

Now, consider the more extensive example in figure 10-3. The PSBGEN for this version of the application specifies three alternate PCBs. The one for the packing list that's routed to a warehouse is probably sent via a modifiable alternate destination. Then, the application program can specify the particular destination that's most appropriate. For example, if an order were to be shipped to Pittsburgh, it makes more sense to fill it from a warehouse in Philadelphia than from one in Denver. Although it's more complicated for the program to figure out what the destination LTERM name should be here than in the simpler example in figure 10-2, the concept is the same.

In contrast, the other two alternate destinations in figure 10-3 are fixed. One copy of the invoice produced by the program should always be routed to the accounting department, so the LTERM name of the printer there would be specified as a fixed alternate destination. As a result, the program cannot change the alternate destination for output processed using this PCB.

The other fixed alternate destination in figure 10-3 specifies a program name, not an LTERM name. As a result, output messages inserted using that alternate PCB are queued as input messages for the named transaction.

How to use alternate PCBs

It's easy to use alternate PCBs in your programs. All you have to know is how to code masks for them in the Linkage Section and how to use the DL/I calls that relate to them.

How to code alternate PCB masks in your application programs
Unlike the I/O PCB, an alternate PCB has a simple format, illustrated in figure 10-4. As you can see, it has only three fields. The first is eight bytes long and contains the destination (LTERM name or transaction code) for output processed via this PCB. The next field is a two-byte filler item that contains data reserved for IMS's use. The last field, also two bytes long, contains the status code.

```
01   ALT-PCB-MASK.
*
     05   ALT-PCB-DESTINATION     PIC X(8).
     05   FILLER                  PIC XX.
     05   ALT-PCB-STATUS-CODE     PIC XX.
*
```

Figure 10-4   The COBOL format for an alternate PCB mask

You code a PCB mask like this for each alternate PCB specified in your program's PSB. Of course, you should use meaningful names for the PCB mask itself and its fields. That's particularly important if your program has more than one alternate PCB mask.

The ENTRY statement at the beginning of the Procedure Division lists the names of all the PCBs that the program uses. They're listed on the ENTRY statement in the same sequence that they're coded in the PSBGEN job. Because you'll usually have to use just one alternate PCB, the sequence you'll use is I/O PCB, alternate PCB, and data base PCB(s).

How to route output to alternate destinations from your application programs   After you've set up your program with an appropriate alternate PCB mask and ENTRY statement, you specify the alternate PCB name on ISRT calls that send output messages to the alternate destination. This is how you code an ISRT call to send a message to an alternate destination:

```
CALL 'CBLTDLI' USING DLI-ISRT
                     ALT-PCB-MASK
                     OUTPUT-MESSAGE-IO-AREA.
```

The only difference between this call and a typical DC ISRT call is that it names the alternate PCB instead of the I/O PCB.

You use this technique to route output to both fixed and modifiable alternate destinations. However, to send output to a modifiable alternate destination, you have to do some preliminary work.

How to route output to modifiable alternate destinations from your application programs   It's only slightly more difficult to send output to a destination via a modifiable alternate PCB. The ISRT call is the same as for a fixed alternate PCB. But before you issue it, you have to be sure the alternate PCB specifies the right destination. To do that, you use a call that you're not familiar with yet: CHNG.

```
CALL 'CBLTDLI' USING DLI-CHNG
                     alt-pcb-name
                     ws-destination-name.
```

Figure 10-5   The format of the CHNG call

The CHNG (change) call tells IMS to store the name of a destination you supply in a modifiable alternate PCB so you can issue ISRT calls against it and have the messages routed properly. Figure 10-5 presents the format of the CHNG call. As you can see, the call has only three arguments. The first, as for all DL/I calls, is the name of a four-byte working storage field that contains the function code; for this call, it's CHNG. In figure 10-5, I've followed my convention by naming that field DLI-CHNG. The second argument on the call is the name of the mask in your program for the PCB whose destination you want to change. Finally, the third argument is the name of an eight-byte working storage field that contains the new destination value (LTERM name or transaction code); don't use the destination name field in the alternate PCB mask for this.

You should always issue the CHNG call between a GU call to the I/O PCB to retrieve a new input message and the first ISRT call that specifies the modifiable alternate PCB for that transaction, even if the destination you want to use is the same as for the previous transaction. That's because the GU call can invalidate the destination stored in the alternate PCB; you can't be sure that the alternate destination you used for one transaction will be retained for the next.

Most applications that use a modifiable alternate PCB send only one message to one alternate destination for each input message. However, there may be times when application specifications call for a single input message to result in output messages that are sent to several alternate destinations, all via the same alternate PCB. If so, you'll have to change the alternate destination specified in a PCB after output has been sent via that PCB for the first destination. You also do that with the CHNG call, but only after you've told IMS that the message to the first alternate destination is complete.

The purge (PURG) call indicates to IMS that the message you've been building through the alternate PCB is complete and you want to build another message for another destination. Figure 10-6 presents its format. (Don't let the name of this call confuse you: "purge" doesn't mean delete the message.)

```
CALL 'CBLTDLI' USING DLI-PURG
                    alt-pcb-name.
```

Figure 10-6   The format of the PURG call

```
MOVE 'LACCTP01' TO ALTERNATE-DESTINATION-NAME.
CALL 'CBLTDLI' USING DLI-CHNG
                    ALT-PCB-MASK
                    ALTERNATE-DESTINATION-NAME.
CALL 'CBLTDLI' USING DLI-ISRT
                    ALT-PCB-MASK
                    OUTPUT-MESSAGE-IO-AREA.
CALL 'CBLTDLI' USING DLI-PURG
                    ALT-PCB-MASK.
MOVE 'LRECVP01' TO ALTERNATE-DESTINATION-NAME.
CALL 'CBLTDLI' USING DLI-CHNG
                    ALT-PCB-MASK
                    ALTERNATE-DESTINATION-NAME.
CALL 'CBLTDLI' USING DLI-ISRT
                    ALT-PCB-MASK
                    OUTPUT-MESSAGE-IO-AREA.
CALL 'CBLTDLI' USING DLI-PURG
                    ALT-PCB-MASK.
MOVE 'LWH05P01' TO ALTERNATE-DESTINATION-NAME.
CALL 'CBLTDLI' USING DLI-CHNG
                    ALT-PCB-MASK
                    ALTERNATE-DESTINATION-NAME.
CALL 'CBLTDLI' USING DLI-ISRT
                    ALT-PCB-MASK
                    OUTPUT-MESSAGE-IO-AREA.
```

Figure 10-7   Sequence of calls to send the same output message to three different terminals, all via the same modifiable alternate PCB

Suppose your COBOL program needs to send the same output message (already formatted in the field OUTPUT-MESSAGE-IO-AREA) to three different terminals, with LTERM names LACCTP01, LRECVP01, and LWH05P01. The sequence of calls it should issue is shown in figure 10-7. Notice that a CHNG call is issued before each ISRT call. And after the first and second ISRT calls, the program also issues a PURG call. A PURG call isn't necessary after the third insert call in this example because no more requests will be made against the alternate PCB for the current input message.

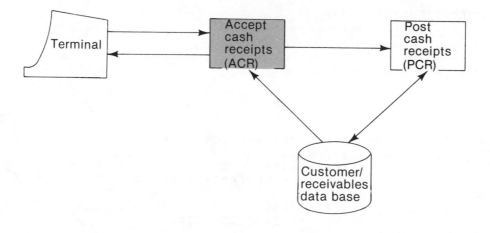

Figure 10-8   The two-program cash receipts application

A two-program cash receipts application

To help you understand how to use alternate destinations, this section
presents another implementation of the cash receipts application
chapter 7 introduced. The difference is that in the implementation in
this section, the entry and posting functions are split and performed by
two separate programs, as figure 10-8 shows.

The first of the two programs, accept cash receipts (transaction
code ACR), performs the operator interaction functions of the program
in chapter 7. That interaction is via a formatted screen that uses a
format set that's almost identical to the one in chapter 7. In fact, the
only difference is that the format set for this application specifies the
transaction code ACR rather than CR. Because the format sets are so
similar, I'm not going to show you the one for this application.

Instead of performing data base calls to replace the receivable
segment and insert a payment segment for each transaction it processes,
the ACR program inserts a second transaction that's bound for the post
cash receipts program (transaction code PCR). The post cash receipts
program can be another MPP that's scheduled immediately by IMS
whenever transactions are present for it, or it can be a BMP program
that's scheduled through JCL. In either case, the COBOL for the
program is the same. As a result, I'll present the post cash receipts
program in the next chapter when I describe BMP programs.

Figures 10-9 and 10-10 present the structure chart and code for the
ACR program. To make it as easy as possible for you to understand this
program, I'm presenting it as a modification of the CR program in

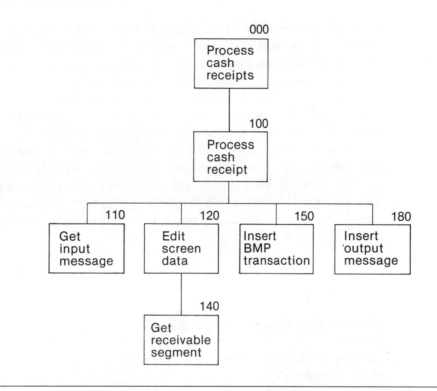

000

Process
cash
receipts

100

Process
cash
receipt

110 | 120 | 150 | 180

Get
input
message

Edit
screen
data

Insert
BMP
transaction

Insert
'output
message

140

Get
receivable
segment

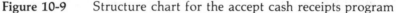

Figure 10-9   Structure chart for the accept cash receipts program

chapter 7. In other words, I've used the same module names and numbers and made only a minimal number of changes to it.

For example, the module numbers in the structure chart aren't continuous. That's because for this version of the program, I simply deleted some modules (130, 160, and 170) from the version of the program in chapter 7. These modules were required to implement data base update functions in the original, but the ACR program doesn't need them.

Now, take a look at the source code for the ACR program in figure 10-10. The alternate PCB mask in the Linkage Section has the same format as the model I presented in figure 10-4. Also, notice that I specified ALT-PCB-MASK on the ENTRY statement at the beginning of the Procedure Division. Because the output that will be sent specifying this PCB will always be headed for the same destination (the transaction PCR), it was specified as a fixed alternate PCB. As a result, I didn't have to worry about coding CHNG and PURG calls in my program.

The next shaded statements format the output message that will be sent to the second program in the application and invoke a module that

actually issues the ISRT call. In this example, I decided to use the input
message I/O area as the output area for the message that will be sent to
the second program. After all, the message formats are almost the same,
and data is already present in the area's fields.

However, I had to change the transaction code in the I/O area to
specify PCR. Also, I moved the current date to the last fields in the I/O
area and included code to set the length and ZZ fields.

Module 150 issues the ISRT call to send the message to the alternate destination. Notice that the call specifies ALT-PCB-MASK, not
IO-PCB-MASK. Also, it names the segment I/O area I'm using for this
message: INPUT-MESSAGE-IO-AREA. Don't let this naming confuse
you. The data here is actually sent out of the program, despite the name
of the I/O area.

Terminology

alternate destination
alternate PCB
modifiable alternate PCB
fixed alternate PCB
modifiable alternate destination
fixed alternate destination

Objectives

1. Describe how alternate destinations are typically used in applica-
    tions.

2. Differentiate between a modifiable alternate destination and a fixed
    alternate destination.

3. Given complete specifications, design and code a COBOL program
    that sends output to one or more alternate destinations.

```
      IDENTIFICATION DIVISION.
    *
      PROGRAM-ID.   ACR.
    *
      ENVIRONMENT DIVISION.
    *
      DATA DIVISION.
    *
      WORKING-STORAGE SECTION.
    *
      01   SWITCHES.
    *
           05   VALID-INVOICE-NO-SW          PIC X          VALUE 'Y'.
                88   VALID-INVOICE-NO                        VALUE 'Y'.
           05   VALID-ENTRY-SW               PIC X          VALUE 'Y'.
                88   VALID-ENTRY                             VALUE 'Y'.
           05   END-OF-MESSAGES-SW           PIC X          VALUE 'N'.
                88   END-OF-MESSAGES                         VALUE 'Y'.
    *
      01   INPUT-MESSAGE-IO-AREA.
    *
           05   IM-LL                        PIC S9(3)   COMP.
           05   IM-ZZ                        PIC S9(3)   COMP.
           05   IM-TRANSACTION-CODE          PIC X(8).
           05   IM-INVOICE-NO                PIC X(6).
           05   IM-INVOICE-NO-NUM            REDEFINES IM-INVOICE-NO
                                             PIC 9(6).
           05   IM-AMOUNT                    PIC X(7).
           05   IM-AMOUNT-NUM                REDEFINES IM-AMOUNT
                                             PIC 9(5)V99.
           05   IM-BANK-NUMBER               PIC X(25).
           05   IM-CHECK-NUMBER              PIC X(16).
           05   IM-DATE.
                10   IM-MONTH                PIC XX.
                10   IM-DAY                  PIC XX.
                10   IM-YEAR                 PIC XX.
    *
      01   OUTPUT-MESSAGE-IO-AREA.
    *
           05   OM-LL                        PIC S9(3)   COMP
                                                         VALUE +145.
           05   OM-Z1-Z2                     PIC S9(3)   COMP
                                                         VALUE ZERO.
           05   OM-INVOICE-NO.
                10   OM-INVOICE-NO-PREFIX.
                     15   OM-INVOICE-NO-CURSOR   PIC X.
                     15   OM-INVOICE-NO-ATTR     PIC X.
                10   OM-INVOICE-NO-DATA          PIC X(6).
           05   OM-AMOUNT.
                10   OM-AMOUNT-PREFIX.
                     15   OM-AMOUNT-CURSOR       PIC X.
                     15   OM-AMOUNT-ATTR         PIC X.
                10   OM-AMOUNT-DATA              PIC X(7).
```

Figure 10-10   Source listing for the accept cash receipts program (part 1 of 6)

```
      05  OM-BANK-NUMBER.
          10  OM-BANK-NUMBER-PREFIX.
              15  OM-BANK-NUMBER-CURSOR    PIC X.
              15  OM-BANK-NUMBER-ATTR      PIC X.
          10  OM-BANK-NUMBER-DATA          PIC X(25).
      05  OM-CHECK-NUMBER.
          10  OM-CHECK-NUMBER-PREFIX.
              15  OM-CHECK-NUMBER-CURSOR   PIC X.
              15  OM-CHECK-NUMBER-ATTR     PIC X.
          10  OM-CHECK-NUMBER-DATA         PIC X(16).
      05  OM-USER-MESSAGE                  PIC X(79).
  *
  01  CONTROL-CHARACTER-DEFINITIONS.
  *
      05  CC-RESET.
          10  CC-RESET-CURSOR      PIC X     VALUE LOW-VALUE.
          10  CC-RESET-ATTR        PIC X     VALUE '\'.
  *
  *                                BINARY VALUE:
  *                                1000 0000
  *                                (X'80')
  *
      05  CURSOR-ON                PIC X     VALUE 'C'.
  *
  *                                BINARY VALUE:
  *                                1100 0000
  *                                (X'C0')
  *
      05  ATTR-CHANGE-TO-BRIGHT    PIC X     VALUE 'H'.
  *
  *                                BINARY VALUE:
  *                                1000 1000
  *                                (X'88')
  *
  *
  01  WORK-FIELDS.
  *
      05  PRESENT-DATE.
          10  PRESENT-YEAR     PIC 99.
          10  PRESENT-MONTH    PIC 99.
          10  PRESENT-DAY      PIC 99.
      05  ERROR-MESSAGE-TEXT.
          10  FILLER           PIC X(8)     VALUE 'INVOICE '.
          10  EMT-INVOICE-NO   PIC X(6).
          10  FILLER           PIC X(11)    VALUE ' NOT FOUND.'.
          10  FILLER           PIC X(54)    VALUE SPACE.
      05  VALID-MESSAGE-TEXT.
          10  VMT-AMOUNT       PIC $$$,$$$.99-.
          10  FILLER           PIC X(15)
                               VALUE ' PAYMENT POSTED'.
          10  FILLER           PIC X(12)
                               VALUE ' TO INVOICE '.
          10  VMT-INVOICE-NO   PIC X(6).
          10  FILLER           PIC X        VALUE '.'.
          10  FILLER           PIC X(34)    VALUE SPACE.
```

Figure 10-10   Source listing for the accept cash receipts program (part 2 of 6)

```
       05   DIVISION-FIELDS.
            10   GOOD-NUMERATOR      PIC S9       COMP-3
                                                  VALUE +1.
            10   BAD-DENOMINATOR     PIC S9       COMP-3
                                                  VALUE ZERO.
*
   01  DLI-FUNCTIONS.
*
       05   DLI-GU                   PIC X(4)     VALUE 'GU  '.
       05   DLI-GHU                  PIC X(4)     VALUE 'GHU '.
       05   DLI-GN                   PIC X(4)     VALUE 'GN  '.
       05   DLI-GHN                  PIC X(4)     VALUE 'GHN '.
       05   DLI-GNP                  PIC X(4)     VALUE 'GNP '.
       05   DLI-GHNP                 PIC X(4)     VALUE 'GHNP'.
       05   DLI-ISRT                 PIC X(4)     VALUE 'ISRT'.
       05   DLI-DLET                 PIC X(4)     VALUE 'DLET'.
       05   DLI-REPL                 PIC X(4)     VALUE 'REPL'.
       05   DLI-CHKP                 PIC X(4)     VALUE 'CHKP'.
       05   DLI-XRST                 PIC X(4)     VALUE 'XRST'.
       05   DLI-PCB                  PIC X(4)     VALUE 'PCB '.
*
   01  RECEIVABLE-SEGMENT.
*
       05   RS-INVOICE-NUMBER        PIC X(6).
       05   RS-INVOICE-DATE          PIC X(6).
       05   RS-PO-NUMBER             PIC X(25).
       05   RS-PRODUCT-TOTAL         PIC S9(5)V99    COMP-3.
       05   RS-CASH-DISCOUNT         PIC S9(5)V99    COMP-3.
       05   RS-SALES-TAX             PIC S9(5)V99    COMP-3.
       05   RS-FREIGHT               PIC S9(5)V99    COMP-3.
       05   RS-BALANCE-DUE           PIC S9(5)V99    COMP-3.
*
   01  INVOICE-NO-SSA.
*
       05   FILLER                   PIC X(9)     VALUE 'CRRECSEG('.
       05   FILLER                   PIC X(10)    VALUE 'CRRECXNO ='.
       05   INVOICE-NO-SSA-VALUE     PIC X(6).
       05   FILLER                   PIC X        VALUE ')'.
*
LINKAGE SECTION.
*
   01  IO-PCB-MASK.
*
       05   IO-PCB-LOGICAL-TERMINAL PIC X(8).
       05   FILLER                   PIC XX.
       05   IO-PCB-STATUS-CODE       PIC XX.
       05   IO-PCB-DATE              PIC S9(7)       COMP-3.
       05   IO-PCB-TIME              PIC S9(6)V9     COMP-3.
       05   IO-PCB-MSG-SEQ-NUMBER    PIC S9(5)       COMP.
       05   IO-PCB-MOD-NAME          PIC X(8).
       05   IO-PCB-USER-ID           PIC X(8).
*
```

Figure 10-10   Source listing for the accept cash receipts program (part 3 of 6)

```
01  ALT-PCB-MASK.
*
    05  ALT-PCB-DESTINATION     PIC X(8).
    05  FILLER                  PIC XX.
    05  ALT-PCB-STATUS-CODE     PIC XX.
*
 01  CR-PCB-MASK.
*
    05  CR-PCB-DBD-NAME         PIC X(8).
    05  CR-PCB-SEGMENT-LEVEL    PIC XX.
    05  CR-PCB-STATUS-CODE      PIC XX.
    05  CR-PCB-PROC-OPTIONS     PIC X(4).
    05  FILLER                  PIC S9(5)       COMP.
    05  CR-PCB-SEGMENT-NAME     PIC X(8).
    05  CR-PCB-KEY-LENGTH       PIC S9(5)       COMP.
    05  CR-PCB-NUMB-SENS-SEGS   PIC S9(5)       COMP.
    05  CR-PCB-KEY              PIC X(22).
*
 PROCEDURE DIVISION.
*
    ENTRY 'DLITCBL' USING IO-PCB-MASK
                          ALT-PCB-MASK
                          CR-PCB-MASK.
*
 000-PROCESS-CASH-RECEIPTS.
*
    ACCEPT PRESENT-DATE FROM DATE.
    PERFORM 100-PROCESS-CASH-RECEIPT
        UNTIL END-OF-MESSAGES.
    GOBACK.
*
 100-PROCESS-CASH-RECEIPT.
*
    PERFORM 110-GET-INPUT-MESSAGE.
    IF NOT END-OF-MESSAGES
        MOVE 'Y' TO VALID-ENTRY-SW
        PERFORM 120-EDIT-SCREEN-DATA
        IF VALID-ENTRY
            MOVE 72            TO IM-LL
            MOVE ZERO          TO IM-ZZ
            MOVE 'PCR    '     TO IM-TRANSACTION-CODE
            MOVE PRESENT-MONTH TO IM-MONTH
            MOVE PRESENT-DAY   TO IM-DAY
            MOVE PRESENT-YEAR  TO IM-YEAR
            PERFORM 150-INSERT-BMP-TRANSACTION.
    IF NOT END-OF-MESSAGES
        PERFORM 180-INSERT-OUTPUT-MESSAGE.
*
 110-GET-INPUT-MESSAGE.
*
    CALL 'CBLTDLI' USING DLI-GU
                         IO-PCB-MASK
                         INPUT-MESSAGE-IO-AREA.
```

Figure 10-10   Source listing for the accept cash receipts program (part 4 of 6)

```
        IF IO-PCB-STATUS-CODE = 'QC'
            MOVE 'Y' TO END-OF-MESSAGES-SW.
*
  120-EDIT-SCREEN-DATA.
*
        MOVE SPACE      TO OM-USER-MESSAGE.
        MOVE CC-RESET TO OM-INVOICE-NO-PREFIX
                         OM-AMOUNT-PREFIX
                         OM-BANK-NUMBER-PREFIX
                         OM-CHECK-NUMBER-PREFIX.
*
        IF IM-CHECK-NUMBER = SPACE
            MOVE CURSOR-ON TO OM-CHECK-NUMBER-CURSOR
            MOVE 'ENTER A CHECK NUMBER.'
                TO OM-USER-MESSAGE.
*
        IF IM-BANK-NUMBER = SPACE
            MOVE CURSOR-ON TO OM-BANK-NUMBER-CURSOR
            MOVE 'ENTER A BANK NUMBER.'
                TO OM-USER-MESSAGE.
*
        IF IM-AMOUNT NOT NUMERIC
            MOVE ATTR-CHANGE-TO-BRIGHT TO OM-AMOUNT-ATTR
            MOVE CURSOR-ON TO OM-AMOUNT-CURSOR
            MOVE 'ENTER A NUMERIC AMOUNT.'
                TO OM-USER-MESSAGE
        ELSE
            IF IM-AMOUNT-NUM NOT > 0
                MOVE ATTR-CHANGE-TO-BRIGHT TO OM-AMOUNT-ATTR
                MOVE CURSOR-ON TO OM-AMOUNT-CURSOR
                MOVE 'ENTER AN AMOUNT GREATER THAN ZERO.'
                    TO OM-USER-MESSAGE.
*
        IF IM-INVOICE-NO NOT NUMERIC
            MOVE ATTR-CHANGE-TO-BRIGHT TO OM-INVOICE-NO-ATTR
            MOVE CURSOR-ON              TO OM-INVOICE-NO-CURSOR
            MOVE 'ENTER A NUMERIC INVOICE NUMBER.'
                TO OM-USER-MESSAGE
        ELSE
            IF IM-INVOICE-NO-NUM NOT > 0
                MOVE ATTR-CHANGE-TO-BRIGHT TO OM-INVOICE-NO-ATTR
                MOVE CURSOR-ON              TO OM-INVOICE-NO-CURSOR
                MOVE 'ENTER AN INVOICE NUMBER GREATER THAN ZERO.'
                    TO OM-USER-MESSAGE
            ELSE
                MOVE IM-INVOICE-NO TO INVOICE-NO-SSA-VALUE
                IF OM-USER-MESSAGE = SPACE
                    PERFORM 140-GET-RECEIVABLE-SEGMENT.
*
        IF OM-USER-MESSAGE = SPACE
            MOVE CURSOR-ON              TO OM-INVOICE-NO-CURSOR
```

Figure 10-10   Source listing for the accept cash receipts program (part 5 of 6)

```
        MOVE SPACE                    TO OM-INVOICE-NO-DATA
                                         OM-AMOUNT-DATA
                                         OM-BANK-NUMBER-DATA
                                         OM-CHECK-NUMBER-DATA
        MOVE IM-AMOUNT-NUM         TO VMT-AMOUNT
        MOVE IM-INVOICE-NO         TO VMT-INVOICE-NO
        MOVE VALID-MESSAGE-TEXT TO OM-USER-MESSAGE
    ELSE
        MOVE IM-INVOICE-NO     TO OM-INVOICE-NO-DATA
        MOVE IM-AMOUNT         TO OM-AMOUNT-DATA
        MOVE IM-BANK-NUMBER    TO OM-BANK-NUMBER-DATA
        MOVE IM-CHECK-NUMBER   TO OM-CHECK-NUMBER-DATA
        MOVE 'N'               TO VALID-ENTRY-SW.
*
 140-GET-RECEIVABLE-SEGMENT.
*
    CALL 'CBLTDLI' USING DLI-GU
                         CR-PCB-MASK
                         RECEIVABLE-SEGMENT
                         INVOICE-NO-SSA.
    IF CR-PCB-STATUS-CODE NOT = SPACE
        MOVE ATTR-CHANGE-TO-BRIGHT TO OM-INVOICE-NO-ATTR
        MOVE CURSOR-ON             TO OM-INVOICE-NO-CURSOR
        MOVE IM-INVOICE-NO         TO EMT-INVOICE-NO
        MOVE ERROR-MESSAGE-TEXT    TO OM-USER-MESSAGE.
*
 150-INSERT-BMP-TRANSACTION.
*
    CALL 'CBLTDLI' USING DLI-ISRT
                         ALT-PCB-MASK
                         INPUT-MESSAGE-IO-AREA.
    IF ALT-PCB-STATUS-CODE NOT = SPACE
        DIVIDE BAD-DENOMINATOR INTO GOOD-NUMERATOR.
*
 180-INSERT-OUTPUT-MESSAGE.
*
    CALL 'CBLTDLI' USING DLI-ISRT
                         IO-PCB-MASK
                         OUTPUT-MESSAGE-IO-AREA.
*
```

Figure 10-10   Source listing for the accept cash receipts program (part 6 of 6)

Chapter 11

How to develop a
batch message
processing application

As you should recall, a batch message processing (BMP) program performs batch-type updates against on-line data bases. Frankly, it's easy to design and code a BMP program if you know how to develop an MPP and a batch program.

BMP program concepts

In a sense, a BMP program is a combination of an MPP and a batch program. Like an MPP and unlike a batch program, a BMP program runs in a dependent region under the control of IMS. It can access on-line data bases and can send and receive messages through the IMS message queues. And logging for a BMP program is done by IMS, on the same set of common log data sets that are used to record MPP activity.

However, unlike an MPP and like a batch program, a BMP program is scheduled through JCL; it's not automatically scheduled by IMS. And unlike an MPP, a BMP program can access MVS data sets; for example, a BMP program can produce a report (a SYSOUT data set) from data extracted from an on-line data base.

Because a BMP program is invoked through JCL, when a transaction for a BMP program is queued, the BMP does not begin to run as soon as possible, even if a BMP region is available. In a sense, transactions are batched by IMS for presentation to the BMP program whenever it is explicitly invoked. Although MPPs can update data bases for each transaction they process (and many do), there is a significant cost to performing on-line updates on a transaction-by-transaction basis. For some entry operations, the system resources required to update the on-line data bases during peak hours can reduce response times so much that the system can seem to crawl. As a result, it's often practical to develop an on-line application that simply captures transactions and queues them for batch-type processing during off-hours.

Why not use traditional batch programs for such updates? To perform true batch processing against data bases used in the DC system, those data bases have to be removed from the control of IMS. Then, the data bases are defined with DD statements in the job that invokes the batch program. Remember, batch programs running in independent regions cannot access on-line data bases, which are allocated to the IMS control region. Although it is possible to remove a data base temporarily from the control of IMS, it might not be reasonable to do so. That's because on-line data bases are often the most important ones at an installation, and removing them from the control of IMS effectively disables the MPPs that use them. So you can see the need for BMP programs.

A simple BMP program

To illustrate how to code BMP programs, I'm going to use the cash receipts example from the last chapter, illustrated in figure 11-1. Recall that the function of the first program in this application (ACR) is to edit operator entries, then queue secondary transactions that will be used by a BMP program to update the customer data base. The format of the message the entry program sends is almost the same as the format of the input message it receives. The only differences are that the entry program changes the value of the transaction code field to specify the BMP program and adds the current date to the transaction.

Figures 11-2 and 11-3 present the structure chart and COBOL source code for the BMP program (PCR). The structure of the program is similar to that for an MPP, except that it doesn't include a module to send a return message for each transaction. That's because the entries that produced the input transaction are complete. (As in the ACR program in chapter 10, the module names and numbers in this program correspond to those in the original cash receipts program in chapter 7.)

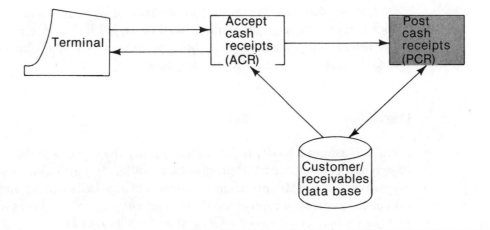

Figure 11-1   The two-program cash receipts application

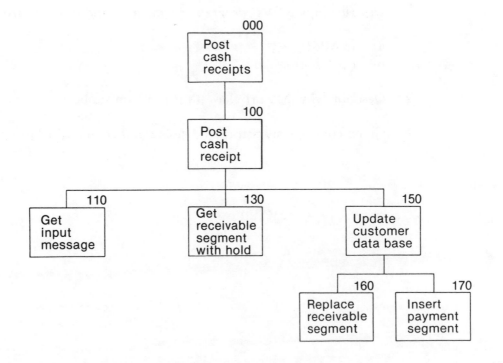

Figure 11-2   Structure chart for the post cash receipts program

The source code is simple too. In fact, all I really want you to notice is that this program could as well be an MPP that doesn't send a reply for each input message. It contains an I/O PCB mask and uses a DC GU call to retrieve its input messages.

Discussion

Although a simple BMP program is essentially the same as an MPP in its design and code, some BMP programs can differ. In particular, it's often necessary for a BMP program to control when IMS checkpoints are taken. In contrast, a typical MPP automatically causes a checkpoint to be taken whenever it issues a GU call against its I/O PCB. You'll learn about checkpointing in chapter 13, which describes error handling in the IMS DC environment.

Objectives

1. Describe how a BMP program is similar to and different from:

   a. an MPP
   b. a batch program

2. Describe why IMS provides BMP program support.

3. Given complete specifications, design and code a BMP program.

```
IDENTIFICATION DIVISION.
*
PROGRAM-ID.  PCR.
*
ENVIRONMENT DIVISION.
*
DATA DIVISION.
*
WORKING-STORAGE SECTION.
*
 01  SWITCHES.
*
     05  END-OF-MESSAGES-SW              PIC X          VALUE 'N'.
         88  END-OF-MESSAGES                           VALUE 'Y'.
*
 01  INPUT-MESSAGE-IO-AREA.
*
     05  IM-LL                   PIC S9(3)     COMP.
     05  IM-ZZ                   PIC S9(3)     COMP.
     05  IM-TRANSACTION-CODE     PIC X(8).
     05  IM-INVOICE-NO           PIC 9(6).
     05  IM-AMOUNT               PIC 9(5)V99.
     05  IM-BANK-NUMBER          PIC X(25).
     05  IM-CHECK-NUMBER         PIC X(16).
     05  IM-DATE                 PIC X(6).
*
 01  WORK-FIELDS.
*
     05  GOOD-NUMERATOR          PIC S9        COMP-3
                                               VALUE +1.
     05  BAD-DENOMINATOR         PIC S9        COMP-3
                                               VALUE ZERO.
*
 01  DLI-FUNCTIONS.
*
     05  DLI-GU                  PIC X(4)      VALUE 'GU  '.
     05  DLI-GHU                 PIC X(4)      VALUE 'GHU '.
     05  DLI-GN                  PIC X(4)      VALUE 'GN  '.
     05  DLI-GHN                 PIC X(4)      VALUE 'GHN '.
     05  DLI-GNP                 PIC X(4)      VALUE 'GNP '.
     05  DLI-GHNP                PIC X(4)      VALUE 'GHNP'.
     05  DLI-ISRT                PIC X(4)      VALUE 'ISRT'.
     05  DLI-DLET                PIC X(4)      VALUE 'DLET'.
     05  DLI-REPL                PIC X(4)      VALUE 'REPL'.
     05  DLI-CHKP                PIC X(4)      VALUE 'CHKP'.
     05  DLI-XRST                PIC X(4)      VALUE 'XRST'.
     05  DLI-PCB                 PIC X(4)      VALUE 'PCB '.
*
```

Figure 11-3   Source listing for the post cash receipts program (part 1 of 4)

```
01   RECEIVABLE-SEGMENT.
*
     05   RS-INVOICE-NUMBER      PIC X(6).
     05   RS-INVOICE-DATE        PIC X(6).
     05   RS-PO-NUMBER           PIC X(25).
     05   RS-PRODUCT-TOTAL       PIC S9(5)V99      COMP-3.
     05   RS-CASH-DISCOUNT       PIC S9(5)V99      COMP-3.
     05   RS-SALES-TAX           PIC S9(5)V99      COMP-3.
     05   RS-FREIGHT             PIC S9(5)V99      COMP-3.
     05   RS-BALANCE-DUE         PIC S9(5)V99      COMP-3.
*
01   PAYMENT-SEGMENT.
*
     05   PS-CHECK-NUMBER        PIC X(16).
     05   PS-BANK-NUMBER         PIC X(25).
     05   PS-PAYMENT-DATE        PIC X(6).
     05   PS-PAYMENT-AMOUNT      PIC S9(5)V99      COMP-3.
*
01   INVOICE-NO-SSA.
*
     05   FILLER                 PIC X(9)      VALUE 'CRRECSEG('.
     05   FILLER                 PIC X(10)     VALUE 'CRRECXNO ='.
     05   INVOICE-NO-SSA-VALUE   PIC X(6).
     05   FILLER                 PIC X         VALUE ')'.
*
01   UNQUALIFIED-SSA            PIC X(9)      VALUE 'CRPAYSEG '.
*
LINKAGE SECTION.
*
01   IO-PCB-MASK.
*
     05   IO-PCB-LOGICAL-TERMINAL PIC X(8).
     05   FILLER                  PIC XX.
     05   IO-PCB-STATUS-CODE      PIC XX.
     05   IO-PCB-DATE             PIC S9(7)         COMP-3.
     05   IO-PCB-TIME             PIC S9(6)V9       COMP-3.
     05   IO-PCB-MSG-SEQ-NUMBER   PIC S9(5)         COMP.
     05   IO-PCB-MOD-NAME         PIC X(3).
     05   IO-PCB-USER-ID          PIC X(8).
*
01   CR-PCB-MASK.
*
     05   CR-PCB-DBD-NAME        PIC X(8).
     05   CR-PCB-SEGMENT-LEVEL   PIC XX.
     05   CR-PCB-STATUS-CODE     PIC XX.
     05   CR-PCB-PROC-OPTIONS    PIC X(4).
     05   FILLER                 PIC S9(5)         COMP.
     05   CR-PCB-SEGMENT-NAME    PIC X(8).
     05   CR-PCB-KEY-LENGTH      PIC S9(5)         COMP.
     05   CR-PCB-NUMB-SENS-SEGS  PIC S9(5)         COMP.
     05   CR-PCB-KEY             PIC X(22).
*
```

Figure 11-3   Source listing for the post cash receipts program (part 2 of 4)

```
PROCEDURE DIVISION.
*
    ENTRY 'DLITCBL' USING IO-PCB-MASK
                          CR-PCB-MASK.
*
 000-POST-CASH-RECEIPTS.
*
    PERFORM 100-POST-CASH-RECEIPT
        UNTIL END-OF-MESSAGES.
    GOBACK.
*
 100-POST-CASH-RECEIPT.
*
    PERFORM 110-GET-INPUT-MESSAGE.
    IF NOT END-OF-MESSAGES
        MOVE IM-INVOICE-NO TO INVOICE-NO-SSA-VALUE
        PERFORM 130-GET-REC-SEG-WITH-HOLD
        IF NOT END-OF-MESSAGES
            PERFORM 150-UPDATE-CUSTOMER-DB.
*
 110-GET-INPUT-MESSAGE.
*
    CALL 'CBLTDLI' USING DLI-GU
                         IO-PCB-MASK
                         INPUT-MESSAGE-IO-AREA.
    IF IO-PCB-STATUS-CODE = 'QC'
        MOVE 'Y' TO END-OF-MESSAGES-SW.
*
 130-GET-REC-SEG-WITH-HOLD.
*
    CALL 'CBLTDLI' USING DLI-GHU
                         CR-PCB-MASK
                         RECEIVABLE-SEGMENT
                         INVOICE-NO-SSA.
    IF CR-PCB-STATUS-CODE NOT = SPACE
        MOVE 'Y' TO END-OF-MESSAGES-SW.
*
 150-UPDATE-CUSTOMER-DB.
*
    SUBTRACT IM-AMOUNT    FROM RS-BALANCE-DUE.
    PERFORM 160-REPLACE-RECEIVABLE-SEG.
    MOVE IM-CHECK-NUMBER TO PS-CHECK-NUMBER.
    MOVE IM-BANK-NUMBER  TO PS-BANK-NUMBER.
    MOVE IM-AMOUNT       TO PS-PAYMENT-AMOUNT.
    MOVE IM-DATE         TO PS-PAYMENT-DATE.
    PERFORM 170-INSERT-PAYMENT-SEGMENT.
*
 160-REPLACE-RECEIVABLE-SEG.
*
    CALL 'CBLTDLI' USING DLI-REPL
                         CR-PCB-MASK
                         RECEIVABLE-SEGMENT.
    IF CR-PCB-STATUS-CODE NOT = SPACE
        DIVIDE BAD-DENOMINATOR INTO GOOD-NUMERATOR.
*
```

Figure 11-3   Source listing for the post cash receipts program (part 3 of 4)

```
170-INSERT-PAYMENT-SEGMENT.
*
    CALL 'CBLTDLI' USING DLI-ISRT
                         CR-PCB-MASK
                         PAYMENT-SEGMENT
                         INVOICE-NO-SSA
                         UNQUALIFIED-SSA.
    IF CR-PCB-STATUS-CODE NOT = SPACE
        DIVIDE BAD-DENOMINATOR INTO GOOD-NUMERATOR.
```

Figure 11-3   Source listing for the post cash receipts program (part 4 of 4)

Chapter 12

How to develop a conversational application

All of the message processing programs you've seen so far in this book process complete transactions. That's how most MPPs work. However, for some more complicated applications, it can be necessary for a program to provide a mechanism to maintain a relationship between data entered during multiple terminal interactions.

For example, consider an order entry application in which the user keys in a customer number and several line items (inventory item and quantity ordered). The application program accepts this message, accesses its data bases to retrieve customer and inventory information, then lets the user enter however many additional line items are required to fill the order. Because the application must retain all the information about the customer and the line items entered until the entry is completed, it's obviously more complicated than an MPP that requires only one input message for a complete transaction.

This chapter describes three techniques you can use to save data between terminal interactions; then it focuses on the most sophisticated of the three: *conversational programming*. A *conversational program* uses special IMS facilities intended specifically for maintaining data between terminal interactions. This chapter presents the details you need to know to develop conversational programs and illustrates them with a complete example. Finally, the chapter deals with an advanced topic: program-to-program message switching with conversational programs.

How to store data between terminal interactions

You can use three techniques to maintain data between terminal interactions. You can (1) store data on the terminal screen, (2) store data in a data base, or (3) store data in an IMS-provided scratch pad area.

Storing data on the terminal screen   The easiest technique is to store data on the user's terminal screen. You do this by transmitting the data to particular fields on the screen, from which it can be retransmitted back to the application program during the next interaction.

The fields you use to store data on the screen should be defined with their modified data tags set to on. As a result, the data in them is always transmitted back to the application program. Often, data stored on the screen between interactions is kept in fields that are defined with the NODISP and PROT attributes; then, the terminal user can't see or change that data.

I recommend you use this technique only when two requirements are met: (1) only a small amount of data is saved and (2) the saved data is non-critical. The size of the terminal screen limits how much data you can store on it and still be able to use it for data entry. And the more data that's transmitted back and forth between the terminal and the host with each iteration, the less efficient the application is.

Also, this technique is suitable only if the data stored on the screen is non-critical. If critical data, perhaps calculated by an application program after a long series of costly data base accesses, is to be stored, it's not a good idea to put it on the screen. Losing it would mean repeating the processing. And even worse from an operator's point of view is losing complex data that he has just entered. (Remember, all the operator has to do to delete an entire screen of data is press the clear key.)

Storing data in a data base   If more than just a little data needs to be stored, you might consider using a data base. The possibilities here are limited only by the amount of data base administration and programming effort you're willing to expend. You can store large amounts of data between terminal interactions like this, of course. However, using a data base for this purpose makes your programs more complicated and less efficient. As you know, data base accesses are expensive in terms of the system resources they use.

When you use this technique, you have to be sure your program can identify the data in the data base that is associated with a particular terminal. A typical way to do this is to use the LTERM name from the I/O PCB, which identifies the terminal from which an input message came, as part of a segment key. Then, when the program receives another message from that terminal, it can retrieve the segment(s) it previously saved for it.

As you can imagine, this technique requires standardization among applications and careful control. Even so, for some situations, it's a practical solution. If it is, the program specifications you receive will certainly indicate how you'll define and use the data base(s).

Storing data in a scratch pad area   The last technique for storing data between terminal interactions is to use a special area IMS provides just for that purpose: the *scratch pad area*, or *SPA*. For a program to be able to use a SPA, it must be specifically enabled during IMS system generation.

If a program can use a SPA, it's a "conversational" program. In other words, it's able to carry on a continuous conversation with the terminal user, even if it processes transactions from other users between terminal interactions or is removed entirely from storage. (In IMS terms, a conversational program must use a scratch pad area; by definition, a program that carries on a conversation with a terminal user by storing data on the screen or in a data base is not conversational.)

A unique SPA is associated with each terminal that's running a conversational transaction. As one of those terminal users works through the conversational program, the SPA is retrieved along with input messages. Then, the program can use the data in the SPA to process the input. When an output message is saved, the SPA is saved too so it can be retrieved for the next terminal interaction.

I want you to be aware of the relationship between SPAs and the application program. Regardless of the number of terminal users running a conversational program, only one copy of the program needs to be scheduled and executed by IMS. However, each terminal user is allocated a separate scratch pad area, so many SPAs may be active at one time for the same program.

How to use the scratch pad area

To develop conversational applications, you need to know how to define and reference the SPA in your COBOL programs. It's easiest to learn how to use the SPA if you think of it as another kind of message segment your program processes. To use a SPA, you need to know how to define the I/O area that will be used for it in your program, and you need to know how to code the DL/I calls that you use to retrieve and save the SPA.

How to define the I/O area for the SPA   As you can see in figure 12-1, the format of the I/O area you define for a SPA is much like that for a message segment. The SPA begins with two binary halfword fields, LL and ZZ, just like a message segment. (Remember, a binary halfword has the COBOL picture S9(4), is defined with COMP usage, and uses two bytes of storage.)

After the LL and ZZ fields, the SPA contains a third binary halfword. This field contains the *conversational identifier*, or *CI*, which IMS uses to keep track of the SPA. The CI identifies a control block (called the *conversational control block*, or *CCB*) that IMS maintains for your conversation. The CCB relates your SPA (among the many that IMS might be keeping track of) to your program and to your terminal. You never need to change the data in the CI field, although you must provide for the space it uses in the definition of the SPA I/O area. (Because it isn't necessary to change the data in the ZZ or CI fields or evaluate them, some programmers define them with a single FILLER field with PIC X(4).)

The data in the SPA follows. The first eight bytes of data (positions 7 through 14) must always contain the transaction code for the application. In a basic conversational program, IMS stores the transaction code in this field; your program does not. After the transaction code, you can define whatever fields you want in the SPA, up to the maximum size specified for it during IMS system generation.

How to use the get calls in a conversational program   The sequence of DC calls (that is, calls to the I/O PCB) you issue in a conversational program differs a little from the sequence you issue in a non-conversational MPP. In a basic MPP, the first DC call you issue for a transaction is a GU to the I/O PCB to retrieve the first message segment from the terminal. Then, if there are any additional input message segments, you retrieve them with GN calls.

In a conversational program, you must retrieve the SPA before you retrieve message segments, and to do that, you issue a GU call against the I/O PCB. For example,

```
CALL 'CBLTDLI' USING DLI-GU
               IO-PCB-MASK
               SPA-IO-AREA.
```

```
 01   SPA-IO-AREA.
 *
      05   SPA-LL                   PIC  S9(4)      COMP.
      05   SPA-ZZ                   PIC  S9(4)      COMP.
      05   SPA-CI                   PIC  S9(4)      COMP.
      05   SPA-TRANSACTION-CODE     PIC  X(8).
      05   SPA-USER-DATA            PIC  X(...).
 *
```

Figure 12-1   Format of the SPA I/O area

retrieves the SPA and stores it in the I/O area I defined in figure 12-1. The status code that results from this call should be spaces; any other value represents an error. Then, to retrieve the first segment of the input message, you issue a GN call, not a GU call as in a basic MPP. Subsequent input message segments are retrieved with GN calls as well. This shouldn't cause you much confusion as long as you think of the SPA as the first segment of the input message.

By the way, the transaction code may not appear in the first segment of the input message in a conversational program. That's because IMS removes the transaction code and stores it in the SPA for the first input message of a conversation. In subsequent messages in the conversation, the transaction code is not removed. You'll see an example of this in a moment.

At the start of a conversation, the data area of the SPA is set to binary zeros. Subsequent interactions return a SPA that contains whatever the program saved during the previous interaction.

How to use insert calls in a conversational program   To save data in the SPA, you issue an ISRT call against the I/O PCB:

```
 CALL 'CBLTDLI' USING DLI-ISRT
                      IO-PCB-MASK
                      SPA-IO-AREA.
```

The first ISRT call issued for an iteration (that is, between DC GU calls) automatically is for the SPA; you must not send an output message segment before you've saved the SPA. The second and subsequent ISRT calls issued against the I/O PCB are for message segments that are to be routed to the originating terminal. Also, you can save the SPA only once during an iteration of the application program. And as with the GU call to retrieve the SPA, any status code other than spaces indicates an error.

The I/O area used for the SPA on output has the same format as it does for input. The program must not modify the data in the first six bytes of the SPA (the LL, ZZ, and CI fields). Note also that the transaction code field is required in positions 7 through 14 of the output message as well as the input message.

For all iterations of a conversation except the last, the program doesn't modify the data in the transaction code field of the SPA; the correct value was supplied when the SPA was retrieved. However, for the last iteration, when the program needs to indicate that the conversation is complete, it moves spaces to the transaction code field before it issues the ISRT call for the SPA. This tells IMS that the conversation is over and the SPA can be released.

A program can also cause IMS to end a conversation if it sends a message to a non-conversational program via an alternate PCB. Or, if a user wants to terminate a conversation before the program does, he can enter an /EXIT or /HOLD command. Typically, though, the program should handle ending the conversation. In the next section, you'll see a conversational program that does this.

Other programming considerations   There are a couple of other important points you need to keep in mind as you design and code conversational programs. First, each iteration in the conversation must include a response back to the terminal user. This makes sense, because failing to send an output message would mean no conversation is going on. The terminal remains locked until the response is received. The response can be through an ISRT call to the I/O PCB or through another conversational program via a call to a properly defined alternate PCB. (I'll describe the second approach later in this chapter when I cover program-to-program message switching.)

The second point has to do with data base updates. As a general rule, it's a good idea to update data bases only during the last iteration of a conversation. As you'll learn in chapter 13, GU calls to the I/O PCB mark synchronization points (points at which the data base updates made thus far are considered to be correct and complete). That means data base updates made during iterations other than the last are committed; they can't be backed out if IMS has to perform its automatic recovery functions. As a result, if a program that has done data base updates in a previous iteration fails, only some of the updates required for the complete transaction are committed, and the integrity of the data base is called into question.

A sample conversational application

To show you how conversational programming works, I want to present still another variation of the display invoice details application you've already seen in section 3. First, I'll present the revised specifications for it, then I'll describe how I designed and coded the program.

Specifications for the conversational display invoice details application

This version of the application is an enhancement of the one I showed you in chapter 8; it lets the user display a financial summary, payment detail, or adjustment detail screen for any specified invoice. From the user's point of view, the program in chapter 8 and this program seem to work in the same way.

However, they differ internally. As you should recall, the program in chapter 8 retrieved the requested segments from the customer data base for each terminal interaction. Although this makes each iteration of the program independent of all others, it can be inefficient if the operator is likely to bounce back and forth from one display to another for the same invoice. When that's the case, the same data base segments may have to be retrieved over and over. And because DL/I data base calls use plenty of system resources, this can be costly.

A solution is to retrieve all the data base segments the operator might need when a new invoice is specified, then store the data necessary to construct any one of the three screens in the SPA. When the user requests a different display for the same invoice, the program simply presents what's already in the SPA; it doesn't have to return to the data base until the user requests information for another invoice.

The format sets for this version of the application are almost iden--tical to those in chapter 8. The only differences are in the PF key specifications:

```
PFK=(PFKIN,
03='DIC      03',
05='DIC      05',
07='DIC      07',
09='DIC      09')
```

Each literal specifies the conversational transaction (DIC) rather than the non-conversational version (DID). Also, they're coded so PF3 doesn't cause MFS to redisplay a menu directly. Instead, it causes the program to be invoked, which (1) saves the SPA with blanks in its transaction code field to end the conversation and (2) issues an ISRT

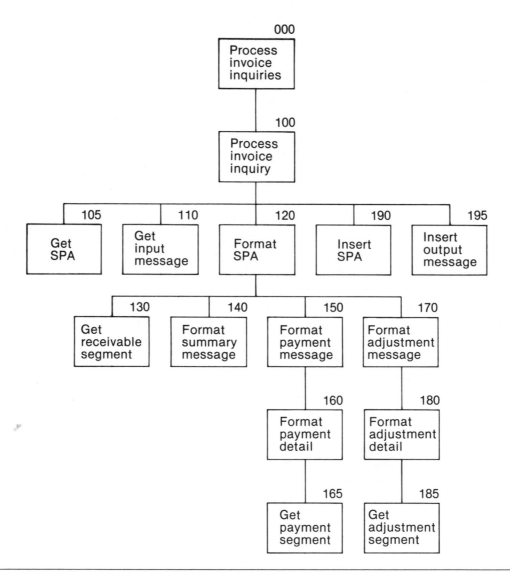

Figure 12-2   Structure chart for the display invoice details program, version 3

call against the I/O PCB with the MOD name MENUO to cause the menu to be displayed.

The structure and code for the conversational display invoice details program   Figures 12-2 and 12-3 present the structure chart and COBOL source code for the conversational display invoice details application. The structure of the program is similar to that of the version in chapter 8. However, notice that I added modules to retrieve the SPA (105) and save it (190).

```
        IDENTIFICATION DIVISION.
      *
        PROGRAM-ID.  DIC.
      *
        ENVIRONMENT DIVISION.
      *
        DATA DIVISION.
      *
        WORKING-STORAGE SECTION.
      *
        01  SWITCHES.
      *
            05   INVOICE-FOUND-SW            PIC X          VALUE 'Y'.
                 88   INVOICE-FOUND                         VALUE 'Y'.
            05   END-OF-MESSAGES-SW          PIC X          VALUE 'N'.
                 88   END-OF-MESSAGES                       VALUE 'Y'.
            05   ALL-DETAILS-PROCESSED-SW    PIC X          VALUE 'N'.
                 88   ALL-DETAILS-PROCESSED                 VALUE 'Y'.
      *
        01  SPA-IO-AREA.
      *
            05   SPA-LL                      PIC S9(4)      COMP.
            05   SPA-ZZ                      PIC S9(4)      COMP.
            05   SPA-CI                      PIC S9(4)      COMP.
            05   SPA-TRANSACTION-CODE        PIC X(8).
            05   SPA-USER-DATA.
                 10   SPA-SUMMARY-TEXT       PIC X(150).
                 10   SPA-PAYMENTS-TEXT      PIC X(835).
                 10   SPA-ADJUSTMENTS-TEXT   PIC X(423).
      *
        01  INPUT-MESSAGE-IO-AREA.
      *
            05   IM-LL                       PIC S9(3)      COMP.
            05   IM-ZZ                       PIC S9(3)      COMP.
            05   IM-TEXT.
                 10   IM-TRANSACTION-CODE    PIC X(8).
                 10   IM-PFKEY-SELECTION     PIC XX.
                      88   IM-RETURN-TO-MENU                VALUE '03'.
                      88   IM-DISPLAY-SUMMARY               VALUE '05'.
                      88   IM-DISPLAY-PAYMENTS              VALUE '07'.
                      88   IM-DISPLAY-ADJUSTMENTS           VALUE '09'.
                 10   IM-INVOICE-NO          PIC X(6).
      *
        01  INPUT-MESSAGE-EDITING-AREA.
      *
            05   FILLER                      PIC X(4).
            05   IMEA-PFKEY-SELECTION        PIC XX.
            05   IMEA-INVOICE-NO             PIC X(6).
      *
        01  OUTPUT-MESSAGE-IO-AREA.
      *
            05   OM-LL                       PIC S9(3)      COMP.
            05   OM-Z1-Z2                    PIC S9(3)      COMP
                                                            VALUE ZERO.
            05   OM-TEXT                     PIC X(835).
```

Figure 12-3   Source listing for the display invoice details program, version 3 (part 1 of 9)

```
*
 01   OUTPUT-MESSAGE-TEXT-BLOCKS.
*
      05   OMTB-SUMMARY-TEXT.
           10   OMTB-S-INVOICE-NO        PIC X(6).
           10   OMTB-S-INVOICE-DATE      PIC 99/99/99.
           10   OMTB-S-PROD-TOTAL        PIC Z(5).99-.
           10   OMTB-S-CASH-DISC         PIC Z(5).99-.
           10   OMTB-S-SALES-TAX         PIC Z(5).99-.
           10   OMTB-S-FREIGHT           PIC Z(5).99-.
           10   OMTB-S-BILLING           PIC Z(5).99-.
           10   OMTB-S-PMTS-ADJS         PIC Z(5).99-.
           10   OMTB-S-BALANCE           PIC Z(5).99-.
           10   OMTB-S-ERROR-LINE        PIC X(79).
*
      05   OMTB-PAYMENT-TEXT.
           10   OMTB-P-INVOICE-NO        PIC X(6).
           10   OMTB-P-INVOICE-DATE      PIC 99/99/99.
           10   OMTB-P-BALANCE           PIC Z(5).99-.
           10   OMTB-P-DETAIL-LINES.
                15   OMTB-P-DETAIL-LINE  OCCURS 12 TIMES.
                     20   OMTB-P-DATE    PIC 99/99/99.
                     20   OMTB-P-BANK    PIC X(25).
                     20   OMTB-P-CHECK   PIC X(16).
                     20   OMTB-P-AMT     PIC Z(5).99-.
           10   OMTB-P-DETAIL-TABLE      REDEFINES OMTB-P-DETAIL-LINES
                                         PIC X(696).
           10   OMTB-P-OVER-12-MSG.
                15   OMTB-P-OVER-12-TITLE PIC X(19).
                15   OMTB-P-OVER-12-TOTAL PIC Z(5).99-.
           10   OMTB-P-PMT-TOTAL         PIC Z(5).99-.
           10   OMTB-P-ERROR-LINE        PIC X(79).
*
      05   OMTB-ADJUSTMENT-TEXT.
           10   OMTB-A-INVOICE-NO        PIC X(6).
           10   OMTB-A-INVOICE-DATE      PIC 99/99/99.
           10   OMTB-A-BALANCE           PIC Z(5).99-.
           10   OMTB-A-DETAIL-LINES.
                15   OMTB-A-DETAIL-LINE  OCCURS 12 TIMES.
                     20   OMTB-A-DATE    PIC 99/99/99.
                     20   OMTB-A-TYPE    PIC X.
                     20   OMTB-A-NO      PIC X(6).
                     20   OMTB-A-AMT     PIC Z(5).99-.
           10   OMTB-A-DETAIL-TABLE      REDEFINES OMTB-A-DETAIL-LINES
                                         PIC X(288).
           10   OMTB-A-OVER-12-MSG.
                15   OMTB-A-OVER-12-TITLE PIC X(19).
                15   OMTB-A-OVER-12-TOTAL PIC Z(5).99-.
           10   OMTB-A-ADJ-TOTAL         PIC Z(5).99-.
           10   OMTB-A-ERROR-LINE        PIC X(79).
*
```

Figure 12-3   Source listing for the display invoice details program, version 3 (part 2 of 9)

```
01    ERROR-LINE.
*
      05    FILLER                    PIC X(8)      VALUE 'INVOICE '.
      05    EL-INVOICE-NO             PIC X(6).
      05    FILLER                    PIC X(10)     VALUE ' NOT FOUND'.
      05    FILLER                    PIC X(55)     VALUE SPACE.
*
 01   OVER-12-TITLE.
*
      05    OVER-12-TITLE-COUNT       PIC ZZ9.
      05    FILLER                    PIC X(16)
                                      VALUE ' OTHERS TOTALING'.
*
 01   SUBSCRIPTS.
*
      05    DETAIL-COUNT              PIC S9(3)     COMP.
*
 01   TOTAL-FIELDS.
*
      05    DETAIL-TOTAL-OVER-12      PIC S9(5)V99     COMP-3.
      05    DETAIL-TOTAL              PIC S9(5)V99     COMP-3.
*
 01   DLI-FUNCTIONS.
*
      05    DLI-GU                    PIC X(4)      VALUE 'GU  '.
      05    DLI-GHU                   PIC X(4)      VALUE 'GHU '.
      05    DLI-GN                    PIC X(4)      VALUE 'GN  '.
      05    DLI-GHN                   PIC X(4)      VALUE 'GHN '.
      05    DLI-GNP                   PIC X(4)      VALUE 'GNP '.
      05    DLI-GHNP                  PIC X(4)      VALUE 'GHNP'.
      05    DLI-ISRT                  PIC X(4)      VALUE 'ISRT'.
      05    DLI-DLET                  PIC X(4)      VALUE 'DLET'.
      05    DLI-REPL                  PIC X(4)      VALUE 'REPL'.
      05    DLI-CHKP                  PIC X(4)      VALUE 'CHKP'.
      05    DLI-XRST                  PIC X(4)      VALUE 'XRST'.
      05    DLI-PCB                   PIC X(4)      VALUE 'PCB '.
*
 01   MFS-FIELDS.
*
      05    MFS-MOD-NAME              PIC X(8).
*
 01   RECEIVABLE-SEGMENT.
*
      05    RS-INVOICE-NUMBER         PIC X(6).
      05    RS-INVOICE-DATE           PIC X(6).
      05    RS-PO-NUMBER              PIC X(25).
      05    RS-PRODUCT-TOTAL          PIC S9(5)V99     COMP-3.
      05    RS-CASH-DISCOUNT          PIC S9(5)V99     COMP-3.
      05    RS-SALES-TAX              PIC S9(5)V99     COMP-3.
      05    RS-FREIGHT                PIC S9(5)V99     COMP-3.
      05    RS-BALANCE-DUE            PIC S9(5)V99     COMP-3.
*
```

Figure 12-3   Source listing for the display invoice details program, version 3 (part 3 of 9)

```
01   PAYMENT-SEGMENT.
*
     05  PS-CHECK-NUMBER        PIC X(16).
     05  PS-BANK-NUMBER         PIC X(25).
     05  PS-PAYMENT-DATE        PIC X(6).
     05  PS-PAYMENT-AMOUNT      PIC S9(5)V99      COMP-3.
*
01   ADJUSTMENT-SEGMENT.
*
     05  AS-REFERENCE-NUMBER    PIC X(6).
     05  AS-ADJUSTMENT-DATE     PIC X(6).
     05  AS-ADJUSTMENT-TYPE     PIC X.
     05  AS-ADJUSTMENT-AMOUNT   PIC S9(5)V99      COMP-3.
*
01   INVOICE-NO-SSA.
*
     05  FILLER                 PIC X(9)     VALUE 'CRRECSEG('.
     05  FILLER                 PIC X(10)    VALUE 'CRRECXNO ='.
     05  INVOICE-NO-SSA-VALUE   PIC X(6).
     05  FILLER                 PIC X        VALUE ')'.
*
01   UNQUALIFIED-SSA.
*
     05  UNQUAL-SSA-SEGMENT-NAME PIC X(8).
     05  FILLER                 PIC X        VALUE SPACE.
*
LINKAGE SECTION.
*
01   IO-PCB-MASK.
*
     05  IO-PCB-LOGICAL-TERMINAL PIC X(8).
     05  FILLER                 PIC XX.
     05  IO-PCB-STATUS-CODE     PIC XX.
     05  IO-PCB-DATE            PIC S9(7)  COMP-3.
     05  IO-PCB-TIME            PIC S9(6)V9 COMP-3.
     05  IO-PCB-MSG-SEQ-NUMBER  PIC S9(5)  COMP.
     05  IO-PCB-MOD-NAME        PIC X(8).
     05  IO-PCB-USER-ID         PIC X(8).
*
01   CR-PCB-MASK.
*
     05  CR-PCB-DBD-NAME        PIC X(8).
     05  CR-PCB-SEGMENT-LEVEL   PIC XX.
     05  CR-PCB-STATUS-CODE     PIC XX.
     05  CR-PCB-PROC-OPTIONS    PIC X(4).
     05  FILLER                 PIC S9(5)  COMP.
     05  CR-PCB-SEGMENT-NAME    PIC X(8).
     05  CR-PCB-KEY-LENGTH      PIC S9(5)  COMP.
     05  CR-PCB-NUMB-SENS-SEGS  PIC S9(5)  COMP.
     05  CR-PCB-KEY             PIC X(22).
*
```

Figure 12-3   Source listing for the display invoice details program, version 3 (part 4 of 9)

```
PROCEDURE DIVISION.
*
    ENTRY 'DLITCBL' USING IO-PCB-MASK
                         CR-PCB-MASK.
*
000-PROCESS-INVOICE-INQUIRIES.
*
    PERFORM 100-PROCESS-INVOICE-INQUIRY
        UNTIL END-OF-MESSAGES.
    GOBACK.
*
100-PROCESS-INVOICE-INQUIRY.
*
    PERFORM 105-GET-SPA.
    IF NOT END-OF-MESSAGES
        MOVE SPA-USER-DATA TO OUTPUT-MESSAGE-TEXT-BLOCKS
        PERFORM 110-GET-INPUT-MESSAGE
        IF NOT END-OF-MESSAGES
            IF IM-LL = 16
                MOVE IM-TEXT TO INPUT-MESSAGE-EDITING-AREA
                MOVE IMEA-PFKEY-SELECTION
                    TO IM-PFKEY-SELECTION
                MOVE IMEA-INVOICE-NO      TO IM-INVOICE-NO.
    IF NOT END-OF-MESSAGES
        IF OMTB-S-INVOICE-NO NOT = IM-INVOICE-NO
            PERFORM 120-FORMAT-SPA.
    IF NOT END-OF-MESSAGES
        IF IM-DISPLAY-PAYMENTS
            MOVE OMTB-PAYMENT-TEXT      TO OM-TEXT
            MOVE 839                    TO OM-LL
            MOVE 'DICPO  '              TO MFS-MOD-NAME
        ELSE IF IM-DISPLAY-ADJUSTMENTS
            MOVE OMTB-ADJUSTMENT-TEXT TO OM-TEXT
            MOVE 431                    TO OM-LL
            MOVE 'DICAO  '              TO MFS-MOD-NAME
        ELSE IF IM-DISPLAY-SUMMARY
            MOVE OMTB-SUMMARY-TEXT      TO OM-TEXT
            MOVE 160                    TO OM-LL
            MOVE 'DICSO  '              TO MFS-MOD-NAME
        ELSE
            MOVE SPACE                  TO OM-TEXT
            MOVE 5                      TO OM-LL
            MOVE 'MENUO  '              TO MFS-MOD-NAME
            MOVE SPACE                  TO SPA-TRANSACTION-CODE.
    IF NOT END-OF-MESSAGES
        PERFORM 190-INSERT-SPA
        PERFORM 195-INSERT-OUTPUT-MESSAGE.
*
105-GET-SPA.
*
    CALL 'CBLTDLI' USING DLI-GU
                         IO-PCB-MASK
                         SPA-IO-AREA.
    IF IO-PCB-STATUS-CODE NOT = SPACE
        MOVE 'Y' TO END-OF-MESSAGES-SW.
```

Figure 12-3   Source listing for the display invoice details program, version 3 (part 5 of 9)

```
*
 110-GET-INPUT-MESSAGE.
*
     CALL 'CBLTDLI' USING DLI-GN
                          IO-PCB-MASK
                          INPUT-MESSAGE-IO-AREA.
     IF IO-PCB-STATUS-CODE NOT = SPACE
         MOVE 'Y' TO END-OF-MESSAGES-SW.
*
 120-FORMAT-SPA.
*
     MOVE 'Y'              TO INVOICE-FOUND-SW.
     MOVE IM-INVOICE-NO TO INVOICE-NO-SSA-VALUE.
     PERFORM 130-GET-RECEIVABLE-SEGMENT.
     PERFORM 140-FORMAT-SUMMARY-MESSAGE.
     PERFORM 150-FORMAT-PAYMENT-MESSAGE.
     PERFORM 170-FORMAT-ADJUSTMENT-MESSAGE.
     MOVE OUTPUT-MESSAGE-TEXT-BLOCKS TO SPA-USER-DATA.
*
 130-GET-RECEIVABLE-SEGMENT.
*
     CALL 'CBLTDLI' USING DLI-GU
                          CR-PCB-MASK
                          RECEIVABLE-SEGMENT
                          INVOICE-NO-SSA.
     IF CR-PCB-STATUS-CODE NOT = SPACE
         MOVE 'N' TO INVOICE-FOUND-SW.
*
 140-FORMAT-SUMMARY-MESSAGE.
*
     MOVE IM-INVOICE-NO TO OMTB-S-INVOICE-NO.
     IF INVOICE-FOUND
         MOVE SPACE            TO OMTB-S-ERROR-LINE
         MOVE RS-INVOICE-DATE  TO OMTB-S-INVOICE-DATE
         MOVE RS-PRODUCT-TOTAL TO OMTB-S-PROD-TOTAL
         MOVE RS-CASH-DISCOUNT TO OMTB-S-CASH-DISC
         MOVE RS-SALES-TAX     TO OMTB-S-SALES-TAX
         MOVE RS-FREIGHT       TO OMTB-S-FREIGHT
         COMPUTE OMTB-S-BILLING =   RS-PRODUCT-TOTAL -
                                    RS-CASH-DISCOUNT +
                                    RS-SALES-TAX +
                                    RS-FREIGHT
         COMPUTE OMTB-S-PMTS-ADJS = RS-BALANCE-DUE -
                                   (RS-PRODUCT-TOTAL -
                                    RS-CASH-DISCOUNT +
                                    RS-SALES-TAX +
                                    RS-FREIGHT)
         MOVE RS-BALANCE-DUE TO OMTB-S-BALANCE
     ELSE
```

Figure 12-3   Source listing for the display invoice details program, version 3 (part 6 of 9)

```
        MOVE ZERO              TO OMTB-S-INVOICE-DATE
                                  OMTB-S-PROD-TOTAL
                                  OMTB-S-CASH-DISC
                                  OMTB-S-SALES-TAX
                                  OMTB-S-FREIGHT
                                  OMTB-S-BILLING
                                  OMTB-S-PMTS-ADJS
                                  OMTB-S-BALANCE
        MOVE IM-INVOICE-NO TO EL-INVOICE-NO
        MOVE ERROR-LINE    TO OMTB-S-ERROR-LINE.
*
 150-FORMAT-PAYMENT-MESSAGE.
*
     MOVE IM-INVOICE-NO TO OMTB-P-INVOICE-NO.
     MOVE SPACE          TO OMTB-P-DETAIL-TABLE.
     IF NOT INVOICE-FOUND
        MOVE ZERO          TO OMTB-P-INVOICE-DATE
                              OMTB-P-PMT-TOTAL
        MOVE ERROR-LINE TO OMTB-P-ERROR-LINE
     ELSE
        MOVE SPACE           TO OMTB-P-ERROR-LINE
        MOVE RS-INVOICE-DATE TO OMTB-P-INVOICE-DATE
        MOVE RS-BALANCE-DUE  TO OMTB-P-BALANCE
        MOVE ZERO            TO DETAIL-COUNT
                                DETAIL-TOTAL
                                DETAIL-TOTAL-OVER-12
        MOVE 'N'             TO ALL-DETAILS-PROCESSED-SW
        MOVE 'CRPAYSEG'      TO UNQUAL-SSA-SEGMENT-NAME
        PERFORM 160-FORMAT-PAYMENT-DETAIL
            UNTIL ALL-DETAILS-PROCESSED
        MOVE DETAIL-TOTAL TO OMTB-P-PMT-TOTAL
        IF DETAIL-COUNT > 12
            SUBTRACT 12 FROM DETAIL-COUNT
                GIVING OVER-12-TITLE-COUNT
            MOVE OVER-12-TITLE        TO OMTB-P-OVER-12-TITLE
            MOVE DETAIL-TOTAL-OVER-12 TO OMTB-P-OVER-12-TOTAL
        ELSE
            MOVE SPACE TO OMTB-P-OVER-12-MSG.
*
 160-FORMAT-PAYMENT-DETAIL.
*
     PERFORM 165-GET-PAYMENT-SEGMENT.
     IF NOT ALL-DETAILS-PROCESSED
        ADD 1                TO DETAIL-COUNT
        ADD PS-PAYMENT-AMOUNT TO DETAIL-TOTAL
        IF DETAIL-COUNT < 13
            MOVE PS-CHECK-NUMBER   TO OMTB-P-CHECK (DETAIL-COUNT)
            MOVE PS-BANK-NUMBER    TO OMTB-P-BANK  (DETAIL-COUNT)
            MOVE PS-PAYMENT-DATE   TO OMTB-P-DATE  (DETAIL-COUNT)
            MOVE PS-PAYMENT-AMOUNT TO OMTB-P-AMT   (DETAIL-COUNT)
        ELSE
            ADD PS-PAYMENT-AMOUNT TO DETAIL-TOTAL-OVER-12.
*
```

Figure 12-3   Source listing for the display invoice details program, version 3 (part 7 of 9)

```
 165-GET-PAYMENT-SEGMENT.
*
    CALL 'CBLTDLI' USING DLI-GNP
                         CR-PCB-MASK
                         PAYMENT-SEGMENT
                         UNQUALIFIED-SSA.
    IF CR-PCB-STATUS-CODE NOT = SPACE
       MOVE 'Y' TO ALL-DETAILS-PROCESSED-SW.
*
 170-FORMAT-ADJUSTMENT-MESSAGE.
*
    MOVE IM-INVOICE-NO TO OMTB-A-INVOICE-NO.
    MOVE SPACE         TO OMTB-A-DETAIL-TABLE.
    IF NOT INVOICE-FOUND
        MOVE ZERO       TO OMTB-A-INVOICE-DATE
                           OMTB-A-ADJ-TOTAL
        MOVE ERROR-LINE TO OMTB-A-ERROR-LINE
    ELSE
        MOVE SPACE          TO OMTB-A-ERROR-LINE
        MOVE RS-INVOICE-DATE TO OMTB-A-INVOICE-DATE
        MOVE RS-BALANCE-DUE  TO OMTB-A-BALANCE
        MOVE ZERO           TO DETAIL-COUNT
                               DETAIL-TOTAL
                               DETAIL-TOTAL-OVER-12
        MOVE 'N'            TO ALL-DETAILS-PROCESSED-SW
        MOVE 'CRADJSEG'     TO UNQUAL-SSA-SEGMENT-NAME
        PERFORM 180-FORMAT-ADJUSTMENT-DETAIL
            UNTIL ALL-DETAILS-PROCESSED
        MOVE DETAIL-TOTAL TO OMTB-A-ADJ-TOTAL
        IF DETAIL-COUNT > 12
            SUBTRACT 12 FROM DETAIL-COUNT
                GIVING OVER-12-TITLE-COUNT
            MOVE OVER-12-TITLE         TO OMTB-A-OVER-12-TITLE
            MOVE DETAIL-TOTAL-OVER-12 TO OMTB-A-OVER-12-TOTAL
        ELSE
            MOVE SPACE TO OMTB-A-OVER-12-MSG.
*
 180-FORMAT-ADJUSTMENT-DETAIL.
*
    PERFORM 185-GET-ADJUSTMENT-SEGMENT.
    IF NOT ALL-DETAILS-PROCESSED
        ADD 1                 TO DETAIL-COUNT
        ADD AS-ADJUSTMENT-AMOUNT TO DETAIL-TOTAL
        IF DETAIL-COUNT < 13
            MOVE AS-ADJUSTMENT-DATE
                TO OMTB-A-DATE (DETAIL-COUNT)
            MOVE AS-ADJUSTMENT-TYPE
                TO OMTB-A-TYPE (DETAIL-COUNT)
            MOVE AS-REFERENCE-NUMBER
                TO OMTB-A-NO   (DETAIL-COUNT)
            MOVE AS-ADJUSTMENT-AMOUNT
                TO OMTB-A-AMT  (DETAIL-COUNT)
        ELSE
            ADD AS-ADJUSTMENT-AMOUNT
                TO DETAIL-TOTAL-OVER-12.
```

Figure 12-3   Source listing for the display invoice details program, version 3 (part 8 of 9)

```
*
  185-GET-ADJUSTMENT-SEGMENT.
*
    CALL 'CBLTDLI' USING DLI-GNP
                         CR-PCB-MASK
                         ADJUSTMENT-SEGMENT
                         UNQUALIFIED-SSA.
    IF CR-PCB-STATUS-CODE NOT = SPACE
       MOVE 'Y' TO ALL-DETAILS-PROCESSED-SW.
*
  190-INSERT-SPA.
*
    CALL 'CBLTDLI' USING DLI-ISRT
                         IO-PCB-MASK
                         SPA-IO-AREA.
*
  195-INSERT-OUTPUT-MESSAGE.
*
    CALL 'CBLTDLI' USING DLI-ISRT
                         IO-PCB-MASK
                         OUTPUT-MESSAGE-IO-AREA
                         MFS-MOD-NAME.
*
```

Figure 12-3   Source listing for the display invoice details program, version 3 (part 9 of 9)

As I mentioned, the approach to the problem is a little different in this version of the program than in the one in chapter 8. Module 120, "Format SPA," is performed only when information for a new invoice is requested. If information for the invoice used in a previous iteration of the conversation is requested, the program simply selects the right data from the SPA and sends it to the terminal.

I've shaded the parts of the source code in figure 12-3 that I particularly want you to notice. First, I coded a data description for the SPA. As you can see, it begins with the four standard fields I've described: LL, ZZ, CI, and transaction code. In this example, the user data component of the SPA has three large fields. Each corresponds to one of the message text groups defined subordinate to OUTPUT-MESSAGE-TEXT-BLOCKS. As a result, each time the SPA is saved, all of the information necessary to display any one of the three screens of the application is stored.

The fields in the input message segment are the same as in the version of the program in chapter 8. Notice, however, that I added a fourth condition name (IM-RETURN-TO-MENU) to accommodate the PF3 option. In addition, remember that IMS removes the transaction code from a conversational program's first input message segment and

Input message format for the first message of a conversation

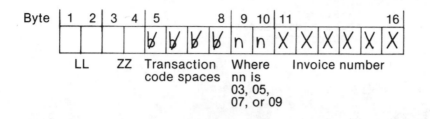
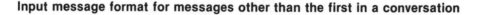

Input message format for messages other than the first in a conversation

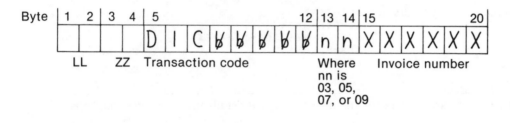

Figure 12-4   Input message formats for the display invoice details program, version 3

stores it in the SPA, but that subsequent input messages contain the transaction code.

To understand how this affects the program, consider figure 12-4. The top part of this figure shows the format of the first input message received in a conversation. As you can see, the message begins with two-byte LL and ZZ fields. Then, the message contains four blanks. Those are the positions in the input message that immediately follow the transaction code (DIC) and the first delimiting character after it. IMS removes those first four bytes, but leaves the four trailing spaces. After these four spaces are the PF key indicator and the invoice number.

The bottom section of figure 12-4 shows the format of input messages other than the first in a conversation. Here, the complete transaction code is passed to the program. That's because IMS doesn't remove it to initialize the SPA; the SPA is already established.

To enable the program to handle either type of message, I coded an editing area right after the input message segment description. If the length of the input message is 16, the program moves the data in the input message field IM-TEXT to INPUT-MESSAGE-EDITING-AREA, then moves the two data fields in the editing area back to the input message segment. That way, the data the program needs in the input message segment is shifted right four bytes so it lines up properly with the fields as they're defined subordinate to INPUT-MESSAGE-IO-AREA.

Now, take a look at the Procedure Division. For each input message, the program first retrieves the SPA by invoking module 105. Notice in that module that the call to retrieve the SPA is like the first call for an input message segment in a non-conversational program. The only difference is that the I/O area it names is for the SPA.

If the SPA is retrieved successfully, module 100 moves the user data stored in it to the group item OUTPUT-MESSAGE-TEXT-BLOCKS and invokes module 110 to retrieve the input message segment; notice in module 110 that the call issued is a get-next, not a get-unique. Next, module 100 formats the input message to accommodate the two possible formats in which IMS can supply the message to the program.

After the SPA and the input message segment have been retrieved, the program compares the invoice number in the input message with the invoice number used during the previous terminal interaction. If they're the same, the program can simply use the data in the SPA to provide whatever response the user wants. However, if they differ, the program performs module 120 to format the SPA for this iteration and subsequent ones.

Next, the program sends one of four output messages. Depending on which selection the operator made, the proper text fields are moved to the output message data component, the length of the output message is set, and the right MOD name is specified. If the program is handling the last message in a conversation (indicated by 03 in the PF key field of the input message), it also moves spaces to the transaction code field of the SPA to tell IMS that the conversation is over.

Finally, after the program has formatted the SPA and output message, it invokes modules 190 and 195 to save the SPA and send the output message. Both modules issue ISRT calls that refer to the I/O PCB. However, the two modules specify different I/O areas: 190 names SPA-IO-AREA and 195 names OUTPUT-MESSAGE-IO-AREA. The SPA is saved before the output message is sent.

How to use program switching in conversational programs

In the last two chapters, you saw examples of program-to-program message switching involving non-conversational programs. This section describes program-to-program message switching between conversational programs. As you'll see, there are two kinds of program-to-program message switches you can use with conversational programs: immediate and deferred.

Switching from one conversational program to another requires that both the SPA and the message to be processed by the second program be transferred. After a conversational program has sent its SPA to another program, it can no longer respond to the originating terminal; the second program assumes that responsibility. Because the SPA is involved, you have to be sure that the SPAs specified for the two programs are compatible. A program with a fixed-length SPA cannot transfer control to a program with a variable-length SPA. However, a program specified with a variable-length SPA can transfer control to a program with a fixed-length SPA.

Immediate program switching   Figure 12-5 illustrates an *immediate program-to-program message switch*, also called simply an *immediate message switch*. As you can see, the program that receives the input message is not the same one that responds to the terminal. Instead, the first program passes its SPA and any other necessary data to another program, which does additional processing and responds to the originating terminal.

The upper right corner of figure 12-5 presents the typical sequence of message calls the first program involved in an immediate switch issues. It retrieves the SPA and the input message as usual (by issuing a GU call and one or more GN calls that reference the I/O PCB), then does whatever processing is appropriate for the application. Next, however, instead of saving its SPA and replying to the originating terminal by issuing ISRT calls against its I/O PCB, it passes the SPA and a message to another program. To pass the SPA, the first program issues an ISRT call that references an alternate PCB. Then, to pass along a message segment, the first program can issue one or more additional ISRT calls that refer to the same alternate PCB. After the first program has done this, it can no longer reply to the originating terminal.

Now, it's up to the second program to reply, which it can do as soon as IMS schedules it. Take a look at the second group of calls in figure 12-5. They're what you'd expect in an independent conversational program, that is, one that isn't involved in a program-to-program message switch. (In other words, the second program isn't any different from an MPP that receives its input messages directly from terminals.) The only PCB referenced for message calls is the I/O PCB. I want you to notice in particular that the second program, not the first, responds to the terminal.

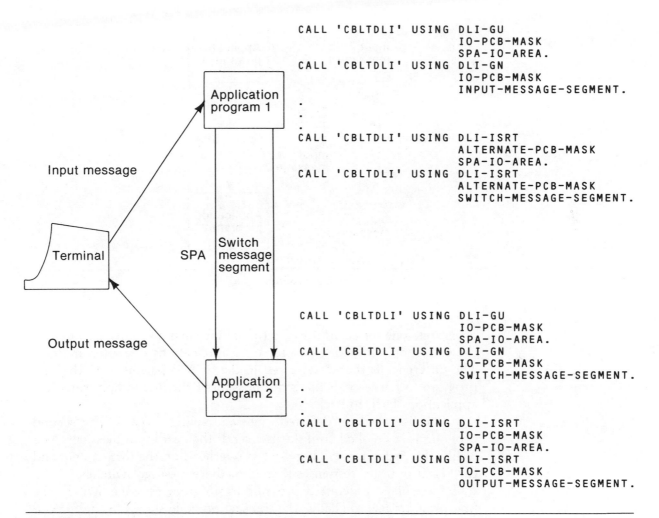

Figure 12-5 Immediate program-to-program message switch

The alternate PCB used in the first program involved in an immediate switch can be fixed or modifiable. If it's modifiable, the first program must issue a CHNG call (to specify the transaction code for the second program) before it issues the first ISRT call against the alternate PCB. In addition, the alternate PCB must be defined to IMS with two additional parameters: ALTRESP and SAMETRM. You shouldn't have to worry about this, though; it's the system administrator's responsibility to make sure the PSB for an application is correct.

Deferred program switching   Figure 12-6 illustrates a *deferred program-to-program message switch*, also called a *deferred message switch*. Here, a single conversation involves two different application

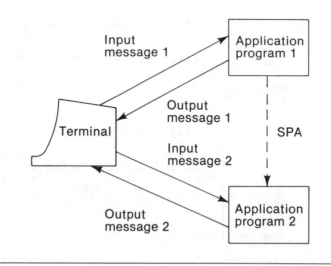

Figure 12-6   Deferred program-to-program message switch

programs, one for each of two terminal interactions. This is similar to the user simply invoking two separate applications one after another. The difference is that data stored in the SPA is passed from the first program to the second; that's not possible if the user simply runs two applications back to back.

This is called a "deferred" message switch because the second program isn't invoked until the user sends the next input message. As a result, this technique can impose less overhead on the IMS system and can result in faster responses than immediate message switches.

To achieve a deferred program-to-program message switch, the first program has to change the transaction code stored in the SPA to that of the second program before it saves the SPA. As a result, when the next input message is received from the terminal, IMS knows that it should schedule the second program because its transaction code is already stored in the SPA. Remember, the SPA is considered to be the first segment of an input message in a conversational program, and the transaction code stored in it—not the transaction code that comes in from the terminal—determines what application program should be scheduled.

Aside from changing the transaction code in the SPA, there are no other special programming considerations you need to keep in mind for developing an application that does a deferred program-to-program message switch.

Terminology

conversational programming
conversational program
scratch pad area
SPA
conversational identifier
CI
conversational control block
CCB
immediate program-to-program message switch
immediate message switch
deferred program-to-program message switch
deferred message switch

Objectives

1. Describe an application in which data needs to be saved between terminal interactions.

2. Describe the advantages and disadvantages of the three techniques that are available for a program to store data between interactions of a program.

3. Describe the format of the I/O area used for a SPA.

4. Describe the data communications calls used in a program that uses a SPA.

5. Given complete specifications, design and code a conversational program.

6. Differentiate between an immediate program-to-program message switch and a deferred program-to-program message switch.

Chapter 13

An introduction to error handling in the IMS DC environment

Failures in an IMS system that can affect data base and message integrity can have a variety of sources. For example, it's possible that the IMS or MVS software or the network hardware will fail. However, it's much more likely that the source of a failure will be an application program. Regardless of the source of a failure, IMS provides facilities to overcome it. Those facilities involve recording information about all the activity of the system (*logging*) and using that information to restart the system and reverse partial changes (*recovery*).

A major strong point of IMS is its set of logging and recovery facilities. This chapter introduces them. However, I want you to keep in mind that application programmers typically have less to do with logging and recovery than systems programmers and operators. And even then, the logging and recovery facilities you'll use will be limited and standardized in your shop. As a result, this chapter just presents the background you need to understand IMS logging and recovery facilities and describes some of the features you may have to integrate into your programs. It does not present specific techniques that you must use.

Logging

Logging is a central, key feature of IMS; it's always active while the DC system is running. Logging records all data base updates, all messages queued, and all programs scheduled, among other things. Figure 13-1, which you first saw in chapter 3, shows how central logging functions

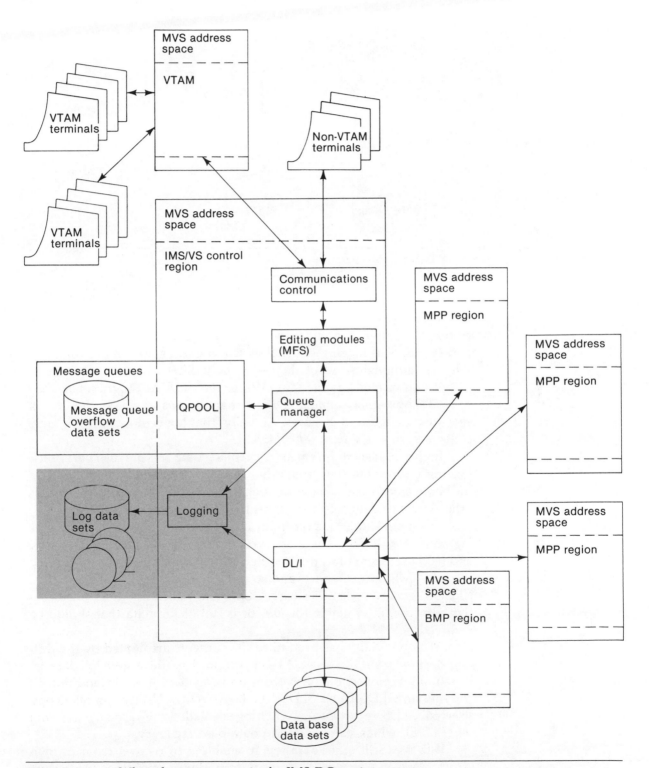

Figure 13-1   Where logging occurs in the IMS DC environment

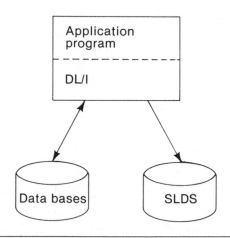

Figure 13-2   Logging for an IMS batch program

are in IMS. Because log information is available, it can be used to restore the system if a failure occurs. This section introduces the terms and concepts of logging under IMS 1.3; the ideas are similar for other releases, although some of the details may differ.

If you've read chapter 9 in *IMS for the COBOL Programmer, Part 1*, you know that a batch DL/I program uses a single "log" as it executes, as figure 13-2 shows. Actually, that log is more appropriately called a *system log data set* (*SLDS*).

In the on-line environment, system log data sets are also part of the logging system, but they aren't the "first line" of logging, as they are in the batch environment. Instead, logging in the on-line environment uses other kinds of data sets as well, as figure 13-3 shows.

The main kind of log file in the DC environment is called an *on-line log data set* (*OLDS*). There are typically several on-line log data sets, and IMS uses them one after another. When one OLDS fills up with log records, IMS uses the next, and so on. Another file, called the *DBRC RECON data set*, identifies each OLDS and indicates whether it's currently in use, is available for use, or is full of log data that should be archived.

After an OLDS has been filled, its contents are copied by the IMS *Log Archive Utility* to an SLDS. So you can see, the system log data set is actually removed one step from on-line operations. In addition to copying an OLDS to an SLDS, the Log Archive Utility can also copy selected OLDS records to another log file called the *recovery log data set* (*RLDS*), which can be used in data base recovery.

IMS uses still other data sets to enable it to recover from its own errors. As IMS executes, it stores information it might need to restart

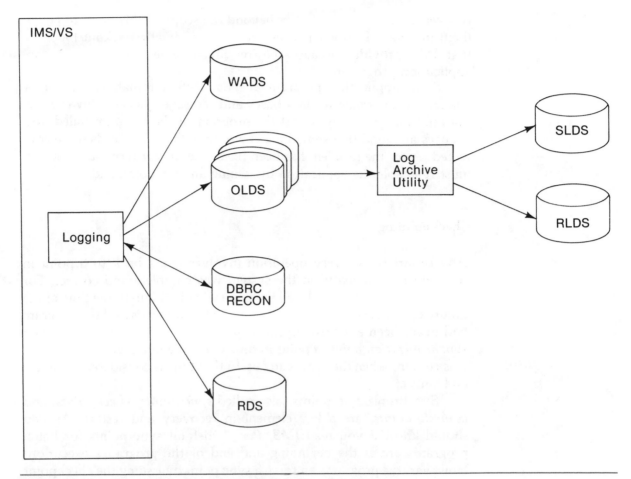

Figure 13-3   Logging data sets in the IMS DC environment

itself in another log file called the *restart data set* (*RDS*). Also, it uses a file called a *write-ahead data set* (*WADS*) to record log data temporarily that will eventually be stored in an OLDS. The WADS enables IMS to write to the OLDS only when enough log data has been accumulated to fill a block, but at the same time not risk losing data in the event of a system failure.

Recovery

Simply storing all the activity of the system in logs isn't worth much if a way isn't provided to use that data to recover the system in the event of a failure. As you'd expect, IMS includes extensive facilities for recovery. Although it's clearly beyond the scope of this book to cover them in detail, I do want to describe the automatic backout facilities that IMS provides because they're directly relevant to you as an application programmer.

If an application program abends, IMS automatically reverses changes it has made to data bases and message queues. However, it does not automatically restart the program. If the program failed, the chances are good that something is wrong with it that needs to be corrected. After the problem has been fixed, the master terminal operator must re-enable the application by issuing an IMS command.

Checkpointing

Any restart or recovery operation involves going back to a point in time when all activity on the system was complete and correct. For example, if a program fails, all the processing it did up to the time of the failure can be reversed. Then, the state of the system is as if the program had never been executed. In this case, the start of the program was a *synchronization point*, a point in time when the integrity of the system was certain, when the processing up to that time is considered complete and correct.

Synchronization points, also called *sync points*, *checkpoints*, and *commit points*, are a key element in recovery and restart. As you should know if you read *IMS, Part 1*, default sync points for batch programs are at the beginning and end of the program's execution. However, the program can force a sync point by issuing the checkpoint (CHKP) call. Then, IMS writes a checkpoint record on the log to indicate that the processing the program has done so far is OK and does not need to be backed out if the program fails.

For an MPP, the system is typically defined so checkpoints are taken automatically with each transaction a program processes. This is called *single-mode processing*. As you know, when a program issues a GU call against its I/O PCB, that indicates that it has finished the processing for the previous transaction. At that time, IMS considers the transaction complete, and it is not backed out in the event of a system failure. Although single-mode processing requires a significant amount of system overhead, it's the rule for typical MPPs because it requires smaller log areas and, more important, makes it less likely that many transactions will have to be reprocessed if there's a failure.

If a program is specified with *multiple-mode processing*, the only automatic checkpoint is at the end of the program. However, the program can force a checkpoint by issuing the checkpoint (CHKP) call, which causes IMS to write a checkpoint record to the log, and in effect declares that all the processing done by the program so far is complete and correct. (Because MPPs typically are defined to run in single mode, you'll probably use the CHKP call only in BMP programs.)

You code the CHKP call like this:

```
CALL 'CBLTDLI' USING DLI-CHKP
                     IO-PCB-MASK
                     INPUT-MESSAGE-IO-AREA.
```

The checkpoint call must reference the I/O PCB. Notice also that you code the name of an I/O area on the call. That's because the CHKP call not only causes IMS to write a checkpoint record to the log, but it also requests the next input message. In this case, the next input message will be stored in the field INPUT-MESSAGE-IO-AREA. If there are no more input messages for your program, the CHKP call returns a QC status code, just like a GU call to the I/O PCB. Because the CHKP call includes the function of a get call, you don't use a GU or GN call when you request a checkpoint.

Like a batch program, a BMP program typically issues a CHKP call after it has processed a certain number of transactions. The checkpoint call should be issued at a logical place in the processing: after all data base updates for a transaction have been completed, but before the next message is retrieved. If you issue the CHKP call right after a message retrieval call, the data from that call is lost because the checkpoint causes a new message to be retrieved.

Error handling in MPPs

Usually, an MPP shouldn't abend. However, it is possible that it might encounter exceptional conditions that it can't handle. For example, suppose an application program that always runs normally receives an unexpected status code as a result of a simple data base call. Perhaps the code indicates that the data base data sets weren't available. If that happens, the program is still in control, but can't do the expected processing.

What happens when your program encounters an unexpected status code depends on your shop's standards. In any case, three steps are generally required. First, the problem needs to be documented so it can be solved by the appropriate personnel. Second, any data base changes the program made need to be reversed. And third, the program probably needs to be terminated and flagged as having experienced an error. Regardless of the techniques I present for meeting these requirements, you must follow your shop's standards.

To document an error, you should include standardized code in your programs to record as much information as necessary to solve the problem. Typically, there are two parts to documenting the error. First, you need to advise the system operator that the program detected an error. To do this, you can insert a message to an alternate PCB. However, since the program will be terminated in a moment and output messages are normally deleted when that happens, you use a special kind of alternate PCB called an *express PCB*, which is defined in the PSBGEN. When a message is inserted via an express PCB, it's routed to its destination immediately, without waiting for the next sync point. Be sure to issue a PURG call after each complete message you send via an express PCB.

You can also use this technique to send a message to another program that is designed to record errors. The format of the message you send depends entirely on what the destination program does. Check to see if your installation uses this kind of "common error-handler" program and, if it does, what the formats of the messages it expects are.

There are other ways to record information about a program error. One is to use another DC call, the LOG call, to record a user message on the log. (The function code for the call is the three letters LOG followed by one space.) After the program formats the data to be stored in the log in an I/O area, it issues the call in this format:

```
CALL 'CBLTDLI' USING DLI-LOG
                     IO-PCB-MASK
                     LOG-USER-DATA.
```

The first five bytes of the user data field have a rigid format. The first two bytes correspond to the LL and ZZ fields on any DC message. You must initialize the LL field to contain the length of the user data plus the five-byte prefix; the ZZ field must contain binary zeros (COBOL LOW-VALUE). The fifth byte contains a code that identifies the record in the log data set; its value must be between hex A0 and EF. There are some restrictions on the size of the I/O area you specify on the LOG call, but they should be taken into account in the program specifications you receive. Many shops do not allow you to store user records in the IMS logs at all, so don't use the LOG call unless your program specifications explicitly require it.

To reverse changes the program has made, you adopt one of two approaches. First, you can rely on IMS's default automatic recovery. To do that, you include code in your program that will certainly result in an abend, like dividing by zero. (I used this technique in the CR program in chapter 7, the ACR program in chapter 10, and the PCR program in chapter 11.) You'll often see this called a *pseudo-abend*. Actually, an intentional abend would be a better term, because there's nothing "pseudo" about it: An abend is an abend.

When you force your program to fail, IMS reverses data base changes made since its last checkpoint and deletes incomplete messages. Obviously, in addition to reversing your changes, this approach also takes care of the third step: it ends your program too.

An alternative approach is to use either the ROLL or ROLB call to roll back the changes to the last sync point. Both calls cause data base updates made since the last checkpoint to be reversed and cancel output messages inserted since then. They differ in what happens next.

If you issue the ROLL call, which has the simple format

```
CALL 'CBLTDLI' USING DLI-ROLL.
```

IMS terminates your program and disables it from being automatically scheduled again. Notice that you don't even name a PCB on the ROLL call. After a program has issued the ROLL call, the system operator has to enable it explicitly before IMS will schedule it again. The input message that was being processed when the call was issued is deleted.

In contrast, the ROLB call does not cause the application program to be terminated. Instead, the program can continue to process other messages that are present on its queue. The ROLB call can be used only in programs that are specified to IMS to run in single processing mode. The input message that was being processed when the call was issued may or may not be deleted, depending on the format of the call.

If you specify an I/O area on the call, as in

```
CALL 'CBLTDLI' USING DLI-ROLB
                     IO-PCB-MASK
                     INPUT-MESSAGE-IO-AREA.
```

the input message that's currently being processed is presented to the program again in the specified area. I suspect that you'll seldom if ever use this option. After all, if it's OK to use the ROLB call to let the program continue, why process what obviously must have been a bad transaction?

You're more likely to use the the ROLB call to delete the current input message and continue execution with the next. Its format is

```
CALL 'CBLTDLI' USING DLI-ROLB
                     IO-PCB-MASK.
```

You only specify the function code field and the name of the I/O PCB; you do not specify an I/O area.

Discussion

I want to stress again that your shop almost certainly has unique error-handling standards. Although the subjects I've described in this chapter are common elements in error-handling schemes, your shop may not use them in the same ways and may use still other techniques. As a result, I encourage you to talk with your supervisor and co-workers and read your shop's programming standards manual to find out exactly what your programs should do.

For more information on the way IMS logging and recovery work, you might be interested in looking into two manuals: *IMS/VS Version 1 Operations and Recovery Guide* and *IMS/VS Version 1 Data Base Recovery Control: Guide and Reference*. They should be available in your shop's reference library.

Terminology

logging
recovery
system log data set
SLDS
on-line log data set
OLDS
DBRC RECON data set
Log Archive Utility
recovery log data set
RLDS
restart data set

RDS
write-ahead data set
WADS
synchronization point
sync point
checkpoint
commit point
single-mode processing
multiple-mode processing
express PCB
pseudo-abend

Objectives

1. Describe when logging occurs in the IMS DC system.

2. Describe the data sets used for IMS DC logging.

3. Distinguish between single- and multiple-mode processing.

4. Describe alternatives for recording a program error in the IMS DC environment.

5. Distinguish between the functions of the ROLL and ROLB calls.

Section 5

Using
Batch Terminal Simulator

As you develop an IMS DC program and its MFS blocks, it's almost certain that you won't be testing them in the production environment. After all, the production system has been carefully tuned so it performs at optimum levels. Instead, you'll probably use an IBM program product called Batch Terminal Simulator, or just BTS, for testing.

This section presents BTS in three chapters. Chapter 14 introduces BTS; it shows you how to interpret BTS output and how to supply input to direct BTS functions. Chapter 15 shows you how to run BTS in a batch job. Finally, chapter 16 shows you how to use BTS Full Screen Support under TSO.

Chapter 14

An introduction to BTS

Batch Terminal Simulator (BTS) is an IMS DC program development tool that I think you'll come to use extensively and appreciate. BTS lets you run your DC applications using real DL/I data bases, MFS format sets, and IMS modules. However, it does that separately from the production DC system. In addition to letting you simply run applications, it can provide you with a wealth of debugging information, both for your COBOL programs and your MFS format sets. In this chapter, I'll describe BTS by showing you (1) what BTS output looks like, (2) how to code BTS input commands, and (3) what processing BTS does.

BTS OUTPUT

As I just mentioned, BTS can provide extensive testing information for applications, both programs and format sets. Regardless of whether you run BTS in the batch or TSO environment, the information is supplied to you in a print (SYSOUT) data set called *BTSOUT*. (Under TSO, that output is not only stored in the BTSOUT data set, but can also be displayed at your terminal as BTS executes.) This section describes what BTSOUT can contain.

For a program, BTS can provide a trace of all DL/I calls it issues, both for DB and DC operations. You can disable the trace feature altogether, or you can request either DB or DC call information,

310

whatever you need to diagnose and solve your debugging problems. For instance, BTS can print any call's function, its I/O area, and its PCB name. And for a DB operation, it also prints the PCB key feedback area and the segment search arguments you used on the call.

For a format set, BTS can provide a printed image of a 3270 screen that you can use to check locations and sizes of fields, data entered into and displayed in them, and their attributes. By combining this information with the contents of input and output message segments processed by application programs, you can see exactly how MFS maps data between device formats and message descriptors. To provide this support, BTS maintains an image of a terminal screen that it updates to reflect changes via simulated operator entry or program action.

How to read BTSOUT screen images

Figure 14-1 shows part of the BTS output for a test run of one of the versions of the invoice summary application you saw earlier in this book. Part 1 of the figure shows the screen displayed after I entered the command

```
/FORMAT DI20
```

and keyed in an invoice number (010000) in line 3, column 12. Notice at the top of the page that BTS indicates the screen displayed is input (ACTION=ENTER) that's to be mapped into a message defined by the MID DI2I.

As you can see, each screen line is identified on the right and left with a line number, and each column is identified on the scale lines that bound the top and bottom of the screen image. In this example, each screen line is displayed in two print lines. The first print line shows what the user would see, while the second shows useful terminal information including attribute bytes, cursor position, and modified fields.

The way BTS displays this additional information can be confusing. That's because some information can overlay other information. To understand, you need to be aware of the sequence in which MFS formats these lines. First, it marks modified fields by underlining them with rows of plus signs. In part 1 of figure 14-1, you can see that the invoice number field is marked like this.

After BTS has identified modified fields on its screen image, it marks the cursor position with a hyphen. In this case, it's in line 3, column 12 because that's the only modifiable field on the screen. Notice, though, that the line and column location of the cursor is included in the heading; that's easier to use than trying to find a single hyphen in the screen image.

Finally, after modified fields and the cursor position have been marked, BTS prints the hexadecimal values of attribute bytes below and immediately before the fields they delimit. To use this information, you have to know what the hexadecimal equivalents are of the bit combinations for the attributes you requested in your format set. At the bottom of each screen image is a legend that can help you decode the hex values. You can use it in conjunction with the conversion table in appendix D to figure out what each attribute byte value means.

For example, the value of the first attribute byte on the screen (in column 1 of line 1) is hex 38. In the table in appendix D, you can see that this is equivalent to binary 0011 1000. And from the legend at the bottom of the screen image, that means the field that follows the attribute byte is protected, has numeric shift, is displayed with bright intensity, and does not have its MDT set to on.

Notice in part 1 of figure 14-1 that the end of each field is marked by an attribute byte with value hex 3C. Those attribute bytes are inserted by MFS to create fields at all screen positions that aren't specified in the format set. Hex 3C means those fields' attributes are protected, numeric, and no-display. Because they combine the protected and numeric attributes, they're considered auto-skip fields.

Attribute byte values are formatted from left to right across a line and from top to bottom on the screen. As they're positioned in the right spots, it's possible that they can overlay other information that has already been formatted, including preceding attribute byte values. To understand this, look at the data entry field on the screen: the invoice number field that begins in line 3, column 12.

The attribute byte that immediately precedes it is hex 11, which indicates that the field is not protected, has normal intensity, is numeric, and has its MDT set on. However, the attribute byte value BTS printed for the data entry field overlays the value for the immediately preceding field, which should appear as 3C. That's because the data entry field follows so closely after the literal field that identifies it. This shouldn't present a problem for you as long as you're aware of it; almost always, the attribute byte value that's hidden is 3C.

Part 3 of figure 14-1 shows the output screen displayed via MFS after the application program has processed the transaction. The fields in the output message, defined in the MOD named DI2O, were mapped to the screen in the positions shown. Note here that no fields have been modified (that is, no field is underlined with a row of plus signs). That's because this screen image represents the data that was sent to the terminal, before the user has made any changes.

PAGE 0004

B T S 3270 FORMATTED SCREEN IMAGE.

B A T C H   T E R M I N A L   S I M U L A T O R   ' B T S O U T '

MID/MOD= DI2I   , CURSOR= L03C012, ACTION= ENTER

```
    ----.----1----.----2----.----3----.----4----.----5----.----6----.----7----.----8
*01* DISPLAY INVOICE SUMMARY                              DATE: 12/27/86 *01*
     38                         3C                      38      328  3C
*02*                                                                    *02*
*03* INVOICE: 010000   DATE:              SUBTOTAL:                     *03*
     38  311-+++3C38   320           3C   38         3C    20      3C
*04*                                      DISCOUNT:                     *04*
                                          38         3C    20      3C
*05*                                      SALES TAX:                    *05*
                                          38         3C    20      3C
*06*                                      FREIGHT:                      *06*
                                          38       3C      20      3C
*07*                                                          3C        *07*
                                                   38      20
*08*                                      BILLING:                      *08*
                                          38         3C  38            *08*
*09*                                      PMTS/ADJS:                    *09*
                                          38         3C    20      3C
*10*                                                 3C                 *10*
                                          38               38
*11*                                      DUE:                          *11*
                                          38   3C          20      3C
*12*                                                                    *12*
*13*                                                                    *13*
*14*                                                                    *14*
*15*                                                                    *15*
*16*                                                                    *16*
*17*                                                                    *17*
*18*                                                                    *18*
*19*                                                                    *19*
*20*                                                                    *20*
*21*                                                                    *21*
*22*                                                                    *22*
*23*                   20                                               *23*
*24*  3C                                                                *24*
    ----.----1----.----2----.----3----.----4----.----5----.----6----.----7----.----8
```

THE FIELD ATTRIBUTE BITS ARE: RRPNDDRM, WHERE P MEANS PROTECTED; N MEANS NUMERIC; M MEANS MODIFIED.
THE MEANING OF THE DD BITS IS: 00=DISPLAY/NO PEN DETECT; 01=DISPLAY/DETECT; 10=BRIGHT/DETECT; 11=DARK/NO PEN DETECT.

Figure 14-1   Sample BTS output (part 1 of 3)

```
PAGE 0005              B A T C H   T E R M I N A L   S I M U L A T O R   ' B T S O U T '

BTS0006I TRANSACTION STARTED: DI2

MBR=DI2      PSB=DCTST    EDIT=        SPA=0      PLC=1      LANG=CBL TYPE=MSG

****  MSG CALL- FUNC=GU , PCB=IOPCB     , STATUS= , MESSAGE NUMBER=000001        LENGTH=000018, PCBN=001     -MSG-  GU

      ----.----1----.----2----.----3----.----4----.----5----.----6----.----7----.----8----.----9----.----1C
IOAREA=    DI2    010000
      0100CCF444444FFFFF
      020149200000010000

******  DB CALL- FUNC=GU , PCB=C9BD     , STATUS= , LEVEL=01, SEGMENT=CRRECSEG  IOLENGTH=000057, PCBN=002     -DB-   GU

      ----.----1----.----2----.----3----.----4----.----5----.----6----.----7----.----8----.----9----.----1C
KFB=010000
    FFFFF                                                                              H
    010000

SSA1=CRRECSEG(CRRECXNO =010000)
     CDDCCECC4CDDCCEDD47FFFFFF5
     39953257D3995375606010000D

      ----.----1----.----2----.----3----.----4----.----5----.----6----.----7----.----8----.----9----.----1C
IOAREA=010000071586
    FFFFFFFFF4444444444444444444402000000000000300189
    010000071586000000000000000000000C000C000C010C008C

BTS0031I MODNAME: DI2O

****  MSG CALL- FUNC=ISRT, PCB=IOPCB     , STATUS= , MESSAGE NUMBER=000001        LENGTH=000160, PCBN=001     -MSG-  ISRT

      ----.----1----.----2----.----3----.----4----.----5----.----6----.----7----.----8----.----9----.----10
IOAREA= 010000071586 200.00      .00        .00      13.00   213.00  104.11- 108.89
    0A00FFFFFF6FF6FF4FF444FF4444FF4444FF444FF4444FF444FF4444444444444444444444
    0000010000071518600200B000000000B000000013B00000104B11000108B89000000000000000000000C
    4444444444444444444444444444444444444444444444444444
    0000000000000000000000000000000000000000000000000000

****  MSG CALL- FUNC=GU , PCB=IOPCB     , STATUS=QC, MESSAGE NUMBER=000001        -ENGTH=000000, PCBN=001     -MSG-  GU   QC

BTS0020I STATISTICS REPORT FOR TRANSACTION:DI2
PCBNAME  GU  GN  GNP  GHU  GN  GHNP  ISRT PURG REPL DLET  DEQ CHKP  LOG STAT XRST CHNG ROLB OPEN CLSE OTHR
IOPCB    2                                                                   1
```

Figure 14-1   Sample BTS output (part 2 of 3)

PAGE 0006   B A T C H   T E R M I N A L   S I M U L A T O R   ' B T S O U T '

B T S   3270 FORMATTED SCREEN IMAGE. MID/MOD= DI20   , CURSOR= L03C012, ACTION= OUTPUT

```
    ----.----1----.----2----.----3----.----4----.----5----.----6----.----7----.----8
*01* DISPLAY INVOICE SUMMARY                                  DATE: 12/27/86  *01*
     38                         3c                            38        328  3c  *02*
*02*
*03* INVOICE: 010000  DATE: 07/15/86                                          *03*
     38      310-  3c38  320  3c
*04*                         SUBTOTAL:   200.00                               *04*
                         38          3c 20        3c
*05*                         DISCOUNT:     .00                                *05*
                         38          3c 20        3c
*06*                         SALES TAX:    .00                                *06*
                         38           3c 20       3c
*07*                         FREIGHT:    13.00                                *07*
                         38         3c 20         3c
*08*                                    ------                                *08*
                                    38           3c
*09*                         BILLING:   213.00                                *09*
                         38         3c 20         3c
*10*                         PMTS/ADJS: 104.11-                               *10*
                         38          3c 20        3c
*11*                                    ------                                *11*
                                    38           3c
*12*                         DUE:      108.89                                 *12*
                         38    3c 20              3c
*13*                                                                          *13*
*14*                                                                          *14*
*15*                                                                          *15*
*16*                                                                          *16*
*17*                                                                          *17*
*18*                                                                          *18*
*19*                                                                          *19*
*20*                                                                          *20*
*21*                                                                          *21*
*22*                                                                          *22*
*23*                                                                          *23*
     20
*24*                                                                          *24*
     3c
    ----.----1----.----2----.----3----.----4----.----5----.----6----.----7----.----8
```

THE FIELD ATTRIBUTE BITS ARE: RRPNDDRM, WHERE P MEANS PROTECTED; N MEANS NUMERIC; M MEANS MODIFIED.
THE MEANING OF THE DD BITS IS: 00=DISPLAY/NO PEN DETECT; 01=DISPLAY/DETECT; 10=BRIGHT/DETECT; 11=DARK/NO PEN DETECT.

Figure 14-1   Sample BTS output (part 3 of 3)

How to read BTSOUT call traces

The processing that was done between the time the screen in part 1 of figure 14-1 was received and the screen in part 3 was displayed is recorded in part 2 of the figure, which traces the application program's calls. The name of the transaction, DI2, is given at the top of the page. The first call after the program was loaded was a GU against the I/O PCB. The I/O area returned by the call, as you can see in the figure, is 18 bytes long, beginning with LL and ZZ fields followed by the eight-byte transaction code (DI2). The last six bytes of the input message contain the invoice number from the entry screen (010000). The first line shown for the I/O area presents its contents in character form; the other two present its contents in hex.

The next call the program issued was a GU for the data base. The BTS output shows the key feedback area after the call (KFB) and the segment search argument used for the call (SSA1). If an SSA is longer than 512 bytes, only the first 512 are printed, and if an SSA's value contains a right parenthesis, the value that's printed ends with that character. Again, the contents of the I/O area are also printed.

The third call was an ISRT to the I/O PCB to respond to the terminal. This time, the message is longer. The last call the program issued was another GU against the I/O PCB. Because there were no other messages queued for the program, IMS returned a status code of QC, and the program ended. The last lines on the page in part 2 contain statistics for the execution of the program. They show how many calls of each type were issued for the program's PCBs.

The example in figure 14-1 is simple. Even so, I think it illustrates how much useful information, both for debugging and documentation, BTS can provide. You're not limited to simple applications like the one in figure 14-1; you can test applications that issue many data base calls against multiple DB PCBs, that are conversational, and that use alternate destinations or paging. However, to test any application under BTS, you have to supply input to BTS that tells it what to do.

BTS INPUT

BTS input comes in three forms: IMS commands, BTS simulator statements, and BTS commands. All are supplied in card-image format through a data set called *BTSIN*.

IMS commands

You can include two IMS commands in a BTS input stream: /EXIT and /FORMAT. The /EXIT command lets you end a conversational program in the middle of a conversation; you'll seldom use it. In contrast, you'll often use the /FORMAT command. It lets you format the BTS screen image by specifying an MFS MOD name.

You should be careful to use a /FORMAT command only when the screen image is unformatted. That's the case at the beginning of a BTS session or after you've cleared the BTS screen image. If BTS encounters a /FORMAT command when the screen is formatted, the results, according to the BTS manual, are "unpredictable."

BTS simulator statements

BTS simulator statements, which are supplied to BTS in card format, provide simulated terminal input. For 3270 operations, each simulator statement represents a complete terminal input transmission. After you've formatted the BTS screen image with a /FORMAT command, you can supply *formatted mode simulator statements*. Each simulator statement can include data that would come from multiple screen fields.

To specify input from a device field, you identify the field with its line and column position and you supply the data that is to be entered. For example, suppose you want to simulate that the value 010000 is to be keyed into the invoice number field of the display invoice application screen, which begins in column 12 of line 3. To do so, code

```
L3C12 '010000'
```

in the simulator statement for the terminal entry. Notice here that you identify the field position with the letter *L* followed by the line number, then the letter *C* followed by the column number. One or more spaces separates the location from the field value, which has to be coded between single quotes.

You can code as many field specifications as you need on a single simulator statement. Just separate them from each other with one or more spaces. You can code these values through column 71. If you need to use more than one line for a single simulator statement, code a nonblank value in column 72 of each line in the statement except the last.

Keyword	Action
ENTER	Simulates the enter key.
CLEAR	Simulates the clear key; enables you to supply another /FORMAT command.
PFx	Simulates a program function key, where x is a number from 1 to 24.
PAx	Simulates a program access key, where x is a number from 1 to 3.

Figure 14-2   Simulator statement terminal action keywords

After you've coded all the field specifications for a single terminal transmission, you need to specify a terminal action. Figure 14-2 lists the values you can code for terminal action. Usually, you'll specify ENTER.

To end a simulator statement, you code the EOM (end-of-message) character. The default is the dollar sign, although you can change this, as you'll see in a moment.

So, a complete simulator statement for the display invoice application would be

```
L3C12 '010000' ENTER $
```

Although this example includes just one field specification, other simulator statements can include many.

When you use BTS under TSO, the terminal is used as if it were an IMS terminal. Formatted input and output are accepted from and sent to it, just as if the application were executing in the production environment. As a result, you don't have to code simulator statements when you use BTS under TSO. However, even though BTS under TSO is running in an interactive environment, it still expects a batch of card-format simulator statements. As a result, the BTS modules that provide TSO full-screen support have to translate actual terminal entries that are just what the IMS application user would make into simulator statements. Fortunately, this is transparent to you. Just realize that this overhead is going on when you use BTS under TSO.

The simulator statements that are generated when you use BTS under TSO are stored in a data set (called *BTSPUNCH*) that you can use later to recreate the exact sequence of entries you made interactively. This can be useful when you're going through repetitive testing and debugging. When you change an application program, it's convenient to be able to test the application again with the same input data to make sure you haven't introduced any new errors. (However,

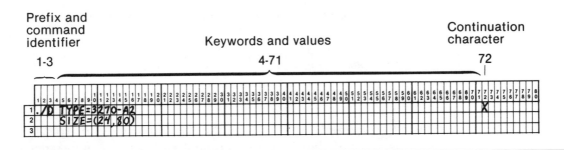

Figure 14-3   The format of a BTS command

changes to format sets that move fields would probably invalidate the simulator statements generated during an earlier test run.)

BTS commands

BTS commands are the third group of statements you can include in the BTSIN data set. You use BTS commands to specify the transaction codes for the programs that can be scheduled, the terminal type to be simulated, and the options to be in effect for the run. First, I'll show you the syntax of BTS commands; then I'll describe how to code the commands you'll use most often.

BTS command syntax   Figure 14-3 shows the format of a BTS command. Each command begins with the characters ./ in columns 1 and 2. After the slash, you code the command identifier; in all cases except one, the command identifier is a single letter. The three most commonly used command identifiers are T, D, and O; the others are C, P, R, S, and SPA.

After you code the command identifier, you supply keywords and associated values that indicate the options you want for the command. At least one space must precede and follow each keyword and the value associated with it. You can code BTS command keywords in any order, and they can extend into column 71.

If a command requires more than one line, you can continue it by coding a non-blank character in column 72. The continued keywords and values can be coded in columns 1 through 71 of the following line(s). You can use as many continuation lines as you need; just be sure to code a continuation character in column 72 on each except the last. Notice that you do not code ./ and the command identifier on continued lines.

If you want to include a comment in a BTS input stream, do so like this:

```
./* comment. . .
```

Code a period, slash, asterisk, and space, then any text you want.

The D command   You use the D command to specify the characteristics of the simulated terminal that will be associated with your program's I/O PCB: your application's primary terminal. Figure 14-4 shows the keywords you can specify for the D command.

The format of the D command you use depends on whether your shop uses symbolic names for 3270 terminal types. If so, you code the command like this for a standard 3270 display station:

```
./D TYPE=3270-A2 SIZE=(24,80)
```

but if not, you code the command like this:

```
./D DDOF=327020
```

In either case, if the terminal you want to simulate is specified with MFS features other than IGNORE, you need to supply the appropriate hexadecimal value that identifies them in the FEAT keyword of the D command. (It's unlikely that you'll need to supply a different value.)

The last keyword figure 14-4 shows for the D command is EOM. You can use it to specify a delimiter character that you code to mark the end of a message in a simulator statement. The default value is the dollar sign ($), which is appropriate for most applications. However, if you need to send a message that contains a dollar sign to a program you're testing under BTS, you have to specify another delimiter with the EOM keyword and use it in all of your simulator statements.

The T command   The T command is the one you'll use most often; it's also the most complicated of the BTS commands. You use it to supply the information BTS needs about destinations, both alternate terminals and transaction codes associated with programs.

Before BTS can run a program, it must have already processed a T command for it. As a result, it's typical to code all the T commands a BTS run requires (you can test more than one transaction type in a single BTS run) at the beginning of the BTS input stream.

Figure 14-5 shows the T command's keywords and the values you can specify for them. A typical T command to define a transaction code

The D command

For a primary terminal
defined with a 3270
symbolic type

```
./D TYPE=3270-An

    SIZE=(ll,ccc)

    [FEAT=hh]

    [EOM=eom-char]
```

For a primary terminal
defined with a 3270 model
identifier

```
./D DDOF=3270xx

    [FEAT=hh]

    [EOM=eom-char]
```

Explanation

3270-An
For n, code 1 through 9 to correspond to the symbolic name associated with a particular 3270 terminal type. Typically, 3270-A2 refers to standard display stations, but this can vary from one installation to another.

ll,ccc
The size of the terminal screen in lines (ll) and columns (ccc); valid only when the terminal type is specified with a symbolic name.

hh
A two-digit hexadecimal value that specifies the combination of features to be simulated for this terminal. If you omit this keyword, the value 7F, which corresponds to FEAT = IGNORE, is used.

eom-char
The delimiter character that will be used in simulator statements to indicate the end of a message. The default is the dollar sign ($).

3270xx
For xx, code 10 for a 3270 model 1 display station or 20 for a 3270 model 2 display station.

Figure 14-4   The D command

for an application is

```
./T TC=DI2 MBR=DI2 PSB=DI2 LANG=CBL TYPE=MSG
```

This command specifies that a transaction whose code is DI2 should invoke a program with the same name and should use a PSB with the same name. Since the PSB name and the program name are the same, I could have omitted the PSB keyword. It's not a BTS requirement that the transaction code, program name, and PSB name all be the same, but they often are. (In the production IMS DC system, the program name

The T command

	For alternate terminals defined with 3270 symbolic types	For alternate terminals defined with 3270 model identifiers
For transactions		
./T TC=trans-code	./T TC=terminal	./T TC=terminal
MBR=program	TYPE=3270-An	TYPE=model
LANG=CBL	SIZE=(ll,ccc)	[FEAT=hh]
TYPE=MSG	[FEAT=hh]	
[PSB=psb-name]		
[SPA=spa-size]		
[PLC=limit-count]		

Explanation

trans-code	One- to eight-character transaction code for the application.
program	Name of the program load module that should be used to process messages associated with the specified transaction code.
psb-name	Name of the PSB for the transaction; if the PSB has the same name as the application program, you can omit the PSB keyword.
spa-size	Size, in bytes, of the SPA to be provided for a conversational transaction. Should be omitted for a non-conversational transaction.
limit-count	The number of successive GU calls the program can issue against the I/O PCB before BTS will cause a QC status code to be returned. The default value is 1, which allows the program to issue two GU calls.
terminal	Logical terminal name of the alternate terminal to be used.
3270-An	For n, code 1 through 9 to correspond to the symbolic name associated with a particular 3270 terminal type. Typically, 3270-A2 refers to standard display stations, but this can vary from one installation to another.
ll,ccc	The size of the terminal screen in lines (ll) and columns (ccc); valid only when the alternate terminal type is specified with a symbolic name.

Figure 14-5   The T command (part 1 of 2)

hh   A two-digit hexadecimal value that specifies the combination of features to be simulated for this alternate terminal. If you omit this keyword, the value 7F, which corresponds to FEAT = IGNORE, is used.

model   Specify 1 or 2 to indicate whether the terminal should be simulated as a 3270 model 1 display station or a model 2 display station.

Figure 14-5   The T command (part 2 of 2)

and the PSB name *must* be the same.) If the application program is coded in COBOL, you specify that with the value CBL for the LANG keyword (its default value is ASM for assembler language). The last keyword in this example (TYPE) indicates that the program is a message processing program (MSG).

There are two other keywords you can use when you specify a transaction: SPA and PLC. If you're going to test a conversational program, you must specify the size of its scratch pad area with the SPA keyword. Simply code the number of bytes the SPA requires. Also, you can limit the processing the program does with the PLC keyword. The value you associate with it indicates how many GU calls the program can issue before BTS will return a QC status code. The default for PLC is 1; if you let it remain in effect, BTS returns a QC status code for the second DC GU call your program issues. If you want to test a program with an unbroken series of input messages, you'll need to specify a larger PLC value.

You also use the T command to specify a terminal as an alternate destination. As figure 14-5 shows, there are two ways you can code the command for this purpose; as with the D command, the one you use depends on how 3270 terminals are defined in your IMS system. If your 3270s are associated with symbolic names, you should use those names in T commands. For example, a standard 3270 terminal that's the destination for a message sent via an alternate PCB might be defined like this:

```
./T TC=LRECVD06 TYPE=3270-A2 SIZE=(24,80)
```

Here, the logical terminal-id is LRECVD06, and the symbolic name is 3270-A2.

Because I didn't specify the FEAT keyword, BTS will use the MFS device formats for the specified terminal type defined with FEAT=IGNORE. If you want to use a format set that specifies different

The O command

```
./O [APS=YES | NO]

    [DB=YES | NO]

    [MSG=YES | NO]

    [SCREEN=INOUT | OUT | NO]

    [ATR=YES | NO]

    [EATR=YES | NO]

    [TSO=YES | NO]

    [TSOMLVL=1 | 0]

    [TSODB=YES | ALL | PROMPT | NO]

    [TSOMSG=YES | ALL | PROMPT | NO]
```

Figure 14-6   The O command (part 1 of 2)

features for the alternate terminal, you have to supply the correct hexadecimal feature code with the FEAT keyword, just as with the D command.

If your shop doesn't use symbolic names for 3270 terminal types, you specify the model number of the 3270 terminal (1 or 2) in the TYPE keyword. For instance,

```
./T TC=LRECVD06 TYPE=2
```

is equivalent to the T command I just showed you.

The O command   You use the O command to specify what information BTS should provide for you as it executes your application. As you can imagine from the simple example I showed you in figure 14-1, the sheer quantity of output BTS can generate can be overwhelming. As a result, it's often useful to limit what's printed.

The O command, illustrated in figure 14-6, lets you limit the output that's presented in the BTSOUT data set and on the TSO screen. The keywords of the O command should be self-explanatory. The first six all control BTSOUT contents; the first three of them let you specify

Explanation

APS   YES specifies that statistics about calls issued by the application program should be printed; NO specifies that they should not.

DB   YES specifies that data base calls should be traced in the print output; NO specifies that they should not.

MSG   YES specifies that message calls should be traced in the print output; NO specifies that they should not.

SCREEN   INOUT specifies that both input and output screen images should be printed; OUT specifies that only output screen images should be printed; NO specifies that screen images should not be printed.

ATR   YES specifies that attribute byte values should be printed with screen images; NO specifies that they should not.

EATR   YES specifies that extended attributes, if present, should be printed with screen images; NO specifies that they should not.

TSO   YES specifies that you want to use TSO full-screen support; NO specifies that you do not. When you invoke BTS under TSO, the default is YES.

TSOMLVL   The value 0 specifies that only IMS screens and BTS error messages should be displayed at the TSO terminal; the value 1 specifies that IMS screens, BTS error messages, BTS informational messages, and call traces (if enabled by the TSODB and TSOMSG keywords) should be displayed.

TSODB   YES specifies that data base calls should be traced at the terminal with one line per call; ALL specifies that data base calls should be traced at the terminal with full detail (I/O area, key feedback area, and SSAs); PROMPT specifies that data base calls should be traced at the terminal with one line per call, followed by a user prompt through which the terminal user can request additional call information; NO specifies that data base calls should not be traced.

TSOMSG   YES specifies that message calls should be traced at the terminal with one line per call; ALL specifies that message calls should be traced at the terminal and should include the I/O area; PROMPT specifies that message calls should be traced at the terminal with one line per call, followed by a user prompt through which the terminal user can request BTS to display the I/O area; NO specifies that message calls should not be traced.

Figure 14-6   The O command (part 2 of 2)

how BTS should report your program's DL/I call activity. The first, APS, indicates whether or not call statistics for the program should be included in the BTSOUT listing. (These are the statistics that are at the bottom of part 2 of figure 14-1.) The next two, DB and MSG, let you control whether or not BTS prints detail trace information for the data base and message calls your application program issues.

The next three keywords relate to how MFS screen images are printed in BTSOUT. SCREEN indicates whether they should be printed at all; it further lets you specify whether all screen images (INOUT) or just output screen images (OUT) should be printed. ATR and EATR indicate whether the hex values of attribute bytes and extended attributes should be printed.

The last four keywords of the O command relate to the TSO environment. The TSO keyword indicates whether or not you want to use the Full Screen Support feature. TSOMLVL indicates whether the interactions at the TSO terminal can include call traces and BTS informational messages. TSODB lets you control how much information is displayed for data base call traces, and TSOMSG does the same for DC call traces.

The default values for the O command keywords are probably what you'll want most of the time. However, if you want to focus your testing on just part of what your application is doing, you can be selective about what BTS provides. For instance, if your application's message handling is acceptable, but its data base processing isn't doing what you think it should, you could code this O command:

```
./O MSG=NO SCREEN=NO
```

to exclude both screen images and message call traces from the BTSOUT listing. However, application program call statistics and data base call traces would still be included because the APS and DB keyword defaults (both YES) were not overridden.

Other commands   There are five other BTS commands, but you'll seldom use them. The ./SPA command lets you initialize a scratch pad area to test a conversational program. Frankly, this is useful only when you want to test a conversational program starting at some point within an active conversation; that's unlikely.

The other four commands are even less useful. The P command lets you patch main storage to change a program dynamically. The R command lets you tell BTS that the simulator statements that follow contain hexadecimal rather than character data. The S command lets you specify a special action that should occur at particular points during testing; you can use it to force a dump or to substitute a status code for the one that IMS would otherwise return for a particular kind of call against a particular PCB. Finally, the C command lets you specify that BTS is to be used in conjunction with the COBOL Interactive Debug facility. If you think you need to use the features any of these commands offer, refer to *Batch Terminal Simulator Program Reference and Operations Manual* for more details.

BTS PROCESSING

Although you don't need to know what components are involved when BTS is executed, it's useful background. A real advantage of BTS is that it can use actual IMS and MFS control blocks and modules, yet still be independent of the production DC system. In this section, I'll give you some perspective on how this works.

BTS has three main program components: the *TSO controller*, the *region controller*, and the *program controller*. The TSO controller is used only in the TSO environment, where it serves as an interface between TSO and the other components involved in BTS.

The region controller simulates the scheduling functions the IMS control region provides in the production environment. The transactions that you request on T commands are scheduled by the region controller. When the region controller gets a message (in a simulator statement), it invokes actual IMS modules to initialize the proper control blocks for the requested transaction. Then, BTS dynamically patches parts of those control blocks so when the application program issues calls, they're intercepted by BTS.

After the region controller has set up the environment so the program's calls will be properly intercepted, the program controller is invoked. It loads and executes the application program. A vital function of the program controller is to intercept and handle DL/I calls the application program issues. Because the program controller intercepts all calls, it's the component of BTS that produces the call traces in the BTSOUT listing.

When the program controller intercepts a DC call, it does not pass it to IMS modules, but handles it itself. BTS invokes MFS modules when appropriate to edit message segments. The internal screen image is updated as necessary to reflect the simulated terminal action.

BTS simulates almost all DC calls and MFS features. However, there are three limitations you should know about. First, the SYSMSG field you can specify in device formats for messages from IMS is not supported; you can use format sets that include SYSMSG, but IMS messages won't be displayed in the related field. Second, the IMS password function isn't supported by BTS. And third, the operator control functions NEXTMSGP, NEXTLP, and NEXTPP aren't supported. (However, the operator physical paging operations associated with PA1 and PA2 do work, and you can also enter operator logical paging commands, like $= +3$, in a properly defined field.) Fortunately, these are all relatively minor details; the essential DC call and MFS features are all supported.

When the program controller intercepts a data base call, it passes it on to IMS, where it's handled normally. As a result, your application programs can perform data base processing under BTS just as if they were running in the production environment. Of course, the data bases you use are test data bases that are not part of the production environment. Even in the test environment, though, preliminary data base administration work has to be done to set up your test data bases.

DISCUSSION

As you can see, BTS gives you two advantages. First, it lets you test your DC applications independent of the production DC system. That enables you to test freely, without worrying about interfering with production work. In addition, it saves the IMS system administrator from having to do extra work to set up the DC environment to support your testing.

Second, and perhaps more important, BTS provides you with all the detailed screen format and call trace information I've described in this chapter. That can save you hours and hours of testing time, especially after you've worked with BTS for a while and get used to it.

The next two chapters show you how to run BTS in batch and under TSO. You can read either or both, depending on your interests and needs.

Terminology

Batch Terminal Simulator
BTS
BTSOUT
BTSIN
BTS simulator statement
formatted mode simulator statement
BTSPUNCH
TSO controller
region controller
program controller

Objectives

1. Interpret the screen images and call traces in BTS output.

2. Describe the components of a BTS input stream.

3. Code appropriate D, T, and O commands to specify the devices, transactions, and options to be used for a BTS run.

4. Describe how BTS can use IMS and MFS modules, yet still be independent of the production DC system.

Chapter 15

How to run BTS
from a batch job

To run BTS in a batch job, you need to know how to code the job control statements to invoke it and the contents of the BTSIN data set to control the processing BTS will do. I'll show you how to do both in this chapter. Then, I'll present and describe the BTSOUT listing for a brief, but complete, BTS batch run.

JCL requirements for BTS in a batch job

Figure 15-1 is a sample job stream that shows how you run BTS. It's for the cash receipts application I presented in chapter 7. As you can see in the EXEC statement in the second line of the job, you invoke BTS by running a procedure named BTSII. (Depending on the release of BTS you're using, the procedure name may be BTS instead of BTSII.)

The BTSII cataloged procedure has only one step, whose name is G. You need to use this step name when you supply overriding DD statements for the data sets used by the procedure. Whenever you run the procedure, you'll have to supply an overriding DD statement for the BTSIN data set. In the procedure, the DD statement

```
//BTSIN    DD  DUMMY
```

defines the BTSIN data set. Because you supply BTS commands and

```
//ECKOLSB JOB  USER=ECKOLS,PASSWORD=...
//           EXEC BTSII,USRNODE=ECKOLS
//G.BTSIN DD   *
./T TC=CR MBR=CR PSB=DCTST LANG=CBL TYPE=MSG
./D DDOF=327020 EOM=$
/FORMAT CRO
L4C17 '010000' L5C17 '1200' L7C17 '192/24-8' L8C17 '127452' ENTER $
L4C17 '011331' ENTER $
/*
//G.DFSVSAMP DD DSN=ECKOLS.DFSVSAMP,DISP=SHR
//G.CR        DD DSN=ECKOLS.CR,DISP=SHR
//G.CRPX      DD DSN=ECKOLS.CRPX,DISP=SHR
//G.CRSX      DD DSN=ECKOLS.CRSX,DISP=SHR
//
```

Figure 15-1   Sample job to invoke the BTS cataloged procedure to test the cash receipts application

simulator statements through BTSIN, you can't let it remain a dummy data set.

Instead, you'll usually want BTSIN to be an in-line data set. When that's the case, you code this DD statement:

```
//G.BTSIN   DD *
```

and follow it with the commands and statements you want to use for the test run. That's what I did in the job in figure 15-1.

As I've mentioned, you can code three kinds of records in the BTSIN data set: (1) BTS commands, (2) the IMS commands /FORMAT and /EXIT, and (3) BTS simulator statements. You supply these statements in the order you want BTS to process them. Usually, you code all of a run's commands at the beginning of the input stream. That's what I did in the job stream in figure 15-1; the two BTS commands I used (T and D) are the first records in the in-stream data set. Then, I coded a /FORMAT command to prepare the terminal to accept a transaction for the cash receipts application. Finally, I coded two simulator statements for that application. You'll see the results of these statements in a moment when I present the job's output.

In addition to providing an override for the BTSIN DD statement, you might also have to provide overrides for other DD statements in the BTS cataloged procedure. For example, it's possible that the partitioned data sets that you'll use to store format sets and application programs for testing won't be the ones specified in the BTS cataloged procedure. When that's the case, you'll have to provide overrides for the affected data sets.

Figure 15-1 shows one way you might be able to do this. I coded

```
USRNODE=ECKOLS
```

on the EXEC statement to specify an overriding value for one of the symbolic parameters in the BTS procedure. In the version of the procedure on my system, the USRNODE symbolic parameter is used as the high-level qualifier in the names of IMS data sets like the program and format libraries. By supplying an overriding value for it, I indicated that my test versions of these data sets (rather than the production data sets) should be used for the BTS run.

However, exactly what overrides are necessary and how you specify them depends on (1) the testing practices your shop or project group follows and (2) changes that have been made to the BTS cataloged procedure at your installation. Because these considerations can vary so much from one shop to another, you should check with your supervisor or a co-worker to find out what specifics you have to code in your BTS jobs.

In addition to overriding some DD statements that are coded in the BTS cataloged procedure, you have to supply additional DD statements to define the data base data sets to be used for the test run. That's what the last four DD statements in figure 15-1 do:

```
//G.DFSVSAMP DD DSN=ECKOLS.DFSVSAMP,DISP=SHR
//G.CR       DD DSN=ECKOLS.CR,DISP=SHR
//G.CRPX     DD DSN=ECKOLS.CRPX,DISP=SHR
//G.CRSX     DD DSN=ECKOLS.CRSX,DISP=SHR
```

The first of these DD statements defines a data set that contains execution-time VSAM parameters. You can code this as an in-line data set too; typically, it requires just one record. Find out from your data base administrator what its contents should be. The other three DD statements define the data base data sets themselves. (When you code a job stream to invoke BTS, you should use the DD and data set names supplied by your data base administrator.)

BTSOUT listing for the BTS batch job

Figure 15-2 presents the BTSOUT listing that was produced as a result of the job in figure 15-1. Each of the parts of the figure is annotated, and I've shaded the parts of it I want you to notice.

BTS is invoked and processes the first three records in the BTSIN data set (a T command, a D command, and an IMS /FORMAT command).

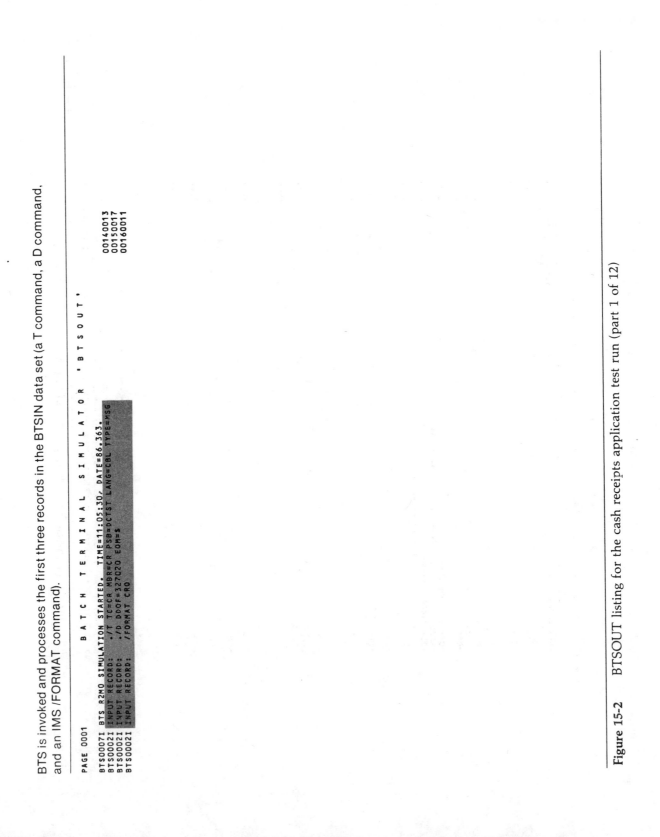

```
PAGE 0001          B A T C H   T E R M I N A L   S I M U L A T O R   ' B T S O U T '

BTS0007I BTS R2MO SIMULATION STARTED.  TIME=11:05:30, DATE=86.363.
BTS0002I INPUT RECORD:  ./T TC=CR MBR=CR PSB=DCTST LANG=CBL TYPE=MSG            00140013
BTS0002I INPUT RECORD:  ./D DDOF=327020 EOM=$                                  00150017
BTS0002I INPUT RECORD:  /FORMAT CRO                                            00160011
```

Figure 15-2   BTSOUT listing for the cash receipts application test run (part 1 of 12)

BTS responds to the /FORMAT command and uses the specified MOD (CRO) to format its internal screen image.

Chapter 15

```
PAGE 0002        B A T C H   T E R M I N A L   S I M U L A T O R   ' B T S O U T '

B T S   3270 FORMATTED SCREEN IMAGE.  MID/MOD= CRO  , CURSOR= L04C017,  ACTION= OUTPUT

     ----.----1----.----2----.----3----.----4----.----5----.----6----.----7----.----8
*01* ENTER CASH RECEIPTS                                        DATE: 12/29/86 *01*
     28                 3c                                   28    328      3c   *02*
*02*                                                                             *03*
*03*                                                                             *04* .
*04* INVOICE:                                                                    *05*
     28    3c     11-++++3c                                                      *06*
*05* AMOUNT:                                                                     *07*
     28    3c     11++++++3c                                                     *08*
*06*                                                                             *09*
*07* BANK NUMBER:                                                                *10*
     28         3c01+++++++++++++++++++++++++++3c                                *11*
*08* CHECK NUMBER:                                                               *12*
     28         301+++++++++++++++++3c                                           *13*
*09*                                                                             *14*
*10*                                                                             *15*
*11*                                                                             *16*
*12*                                                                             *17*
*13*                                                                             *18*
*14*                                                                             *19*
*15*                                                                             *20*
*16*                                                                             *21*
*17*                                                                             *22*
*18*                                                                             *23*
*19*                                                                             *24*
*20*
*21*
*22*
*23*
     20
*24*
     3c
     ----.----1----.----2----.----3----.----4----.----5----.----6----.----7----.----8
```

THE FIELD ATTRIBUTE BITS ARE: RRPNDDRM, WHERE P MEANS PROTECTED; N MEANS NUMERIC; M MEANS MODIFIED.
THE MEANING OF THE DD BITS IS: 00=DISPLAY/NO PEN DETECT; 01=DISPLAY/DETECT; 10=BRIGHT/DETECT; 11=DARK/NO PEN DETECT.

Figure 15-2   BTSOUT listing for the cash receipts application test run (part 2 of 12)

BTS processes the fourth record in the BTSIN data set, the first simulator statement. The simulator statement supplies values for the four data entry fields on the screen.

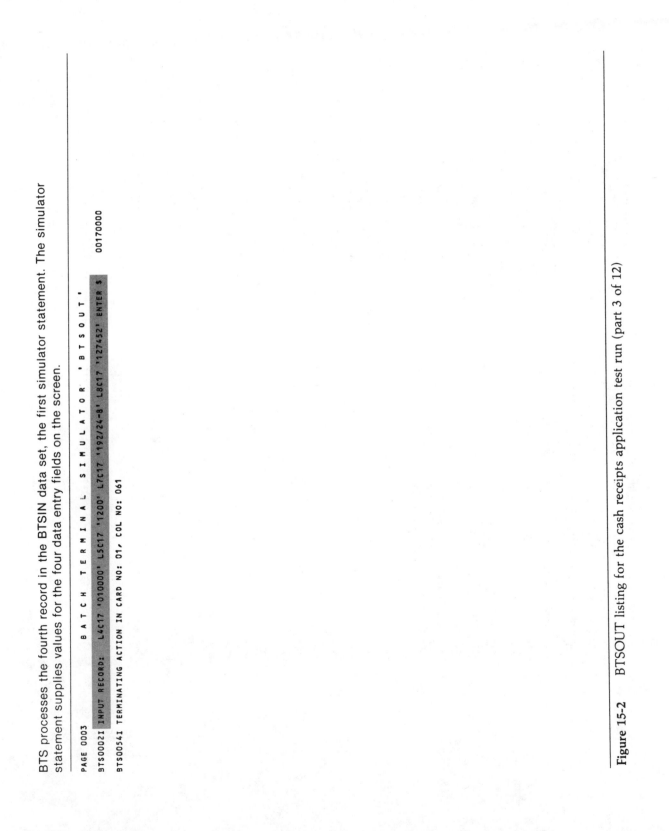

```
PAGE 0003          B A T C H   T E R M I N A L   S I M U L A T O R   ' B T S O U T '

BTS0002I INPUT RECORD:  L4C17 '010000' L5C17 '1200' L7C17 '192/24-8' L8C17 '127452' ENTER $    00170000

BTS0054I TERMINATING ACTION IN CARD NO: 01, COL NO: 061
```

Figure 15-2 BTSOUT listing for the cash receipts application test run (part 3 of 12)

BTS updates its internal screen image using the values supplied in the simulator statement. The data in the screen image is then mapped into an input message according to the specifications in the MID CRI.

```
PAGE 0004        B A T C H   T E R M I N A L   S I M U L A T O R   ' B T S O U T '

B T S   3270 FORMATTED SCREEN IMAGE.  MID/MOD= CRI    , CURSOR= L04C017, ACTION= ENTER

         ----.----1----.----2----.----3----.----4----.----5----.----6----.----7----.----8
    *01* ENTER CASH RECEIPTS                                     DATE: 12/29/86 *01*
         28                                                    28    328           3C
    *02*                                                                          *02*
    *03*                                                                          *03*
    *04* INVOICE:    010000                                                       *04*
         28      3C  11--+++3C
    *05* AMOUNT:     1200                                                         *05*
         28      3C  11++++3C
    *06*                                                                          *06*
    *07* BANK NUMBER:  192/24-8                                                   *07*
         28         3C01+++++++++++++++++++++++++3C
    *08* CHECK NUMBER:  127452                                                    *08*
         28           301+++++++++++++3C
    *09*                                                                          *09*
    *10*                                                                          *10*
    *11*                                                                          *11*
    *12*                                                                          *12*
    *13*                                                                          *13*
    *14*                                                                          *14*
    *15*                                                                          *15*
    *16*                                                                          *16*
    *17*                                                                          *17*
    *18*                                                                          *18*
    *19*                                                                          *19*
    *20*                                                                          *20*
    *21*                                                                          *21*
    *22*                                                                          *22*
    *23*                                                                          *23*
         20
    *24*                                                                          *24*
         3C
         ----.----1----.----2----.----3----.----4----.----5----.----6----.----7----.----8
```

THE FIELD ATTRIBUTE BITS ARE: RRPNDDRM, WHERE P MEANS PROTECTED; N MEANS NUMERIC; M MEANS MODIFIED.
THE MEANING OF THE DD BITS IS: 00=DISPLAY/NO PEN DETECT; 01=DISPLAY/DETECT; 10=BRIGHT/DETECT; 11=DARK/NO PEN DETECT.

Figure 15-2   BTSOUT listing for the cash receipts application test run (part 4 of 12)

BTS invokes the application program CR; the processing limit count for this scheduling of the program is 1. The program issues a GU call against the I/O PCB to retrieve the input message segment. Then, it issues a GHU call against the data base PCB to retrieve the specified receivable segment occurrence, and it updates the data base by replacing that segment and inserting a new payment segment occurrence.

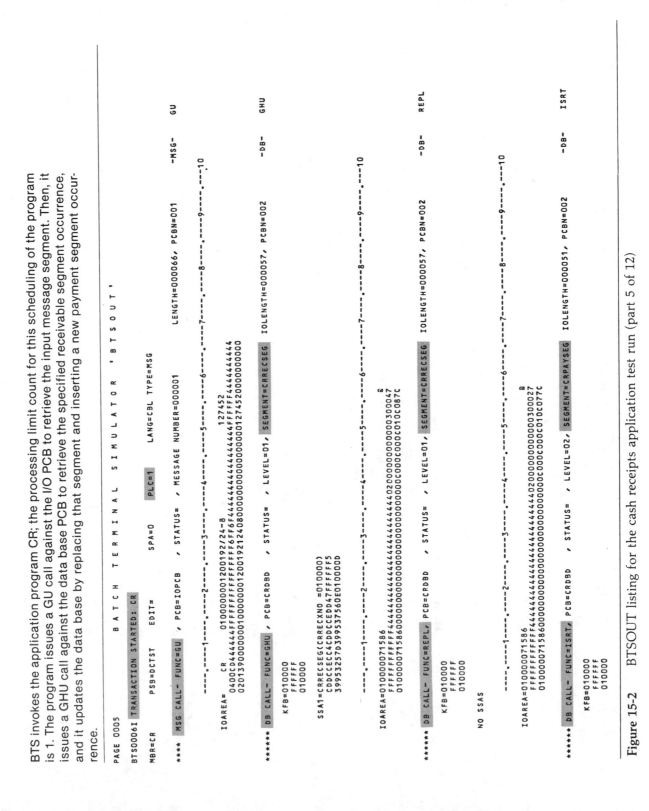

```
PAGE 0005                 B A T C H   T E R M I N A L   S I M U L A T O R   ' B T S O U T '

BTS0006I TRANSACTION STARTED: CR

MBR=CR        PSB=DCTST     EDIT=          SPA=0      PLC=1      LANG=CBL TYPE=MSG

****  MSG CALL- FUNC=GU  , PCB=IOPCB   , STATUS=  , MESSAGE NUMBER=000001        LENGTH=000066, PCBN=001       -MSG-    GU

        ----.----1----.----2----.----3----.----4----.----5----.----6----.----7----.----8----.----9----.---10

     IOAREA=    CR      0100000001200192/24-8                    127452
        0400CD444444FFFFFFFFFFFFFFFF6FF6F4444444444444444FFFFFF444444444
        0201390000000100000001200192124080000000000000000127452000000000

****** DB CALL- FUNC=GHU , PCB=CRDBD   , STATUS=  , LEVEL=01, SEGMENT=CRRECSEG  IOLENGTH=000057, PCBN=002      -DB-    GHU

     KFB=010000
        FFFFFF
        010000

     SSA1=CRRECSEG(CRRECXNO =010000)
        CDDCCECC4CDDCCEDD47FFFFFF5
        39953257D399537560E010000D

        ----.----1----.----2----.----3----.----4----.----5----.----6----.----7----.----8----.----9----.---10

     IOAREA=010000071586                                           &
        FFFFFFFFFFFF444444444444444444444444402000000000000300047
        010000071586000000000000000000000000000C000C000C010C087C

****** DB CALL- FUNC=REPL, PCB=CRDBD   , STATUS=  , LEVEL=01, SEGMENT=CRRECSEG  IOLENGTH=000057, PCBN=002      -DB-    REPL

     KFB=010000
        FFFFFF
        010000

     NO SSAS

        ----.----1----.----2----.----3----.----4----.----5----.----6----.----7----.----8----.----9----.---10

     IOAREA=010000071586                                           @
        FFFFFFFFFFFF444444444444444444444444402000000000000300027
        010000071586000000000000000000000000000C000C000C010C077C

****** DB CALL- FUNC=ISRT, PCB=CRDBD   , STATUS=  , LEVEL=02, SEGMENT=CRPAYSEG  IOLENGTH=000051, PCBN=002      -DB-    ISRT

     KFB=010000
        FFFFFF
        010000
```

Figure 15-2 BTSOUT listing for the cash receipts application test run (part 5 of 12)

The program responds to the originating terminal by issuing an ISRT call against the I/O PCB. Next, the program issues another DC GU call to retrieve another input message. However, because the PLC is 1 for this test run, BTS returns a QC status code, and the program ends.

```
PAGE 0006        B A T C H   T E R M I N A L   S I M U L A T O R   ' B T S O U T '

SSA1=CRRECSEG(CRRECXNO =01000J)
     CDDCCEC4CDDCCEDD47FFFFF5
     3995325703995375560E01000OD

SSA2=CRPAYSEG
     CDDCEECC4
     397182570

     ----.----1----.----2----.----3----.----4----.----5----.----6----.----7----.----8----.----9----.---10

IOAREA=127452       192/24-8         122986
       FFFFFF4444444444FFF6FF4444444444444FFFFFF0020 ,
       1274520000000000019212408000000000000000000122986010C

BTS0031I MODNAME: CRO

**** MSG CALL- FUNC=ISRT,  PCB=IOPCB   , STATUS=   , MESSAGE NUMBER=000001        LENGTH=000145, PCBN=001        -MSG-    ISRT

     ----.----1----.----2----.----3----.----4----.----5----.----6----.----7----.----8----.----9----.---10
                                                                                  $12.00    PAYMENT POSTED TO INVO
IOAREA=J C
       09D0C84444444444444444444444444444444444444444444445FF4FF44DCEDCDE4DDEECC4ED4CDED
       010000000000000000000000000000000000000000000000000B12B0000718455307623540360 9556

       ICE 010000.
       CCC4FFFFF4444444444444444444444444444444444444444
       93500100000B00000000000000000000000000000000000

**** MSG CALL- FUNC=GU ,  PCB=IOPCB   , STATUS=QC,  MESSAGE NUMBER=00C001        LENGTH=000000, PCBN=001        -MSG-    GU    QC

BTS0020I STATISTICS REPORT FOR TRANSACTION:CR
PCBNAME  GU  GN  GNP  GHU  GHN  GHNP  ISRT  PURG  REPL  DLET  DEQ  CHKP  LOG  STAT  XRST  CHNG  ROLB  OPEN  CLSE  OTHR
IOPCB     2                             1     1
CRDBD         1                         1           1
```

Figure 15-2   BTSOUT listing for the cash receipts application test run (part 6 of 12)

BTS maps the data from the output message inserted by the program into its internal screen image.

```
PAGE 0007        BATCH TERMINAL SIMULATOR 'BTSOUT'

BTS  3270 FORMATTED SCREEN IMAGE. MID/MOD= CRO    , CURSOR= L04C017, ACTION= OUTPUT

    ....-1----.----2----.----3----.----4----.----5----.----6----.----7----.----8
*01* ENTER CASH RECEIPTS                                     DATE: 12/29/86 *01*
     28                                                          28   328    3C
     3C
*02*                                                                        *02*

*03*                                                                        *03*

*04* INVOICE:     11-++++3C                                                 *04*
     28    3C
*05* AMOUNT:      11+++++3C                                                 *05*
     28    3C
*06*                                                                        *06*

*07* BANK NUMBER:                                                           *07*
     3C01++++++++++++++++++++++3C
     28
*08* CHECK NUMBER:                                                          *08*
     301++++++++++++++3C
     28
*09*                                                                        *09*
*10*                                                                        *10*
*11*                                                                        *11*
*12*                                                                        *12*
*13*                                                                        *13*
*14*                                                                        *14*
*15*                                                                        *15*
*16*                                                                        *16*
*17*                                                                        *17*
*18*                                                                        *18*
*19*                                                                        *19*
*20*                                                                        *20*
*21*                                                                        *21*
*22*                                                                        *22*
*23*  $12.00  PAYMENT POSTED TO INVOICE 010000.                            *23*
     20
*24*                                                                        *24*
     3C
    ....-1----.----2----.----3----.----4----.----5----.----6----.----7----.----8

THE FIELD ATTRIBUTE BITS ARE: RRPNDDRM, WHERE P MEANS PROTECTED; N MEANS NUMERIC; M MEANS MODIFIED.
THE MEANING OF THE DD BITS IS: 00=DISPLAY/NO PEN DETECT; 01=DISPLAY/DETECT; 10=BRIGHT/DETECT; 11=DARK/NO PEN DETECT.
```

Figure 15-2 BTSOUT listing for the cash receipts application test run (part 7 of 12)

BTS processes the fifth record in the BTSIN data set, the second simulator statement. The simulator statement supplies a value for only one data entry field; it's an invalid transaction.

```
PAGE 0008          B A T C H   T E R M I N A L   S I M U L A T O R   ' B T S O U T '

BTS0002I INPUT RECORD:   L4C17 '011331' ENTER $                          00180000

BTS0054I TERMINATING ACTION IN CARD NO: 01, COL NO: 016
```

Figure 15-2   BTSOUT listing for the cash receipts application test run (part 8 of 12)

BTS updates its internal screen image using the data supplied in the simulator statement. The data in the screen image is then mapped into an input message according to the specifications in the MID CRI.

```
PAGE 0009          B A T C H   T E R M I N A L   S I M U L A T O R   ' B T S O U T '

B T S  3270 FORMATTED SCREEN IMAGE.  MID/MOD= CRI    , CURSOR= L05C017,  ACTION= ENTER

     ----.----1----.----2----.----3----.----4----.----5----.----6----.----7----.----8
*C1* ENTER CASH RECEIPTS                                        DATE:  12/29/86   *01*
    28                                                          28    328    3C    *02*
*C2*                                                                               *03*
*03*                                                                               *04*
*C4* INVOICE:   011331                                                             *05*
    28      3C     11-+++++3C                                                      *06*
*C5* AMOUNT:                                                                       *07*
    28      3C     11--+++++3C                                                     *08*
*06*                                                                               *09*
*C7* BANK NUMBER:                                                                  *10*
    28    3C01++++++++++++++++++++++++++++++3C                                     *11*
*C8* CHECK NUMBER:                                                                 *12*
    28    3C1+++++++++++++3C                                                       *13*
*09*                                                                               *14*
*10*                                                                               *15*
*11*                                                                               *16*
*12*                                                                               *17*
*13*                                                                               *18*
*14*                                                                               *19*
*15*                                                                               *20*
*16*                                                                               *21*
*17*                                                                               *22*
*18*                                                                               *23*
*19*                                                                               *24*
*20*
*21*
*22*
*23*        $12.00   PAYMENT POSTED TO INVOICE 010000.
*24*
    20
    3C
     ----.----1----.----2----.----3----.----4----.----5----.----6----.----7----.----8
```

THE FIELD ATTRIBUTE BITS ARE: RRPNDDRM, WHERE P MEANS PROTECTED; N MEANS NUMERIC; M MEANS MODIFIED.
THE MEANING OF THE DD BITS IS: 00=DISPLAY/NO PEN DETECT; 01=DISPLAY/DETECT; 10=BRIGHT/DETECT; 11=DARK/NO PEN DETECT.

Figure 15-2   BTSOUT listing for the cash receipts application test run (part 9 of 12)

BTS invokes the application program CR again. The program issues a GU call against the I/O PCB to retrieve the input message segment. Then, it issues a GU call against the data base PCB to retrieve the specified receivable segment occurrence. (The program issues a GU call rather than a GHU call because other fields in the input message were invalid.) Because the invoice number supplied in the simulator statement doesn't exist in the data base, the GU call results in a GE status code. The program responds to the originating terminal by issuing an ISRT call against the I/O PCB. Notice in the I/O area that cursor-positioning and attribute modification values are present in the output stream to indicate invalid fields. Finally, the program issues another DC GU call to retrieve another input message. However, because the PLC is 1 for this test run, BTS returns a QC status code, and the program ends.

```
PAGE 0010              B A T C H   T E R M I N A L   S I M U L A T O R   ' B T S O U T '

BTS0006I TRANSACTION STARTED: CR

MBR=CR    PSB=DCTST    EDIT=         SPA=0    PLC=1    LANG=CBL TYPE=MSG

****  MSG CALL- FUNC=GU  , PCB=IOPCB  , STATUS=   , MESSAGE NUMBER=000001    LENGTH=000066, PCBN=001    -MSG-    GU

     IOAREA=    CR    011331
            ----+----1----+----2----+----3----+----4----+----5----+----6----+----7----+----8----+----9----+---10.
            0400CD4444444FFFFF4444444444444444444444444444444444
            0201390000000113310000000C0000000000000000000000000CC0

******  DB CALL- FUNC=GU  , PCB=CRDBD  , STATUS=GE, LEVEL=00, SEGMENT=      IOLENGTH=000000, PCBN=002    -DB-    GU    GE

     KFB=

     SSA1=CRRECSEG(CRRECXNO =0113331)
          CDDCCECC4CDDCCEDD47FFFFFF5
          39953257D399537560E011331D

BTS0031I MODNAME: CRO

****  MSG CALL- FUNC=ISRT, PCB=IOPCB  , STATUS=   , MESSAGE NUMBER=000001    LENGTH=000145, PCBN=001    -MSG-    ISRT

            ----+----1----+----2----+----3----+----4----+----5----+----6----+----7----+----8----+----9----+---10
                                                           INVOICE 011331 NOT FOUND.
     IOAREA= J [H011331CH    [C8444444444CDEDCCC4FFFFFF4DDE4CDEDC44444444444
            0900C8FFFFFFC84444444444444444444444444444444
            0100080113310B0000000000000000000000000009556935001133105630664548B000000000

            4444444444444444444444444444444
            0000000000000000000000000000000

****  MSG CALL- FUNC=GU  , PCB=IOPCB  , STATUS=QC, MESSAGE NUMBER=000001    LENGTH=000000, PCBN=001    -MSG-    GU    QC

BTS0020I STATISTICS REPORT FOR TRANSACTION:CR
PCBNAME  GU  GN  GNP  GHU  GHN  GHNP  ISRT  PURG  REPL  DLET  DEQ  CHKP  LOG  STAT  XRST  CHNG  ROLB  OPEN  CLSE  OTHR
IOPCB     2   1
CRDBD     1
```

Figure 15-2   BTSOUT listing for the cash receipts application test run (part 10 of 12)

BTS maps the data from the output message inserted by the program into its internal screen image.

```
PAGE 0011        B A T C H   T E R M I N A L   S I M U L A T O R   ' B T S O U T '

B T S  3270 FORMATTED SCREEN IMAGE. MID/MOD= CRO    , CURSOR= L04C017, ACTION= OUTPUT

      ----.----1----.----2----.----3----.----4----.----5----.----6----.----7----.----8
*01* ENTER CASH RECEIPTS                                           DATE: 12/29/86 *01*
      28                    3C                                28        328      3C
*02*                                                                             *02*
*03*                                                                             *03*
*04* INVOICE:    011331                                                          *04*
      28       3C  19-+++3C
*05* AMOUNT:     3C  19++++++3C                                                  *05*
      28       3C
*06*                                                                             *06*
*07* BANK NUMBER:                                                                *07*
      28        3C01+++++++++++++++++++++++++++++3C
*08* CHECK NUMBER:                                                               *08*
      28        301++++++++++++++3C
*09*                                                                             *09*
*10*                                                                             *10*
*11*                                                                             *11*
*12*                                                                             *12*
*13*                                                                             *13*
*14*                                                                             *14*
*15*                                                                             *15*
*16*                                                                             *16*
*17*                                                                             *17*
*18*                                                                             *18*
*19*                                                                             *19*
*20*                                                                             *20*
*21*                                                                             *21*
*22*                                                                             *22*
*23* INVOICE 011331 NOT FOUND.                                                   *23*
      20
*24*  3C                                                                         *24*
      ----.----1----.----2----.----3----.----4----.----5----.----6----.----7----.----8
```

THE FIELD ATTRIBUTE BITS ARE: RRPNDDRM, WHERE P MEANS PROTECTED; N MEANS NUMERIC; M MEANS MODIFIED.
THE MEANING OF THE DD BITS IS: 00=DISPLAY/NO PEN DETECT; 01=DISPLAY/DETECT; 10=BRIGHT/DETECT; 11=DARK/NO PEN DETECT.

Figure 15-2   BTSOUT listing for the cash receipts application test run (part 11 of 12)

BTS reaches the end of the BTSIN data set and terminates.

```
PAGE 0012         B A T C H   T E R M I N A L   S I M U L A T O R   ' B T S O U T '

BTS0008I END OF INPUT DATA SET ENCOUNTERED.

BTS0005I END OF BTS RUN.
```

Figure 15-2   BTSOUT listing for the cash receipts application test run (part 12 of 12)

Discussion

Although BTS in batch mode is useful, it's difficult and tedious to code all the simulator statements you need to do a thorough test of any but the simplest of applications. As a result, you're more likely to use BTS Full Screen Support under TSO; the next chapter describes it.

Objective

Given details about your shop's BTS cataloged procedure, code a job stream to run BTS in batch mode.

Chapter 16

How to run
BTS under TSO

When you use BTS under TSO, it executes in a foreground address space and it provides all the features it does in a batch job. Input is supplied from the BTSIN data set, and print output is stored in the BTSOUT data set, just as in batch. However, your TSO terminal becomes an additional source of input and destination for output. With *Full Screen Support (FSS)*, your TSO terminal can be used just like the 3270 on which your application will eventually run on the production system. And you can follow the execution of your application as it executes, rather than after the fact, as you must with BTS in batch.

This chapter describes the considerations you need to keep in mind as you find out how to use BTS FSS at your shop. Then, it presents a test run of the cash receipts application presented in chapter 7. If you've read chapter 15, you'll find that the tests done are the same as in the batch job illustrated in that chapter, but here, they're done in the TSO environment.

TSO requirements for running BTS FSS

The way you'll use BTS under TSO depends heavily on how BTS has been installed on your system. At the very least, a standardized TSO

CLIST (*command list*) to invoke BTS and allocate the required data sets should be available. (The name IBM recommends for the CLIST is BTS.) For some development projects, customized CLISTs might be available that include allocations for test data base data sets. And in other shops, like mine, BTS FSS might be implemented through ISPF dialogs to make it even easier to use.

As you know, before a program you run under TSO can use a data set, that data set has to be allocated. The data sets BTS uses fall into two categories: data base data sets and BTS data sets.

If you use the standard TSO BTS CLIST, you'll have to allocate data base data sets explicitly. To do so, you issue the ALLOC command in this format:

```
ALLOC F(ddname) DA(data.set.name)
```

where *ddname* is the symbolic name specified by the data base administrator for the data base and *data.set.name* is the name of the file as it's stored on DASD. For example, suppose I need to allocate a data base data set named ECKOLS.CRPX (ECKOLS is my TSO user-id) which has to be associated with the ddname CRPX. To do so, I'd enter the command

```
ALLOC F(CRPX) DA(CRPX)
```

I don't need to enter the high-level qualifier on the data set name because TSO automatically supplies the user-id for it.

In contrast, to allocate the BTS data sets (like BTSIN, BTSOUT, and others), you probably won't have to issue explicit ALLOC commands. That's because the BTS CLIST includes those commands for you. When you invoke the standard BTS CLIST, it displays this prompt:

```
CHOOSE ONE OF THE FOLLOWING:
ALLOC ALLOCDS FREE DELETE OR JUST HIT ENTER
```

If you enter ALLOC, the CLIST assumes that all the necessary BTS data sets exist, and it allocates them. If you enter ALLOCDS, the BTS CLIST allocates new data sets. In either case, after the data sets have been allocated, BTS is invoked.

On the other hand, the FREE and DELETE functions do not cause BTS to be invoked; they're provided just to help you manage your BTS data sets. If you enter FREE, the BTS data sets are deallocated, but not deleted. If you specify DELETE, all the BTS data sets are deallocated, and ones that don't need to be kept are deleted.

If you've already run BTS once during a terminal session and all the data sets you need have already been allocated, there's no need to allocate them again. When that's the case, all you do is press the enter key when the prompt above is displayed. Then, BTS is invoked immediately, and no data set management functions are performed.

How to interact with BTS FSS

After BTS has been invoked, it first reads the statements in the BTSIN data set. When you use BTS under TSO, BTSIN should be a sequential data set with 80-character records. The default data set name for it is BTSIN, prefixed with your user-id as the high-level qualifier. For me, the data set name is

    ECKOLS.BTSIN

You can use your editor to make sure the BTSIN data set contains the commands you want processed.

Complete Full Screen Support isn't enabled until BTS has processed all of the records in the BTSIN data set. In effect, you code all of the commands you need to set up the FSS environment in the BTSIN data set, and they're processed automatically for you. Typically, this includes D and T commands for the devices and transactions you want to test, plus an O command to specify the options you want to be in effect for the test run. It's also possible to include simulator statements in the BTSIN data set. When you do, they're processed before full-screen interaction begins.

When BTS reaches the end of the BTSIN data set, the Full Screen Support facility is invoked. Then, you can interact with BTS. At the beginning of an interactive BTS session, the terminal screen is in unformatted mode. When that's the case, you can enter other BTS commands (if, for instance, you want to change a specification made in a command in the BTSIN data set) or an IMS /FORMAT command to prepare the terminal to simulate an application. You'll see an example of this in a moment.

After you've formatted the screen, you key in data using the actual MFS screen format. Data you enter on the formatted screen is converted by BTS into a simulator statement, then processed as if it had come from the BTSIN data set.

If you want to enter a BTS command or an IMS command after you've started formatted entry, you have to do so from an unformatted, cleared screen. Clearing the screen is a two-step process. First, you press the clear key to clear your TSO terminal's screen. But then you also have to clear the BTS screen image. To do that, you key in the command

```
&&CLEAR
```

and press the enter key. (The two leading ampersands may or may not be required on your system; however, the command always works if you include them.)

When you've finished your BTS session, you clear the screen (using the technique I just described), then key in

```
/*
```

and press enter. This signals to BTS that there's no more input, and the session ends.

A sample BTS FSS session

Now, I want to illustrate BTS under TSO with a sample FSS session. Figure 16-1 shows a test run of the cash receipts application presented in chapter 7 (this is the same testing I did in the batch BTS job in the last chapter). I've annotated each part of the figure and shaded the parts I particularly want you to notice. This test run was done through an ISPF dialog, not through the standard BTS procedure I described earlier in this chapter. However, the BTS output is the same in either case.

To invoke BTS, I select option 1 from the menu.

```
------------------------- BTS/IMS SELECTION MENU --------------------------------
SELECT OPTION ===> 1


     1.   IMS/BTS        EXECUTE IMS UNDER BTS
     2.   SPECIFY        DISPLAY/SPECIFY DATA SET NAMES
     3.   DICTIONARY     IMS/VS DATA DICTIONARY SUPPORT
     4.   ADF-II         IMS/VS ADF-II SUPPORT
     5.   SAMPLE         FSS SAMPLE SUPPORT






  PRESS END KEY TO TERMINATE
```

Figure 16-1   A sample BTS FSS session (part 1 of 15)

BTS displays progress messages as data sets are allocated.

```
BEGINNING ALLOCATIONS FOR USER IMS APPLICATION
BEGINNING ALLOCATIONS FOR BTS
CONTINUING ALLOCATIONS FOR BTS
BEGINNING ALLOCATIONS FOR IMS LIBRARIES
INVOKING BTS
```

Figure 16-1   A sample BTS FSS session (part 2 of 15)

BTS displays the records it processed from the BTSIN data set. Notice that I coded many T commands in this example. As a result, I can test a variety of applications during one FSS session. Here, I've keyed in the command /FORMAT CRO to prepare the terminal for the cash receipts application.

```
BTS0007I BTS R2M0 SIMULATION STARTED.  TIME=11:12:45, DATE=86.363.
./T TC=ACR MBR=ACR PSB=ACR LANG=CBL TYPE=MSG
./T TC=PCR MBR=PCR PSB=PCR LANG=CBL TYPE=MSG
./T TC=CR MBR=CR PSB=DCTST LANG=CBL TYPE=MSG
./T TC=CRT MBR=CRT PSB=DCTST LANG=CBL TYPE=MSG
./T TC=DI1 MBR=DI1 PSB=DCTST LANG=CBL TYPE=MSG
./T TC=DI2 MBR=DI2 PSB=DCTST LANG=CBL TYPE=MSG
./T TC=DID MBR=DID PSB=DCTST LANG=CBL TYPE=MSG
./T TC=DIC MBR=DIC PSB=DCTST LANG=CBL TYPE=MSG SPA=1422
./T TC=DIL MBR=DIL PSB=DCTST LANG=CBL TYPE=MSG
./O TSOMSG=ALL TSODB=ALL
./D LTERM=IOPCB EOM=$ DDOF=327020 FEAT=7F
/*
BTS0004W NO TRANSACTION INFORMATION SUPPLIED. UNABLE TO SCHEDULE TRANSACTION:/
*
BTS0011I CONTINUING WITH NEXT TRANSACTION.
ENTER BTS COMMAND OR /FORMAT OR /*
/FORMAT CRO
```

Figure 16-1   A sample BTS FSS session (part 3 of 15)

BTS formats the screen with the MOD I requested (CRO), and I key data into four fields.

```
ENTER CASH RECEIPTS                                       DATE:  12/29/86


  INVOICE:        010000
  AMOUNT:         1200

  BANK NUMBER:    192/24-8
  CHECK NUMBER:   127452
```

Figure 16-1   A sample BTS FSS session (part 4 of 15)

BTS displays informational messages telling me it has started my program. The first call issued by the program is a DC GU, and it's followed by a GHU for the specified receivable segment from the customer data base. Notice that the I/O areas used for the calls are displayed (because the O command in the BTSIN data set specified TSOMSG = ALL and TSODB = ALL). Also, notice that to make the call trace output fit on the screen, the lines are shortened. The three asterisks at the bottom of the screen are a cue for the user to press the enter key to display more output.

```
BTS0100I ATTACHING DFSRRC00, PARM=DLI,BTSPC000,DCTST   ,12,01
BTS0006I TRANSACTION STARTED: CR          .
MBR=CR       PSB=DCTST    EDIT=          SPA=0      PLC=1      LANG=CBL TYPE=MSG
**** MSG CALL- FUNC=GU  , PCB=IOPCB  , STATUS= , MESSAGE NUMBER=000001
    LENGTH=000066, PCBN=001        -MSG-    GU
            ----.----1----.----2----.----3----.----4----.----5 (  1-  50)
    IOAREA=    CR      0100000001200192/24-8
            0400CD444444FFFFFFFFFFFFFFFF6FF6F4444444444444444444
            0201390000000100000001200192124080000000000000000000
            ----.----6----.-                                     ( 51-  66)
            127452
            FFFFFF4444444444
            1274520000000000
****** DB CALL- FUNC=GHU , PCB=CRDBD  , STATUS= , LEVEL=01, SEGMENT=CRRECSEG
  IOLENGTH=000057, PCBN=002        -DB-    GHU
            ----.-                                               (  1-   6)
    KFB=010000
        FFFFFF
        010000
            ----.----1----.----2----.-                           (  1-  26)
    SSA=CRRECSEG(CRRECXNO =010000)
        CDDCCECC4CDDCCEDD47FFFFFF5
        39953257D399537560E010000D
***
```

Figure 16-1   A sample BTS FSS session (part 5 of 15)

The I/O area at the top of this screen is for the DB GHU call whose trace began on the previous screen. The second call trace is for a replace call issued for the receivable segment. Again, the three asterisks at the bottom of the screen mean that another output screen follows.

```
                ----.----1----.----2----.----3----.----4----.----5 (   1-  50)
         IOAREA=010000071586
                FFFFFFFFFFFF44444444444444444444444444440200000000000
                0100000715860000000000000000000000000000C000C000C0
                ----.--                                          (  51-  57)
                      @
                0300027
                10C077C
******  DB CALL- FUNC=REPL, PCB=CRDBD   , STATUS=  , LEVEL=01, SEGMENT=CRRECSEG
        IOLENGTH=000057, PCBN=002       -DB-    REPL
                ----.-                                           (   1-   6)
            KFB=010000
                FFFFFF
                010000
                NO SSA IN THIS CALL
                ----.----1----.----2----.----3----.----4----.----5 (   1-  50)
         IOAREA=010000071586
                FFFFFFFFFFFF44444444444444444444444444440200000000000
                0100000715860000000000000000000000000000C000C000C0
                ----.--                                          (  51-  57)
                      @
                0300007
                10C067C
 ***
```

Figure 16-1   A sample BTS FSS session (part 6 of 15)

This call trace is for the ISRT call to add a payment segment occurrence to the customer data base. At the bottom of the screen is the first line for the call trace for the DC ISRT call that sends the output message back to the terminal. Again, the three asterisks mean more output follows on the next screen.

```
****** DB CALL- FUNC=ISRT, PCB=CRDBD    , STATUS=   , LEVEL=02, SEGMENT=CRPAYSEG
    IOLENGTH=000051, PCBN=002         -DB-    ISRT
                ----.-                                        (   1-   6)
        KFB=010000
            FFFFFF
            010000
            ----.----1----.----2----.-                       (   1-  26)
        SSA=CRRECSEG(CRRECXNO =010000)
            CDDCCECC4CDDCCEDD47FFFFFF5
            39953257D399537560E010000D
            ----.----                                         (   1-   9)
        SSA=CRPAYSEG
            CDDCEECC4
            397182570
            ----.----1----.----2----.----3----.----4----.----5 (   1-  50)
    IOAREA=127452          192/24-8              122986
        FFFFFF4444444444FFF6FF6F44444444444444444FFFFFF002
        1274520000000000019212408000000000000000000122986010
        -                                                     (  51-  51)
        0
        C
BTS0031I MODNAME: CRO
 ****  MSG CALL- FUNC=ISRT, PCB=IOPCB    , STATUS=   , MESSAGE NUMBER=000001
 ***
```

Figure 16-1   A sample BTS FSS session (part 7 of 15)

The data at the top of this screen is the remainder of the DC ISRT call trace that began on the previous screen. The last call trace is for another DC GU call to retrieve an input message; that call yielded a QC status code, and the program ended. After the last call trace on this screen is a summary of the calls the program made. Finally, the user is prompted to press the enter key to return to the IMS screen display.

```
    LENGTH=000145, PCBN=001        -MSG-      ISRT
              ----.----1----.----2----.----3----.----4----.----5 (   1-  50)
      IOAREA= J   :
              0900C84444444084444444084444444444444444444444444408
              0100000000000000000000000000000000000000000000000000
              ----.----6----.----7----.----8----.----9----.--10 (  51- 100)
                             $12.00   PAYMENT POSTED TO INVO
              4444444444444444444445FF4FF44DCEDCDE4DDEECC4ED4CDED
              0000000000000000000000B12B000071845530762354036095 56
              ----.----1----.----2----.----3----.----4----.      ( 101- 145)
              ICE 010000.
              CCC4FFFFFF4444444444444444444444444444444444444444
              9350010000B00000000000000000000000000000000000000
   **** MSG CALL- FUNC=GU   , PCB=IOPCB    , STATUS=QC, MESSAGE NUMBER=000001
      LENGTH=000000, PCBN=001        -MSG-      GU   QC
   BTS0020I STATISTICS REPORT FOR TRANSACTION:CR           .
   PCBNAME    GU   GN   GNP  GHU  GHN GHNP ISRT PURG REPL DLET  DEQ CHKP  LOG STAT
    XRST CHNG ROLB OPEN CLSE OTHR
   IOPCB       2                                  1
   CRDBD                 1                         1         1
   ENTER NULL LINE TO OBTAIN IMS-SCREEN FOR PCB(IOPCB    )
```

Figure 16-1   A sample BTS FSS session (part 8 of 15)

BTS has formatted the output message using the MOD CRO, and I've entered data for a new transaction. Here, I've just keyed in an invoice number (not the other three fields that make up a complete entry).

```
ENTER CASH RECEIPTS                                    DATE:   12/29/86


INVOICE:       011331
AMOUNT:

BANK NUMBER:
CHECK NUMBER:

















     $12.00  PAYMENT POSTED TO INVOICE 010000.
```

Figure 16-1   A sample BTS FSS session (part 9 of 15)

BTS starts the application program, which successfully issues a DC GU call to retrieve the input message. The program detects errors in the input message because not all fields were entered, so it issues a GU (not GHU) call for the requested receivable segment. That call is unsuccessful; the GE status code indicates the requested receivable segment wasn't found. Since no data base updates are done for an invalid transaction, the program replies immediately to the terminal with a DC ISRT call.

```
BTS0006I TRANSACTION STARTED: CR
MBR=CR        PSB=DCTST     EDIT=          SPA=0      PLC=1      LANG=CBL TYPE=MSG
**** MSG CALL- FUNC=GU   , PCB=IOPCB  , STATUS=  , MESSAGE NUMBER=000001
    LENGTH=000066, PCBN=001        -MSG-    GU
       ----.----1----.----2----.----3----.----4----.----5 (   1-  50)
     IOAREA=    CR      011331
            0400CD444444FFFFFF444444444444444444444444444444444
            0201390000000011331000000000000000000000000000000000
            ----.----6----.-                                    (  51-  66)
            444444444444444
            0000000000000000
****** DB CALL- FUNC=GU   , PCB=CRDBD  , STATUS=GE, LEVEL=00, SEGMENT=
    IOLENGTH=000000, PCBN=002        -DB-     GU   GE
       ----.----1----.----2----.-                               (   1-  26)
       SSA=CRRECSEG(CRRECXNO =011331)
          CDDCCECC4CDDCCEDD47FFFFFF5
          39953257D399537560E011331D
BTS0031I MODNAME: CRO
**** MSG CALL- FUNC=ISRT, PCB=IOPCB  , STATUS=  , MESSAGE NUMBER=000001
    LENGTH=000145, PCBN=001        -MSG-    ISRT
       ----.----1----.----2----.----3----.----4----.----5 (   1-  50)
     IOAREA= J  :H011331:H       :                             :
            0900C8FFFFFFC84444444C844444444444444444444444444C8
***
```

Figure 16-1   A sample BTS FSS session (part 10 of 15)

The top of this screen shows part of the I/O area for the DC ISRT call. Then, the program issues another DC GU call, and receives a QC status code. As a result, it ends, and the operator is prompted to press the enter key to display the IMS screen.

```
           0100080113310800000000000000000000000000000000000000
           ----.----6----.----7----.----8----.----9----.--10 (  51- 100)
                         INVOICE 011331 NOT FOUND.
           444444444444444CDEDCCC4FFFFFF4DDE4CDEDC4444444444
           0000000000000000095569350011331056306645 4B000000000
           ----.----1----.----2----.----3----.----4----.        ( 101- 145)
           44444444444444444444444444444444444444444444444
           000000000000000000000000000000000000000000000
    ****  MSG CALL- FUNC=GU    , PCB=IOPCB     , STATUS=QC, MESSAGE NUMBER=000001
       LENGTH=000000, PCBN=001        -MSG-      GU    QC
    BTS0020I STATISTICS REPORT FOR TRANSACTION:CR           .
    PCBNAME      GU   GN  GNP  GHU  GHN GHNP ISRT PURG REPL DLET  DEQ CHKP  LOG STAT
     XRST CHNG ROLB OPEN CLSE OTHR
    IOPCB        2                                  1
    CRDBD        1
    ENTER NULL LINE TO OBTAIN IMS-SCREEN FOR PCB(IOPCB    )
```

Figure 16-1   A sample BTS FSS session (part 11 of 15)

BTS formats the output message using the MOD CRO, and redisplays the IMS screen.

```
ENTER CASH RECEIPTS                                    DATE:   12/29/86


INVOICE:        011331
AMOUNT:

BANK NUMBER:
CHECK NUMBER:













INVOICE 011331 NOT FOUND.
```

Figure 16-1   A sample BTS FSS session (part 12 of 15)

I'm finished with my test run, so I press the clear key, then key in CLEAR on the unformatted screen and press the enter key. (My system doesn't require that I use the && prefix for the CLEAR command.)

```
CLEAR
```

Figure 16-1   A sample BTS FSS session (part 13 of 15)

BTS displays informational messages and prompts me for an entry. At this point, I could enter the /FORMAT command to test another application. Instead, I enter /* to end the session.

```
    BTS0034I THE SCREEN IS CLEARED AND UNFORMATTED.
    BTS0032I OUTPUT QUEUE NOT EMPTY AT A/P RETURN. NUMBER OF MESSAGES: 00001
    ENTER BTS COMMAND OR /FORMAT OR /*
    /*
```

Figure 16-1   A sample BTS FSS session (part 14 of 15)

BTS displays a termination message and ends. When I press enter, TSO returns me to the ISPF menu in part 1 of the figure.

```
   BTS0034I THE SCREEN IS CLEARED AND UNFORMATTED.
   BTS0032I OUTPUT QUEUE NOT EMPTY AT A/P RETURN. NUMBER OF MESSAGES: 00001
   ENTER BTS COMMAND OR /FORMAT OR /*
/*'
   BTS0008I END OF INPUT DATA SET ENCOUNTERED.
   BTS0005I END OF BTS RUN.
   ***
```

Figure 16-1   A sample BTS FSS session (part 15 of 15)

Advanced topics for BTS under TSO

There are a couple of additional points that you should be aware of when you use BTS under TSO. In this section, I'll describe how to control call traces and how to use the BTSPUNCH and BTSOUT data sets.

How to control call traces   Three of the four O command keywords for TSO let you control what call trace information is displayed when you execute BTS under TSO. TSOMLVL lets you disable call traces altogether. When you specify

```
TSOMLVL=0
```

on an O command, only IMS screens and BTS error messages are displayed at your TSO terminal. Because BTS error messages are unusual, requesting this option makes your TSO terminal behave just like the 3270s that will be used for your application on the production system.

If you don't specify the TSOMLVL keyword on the O command, the default (1) is in effect. Then, in addition to BTS error messages and IMS screens, call traces and BTS informational messages are also displayed at your terminal. When this is the case, the specifications you make on the TSOMSG and TSODB keywords come into play.

As their names imply, the TSOMSG keyword controls the information displayed for message call traces, and the TSODB keyword controls the information displayed for data base call traces. The values you can code for both are the same, so I'll describe just the TSOMSG keyword.

To disable call traces for message calls, you code

```
TSOMSG=NO
```

on the O command. To display complete message call traces, which include an identifying line and the I/O area, you code

```
TSOMSG=ALL
```

(For the TSODB keyword, ALL also causes SSAs and the key feedback area to be displayed.) The default for the keyword,

```
TSOMSG=YES
```

displays only the one-line call identifier that's part of the output that's produced with the ALL option.

In addition to these three options, you can also specify that you should receive control after each call, at which time you can request the trace information to be displayed. To receive control at the completion of each call, code

```
TSOMSG=PROMPT
```

on the O command. Then, for each call, you're prompted with this message:

```
ENTER 'L CALL', 'L IOAR', 'END' OR NULL LINE
```

The first option, L CALL, displays the one-line call identifier; the second, L IOAR, displays the call I/O area and, for a DB call, the key feedback area and SSAs. The third option, END, resets the option to TSOMSG=YES so you are no longer prompted for each call. When you press the enter key without entering an option value (NULL LINE), processing continues.

How to use the BTSOUT and BTSPUNCH data sets   As BTS executes under TSO, it writes output to the BTSPUNCH and BTSOUT data sets. The contents of the BTSOUT data set are just what you'd get if you ran BTS in a batch job. To print BTSOUT, you can code and submit a simple IEBGENER job to copy the data set to a printer.

The BTSPUNCH data set contains all the input records that were supplied to BTS during the test session, both those that were supplied through BTSIN and the ones generated as a result of your full-screen terminal entries. As a result, you can use BTSPUNCH to repeat a test run exactly. You can do this in two ways. First, you can use the contents of BTSPUNCH for BTSIN in a subsequent BTS run under FSS. Alternatively, you can specify the name of the BTSPUNCH data set on the BTSIN DD statement in a BTS batch job.

You should realize that the usefulness of this regression test data can be limited. For example, if you change a format set so fields are moved, the simulator statements generated during a previous test run probably won't match up with the new screen format.

Terminology

Full Screen Support
FSS
CLIST
command list

Objective

Given details about your shop's implementation of BTS Full Screen
Support, test an application under TSO.

Appendix A

DL/I status codes

This appendix contains the DL/I status codes that can be returned as a result of calls issued in the DC environment. For each status code, there's a brief description followed by the call functions that can result in the code. (When one of the data base get functions is indicated for a status code, the get-hold form of that call can also cause the condition to be raised; for example, if the data base GN call can cause a particular status code to be returned, the GHN call can too.) Although the descriptions that follow are brief, they're adequate for most problems. If you find that you need more information for a particular code, consult the *IMS/VS Version 1 Application Programming* manual.

AB

The call did not specify a segment I/O area. This is a programming error.

Calls: All

AC

The call included an SSA with a hierarchical error. This is a programming error.

Calls: All data base get calls and ISRT

AD

The function code field specified for the call contains an incorrect value. This is a programming error.

Calls: All

AH

The call requires at least one SSA. This is a programming error.

Calls: Data base ISRT

AI

An error occurred when trying to open the data base data set. The most common cause of the AI status code is an error in the JCL defining the data base data set. You might also get this status code if you try to load an existing data base or do other than load processing on an empty data set.

Calls: All data base calls

AJ

The call specifies an invalid SSA. This is a programming error. The PCB's segment level field contains the level number of the segment for which the SSA is invalid. The first thing you should check is the format of the SSA itself. If it seems to be correct, make sure the call doesn't specify an invalid SSA type. For an ISRT call, the lowest-level SSA must be unqualified. For a REPL call, there may not be a qualified SSA. And for a DLET call, there may be only one SSA, and it must be unqualified.

Calls: All data base calls

AK

The field you named on a qualified SSA isn't correct. This is a programming error.

Calls: All data base get calls and data base ISRT

AM

The call attempted an unauthorized operation, that is, one not allowed by the processing options or sensitive segments specified in the PCB. This is a programming error.

Calls: All data base calls

AO

The call caused an operation that resulted in a physical I/O error. This is a serious error that probably requires intervention by a systems programmer.

Calls: All data base calls

AT

The I/O area the call specified is too large. This is usually a programming error, but the program's PSB may be incorrect.

Calls: Data base DLET, REPL, and ISRT

AU

The SSAs specified on the call exceeded the maximum length allowed for them in the PSB. This usually is a programming error, but the PSB may be incorrect.

Calls: All data base calls

A1

The destination name specified is invalid. This is usually a programming error.

Calls: CHNG

A2

The program tried to change the destination associated with a fixed alternate PCB. This is a programming error.

Calls: CHNG

A3

The program tried to send a message to a modifiable alternate PCB, but no destination had been associated with it. This is a programming error.

Calls: Message ISRT and PURG

A5

The program specified a MOD name for a segment other than the first in an output message. This is a programming error.

Calls: Message ISRT and PURG

DA

The sequence field (or a non-replaceable field) has been changed in the program's I/O area.

Calls: Data base DLET and REPL

DJ

The call wasn't immediately preceded by a successful get-hold call.

Calls: Data base DLET and REPL

DX

The call violated a delete rule for a segment. This is usually a programming error.

Calls: Data base DLET

GA

A higher-level segment was retrieved during sequential retrieval. Usually a GA isn't an error, but an expected condition.

Calls: Unqualified data base GN and GNP

GB

The end of the data base was reached during sequential retrieval.

Calls: Data base GN

GD

Position was lost before the call could be completed, probably because a segment in the path to it was deleted through another PCB.

Calls: Data base ISRT

GE

A segment occurrence meeting all the specified qualifications wasn't found (for a get call) or couldn't be added due to an error in the specified path (for an ISRT).

Calls: All data base get calls and ISRT

GK

A segment of a different type but at the same hierarchical level was retrieved during sequential retrieval. Usually, a GK isn't an error, but an expected condition.

Calls: Unqualified data base GN and GNP

GP

Proper parentage isn't in effect. This is usually a programming error.

Calls: GNP

II

The segment already exists in the data base.

Calls: Data base ISRT

IX

The call violated an insert rule for a segment. This is usually a programming error.

Calls: Data base ISRT

LB

The segment already exists in the data base.

Calls: Data base ISRT

LC

The input data is not in hierarchical sequence.

Calls: Data base ISRT

LD

One or more segments in the path to the segment being loaded are missing (an error in hierarchical sequence).

Calls: Data base ISRT

LE

The sequence of segment types at the same level isn't the same as that specified in the DBD (an error in hierarchical sequence).

Calls: Data base ISRT

NO

The call caused an operation that resulted in a physical I/O error on a secondary index. This is a serious error that probably requires intervention by a systems programmer.

Calls: Data base DLET, REPL, ISRT

QC

No more input messages are present for the program. This is a condition your programs should anticipate.

Calls: Message GU

QD

No more segments are present for the current input message. This is a condition your programs should anticipate.

Calls: Message GN

QE

The program issued a message GN call before a message GU call. This is a programming error.

Calls: Message GN

QF

The message segment is five characters long or less (including the four-character prefix). For an output call, this is a programming error. For a GU call, it's a system error.

Calls: Message GU, ISRT, and PURG

QH

The destination of the output message (logical terminal or transaction) is undefined. This can have a variety of causes. The program may have issued an ISRT call before issuing a GU; this is a programming error.

Calls: Message ISRT and PURG

RX

The call violated a replace rule for a segment. This is usually a programming error.

Calls: Data base ISRT

V1

A variable-length segment longer than the maximum segment size was specified.

Calls: Data base DLET, REPL, ISRT

XA

The program has already responded to the originating terminal, but is trying to pass the SPA to another program. This is a programming error.

Calls: Message ISRT

XB

The program has already passed the SPA to another program, but is trying to send an output message to the originating terminal. This is a programming error.

Calls: Message ISRT

XC

The program sent a message whose Z1 field has a value other than binary zeros. This is a programming error.

Calls: Message ISRT

XF

A logical terminal involved in a conversation is not defined properly to IMS. This is a systems programming problem.

Calls: Message ISRT

XG

The size of the SPA the program tried to insert isn't correct. This is a programming error.

Calls: Message ISRT

X1

An I/O error occurred while IMS was accessing the SPA. This is a serious error that probably requires intervention by a systems programmer.

Calls: Message GU and ISRT

X2

The first output message of a conversational program was not the SPA. This is a programming error.

Calls: Message ISRT and PURG

X3

The SPA is invalid because the program altered its first six bytes. This is a programming error.

Calls: Message ISRT

X4

The program tried to perform a message switch to a non-conversational program by passing the SPA to it. This is a programming error.

Calls: Message ISRT

X5

The program tried to perform a message switch to a program by passing the SPA to it more than once. This is a programming error.

Calls: Message ISRT

X6

The program tried to perform a message switch to a transaction that isn't defined; that is, the program stored an invalid transaction code in the SPA. This is a programming error.

Calls: Message ISRT

X7

The SPA is invalid because the program altered its first six bytes. This is a programming error.

Calls: Message ISRT

X8

A system or I/O error occurred when IMS attempted to store a SPA for a program-to-program message switch. This is a serious error that probably requires intervention by a systems programmer.

Calls: Message ISRT

X9

The SPA the program tried to insert is larger than the value specified for it in the PSB. This is probably a programming error, but the PSB may be wrong.

Calls: Message ISRT

bb (spaces)

The call was executed normally.

Calls: All

Appendix B

JCL to compile an
IMS DC program

Figure B-1 shows a job stream that uses the COBUCL procedure to compile and link a COBOL DL/I program (either a DC or a DB program). Here, the program name is INV2300. Although this job is much like the procedure to compile and link a non-DL/I program, a DD statement for LKED.SYSLMOD specifies the partitioned data set (PDS), or library, that contains DL/I programs; in this case, it's named ECKOLS.IMSVS.PGMLIB. Your program specs should indicate the name of the library that will contain the load module.

You can specify the name of the load module in two places in the job. You can code it in parentheses after the PDS data set name on the DD statement for LKED.SYSLMOD, or you can supply a NAME linkage editor control statement after the LKED.SYSIN DD statement. If you use the second technique and you want to replace an existing version of the member in the library, you have to follow the name with an R in parentheses (the first technique replaces the existing member automatically). If you like, you can use both techniques, as I did in figure B-1.

You need to include two other linkage editor control statements after the LKED.SYSIN DD statement:

```
INCLUDE RESLIB(CBLTDLI)
```

and

```
ENTRY DLITCBL
```

```
//ECKOLSC    JOB    USER=...
//COBLK      EXEC PROC=COBUCL,
              PARM.COB='APOST',
              PARM.LKED='MAP,LET,LIST'
//COB.SYSIN DD   *
      IDENTIFICATION DIVISION.
     *
      PROGRAM-ID.    INV2300.
     *
              .
              .
              .
/*
//LKED.SYSLMOD DD   DSN=ECKOLS.IMSVS.PGMLIB(INV2300),DISP=SHR
//LKED.SYSIN    DD   *
   INCLUDE RESLIB(CBLTDLI)
   ENTRY    DLITCBL
   NAME     INV2300(R)
//LKED.RESLIB   DD   DSN=IMS1.IMSVS.RESLIB,DISP=SHR
//
```

Figure B-1   Sample job to compile and link an IMS/VS COBOL program

These are the same for all COBOL DL/I programs.

Finally, be sure to provide an overriding statement for LKED.RESLIB that specifies the correct data set name. Here, it's IMS1.IMSVS.RESLIB.

Your shop probably has a special procedure to compile and link DL/I programs. Or, IMSCOBOL, which is supplied with IMS, may be tailored to your installation's requirements. Check with a co-worker, your supervisior, or your DBA to find out if it or a similar procedure is available.

Appendix C

JCL to translate an MFS format set

As I mentioned when I described the MFS Language Utility in chapter 5, you may not be allowed to translate format sets at all. And if you are, your shop may well have customized procedures you'll use. If that's the case, you should find out what the unique JCL requirements are for those procedures.

In this appendix, I want to show you how to use the MFSTEST procedure, one of several supplied by IBM with MFS to translate format sets. The MFSTEST procedure causes the translated blocks to be stored in the test format library (IMSVS.TFORMAT is the default data set name). Figure C-1 shows a sample job for running MFSTEST.

On the EXEC statement that invoked the procedure, I specified overriding values for two symbolic parameters. The first,

```
PCOMP=COMP
```

tells MFS to print statements generated as a result of DO and ENDDO statements. If your format set does not contain DO or ENDDO statements, you can omit this parameter. The second overriding value I supplied,

```
PSUBS=SUBS
```

tells MFS that it should perform any substitutions requested by EQU

```
//ECKOLSM  JOB   USER=...
//MFSTRANS EXEC  PROC=MFSTEST,PCOMP=COMP,PSUBS=SUBS
//S1.SYSLIB DD   DSN=ECKOLS.MFS.COPYLIB,DISP=SHR
//S1.SYSIN  DD   *
          PRINT ON,NOGEN
DI2DF     FMT
            .
            .
            .
          MSGEND
          END
/*
//S2.FORMAT DD   DSN=ECKOLS.TFORMAT,DISP=SHR
//
```

Figure C-1   Sample job to translate an MFS format set

statements in the format set. If your format set doesn't contain any EQU statements, you can omit this parameter.

The MFSTEST procedure has two steps, named S1 and S2. You'll probably need to supply one or two overriding DD statements for the first step. In figure C-1, I supplied two. The first identifies a partitioned data set that MFS will search to find members named on COPY statements in the format set. If you don't use any COPY statements in your format set, you can omit this DD statement.

The second overriding DD statement I supplied for step S1 is for the SYSIN data set. It contains the control statements that are to be processed by the MFS Language Utility. Here, I coded SYSIN as an instream data set. However, you might also refer to a member of a partitioned data set with a DD statement like this:

```
//S1.SYSIN DD   DSN=ECKOLS.MFS.SOURCE(DI2),DISP=SHR
```

I only coded one overriding DD statement for step S2. It's for the test format library (ddname FORMAT) in which the MFS Language Utility will store the blocks it creates from your format set statements. When you work in a test environment, it's likely that you'll use a test format data set, not the one named in the procedure.

Appendix D

Binary, hexadecimal, and character conversion table

Binary	Hex	Character
0000 0000	00	
0000 0001	01	
0000 0010	02	
0000 0011	03	
0000 0100	04	
0000 0101	05	
0000 0110	06	
0000 0111	07	
0000 1000	08	
0000 1001	09	
0000 1010	0A	
0000 1011	0B	
0000 1100	0C	
0000 1101	0D	
0000 1110	0E	
0000 1111	0F	

Binary	Hex	Character	Binary	Hex	Character
0001 0000	10		0011 0000	30	
0001 0001	11		0011 0001	31	
0001 0010	12		0011 0010	32	
0001 0011	13		0011 0011	33	
0001 0100	14		0011 0100	34	
0001 0101	15		0011 0101	35	
0001 0110	16		0011 0110	36	
0001 0111	17		0011 0111	37	
0001 1000	18		0011 1000	38	
0001 1001	19		0011 1001	39	
0001 1010	1A		0011 1010	3A	
0001 1011	1B		0011 1011	3B	
0001 1100	1C		0011 1100	3C	
0001 1101	1D		0011 1101	3D	
0001 1110	1E		0011 1110	3E	
0001 1111	1F		0011 1111	3F	
0010 0000	20		0100 0000	40	
0010 0001	21		0100 0001	41	
0010 0010	22		0100 0010	42	
0010 0011	23		0100 0011	43	
0010 0100	24		0100 0100	44	
0010 0101	25		0100 0101	45	
0010 0110	26		0100 0110	46	
0010 0111	27		0100 0111	47	
0010 1000	28		0100 1000	48	
0010 1001	29		0100 1001	49	
0010 1010	2A		0100 1010	4A	¢
0010 1011	2B		0100 1011	4B	.
0010 1100	2C		0100 1100	4C	<
0010 1101	2D		0100 1101	4D	(
0010 1110	2E		0100 1110	4E	+
0010 1111	2F		0100 1111	4F	|

Binary	Hex	Character	Binary	Hex	Character
0101 0000	50	&	0111 0000	70	
0101 0001	51		0111 0001	71	
0101 0010	52		0111 0010	72	
0101 0011	53		0111 0011	73	
0101 0100	54		0111 0100	74	
0101 0101	55		0111 0101	75	
0101 0110	56		0111 0110	76	
0101 0111	57		0111 0111	77	
0101 1000	58		0111 1000	78	
0101 1001	59		0111 1001	79	`
0101 1010	5A	!	0111 1010	7A	:
0101 1011	5B	$	0111 1011	7B	#
0101 1100	5C	*	0111 1100	7C	@
0101 1101	5D	)	0111 1101	7D	'
0101 1110	5E	;	0111 1110	7E	=
0101 1111	5F	¬	0111 1111	7F	"
0110 0000	60	−	1000 0000	80	
0110 0001	61	/	1000 0001	81	a
0110 0010	62		1000 0010	82	b
0110 0011	63		1000 0011	83	c
0110 0100	64		1000 0100	84	d
0110 0101	65		1000 0101	85	e
0110 0110	66		1000 0110	86	f
0110 0111	67		1000 0111	87	g
0110 1000	68		1000 1000	88	h
0110 1001	69		1000 1001	89	i
0110 1010	6A	¦	1000 1010	8A	
0110 1011	6B	,	1000 1011	8B	
0110 1100	6C	%	1000 1100	8C	
0110 1101	6D		1000 1101	8D	
0110 1110	6E	>	1000 1110	8E	
0110 1111	6F	?	1000 1111	8F	

Binary	Hex	Character	Binary	Hex	Character
1001 0000	90		1011 0000	B0	
1001 0001	91	j	1011 0001	B1	
1001 0010	92	k	1011 0010	B2	
1001 0011	93	l	1011 0011	B3	
1001 0100	94	m	1011 0100	B4	
1001 0101	95	n	1011 0101	B5	
1001 0110	96	o	1011 0110	B6	
1001 0111	97	p	1011 0111	B7	
1001 1000	98	q	1011 1000	B8	
1001 1001	99	r	1011 1001	B9	
1001 1010	9A		1011 1010	BA	
1001 1011	9B		1011 1011	BB	
1001 1100	9C		1011 1100	BC	
1001 1101	9D		1011 1101	BD	
1001 1110	9E		1011 1110	BE	
1001 1111	9F		1011 1111	BF	
1010 0000	A0		1100 0000	C0	{
1010 0001	A1	~	1100 0001	C1	A
1010 0010	A2	s	1100 0010	C2	B
1010 0011	A3	t	1100 0011	C3	C
1010 0100	A4	u	1100 0100	C4	D
1010 0101	A5	v	1100 0101	C5	E
1010 0110	A6	w	1100 0110	C6	F
1010 0111	A7	x	1100 0111	C7	G
1010 1000	A8	y	1100 1000	C8	H
1010 1001	A9	z	1100 1001	C9	I
1010 1010	AA		1100 1010	CA	
1010 1011	AB		1100 1011	CB	
1010 1100	AC		1100 1100	CC	
1010 1101	AD		1100 1101	CD	
1010 1110	AE		1100 1110	CE	
1010 1111	AF		1100 1111	CF	

Binary	Hex	Character	Binary	Hex	Character
1101 0000	D0	}	1111 0000	F0	0
1101 0001	D1	J	1111 0001	F1	1
1101 0010	D2	K	1111 0010	F2	2
1101 0011	D3	L	1111 0011	F3	3
1101 0100	D4	M	1111 0100	F4	4
1101 0101	D5	N	1111 0101	F5	5
1101 0110	D6	O	1111 0110	F6	6
1101 0111	D7	P	1111 0111	F7	7
1101 1000	D8	Q	1111 1000	F8	8
1101 1001	D9	R	1111 1001	F9	9
1101 1010	DA		1111 1010	FA	|
1101 1011	DB		1111 1011	FB	
1101 1100	DC		1111 1100	FC	
1101 1101	DD		1111 1101	FD	
1101 1110	DE		1111 1110	FE	
1101 1111	DF		1111 1111	FF	
1110 0000	E0	\			
1110 0001	E1				
1110 0010	E2	S			
1110 0011	E3	T			
1110 0100	E4	U			
1110 0101	E5	V			
1110 0110	E6	W			
1110 0111	E7	X			
1110 1000	E8	Y			
1110 1001	E9	Z			
1110 1010	EA				
1110 1011	EB				
1110 1100	EC				
1110 1101	ED				
1110 1110	EE				
1110 1111	EF				

Index

Comment Form

Your opinions count

If you have comments, criticisms, or suggestions, I'm eager to get them. Your opinions today will affect our products of tomorrow. If you have questions, you can expect an answer within one week of the time we receive them. And if you discover any errors in this book, typographical or otherwise, please point them out so we can make corrections when the book is reprinted.

Thanks for your help.

Mike Murach
Fresno, California

Book title: IMS for the COBOL Programmer, Part 2

_____

_____

_____

_____

_____

_____

_____

_____

_____

_____

_____

_____

_____

_____

_____

_____

_____

Name and Title_____

Company (if company address)_____

Address_____

City, State, Zip_____

Fold where indicated and tape.
No postage necessary if mailed in the U.S.